THE ENIGMATIC MR DEAKIN

ALSO BY JUDITH BRETT

Robert Menzies' Forgotten People

*Australian Liberals and the Moral Middle Class:
From Alfred Deakin to John Howard*

*Ordinary People's Politics: Australians Talk about
Life, Politics and the Future of Their Country*
(with Anthony Moran)

THE ENIGMATIC MR DEAKIN

JUDITH BRETT

TEXT PUBLISHING MELBOURNE AUSTRALIA

textpublishing.com.au
The Text Publishing Company
Swann House
22 William Street
Melbourne Victoria 3000
Australia

First published by The Text Publishing Company in 2017

Book design by W.H. Chong

Typeset by J&M Typesetting

Index by Karen Gillen

Map by Simon Barnard, adapted from Whitehead's Map of Melbourne and Suburbs, 1892

Cover image of Alfred Deakin at Point Lonsdale front beach, 1910, courtesy of Brookes family and Deakin University Library

Printed and bound in Australia by Griffin Press, an accredited ISO/NZS 1401:2004 Environmental Management System printer

National Library of Australia Cataloguing-in-Publication entry

ISBN: 9781925498660 (hardback)

ISBN: 9781925410884 (ebook)

Creator: Brett, Judith Margaret, 1949–, author.

Title: The enigmatic Mr Deakin / by Judith Brett.

Subjects: Deakin, Alfred, 1856–1919. Prime ministers—Australia—Biography. Politicians—Australia—Biography. Statesmen—Australia—Biography. Journalists—Australia—19th century—Biography. Australia—History— Federation, 1901. Australia—Politics and government—To 1900. Australia—Politics and government—1901–1914.

To the memory of
Alan Davies and John Hirst

CONTENTS

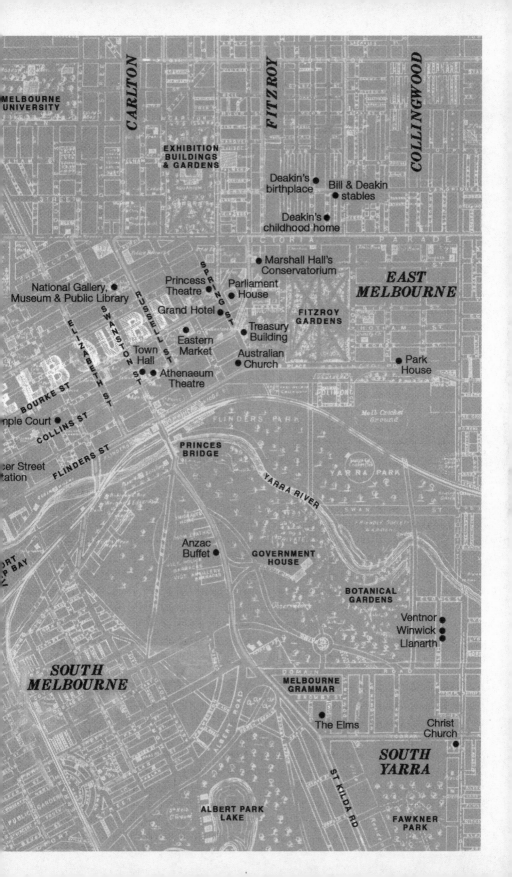

The Real is what the senses see.
The Ideal is what the Soul sees.

ALFRED DEAKIN, 1879

INTRODUCTION

ALFRED DEAKIN WAS born two years after Ned Kelly in the new British colony of Victoria. Kelly's parents were an Irish ex-convict from Van Diemen's Land and his spirited young Irish wife. Deakin was the only son of respectable goldrush immigrants, one of the thousands of young couples who left England in the late 1840s for a better life abroad. When Kelly's father crossed Bass Strait in 1848 at the expiry of his sentence, it was only fourteen years since the Henty Brothers had settled at Portland and begun to open up the Port Phillip District to Europeans and their sheep. The white population was fifty thousand, with fifteen thousand of them living in Melbourne, which was already established as the capital.[1] The indigenous population had been decimated by smallpox and venereal disease which had travelled ahead of the invaders, by the destruction of food sources when the men and sheep arrived, and by frontier violence. Richard Broome estimates that by 1850 the indigenous population of the District was a mere 10 per cent of pre-invasion levels.[2]

In 1850 the British government legislated for the separation of

a new colony from New South Wales, and it was named Victoria
after the reigning queen. Soon afterwards, gold was discovered in the
Central Highlands and the rush was on. William and Sarah Deakin
were already in Adelaide with their baby daughter. Along with much
of Adelaide they headed for the goldfields. By 1856, when Alfred was
born, they were in Melbourne, living in Fitzroy, and William was
running a coach to Bendigo.

Gold transformed Victoria from a minor pastoral settlement into
Britain's most prosperous and progressive colony. The speed of the
transformation was astonishing. Within a decade Victoria had half a
million new settlers. Most were literate and the proportion of skilled
artisans was higher than in the other Australian colonies. Their politics
had been shaped by Chartism, the working-class political movement
which demanded democratic reform of Britain's class-bound political
institutions, and the immigrants were determined to avoid recreating
the hierarchies and inequalities of the old world. Ten years after being
granted self-government Victoria had achieved most of the Chartists'
democratic demands: regular elections for both houses of parliament,
no property qualifications for members, manhood suffrage for the
lower house, the secret ballot and regular electoral redistributions.
The ramshackle unpaved town on the banks of the Yarra had been
replaced by a modern metropolis with grand stone buildings, well-lit
streets, elegant parks and gardens, and fashionable shops and villas.
During the 1850s a public library, an art gallery and a university were
founded, government buildings erected, and Parliament House begun
on the hill east of the city. It was a new beginning and people spoke of
the time before the gold as if it were another country.[3]

By 1888, when the centenary of the First Fleet's arrival was celebrated,
Victoria was far and away the leading Australian colony and Marvellous Melbourne a world-class metropolis. Thirty-two-year-old Alfred
Deakin was chief secretary, a political wunderkind who had been a
member of parliament for almost a decade. Ned Kelly was already dead,
hanged on 11 November 1880 for murdering a policeman. Deakin saw
the hanging, most likely as a reporter for the *Age*, one of the fifty men
allowed inside the Melbourne Gaol to witness the drop.[4]

The differing fates of these two native sons, outlaw and lawmaker, exemplified the profound shifts that had taken place in Victoria since their births in the mid-1850s. Kelly was born into rural poverty in the hills in northern Victoria, his extended family supplementing their meagre incomes with horse and cattle duffing. The lawless frontier daredevilry of the Kelly Gang had no place in the respectable society the goldrush immigrants were building for themselves and their children. But it is the outlaw who has survived more vividly in popular memory. His homemade armour is etched into the national myth by Sidney Nolan's jaunty silhouette and his crazy bravery has become a symbol of the defiance of authority so many Australians like to believe is part of our character.

Deakin is remembered too, but not so vividly, more as a bearded worthy than a national icon. He was Australia's most important prime minister in its first ten years after federation, but he sits uneasily as a representative Australian figure. He is too intellectual, too respectable, for the larrikin masculinity of the Australian legend that runs from convicts and bushrangers like the Kellys through the drovers and shearers and men from Snowy River, the early labour unions and the Anzacs, to Crocodile Dundee and footballers out on a spree, that long, meandering line-up of mates who stagger and stride through our national story.

Deakin was never a mate. He didn't swear and rarely drank. He didn't play organised sport nor fight in the Great War, was unfailingly courteous and, although many loved him, he always held himself a little aloof. He was also enormously well read, in philosophy, theology, comparative religion and the world's literature, including poetry, his first love. In short, he was middle-class, well-educated, urbane and supremely self-confident, like the city and the colony in which he grew to manhood. When he first visited England in 1887 to attend the Colonial Conference, Britain's political leaders were captivated by his charm and his gifted oratory and astonished by his audacity in arguing with them about imperial foreign policy. After all, he was only a thirty-year-old colonial. In 1887 he was the voice of young Australia holding its own at the centre of empire, Australia's greatest native son, and young, native-born men like himself were thrilled when he refused a knighthood. He was their representative.

Deakin became a politician, almost by accident, when other ways of making a living eluded him. He had qualified for the bar, but briefs were scarce for a young man with few connections. To earn money he began writing for the *Age*, where he became close to David Syme, its powerful editor. In 1879 Syme suggested him as the Liberal candidate to a local electoral committee and to everyone's surprise, including his own, he won the seat.

During this first campaign Deakin revealed himself as an extraordinary orator. Political oratory was at its height, with public political meetings sites of entertainment as well as persuasion. Supporters would cheer and applaud in the call-and-response structure of evangelical preaching and hostile interjectors would be dispatched with wit. For the successful orator it was an exhilarating experience, and Deakin was brilliant at it. With rapid delivery, words, phrases, images, arguments, quotations and examples streamed from his mouth in complex, well-shaped sentences as he strode around the platform, gesturing for emphasis, his voice rising on crescendos of fervour and gliding down to quiet appeals. Tall and strong, with thick dark hair and mesmeric brown eyes, Deakin had the compelling physical presence of a great actor and the stamina for long performances in which body, mind and voice worked in unison.

Deakin knew he was special, and he had something of the narcissist's intense self-focus, but he sought to harness his gifts and his energy to higher ends. He dabbled in spiritualism, mainly in his late teens and early twenties, as did many others in this period when conventional Christian beliefs were being undermined by discoveries in geology and archaeology and by Darwin's theory of evolution. Spiritualism retained Christianity's faith in an immortal soul and in the divine order of the universe, and believed that the dead could communicate from beyond the grave. Some prophecies early in his political life persuaded Deakin that his destiny lay in politics, as a servant of divine progress towards a more humane and equal society.

As he matured his religious beliefs became more conventional, but his politics retained their strong religious foundation. Many times he contemplated other paths, but he always returned to politics as the realm in which he was best fitted to serve.

His doubts were greatest in the early 1890s, after the land boom crashed, taking Victoria's prosperity and optimism with it. Deakin spent the decade as a backbencher, refusing all offers of office and supplementing his income at the bar. He stayed in politics because of the prospect of federation, which became something of a redemption project for him. To help create a nation was, he felt, a cause worthy of his service. Deakin had a sharp sense of the transience of moments of political opportunity—of how fleeting they were, how easily they could be lost. Federation was one such moment and he put his all into making it happen.

Once the federal constitution had been accepted, and the Commonwealth inaugurated, Deakin believed that it was the duty of those who had argued for federation to make it work. Federal institutions had to be built and the promise of the nation embodied in the constitution had to be made real as Australians learned to put aside their parochial state-based and sectional interests for the wider national interest. Deakin was the first attorney-general and three times prime minister in our Commonwealth's unstable first decade of minority governments. He governed twice with the support of the Labor Party and once as leader of the Fusion government, in which he reluctantly joined with his erstwhile enemies, the Conservatives, to form a single anti-Labor party. The government was roundly defeated in 1910 by the Labor Party led by Andrew Fisher, who became the first prime minister to lead a majority government.

As the leader of minority governments Deakin achieved a great deal by keeping his eyes fixed on the policies and legislation he wanted to achieve. For him, policies always came first and party-political considerations second. He did not think this made him weak, and if others criticised him for it he did not greatly care. Deakin always claimed he had little personal ambition for himself—and I don't believe this was self-deception.

Deakin was a robust debater, but he did not like personal conflict, nor believe it to be productive. Nor did he ever use anger and a sense of grievance to harness political support. Charm and persuasion were his tools as he sought for co-operation and areas of compromise, and so turned minority government to his advantage to construct a centre for Australian federal politics. He said in 1909 that the hundred or so acts passed since federation did not belong to any one party because passing them had always required the co-operation of two.[5]

For Deakin the centre was the place where politics connected with Australians' lived experience and with the nation's needs—for defence, for development, for population, for workable institutions of governance, for civilised wages and working conditions. The politician's first task was to serve that centre through good policy; party was only ever a means. Because they were developed with cross-party support, many of the policies he oversaw lasted for more than three-quarters of a century. Paul Kelly calls the policies of White Australia, tariff protection, state paternalism, compulsory conciliation and arbitration, and a foreign policy dependent on a great and powerful northern-hemisphere friend the Australian Settlement. They have also been called the Deakinite Settlement.[6]

Politics was not Deakin's whole life. He was a devoted son and brother, husband and father, who loved pottering about the garden with the dogs, cycling with his daughters, strolling with Pattie, his wife, and swimming naked in the sea. For as long as he was able, he read and wrote to try to understand the universe and his place in it. I have tried to give each of the three strands of Deakin's life its due: his intense inner world, his public life in politics and his family relationships, following the daily, weekly and yearly rhythms, as well as the arc of his life's physical and psychic energies. My quest has been for the changes and the enduring patterns, the moments of decision and the paths not taken. The book is a life, not a life-and-times; its starting questions are what events meant to Deakin rather than what he contributed to events, though I hope I shed light on this too.

To show events as he experienced them, wherever possible I have used his words to describe them. Deakin wrote two manuscripts on political events which were intended for publication: 'The Crisis in Victorian Politics' and 'The Inner History of the Federal Cause, 1880–1900'. Both are vivid accounts of political events in which he was a key player. Further vivid accounts are in the anonymous letters he wrote from 1900 until 1913 as the Australian correspondent for the conservative London daily the *Morning Post*, which included accounts of the parliamentary twists and turns of the first decade. In fact, my title for the book derives from one of these letters. As he struggled with the inevitability of a Fusion government, Deakin told his English readers that 'For reasons known only to himself, which are a perpetual subject of controversy in our Press, Mr Deakin pursues his enigmatic methods of action.'[7] It was not until after his death that Australians knew this was their prime minister writing about himself. Then there are his speeches, to parliament and to public meetings, as well as letters to friends, family and colleagues. All these give us access to the public, outer life. But there is much, much more.

After Deakin died, his family found notebooks filled with epigrams and observations, verse, prayers, soliloquies, religious writing and records of his voluminous reading. They were in locked cupboards in his study and not intended to be read by others, but in his last years dementia overtook Deakin and they survived. In 1884 he started a prayer diary which he maintained intermittently until 1913, talking to his God about his innermost doubts and expressing his gratitude for his fortunate life. Only rarely did he refer to political events but the prayer diary, together with other of his introspective private writings, provides remarkable access to his intimate inner life and allows us to explore the connections between the private man and the public world of events and actions.

After 1907 Deakin began to complain about lapses of memory. He was still a comparatively young man, only fifty-one, but over the next decade his mind disintegrated and when he died in 1919 he no longer knew who he was. Always an acute self-observer, he recorded with bleak honesty the erosion of his remarkable mind and memory until he had become 'a mere juggler with myself—misleading and misconstruing myself…my helpless attempts to read the riddle of my mind and thought must be frankly abandoned.'[8]

*

I wrote this book to bring Deakin back into Australia's contemporary political imagination, to understand how he shaped the country we live in today, and for the lessons he could teach us about how to handle unstable parliaments. I wanted to understand the handsome young man with the silver tongue and mesmeric eyes who sought his destiny in the politics of a colony that he believed to be at the forefront of liberal progress, his disillusionment in midlife when Victoria's prosperity crashed, his redemptive dedication to achieving federation, his determination, once the Commonwealth was launched, that it would succeed, and the puzzles about his motivations as the party system remade itself around him and liberalism's progressive energies shifted to the Labor Party.

The core challenge of political biography is to answer the question: Why politics? Why did Deakin choose politics for his life's work? What needs did it fulfil, and what emotional and psychological resources did he muster for its accomplishment? Deakin's papers reveal a solitary man who found much about political life deeply distasteful, with its unabashed self-interest, its double dealing and its mediocre appeal to the intellect. When Walter Murdoch published the first biography of Deakin, in 1923, he suggested that a quiet, literary life may have suited Deakin better than politics. But we have to judge a man's life not just by what he says but what he does.

Politics provided the young Deakin with drama, excitement and a great deal of attention from important older men. Deakin described himself as 'whirled into politics'.[9] Whirling is an image of motion and energy, worldly, natural, cosmic or spiritual, and with it Deakin aligned his entry into public life with larger forces. The conviction that he was singled out by higher powers to do great work on behalf of a cause was deeply embedded in Deakin's psyche and would never leave him.[10] As his life in politics unfolded, he did have periods of doubt; and he soon learned that public life had its fair share of tedium and repetition. But by then he was too deeply in to leave. And he persisted as long as he was able.

My biggest debts in writing this book are to the two historians of Melbourne Geoffrey Serle and Graeme Davison, for Deakin's is a Melbourne story, and to Deakin's previous biographers, whose books I have read over and over as I searched for the patterns of Deakin's life. The first was by Walter Murdoch, who wrote *Alfred Deakin: A Sketch* soon after Deakin's death when memories of him were fresh, including Murdoch's own. More than forty years later John La Nauze published his magisterial, meticulously researched two-volume study, *Alfred Deakin: A Biography*. La Nauze was most interested in Deakin as a nation-builder during the early years of the Commonwealth. He was somewhat nonplussed by his inner life, which he crammed into a single chapter, and little interested in relations within the family. La Nauze also brought several of Deakin's manuscripts into print: *The Crisis in Victorian Politics* in 1957 (with Max Crawford), a new edition of *The Federal Story* in 1963, and in 1968 a selection of his letters for the *Morning Post*, which he titled *Federated Australia*.

Two further biographical studies of Deakin appeared in the 1990s: Al Gabay's *The Mystic Life of Alfred Deakin*, which investigates his eclectic religious beliefs and voluminous religious writing, and has much detail on his spiritualism; and John Rickard's *A Family Romance: The Deakins at Home*, which emphasises the spiritualist context of Pattie and Alfred's courtship and uses Catherine Deakin's papers to probe the tensions in the triangular relationship between sister, brother and wife. These two studies, though immensely valuable, are partial: with the politics in the background, they assume the reader already knows why Deakin matters. Partial too are the handful of published articles and book chapters on Deakin. He is a complicated man, with multifarious interests, a propensity for temporary enthusiasms and a large archive. To trace just one theme through all this risks distortion.

I have dedicated the book to Alan Davies and John Hirst. Davies tried to interest me in writing about Deakin when I was a PhD student in the 1970s. He gave me a photocopy of *The New Pilgrim's Progress*, dictated by the spirit of John Bunyan to the nineteen-year-old Deakin. I did not take his advice on Deakin, but I did learn a great deal from him about the tasks of political biography. John Hirst read the first four chapters of the manuscript and it is an enduring grief he is not around to see the book published. I am grateful to Stuart Macintyre, Graeme Davison and Frank Bongiorno for their generous reading of the final manuscript and to my husband, Graeme Smith, for putting up with hours of pillow talk about Deakin. He also read the final manuscript, as did my friend Susan Lever. The Australian Research Council gave me a grant early in the research, and the Prime Ministers' Centre at Old Parliament House a fellowship towards the end. Alex McDermott provided valuable research assistance in the early days of the project, particularly with untangling Deakin's activities during the financial crises of the early 1890s, and John Rickard provided me with his notes on Alfred's letters to Pattie, which are still in the family's hands. The manuscript staff at the National Library of Australia were unfailingly courteous and helpful, and Trove is a researcher's dream, making Australian newspapers available from one's desk at home.

Judith Harley, Deakin's last surviving grandchild, has been generous with her time and memories, particularly of her beloved grandmother. Other of Deakin's descendants have also shared their memories and assisted with the illustrations. Particular thanks to Tom Harley and Sev Clarke. When I began to work on Deakin I spent several weeks at Ballara, his and Pattie's seaside retreat at Point Lonsdale, sitting on the verandah reading Deakin on himself, starting to think myself into his mind and world. Writing biography is an invasive business, and perilous, as one looks for the most plausible paths through the surviving evidence. I have done my best.

1

IMMIGRANTS' CHILD

ALFRED DEAKIN REMEMBERED himself as an unhappy child, a timid, lonely little boy made miserable by intensities of emotion he could barely contain, happy only when reading and occasionally at play. Others saw a different child, engaging and curious, an early talker and precocious reader, a restless, charming little chatterbox. The adult Deakin puzzled about the detachment he often felt from his busy, happy and successful everyday self: 'Living at the heart of things, a most untiring agent in the executive and legislative life of politics, with pulse oftener at fever pitch than those of the most compulsive gambler or speculator, I feel and have always felt "aloof".'[1] Occasionally he felt moments of overwhelming despair, more often just a sense of calm detachment. As with the child, others saw a different man, charming, responsive and quick-witted, a gifted orator and an effective politician. Both are true, and the challenge is to understand how they are related.

Deakin was born on Sunday, 3 August 1856, the only son of William and Sarah Deakin, who named him after the poet laureate, Alfred,

Lord Tennyson. They were good parents, and they loved him dearly, indulging his whims, nurturing the gift for language on which he would base his political career, and giving him the best education Melbourne could offer. But something in his early years laid down a residue of pain and a detachment he lost only towards the end, when his mind was failing, a small stone of unhappiness that ground away inside him, carving out the space for his richly lived inner life. The parents are the child's first world. To understand Deakin's childhood and its resonances in his later life we need to know his parents as well as we are able.

The major sources are the idealised portraits written long after childhood by Deakin and his sister, Catherine, Katie to the family.[2] She was six years his senior. Although recalled by the adult siblings, these are portraits from childhood, when the parents constitute the indissoluble unity that creates the world and their children cannot imagine it any other way. To Deakin, 'Neither ever seemed to have thought of the…possibility of there being any other partner in the world or person who could replace or displace their mutual attachment…They were complementary to each other in disposition and talent while they matched excellently in physique.' With the family, friends and places of their parents' youth on the other side of the world, how would the children know? There were no aunts or family friends in the colony to gossip about disappointed romances, no grandparents to recount stories of their parents' childhoods, few ways of understanding what had made their parents who they were.

Alfred and Catherine also agreed that, apart from providing a loving and supportive home, their parents had little overt influence on the direction of their lives and interests. Many children of immigrants no doubt feel that they made their own way in the new land. But children do not bring themselves up, and the Deakin home was close. Nor did Alfred or Catherine ever ponder what emigration meant for their parents or wonder about their states of mind in their early years in the colony.

Deakin's fullest portrait of his parents was written in 1908 on the day his mother died. Her eighty-five-year-old self fell away, and he remembered the comely young woman of his childhood, the feel of her body and his own adoring gaze: 'I was conscious of her beauty even when still a very young child feeling the gracefulness of her figure, admirably proportioned, supple and strong though slight—the delicate tone of her complexion, pale but easily flushed—her clear grey eyes always calm and calming, clear and still.' Both her children saw Sarah's life as centred on her home and family. To Deakin, she was 'wife and mother first and last, all her womanhood expressed in those relations—There was no life for her outside them, and no thought of hers that did not begin and end in them.'

The family's link to the outside world was William. Deakin's portrait of his father is of a passionate, sociable, excitable man: 'Sensitive in the extreme, ambitious, variable, imitative, talkative, fond of praise and approval, rapid in adapting himself to strangers and fond of meeting them…emotional, affectionate, expressive, versatile, impressionable and reckless'. He was 'susceptible to the beauties of nature, of men and women, of music and literature…often witty, a capital mimic, an admirable reader aloud, a vivacious story teller with natural taste, verve and effectiveness'. Much of this could also be said of the adult Deakin.

William and Sarah Deakin arrived in the colony of South Australia as newlyweds in 1850. The couple had met in the Welsh market town of Abergavenny near the English border sometime during 1849 and, according to their son, they at once 'fell in love'. Family lore has it that an old gypsy woman in the west of England told William Deakin that within a few weeks he would meet and fall in love with his future wife and they would travel to the other side of the world and have two children. The gypsy's assessment was shrewd. In 1849 more than three hundred thousand people a year were leaving Britain and Ireland. Many were just married and the average age of the men was thirty, the same age as William. He had been working since he was fourteen, when his father died, and was visiting Abergavenny as a travelling grocer. His mother was living in Witney in Oxfordshire, and he wrote regularly to family members, but at the time he emigrated he was used to travelling and had no settled home.[3]

Sarah's life was very different. Twenty-seven and still living at home on a large, prosperous tenant farm, she was the fifth of the ten children of William and Sarah Bill, all born in the parish of Llanarth in the beautiful border country between Wales and England. The family farm was Long Barn, and when William Bill married Sarah Jones from the neighbouring village of Penrose in 1815, he regarded himself as of sufficient social standing to announce it in the *New Monthly Magazine*, a recently established Tory periodical.[4] When their daughter Sarah was born on Christmas Day, 1822, he was the tenant of Great House on the same estate as Long Barn, where his brother Richard was now the farmer. The brothers occupied the second- and third-most valuable farms in the parish, and took their turns with the other farmers to act as overseers of the poor. William's graceful copperplate hand records the distribution of weekly payments and in-kind support to the poor of the parish. Sarah came from a family of some local standing, literate and with a history of taking responsibility for local affairs. Her cultural and social identifications were English, and her son Alfred never claimed any Welsh heritage.[5]

Sometime after 1833, when the last of their children was baptised and Sarah was around ten, the Bill family moved to the large farm of Great Campston about seven miles to the north of Llanarth, near the village of Grosmont on the Herefordshire border. It was a step up in the world. The farm was substantial, 332 acres, employing a number of servants and labourers, and the family lived in a seventeenth-century manor house. Grosmont was also considerably bigger than Llanarth. Once a Norman garrison town, it had a ruined castle, a large church, a market square and a school. Llanarth, though, remained the village closest to the family's heart. William and Sarah Bill went to some trouble to be buried there and Deakin later chose the name for the house he and his wife Pattie built in Melbourne.[6]

The Bills were still living at Great Campston when the 1851 census was taken. Soon after, William died in the neighbouring parish. He was sixty-two when his daughter Sarah met William Deakin. It is likely his health was failing and Sarah was under pressure to find herself a husband, though a surviving courtship letter from William suggests that he did not gain immediate approval from her friends, who saw him as unequal to her in birth, education and wealth. Professing the ardour of his affection, he also tells her that 'I cannot compromise one iota of my independence.'[7]

After a short courtship the couple married on 18 October 1849 at St Nicholas', Grosmont. On his marriage certificate William recorded his occupation as grocer and his father's as currier, the leather-industry trade which finishes the hides. By the time of William's death in Melbourne in 1892, his father's occupation had been elevated to civil servant, perhaps to make him a more fitting forebear of one of the colony's leading politicians.[8] There is no record of a honeymoon, or of their living arrangements as man and wife, but when they embarked for Australia on 29 December, Sarah was already pregnant. Friends from Grosmont, James Bevan and his sister, were on the same boat, part of an exodus of young people from the district. Richard Bill, Sarah's brother, followed in 1853.

With seasickness on top of morning sickness, Sarah spent the eighty-six-day voyage mainly below deck while her new husband acted as chambermaid. He wrote to his sister that had he known she would be so ill, he would not have left England. Apart from this, he did not regret the decision as once they arrived in Adelaide he was confident they would soon get ahead, noting the ways men of small capital could make money with investments and property.[9] Still, it was not a great way to start a marriage between two people who scarcely knew each other.

As a commercial traveller, William was used to the peripatetic life and the society of strangers. Emigration was not the wrench for him that it was for Sarah, who had lived all her life in a close-knit rural community. She brought with her two small leather-covered notebooks of poems, some written by her, some by friends and family, and some copied from popular poets. One notebook is dated 1844, when she was twenty-two; the other is later and includes a number of poems of farewell from just before their embarkation. Sarah's own poems in her spidery hand are typical of the domestic poetry popular in the middle decades of the nineteenth century, four-line verses about loss, memory, parting, and affection for home and family, with titles such as 'Farewell', 'The Departure', 'Forget Thee No', 'The Forsaken', 'The Lock of Hair' and 'Grief Under Smiles'. One poem seems to suggest a

dead sweetheart. In 1847, when she was visiting Manchester, she wrote
'My Home'. These verses have a particular poignancy for a young
woman destined for emigration.

> I sit amidst a stranger's Home
> I join in strangers' mirth
> And my heart is in my native land
> And by my father's hearth...
>
> But still my Mother's smile is there
> And her tone of love to warm
> And my sweet young sister bright and fair
> With touches of fairy form.

An affectionate undated poem of William's, 'To My Dearest Sarah',
acknowledges how painful it was for Sarah to part from those she loved,
and her dread of 'the moment we utter Farewell'.[10]

The couple's first few years were unsettled. Catherine was born in July
1850 in Adelaide and named after William's mother. A year later they
joined the rush to Victoria after gold was discovered, and William became
one of the legions of unsuccessful diggers in the Central Goldfields.
For Sarah these few years must have been extremely difficult, caring
for the infant Catherine as they lived in temporary accommodation,
enduring the heat and flies of the Australian summer, and attempting
to keep themselves clean and respectable in the chaos of the goldfields.
As well, mingling with people from all over the world and of all classes
and religions would have been confronting for a shy woman who had
rarely ventured outside the district in which she was born. Sarah's brother
Richard arrived in 1853, and sometime after that he and William set
up a coaching business. Bill and Deakin's People's Line of Coaches ran
from Melbourne through Kyneton and Gisborne to Bendigo.[11]

By the time their son was born in 1856, the better prospects they
had emigrated to find were starting to take shape. They were living in
a rented cottage in George Street, in an area soon to be Fitzroy, on the

northern edge of the city of Melbourne. The coaching business had its
stables in nearby Gertrude Street. The neighbourhood was filling fast
with new immigrants. Their friend from Grosmont, James Bevan, was
two doors down, the proprietor of a booming road-contracting business.
Richard Bill and his family were in Gore Street. The Deakins were
doing well enough to employ a maid and a nurse to help Sarah with the
new baby. Soon after, they moved to a larger house at 27 Gore Street, on
the corner of Little Victoria Street. It was a good position, on the ridge
before the land plunges down to the Collingwood flats, with a view
across the bush stretching to the Dandenongs on the eastern horizon.[12]

What was the state of Sarah's heart when her son was born? She
was thirty-three and had been in the colonies a little more than six
years. Although Catherine was born in the first year of her married
life, there had been no more babies until Alfred and he would be their
last child. The average married woman had six live births, and large
families of ten or more were common. And the beloved home she had
left was no more. In the early 1850s, her father and mother moved to
the next county, perhaps to live with a married daughter, and both
died soon after: her father in 1852, her mother in 1855.[13] To a woman
still feeling the pain of emigration, this was a final severance from the
home of her childhood and youth.

No letters survive from this period, but Deakin's later memories
of Sarah's self-containment and suppression suggest a mother who
may have been emotionally unavailable as she grieved her parents'
deaths and the loss of home, leaving him, as in the lines he loved from
Tennyson's poem *In Memoriam: A. H. H.*,

> An infant crying in the night:
> An infant crying for the light:
> And with no language but a cry.[14]

All his life Deakin sought solace in the belief in a divine universe, and
yearned to lose himself in a mystically experienced oneness.

Catherine was six when her brother was born, beginning a lifelong
devotion: 'I worshipped the baby as I have the man during all our lives.'

She spent her savings to make her first purchase, her own rocking chair to nurse him in.[15] Catherine was a serious child, small and plain, who spent her life in her brother's shadow, seemingly without conscious resentment. In a photo of the family when Alfred is about one, he is sitting snugly on his father's knee while she stands somewhat to the side of her mother, with a hand resting in her lap.

William and Sarah wanted a far better education for Catherine than was available at the overcrowded school at St Mark's in George Street, or at the local Dame schools. In 1858, when she was eight, she became a pupil at a newly established Ladies' School in Kyneton. A pretty town about eighty-five kilometres to the north of Melbourne, Kyneton was a staging post on the route between Melbourne and Bendigo, and the Bill and Deakin coaches stopped there regularly. The school, run by the Misses Thompson, was typical of the nineteenth-century ladies' academies which offered middle-class girls both knowledge and polish: a sound education in English, history and geography, with the refined accomplishments of music, French, drawing and dancing. Louisa Thompson, who was head of music, was a skilled teacher and Catherine developed into a fine musician.[16]

After she had been there two years, and when Alfred was only four, Sarah and William made the extraordinary decision to send him to join her. Sarah and William's commitment to the education of their children is one of the most striking features of their parenting. The goldrush immigrants produced Melbourne's first baby boom, but only a minority of these children received more than three years of education. When Alfred joined Catherine he was 'the only male among dozens of girls of all ages'.[17] According to Catherine, it was she who persuaded her parents to let him join her.

Catherine no doubt missed her home and may indeed have pleaded for the company of her darling little brother, but why did William and Sarah agree? Four is a very young age to send a child away from his mother. And the combined cost of two children boarding was ninety guineas a year, the annual income of an unskilled labourer. This was a hefty sum. Deakin later claimed that his father's income was never more than three hundred pounds a year, the bare minimum to qualify for entry into the middle class.[18] This is likely an understatement by the son honouring the sacrifices his parents made for him, but to send both children to boarding school was still an unusual decision for a family of their relatively modest means.

Catherine recalled that she was sent to Kyneton for the bracing climate, and Deakin agreed that it was partly for their health.[19] Although there is no evidence that either child was sickly, Melbourne in the late 1850s was not a safe place for young children. It had no sewerage system and infectious diseases were rife. Sixteen hundred people died of infectious diseases in the city in 1860, most of them children. In 1857 James Bevan's first born had died of 'congestion of the brain' at seven months; and in 1859 William Deakin was in the room when Richard Bill's nine-month-old son died of 'exhaustion from bilious derangement', a distressing experience he may well have taken as an omen, particularly as he and Sarah were not a fertile couple.[20]

Sarah's own physical or mental health may also have been a reason. With only two children, her household duties were not demanding, particularly as the family had a maid, Alfred had a nurse and Catherine was at boarding school. And, with William an effective breadwinner, she had no need to work to supplement the family's income. Likely there were miscarriages or stillbirths. One of Deakin's fragmentary childhood memories is of burying a doll with a wooden spade; perhaps he had been promised a baby, who died.[21]

Whatever the reasons she and William had for sending their children to boarding school, it was a fateful decision for Alfred, who compensated for his confused loneliness with a vivid fantasy life. Deakin's most extended piece of autobiographical writing on his childhood is an essay called 'Books and a Boy' that he wrote in 1910 for a small circle of family and friends. It is a somewhat contrived piece, in which a quote from St John's Gospel introduces a sentimental family tableau:

'In the beginning was the Word' half encircles a little vignette, lightly tinted according to the vogue of half a century ago... Nothing could be simpler than its presentation of an old-fashioned cottage room with the open fire place, universal in early colonial

days, a loving mother, infant on knee, white-gowned and glowing
from his hot bath, out of which his sister had just tenderly lifted
him, while the father sitting by the oil lamp watches the effect of
his first gift to his boy.[22]

The gift is a stiff-leaved calico picture book with images of lions and
elephants and other exotic animals, and the boy is entranced. Mother,
father and sister all look at him adoringly, but he is looking elsewhere,
into another world to which books are the door.

2

MELBOURNE GRAMMAR

IN 1863 THE Misses Thompson moved their school from Kyneton to South Yarra, and Catherine and Alfred moved back to the family home.[1] Seven-year-old Alfred recited a humorous piece at the Christmas party to great acclaim from the largely female audience, who were charmed by the pretty boy. He accompanied Catherine to and from school and, according to her, 'was rarely out of her control'. In 1864 one of the Misses Thompson boxed his ears and repeated it after he threatened to tell his father. As a result, William and Sarah removed Alfred from the girls' school and enrolled him as a day boy at Melbourne Grammar, where the boys teased him for his girlish ways and looks. He was now nearly eight, and had spent the last four years largely with women and girls who petted and made much of him. Now he needed to learn to live among boys.[2]

To enable Catherine and Alfred to continue their schooling, the family left the crowded streets of Fitzroy for the new suburb of South Yarra, with its larger blocks and more open space. At first they rented, but in 1865 William paid £225 for a block of almost half an acre in Adams Street, which runs into Toorak Road a block back from St Kilda Road.[3] He moved the wooden house from Gore Street and bolstered it with brick nogging. At the north end of Adams Street were the fields and new bluestone buildings of Melbourne Grammar, at the south the newly created Fawkner Park. Opposite was the Blue Lagoon, which became Albert Park Lake, filled with waterbirds. They called the house The Elms and Sarah began to plant a garden.

The family was now settled and this remained the family home until Catherine's death in 1937, though some of the land was sold as Melbourne's real-estate prices skyrocketed over the next few decades. William also bought and sold other land. In an 1883 notebook he records instructions to sell the remaining block of land in Toorak Road for £1,450 and one in Adams Street for fifteen hundred pounds, along with two lots in nearby Walsh Street.[4] William may have been a clerk on only three hundred pounds a year, and he may have made some unwise investments as his son later claimed, but he also made some very profitable ones.

Around 1860 the Bill and Deakin coaching business merged with one run by James Bevan, who had moved his family to Caulfield where he built a mansion and called it Grosmont. The families remained close. In 1866 Bevan and his wife were drowned returning to Australia from a trip home on the steamer *London*. Overloaded with coal, it sank in the Bay of Biscay. The combined coaching business was taken over by Cobb and Co., and William worked there until his retirement, possibly as manager of the Melbourne to Bendigo route.[5] When the two orphaned Bevan children were taken back to Wales by their paternal relatives, the Deakin family was at the docks to farewell the weeping children. Jimmy was to become the first captain of the Welsh rugby team.[6]

The Elms was across the paddock from Melbourne Grammar, which had been established by Archbishop Perry in 1858 to provide the sons of Melbourne's Anglican elite with 'education of the highest order'.[7] Initially it aimed to replicate the great English boarding schools like Eton and Harrow, which removed boys from their parents to be moulded by the school. But the Melbourne middle class wanted a day school. Fees were about twenty pounds a year, with gymnastics, dancing and singing extra, and when Deakin started there were around two hundred pupils, most of them day boys like him.[8]

Deakin's early memories of school are of being teased by the boys for his effeminate looks and ways, and being chastised by the masters for his ceaseless talking. 'Deakin, you are a truthful boy, generally a well-meaning boy, sometimes a good boy, but always the most incorrigible vexatious restless and babbling creature I ever met,' said one. Upper primary and lower secondary he remembered as a 'drudgery lived without an interest or an end except when history, geography or some similar subject appealed to me and then memory made it easy for me to scramble thro'—Grammar I detested. Language brought no material for dreams.' Deakin did poorly in Latin, Greek and French, all of which required discipline and persistence. Nor, he claimed, was he motivated by competitiveness: his 'place in class was a matter of supreme indifference'.

He was dreamy, restless in class, and one of a group who made the life of the French master 'almost unbearable'. Deakin also remembered 'an indifferent despotic sneering master' and a writing master who drank, but none of the traumas of persecution and brutality associated with British nineteenth-century public schooling. Every day he went home to his indulgent parents and adoring sister, to well-cooked meals, and to his books and daydreams.

He 'read anything that came his way' until 'the dreams they bred became by degree the staple of his existence…For him indeed his books filled background, foreground and middle distance.' Books became 'the mirror of life, however faulty, over which he hung as if enchanted', and the door to a world of fantasy and make-believe. 'I spun romance after romance based on my favourite books in which I was the culmination of all heroes…winning a long line of peerless beauties under the most desperate and amazing circumstances.'[9]

In his daydreams he tried out different careers, creating worlds to match, complete with geography, characters, cities, seaports, armies, courts and industries, always with himself as the hero. From his father's shelves stocked with the English classics from Bunyan to Dickens, to books begged and borrowed from friends and neighbours, young Deakin read greedily as he grew, and with no discrimination. When old enough to travel alone, he spent Saturdays, holidays and after school at the new Melbourne and Prahran public libraries.[10]

All over the British empire, clever, restless young men and women were eagerly reading the books and magazines that were pouring from England's presses, seeking escape and pleasure, but also knowledge and ideas, and with these membership of larger cultural worlds beyond village and town, household and colony. One cannot over-emphasise the transporting and transforming power of books in the Victorian era. When Philip Wakem offers Maggie Tulliver a book in George Eliot's *The Mill on the Floss*, she refuses it 'because it would make me long to see and know many things—it would make me long for a full life'.

In 1866, when she was fifteen, Catherine started a diary in which she recorded the comings and goings of the little household for the next twelve years. She was no longer attending the Misses Thompson's school, but she continued with private music and French lessons, and was becoming an accomplished musician. She occupied her days with sewing, music practice and household chores, exchanging visits with friends, family drives with Papa at the reins, shopping with Mama, trips to the theatre, to concerts and to church, and occasional holidays in the country or at the seaside.

She records family birthdays and anniversaries, and, as she gets a little older, her romantic interests. And she gives us glimpses of young Alfie, accompanying her to church, getting measles, giving and receiving birthday presents, falling in the water while fishing, listening to Papa read Dickens to them all, attending the races with Papa and losing two pounds, the weekly wage of a labourer. Occasionally, William, who remained a country man at heart, returned from a shooting trip with ducks for the table.

It was a quiet, orderly life. Melbourne's burgeoning recreational opportunities far outstripped those available in rural Wales. The city was on the international touring circuits of the leading British performers, and Deakin when very young saw Sir William Don as a pantomime dame and the Irish Shakespearean actor Barry Sullivan. The seeds were sown for his love of theatre and the dramatic entrance. In November 1867 the family was on the streets to welcome the colony's first royal visitor, Queen Victoria's second son, the twenty-three-year-old Prince Alfred, who visited Melbourne to a rapturous reception. The Deakins cheered as his ship came up the bay, saw the Illuminations decorating the city streets, watched as he laid the foundation stone of the new Melbourne Town Hall and joined in the crowd at the torchlight procession. At a combined speech day of the four principal boys' schools in Melbourne, His Royal Highness presented Alfie with two book prizes. One was the complete *Robinson Crusoe*.[11]

In 1869, when he was twelve, Deakin transferred to the upper school, where his hero worship for one of the masters began to draw him out of his dream worlds. The master was John Henning Thompson, brother of the Misses Thompson, who had been in the school's first intake and had twice served as its captain.[12] Compared with the middle-aged immigrant masters, Thompson was a man a native-born boy could identify with: 'over 6 feet, handsome as Apollo, voice like a bugle, eyes beautiful as a woman's…His influence over me was the most potent yet formed', and to please him Deakin began to apply himself to his studies.[13] Thompson remembered Deakin at this age as quick and clever, excelling in history and with 'very great discrimination and fastidiousness in the choice and use of words'. He also remembered that although he was 'like most healthy boys, full of mischief', he was 'one of Nature's gentlemen, never wantonly saying or doing anything to cause needless pain'. Another memory of Thompson's shows the young Deakin's remarkable self-confidence. The headmaster, Dr Bromby, was chastising the assembled boys for some misdemeanour, denouncing the perpetrator and declaring that if he did not come forward the whole school must suffer.

> When the torrent of reproof had ceased, a handsome and refined looking child—he did not seem more than ten at most—was seen to rise at the far end of lower school, and in his childish voice, thin and piping but delightfully audible, explained, with an entire absence of self-consciousness, and with perfect self-possession, and

without the least hesitation or lack of appropriate words, how the
Doctor was under a misapprehension, and it was all a mistake.[14]

The old man smiled and accepted the explanation. What is remarkable
about this story is not just Deakin's verbal fluency but his trust in the
rationality and responsiveness of authority, evidence of a family life
in which he expected to be listened to and had no fear of arbitrary
punishment.

Bromby had a lasting influence on Deakin. His life of spartan
simplicity—morning exercise such as wood chopping or gardening,
a disciplined diet and no alcohol—provided the growing boy with a
model of vigorous, disciplined manhood. And his talks to his pupils
were a model of sustained public speaking. A description of Bromby
delivering a lecture with 'a rhythm of rise and swell in the inflection like
a running stream with successive cascades' could well have described
Deakin at the height of his powers.[15]

Bromby's curriculum included science and modern languages alongside the classics. His Friday afternoon talks with the upper school about
developments in the sciences captured Deakin's wandering attention.
In the great mid-century debates between science and religion, Bromby
took the side of science, arguing that its discoveries posed no threat to
religious truth. With evidence from geology and archaeology attesting
to the antiquity of the earth, the Bible, he said, must be regarded as a
book of spiritual not literal truth, and he told them about the new theory
of evolution. When Bromby repeated these controversial arguments in
public lectures on 'Prehistoric Man' and 'Creation versus Development',
he was accused by defenders of the Bible of substituting apes for God
in the story of man's creation.[16]

Deakin did well in the subjects Bromby taught, but Bromby did
not regard him as particularly gifted. His testimonial recommended
him as 'a useful hand either in drilling junior classes in a school or in
private tuition'.[17] In his last years at school Deakin became less shy and
solitary, a transformation he attributed to the arrival of Theodore Fink,
a confident boy with plenty of cheek 'and a cheerful mastery of abusive
and insulting epithets'. Deakin became his admiring ally, learning

from him how to argue back. 'His want of reverence for anything and anybody except the Dr and his cool courage when assailed conveyed invaluable lessons.' With precocious business and organisational skills, Fink started a handwritten school newspaper, formed an orchestra to encourage the football team, and organised lotteries with a currency of nibs, penholders and blotting paper, which grew to such proportions that the careless were bankrupted of the necessities of schoolwork.[18]

By Fink's side, Deakin was now in the thick of schoolyard activities. Writing to Catherine in 1871, when he was fourteen and in his last year at school, he recounted an elaborate schoolyard role play in which one Thomas Martin and two Irish boys conspire to blow up the governor and the volunteers in the militia. They would then march into town, where they would be joined by all the Roman Catholics and form a republic. A general massacre of Protestants was to follow, war to be declared against England and Ireland to be freed.

> We may all be thankful that this dark and bloody plot did not succeed. Martin is to be arrested and tried in the school room on Friday…A Law Court has been started at the school, and you will be glad to hear that I am doing a splendid business as a solicitor and Queen's Counsel and I am at present occupied with the case of 'The Crown v Martin' for High Treason.[19]

Loyal British Protestant suspicions of Irish Roman Catholics had been confirmed three years earlier when a mentally unstable Irishman shot Prince Alfred in the back at a fundraising picnic in New South Wales during his Australian visit. The prince survived but sectarian tensions in the colony were inflamed, and suspicion of Irish Catholics became part of every Protestant schoolboy's common sense.

Later that same year, Deakin enrolled in a volunteer militia, the Southern Rifles. The minimum lawful age was seventeen, and he made no attempt to disguise his youth, but the old sergeant winked and passed him in. He was tall for his age, already five foot eight, slender and with a slight stoop. He grew fast, and fifty years later could still remember his heights: five foot eleven at seventeen, before reaching his

final height of six foot two inches. The Southern Rifles had a debating
society where he would rattle off his hastily formed opinions, but his
military career lasted only three years. He resigned in 1874, 'having
become an advocate for peace'.[20]

Deakin grew to manhood before the jingoism and hardening of
masculinity that took place in the British empire in the last decades of
the nineteenth century. He was never troubled by his lack of martial
skills and, despite his commitment to vigorous daily exercise, he had
little interest in competitive sport. In the 1860s the education of a middle-
class boy was a combination of cultural cultivation heavily influenced
by a romantic sensibility, and the evangelical revival's inculcation of
moral uprightness and a sense of duty and service. As yet there were
no stiff upper lips.

Deakin went up for matriculation in 1871, a decision he remembered
as largely left to himself to make. He passed Latin and English and did
well in Algebra, Euclid and History, but he was not at all sure what he
would do with himself.[21] In this he was not alone. An observer of the
goldrush immigrants' children commented that 'the transition from
boyhood to manhood is an indefinite question…the colonial boy is
allowed to draft himself.'[22] When Deakin was fifteen, 47.5 per cent of
the colony's population was under twenty, with just 0.8 per cent aged
seventy and over: so many young boys to absorb into the workforce, so
many girls to keep respectable, with the paths into adulthood unclear
in a new society.[23]

Most of these young people had no grandparents or older relatives
to provide role models or give them a leg up. The big decision of their
parents' early adult lives had been to emigrate. For them the question
was how to make a living and settle down. Like many other colonial
immigrant parents, William and Sarah had no definite plans for Alfred.
According to Catherine, their idea was to 'put him in the way and let
him blaze the track in any direction, so that he becomes an honourable
man'.[24]

While the lack of a clear pathway into manhood was common
for his generation, in other ways Deakin was very different. His life

had been sheltered and privileged. The family's unusually small size meant William could afford to give his only son the best education the colony could provide. The contrast was not just with the ragged urchins and newsboys who ran through Melbourne's streets and lanes; it was also with his middle-class peers, most of whom were out working as clerks or pupil teachers after only a couple of years of secondary school. Matriculants, who qualified for university entrance, were rare. In 1871 only forty-eight boys from Melbourne's four leading schools presented themselves for the exam, and only thirty-nine were successful.[25]

His parents' light touch of authority was not so unusual, as parenting in the colonies was generally more easy-going than that back Home.[26] William was no authoritarian patriarch instilling guilt and fear via the word of God, but a nurturing father closely involved in his children's lives. Catherine remembered her mother and father as great believers in good manners and the customs of well-bred English folk and with a strong sense of duty, but otherwise broadminded and unconventional.[27] It is hard to know quite what she means by this: perhaps their support for her own education and their tolerance of her and Alfred's later interest in spiritualism; perhaps that they left much up to their children to decide for themselves.

At fifteen Deakin was addicted to reading, daydreaming and to writing his own stories and dramas. In so far as he had any definite aspirations, they were for the stage, which promised poetry and romance, spectacle and passion. He imagined becoming an actor manager 'whose life was devoted to the elevation of the stage by poetic drama filled with passion and power and devoted to high ideals of life, faith and prophecy'.[28] Spectacle and passion he would find in politics; the poetry and romance turned into a lifelong intellectual and spiritual quest for the meaning of life and the universe.

3

AFTER SCHOOL

DEAKIN KNEW HE had to settle on his life's work, but what was it to be? For most of 1872, the year after he finished school, he 'drifted rudderless', doing little 'but delve with delight' into his books and extending his circle of friends. He formed intense friendships with two men ten or so years older than himself: David Mickle, and Arthur Patchett Martin, who a few years later was a co-founder of the *Melbourne Review.*

> For two years we walked and talked together always on Sundays… sometimes two or three afternoons and evenings during the week. I read hard to catch up to them and with the memory I then possessed carried most of my reading with me…The gates of knowledge, judgment and speculation were swung wide open day and night as the three inveterate talkers wrestled with the latest books or articles in the reviews to keep abreast of the times.[1]

He may have met David and Arthur through Catherine, who was now in her early twenties and of an age to marry. Brother and sister were very close, and Alfred frequently accompanied her to parties and the theatre. In 1873 William and Sarah added a music room to The Elms, where Catherine and Alfred entertained their friends at parties and dances, and in early 1874 held a spirit circle. The parents must have enjoyed making their children's friends welcome, particularly William, who had left home at fourteen to earn his living. A sociable man, he entered enthusiastically into the young people's arguments and discussions. Although William and Sarah were leaving them to choose their own way, the reserved Catherine might have benefited from a little help in the business of marriage. From the evidence of her diary there were suitors, and she wanted to marry, but chances slipped away.

Doting and indulgent as William and Sarah were, they were also attuned to the practical necessity for their son to earn his bread. Sometime during 1872 William, no doubt a little exasperated by Alfred's drifting, read aloud to him and Catherine Thomas Carlyle's 1866 address to the students at the University of Edinburgh in which he tells them that 'the first of all problems for a man [is] to find out what kind of work he is to do in the universe.' This was just the problem the young Deakin was facing and on impulse he bought, for two shillings, Carlyle's *Sartor Resartus*, which he later described as the first work that directed his thought along serious channels.[2]

Sartor Resartus, first published in 1833, is a difficult book for the modern reader—the life of Professor Teufelsdröckh (devil's shit) reconstructed by a putative editor from fragmentary documents. In form it recalls the eighteenth-century satires of Sterne and Swift, with some debt to Bunyan's *Pilgrim's Progress*. It offers spiritual advice to young men and women whose sense of life's purpose has been shaped by religion, yet who are unable to live comfortably inside the old dogmas and institutional forms. Teufelsdröckh's journey takes him from his youth as a briefless barrister trying to become a writer, to an embrace of duty and an apprehension of the divinity and spiritual unity of the world; a journey from the Everlasting No, through the city of Indifference, to the Everlasting Yea, where the pilgrim embraces the world and his faith in God:

'Do the Duty which lies nearest thee', which thou knowest to be a Duty!…When your Ideal World, wherein the whole man has been dimly struggling and inexpressibly languishing to work, becomes revealed, and thrown open; and you discover, with amazement enough, like the Lothario in *Wilhelm Meister*, that your 'America is here or nowhere'? The Situation that has not its Duty, its Ideal, was never yet occupied by man. Yes, here, in this poor, miserable, hampered, despicable Actual, wherein thou even now standest, here or nowhere is thy Ideal…Fool! The Ideal is in thyself, the impediment too is in thyself.[3]

Carlyle's injunction to the active life was particularly well suited to the uncertainties of a new colony, and Carlyle was a large presence in Victoria. A good few among the goldrush literati knew him personally, and numerous reading groups and literary societies discussed his books.[4] Over the next few years Deakin and Catherine also read Carlyle's *The French Revolution: A History*, *Chartism* and *Past and Present*; and Carlyle introduced him to the idealist writings of the American Transcendentalists Ralph Waldo Emerson and Henry Thoreau. A serious young man finding his way in a new land, Deakin devoured the Transcendentalists, who gave shape to his own emerging spiritual identity. Why, asked Emerson, should we not throw off the sepulchres of the past, to 'enjoy an original relation to the universe? Why should not we have a poetry and philosophy of insight and not of tradition, and a religion by revelation to us?…There are new lands, new men, new thoughts. Let us demand our own works and laws and worship.'[5] The Transcendentalists' faith that the Divine was to be sought within, through intuition, suited his introspective nature, and their belief in the fundamental continuity between humanity, Nature and God accorded with lessons he was already drawing from his reading of the English Romantic poets William Wordsworth and Samuel Taylor Coleridge.

By sixteen, Deakin had already rejected conventional religion. William and Sarah, nominally Church of England, were not particularly devout, although Catherine attended church regularly and Alfred often accompanied her. Around 1869 he volunteered as a Sunday

School teacher, until he was required to prepare for confirmation. In his 1910 reminiscences, he gives two explanations for his refusal to be confirmed: 'my father's feeling was against conformity'; and 'Christianity as I understood it was wider than any or even all of the Churches and therefore acceptance of any formal limitations was impossible.'[6] Catherine organised her own confirmation when she was twenty.[7]

About this time Deakin became a strict vegetarian. He was likely influenced by his humanist commitment to animal welfare, but perhaps also by a temperamental digestion which plagued him all his life.[8] He describes this as 'one of his first departures' but, as he did not cook, 'the brown flour revolution' he brought to the family table depended on Sarah's indulgence.[9] He also became a temperance man, and, with a teenager's excessive asceticism, gave up tea and coffee as well.

It took Deakin most of 1872 to settle on some direction. Towards the end of the year he enrolled as a 'student at law' at the University of Melbourne, largely at the urging of Theodore Fink and for the practical reason that one could study in the evening and earn a living during the day. After three years of study, a student at law received a certificate of admission to the Victorian bar. This was a lesser qualification than the Bachelor of Laws, which required arts subjects with daytime lectures.[10] Deakin was one of the last to enrol before the rules changed and a Bachelor of Laws was required for admission to the bar. He enrolled only six weeks before the final first-year exams, and passed with the aid of his excellent memory.[11] There was little sense of vocation in this decision, but it was at least a temporary answer to the question of what he was to do with himself.

During his law studies in 1873 and 1874 Deakin had a number of jobs, none of which lasted very long. He worked briefly as a junior teacher at two nearby schools, and as a private tutor to the sons of Colonel William Anderson, the commander of the colony's volunteer forces, who lived nearby in South Yarra. Anderson's wife, Caroline, found him an energetic and painstaking teacher of her sons, whose affection and respect he won.[12] He also volunteered as a teacher at the Gospel Hall Free Night School for ragged boys in an alley off Bourke

Street, where he captivated his young audience with his 'illustrative story telling'.

Here he caught the eye of a Methodist layman involved in running the school, a Mr Evans, who approached William Deakin with a business proposition. He told William that 'he had always been attracted' to his son, and that he would like him to come into his stationery business. William agreed, and invested in the business to give Alfred the opportunity to develop commercial skills, possibly raising the funds by taking out a mortgage on the Adams Street property.[13] But Mr Evans was drifting towards bankruptcy. 'Poor Papa and all of us dreadfully anxious about business,' records Catherine.[14] It ended badly and William lost a hefty sum of money. Alfred 'returned with redoubled zeal to my possible profession and to endeavor to master some kind of literary craftsmanship in poetry or prose'.[15] Evans was the first of the older men who offered to help the talkative young Deakin get on in the world.

While studying law, Deakin hoped he might become a man of letters. He had added an addiction to writing to his addictive reading, and in the years between sixteen and twenty-two words poured from his pen—poems, verse dramas and literary essays, most of them derivative adaptations from his reading. His first attempt at verse in 1872 was based on *The Phantom Ship*, Frederick Marryat's novel about the ghostly Flying Dutchman. It began, 'How haunting is the mystic ancient legend of the sea.' His nature poems expressed Wordsworthian awe at Nature. 'Great trances of ecstasy' were evoked 'by my brief and rare contact with beauty—forests, mountains, streams and the seasons peculiar to Australia'. Sunsets were his keenest source of delight, 'for in a city like Melbourne without features for relief, the sky obtains... an enormous transcendancy of space.' He did not try to publish his poems and dramas, but he did read them to his always appreciative sister and mother.[16] After 1910 he destroyed the surviving manuscripts, leaving only the titles and occasional fragments: 'Raglan Island or the Wreck of the Nelson'; 'Guy Evelyn or In the Far Pacific'; 'Sea Strays, a condensed novel after Bret Harte'.[17]

One survivor is a verse drama, *Quentin Massys*, written in 1873 and 1874, and printed at his own expense in 1875 in the hope that it might find a commercial production, preferably with Deakin in the leading role of the poor but gifted young blacksmith who becomes a painter to win the hand of his beloved. It is based loosely on legends about the early life of the sixteenth-century Flemish artist Quentin Matsys and in form on Shakespeare's five-act plays in blank verse. Deakin personally took a copy of his play to the St Kilda home of actor manager Henry R. Harwood, whose usual fare was burlesque and light opera and who showed no interest. Deakin also sent a copy to the bookseller and publisher George Robertson, whose manager of publishing judged it poor in every way, 'the style too loose and turgid…words linked together only for a supposed effectiveness, but with entire absence of propriety and often of meaning'. Deakin subsequently destroyed most copies of the play.[18]

Meanwhile, he was doing more disciplined reading and writing at university. Charles Pearson, who lectured in history and political economy, was his most influential university teacher. Pearson was a published historian, and had been professor of modern history at King's College London. He had migrated to Australia for its liberal political possibilities and his health. In his mid-forties, he was a worldly, travelled scholar who knew personally many of the men Deakin was reading so assiduously in the quarterly magazines, men of letters like Leslie Stephen and Henry Sidgwick, and radical liberal politicians like Charles Dilke and Joseph Chamberlain.

Pearson was writing leaders for the colony's chief organ of liberal views, David Syme's *Age*. At the end of 1874 he became the foundation headmaster of the new Presbyterian Ladies' College, the first in Australia to offer girls an education equivalent to boys.[19] Catherine enrolled as a mature-age student, and later taught there for a short time, but by then the liberal Pearson had been driven out by the conservative Presbyterian establishment for advocating a land tax on large estates.

In June 1874, before he took up the headmastership, Pearson inaugurated the University Debating Society, modelled on the Oxford Union, to provide a proving ground for future public men. Deakin became a member, along with other bright young Melbourne men of his generation: the future Justice Henry Bournes Higgins, the future

Victorian premier William Shiels, his school friend Theodore Fink, and Richard Hodgson, who was to become an international researcher into psychic phenomena.[20]

Deakin credited Pearson with deflecting his political sympathies from those of the conservative *Argus* newspaper, which his family took, towards liberal causes.[21] He now supported equal education for females, scientific rather than classical studies, universal suffrage, cremation, the theory of evolution and temperance. In debate his verbal fluency was drawing attention. One professor was so impressed that he suspected Deakin must be writing his speeches and learning them off by heart, a procedure for which, in fact, he 'had no patience and no need'.[22] Fellow law student Henry Bournes Higgins came upon Deakin one evening in the cloisters of the university quadrangle, 'a tall, thin, handsome young man holding forth to a few fascinated students (including Dick Hodgson) on the futility of our studying classics, mathematics, logic, history, and all the rest'. With the philosophy of Herbert Spencer, Deakin claimed, the world was entering a new epoch of history.[23] Extravagant enthusiasm expounded to a captive audience in torrents of words—this was Deakin's style, along with a confident dismissal of anything that smacked of dogma and orthodoxy.

Melbourne in the 1870s had a small but vibrant intellectual life, and in 1874 Deakin began attending meetings of the Eclectic Association, where the city's progressive elite discussed the leading questions of the day. After some months Deakin spoke for the first time, following the ever confident Theodore Fink. The topic was Women's Rights, of which they were both 'ardent defenders'. He later delivered papers, including one on Morality and its Development. These were his first public performances.[24] The extensive Eclectic Association library held every important work in nineteenth-century English popular free thought, from David Hume and Thomas Paine in the eighteenth century to John Stuart Mill and the secularist George Holyoake. For a time Deakin was its librarian, with ample time to read its contents.[25]

At the Royal Society, where he was also a librarian, he read the best English magazines and the latest literary, scientific and critical books.[26] By his early twenties he was as well and widely read as any young man of his age in the English-speaking world, his head full of ideas, theories, quotations and many passages of prose and poetry, all retained in his remarkable memory.

The big debate of the day was between science and religion, to which Dr Bromby had already introduced him. The few thousand years of Biblical time stretched into millennia, the cosmos expanded into an infinite vastness, and man seemed on his own to make sense of it all. It was bewildering and for many profoundly shocking. Higgins, the son of a pious Methodist minister, recalled that reading George Grote's account of the origins of the myths of Ancient Greece at university 'shook my spiritual world like an earthquake...It led me to think of the creed in which I had been nurtured, had it not foundations?'[27]

Deakin experienced no such moment of doubt and upheaval and, with parents who wore their religion lightly, there was no inner drama of rebellion and guilt. But like many intellectually minded and gifted young people before and since, Deakin's search for his life's work was also a search for life's meaning. Where did his small existence fit in this vast cosmos? How should he use his sliver of time? What was he to do with his surging energies and God-given gifts? Dreamy, speculative and intensely self-focussed, Deakin longed to live at the centre of a world filled with meaning. This is what drew him to spiritualism.

4

THE PLUNGE INTO SPIRITUALISM

IN 1848 TWO young sisters in upstate New York claimed that knocking noises in their house were messages from spirits. Here, supposedly, was proof of life after death, and spiritualism quickly became both a new religion and a novel form of sensationalist entertainment. Mediums joined magicians on the concert stage, but it was séances in the home that turned the movement into a craze. Sitting in the dark holding hands around a ouija board or a planchette was much more compelling after-dinner entertainment than a game of whist.

Before he left school Deakin had already dabbled a little. He had used the planchette at the home of some American friends of the family and he had experimented with mesmerism at a party. 'One exciting evening when my keen interest in its mysteries was intended to be ridiculed, the charming young lady who was to affect to be mesmerised found herself speechless and helpless, falling into a kind of swoon.'[1] Deakin does not record his response to this revelation of his mesmeric power, but it no doubt delighted him to have such an effect on a young lady.

A few years later, in 1872, he found himself able to exercise extraordinary hypnotic powers over a young man. Focussing his will on him when he was in another room he could command him to come, and by merely drawing his hands around his body he could imprison him as if by an invisible chain, 'as Merlin was by Vivien'.[2] These powers alarmed him and he broke off the experiments.

Deakin dates his 'plunge into spiritualism' to the first half of 1874, when he visited two mediums and began to read the literature.[3] One of the mediums was William Henry Terry, founder of the Victorian Association of Progressive Spiritualists and editor and publisher of its periodical, the *Harbinger of Light*. Melbourne was the only Australian city with a strong spiritualist organisation, largely owing to Terry, whose bookstore and herbarium in Russell Street was an informal organisational centre. For Terry the first duty of the spiritualist was 'to remove the cramped fetters so long imposed on free and independent thought',[4] and his shop stocked progressive literature on a wide range of subjects, such as women's rights, capital punishment, health and physiology, including marriage guides.[5]

Terry was also a psychic healer and Deakin consulted him about various physical complaints, probably arising from his troublesome digestion. He was impressed by the answers, which confirmed his already established practices of bodily control. To maintain the harmony of body and spirit, many spiritualists undertook regular rhythmic exercise and abstained from meat and alcohol. This stress on bodily control no doubt also helped the young man maintain his sexual purity amid the temptations of the many prostitutes on Melbourne's streets.

The second medium was George Stow, one of the two regular mediums at the circle of Dr Motherwell, 'at that time the chief assembly of the kind in Australia'. In May, when Alfred and Catherine decided to start a spirit circle in the family home at Adams Street, they invited him to attend. On arrival, Stow revealed that he had been told that 'a great medium' would be present 'who would develop and occupy a very prominent place'.[6] Soon after, Deakin and Catherine were invited to join Motherwell's circle and the Adams Street circle petered out.[7]

Motherwell, a prominent Melbourne doctor who had been converted to spiritualism by the veracity of Terry's psychic diagnoses, shows the interconnectedness of spiritualism with progressive free thought and political activism. A founder of the Melbourne Unitarian Church and a member of the council of the University of Melbourne, he was instrumental in establishing its medical school and a persistent advocate for women's admission into the university. His small, select spiritualist circle met in his consulting rooms in Collins Street and invitations to participate were rare. The circle included Motherwell's sister, Terry and Walter Richardson, whose daughter Ethel was to become the famous novelist Henry Handel Richardson.[8] All were many years older than Deakin, goldrush immigrants who had done well. To be singled out to join the circle was a great honour for a youth not yet eighteen.

Motherwell's circle met twice weekly, once to listen to trance speaking and once for spirit writing. The meetings began with a prayer and a little music, the atmosphere as reverent as a church service, before the gas was turned down and participants waited for the spirits to arrive. After many months of attendance, when the usual medium Stow was in England, Deakin came under pressure to speak:

> without entering a trance or claiming any authority I spoke in his stead impromptu, without preparation or consideration on some theme that rose to my lips. I took no conscious part in the preparation or elaboration of the subject suddenly presented yet it obviously contented the Dr. and his circle.

His performance was wonderful, Catherine thought, and greatly lifted the spiritual and philosophic tone.[9]

Before he died Motherwell passed nine volumes of transcripts of these sessions to Terry, who published them in 1908, including messages conveyed by the spirit to Mr A, 'a gentleman studying for the legal profession', as Deakin was described. An example from October 1875:

> Like children playing on the shore of the ocean, who look over the heaving billows and in the far off distance they see the blending of sea and sky and that is all their vision can reach…Life passes

away like a dream, but in reality it rolls slowly along, till purged
from earthly impurities, when it gains new speed and brightens
from the eternal fires, and souls soar thru' out the vast infinity.[10]

Young Deakin became a successful medium. Twenty years later,
when he wrote a long manuscript, 'Personal Experiences of Spiritism',
he concluded that the messages he received from the spirits were 'just
such as I should have delivered myself if I had possessed the courage
to speak upon such subjects without nervousness and without special
preparation…Indeed although there were supposed to be many "spirits"
speaking, they never departed much from my own opinions.'[11] Deakin's
greedy reading had filled his retentive memory with the images, ideas
and words of the great masters of English literature. Believing that it
was the words of others that were commanding his listeners' attention, he was able to overcome his initial self-consciousness and, at the
centre of a circle of admiring and supportive older men, to develop
the oratorical skills and performative self on which he was to base his
later political success.

In 'Personal Experiences' he also described the submissive, empty
mind required to communicate with the spirits. 'Writing under inspiration I was accustomed…simply to write what occurred to me just as it
came, rarely modifying an expression, never forecasting what was to
follow…it was my consistent endeavor to abstract myself altogether
and allow the inspiration to go its own way.'[12] The older Deakin felt
it was 'by no means a manly state of mind'; nor was it a wise practice
'to relax the control of the brain and to allow it to be operated upon
either by subliminal forces in oneself, or by an influence from without'.
Such a habit of self-surrender, he feared, may permanently weaken
one's self control.[13]

In Vienna a couple of decades after Deakin's early experiences as a
medium, Sigmund Freud would develop free association as a tool for the
exploration of the unconscious, and in the twentieth century surrealist
artists would experiment with automatic writing. Deakin was gifted in
experiences of reverie, with a porous relationship between his conscious
and unconscious. Poems fell into his mind between sleeping and waking,

'sudden inexplicable visitations of verse arriving without warning as if from without me'.[14] He had occasional auditory hallucinations and out-of-body experiences; and his remarkable memory effortlessly offered up its copious contents. With its belief that the human mind encompassed more than its conscious capacities, spiritualism offered Deakin a framework for exploring and understanding such experiences. This, as much as what he believed to be the veracity of various prophecies, provided an experiential basis for Deakin's lifelong interest in spiritualism.

At the time it also provided him with a religion. Spiritualism was one response to the crisis of orthodox religious belief, rejecting dogma and sectarian differences for a universal religious faith, and retaining Christianity's belief in an afterlife. Its distinctive conviction was that the spirits of the departed could communicate from beyond the grave and that this was provable. If there were more things in heaven and earth than had hitherto been dreamed of, then their existence could be established by the rigorous application of scientific method. Such scientific proof, early spiritualists believed, would free people from the tyranny of superstition and the fear of hell peddled by the Christian churches and so enable them to live according to reason alone.[15]

Spiritualism reinforced Deakin's growing liberalism. It was essentially a Protestant religion, but without the pessimism and misanthropy of Protestantism's more Calvinist strains and without the belief in Original Sin. For spiritualists, evil was the result of misdirection or adverse circumstances, and the task of reform was to tackle ignorance and provide the circumstances for individuals to flourish. This optimistic faith in the natural goodness of people was shared by progressive liberals and motivated a wide range of nineteenth- and early twentieth-century liberal reform movements, from prison reform to progressive education and campaigns against poverty. Social reformers put their faith in education and wholesome environments, spiritualists in enlightenment. But neither liberalism nor spiritualism had any systematic way of explaining or resolving entrenched social conflict. Spiritualists simply avoided the question with a joyous faith in a harmonious universe in which all contradictions dissolved.

In 1874 Deakin became a 'leader' in the Melbourne Progressive Lyceum, which was the spiritualists' Sunday School. Here he first met Pattie Browne, who was then eleven.[16] Eight years later she would become his wife. Pattie was the eldest daughter and third child of Hugh Junor Browne, a new convert to spiritualism. The son of a parson, Browne had followed the orthodox faith of the Church of Scotland until he was about forty when, unsettled by the contemporary religious controversies, 'his mind craved secure foundations on which to rest.' He sought out a visiting American medium, who conveyed communications from his long-dead father, his little daughter Ada who had died in infancy and a 'Kaffir-speaking' man who had worked for him in Natal before Browne settled in Melbourne. Browne was converted and soon after held an informal family séance. When the pencil was passed to Pattie, she said, 'Oh Mama, I'm so frightened, my hand is writing.' With a medium in the family, Browne established a regular séance circle in his home, with Pattie at its centre. Although she later complained of the tedium of the séance, it must have been a heady experience for a young girl.

Browne hosted another regular séance circle to receive messages from 'the spirit of a great dramatist', Shakespeare. Pattie was not the medium, but she occasionally participated, and the spirit would sometimes address his 'young friend' directly. As 'a medium of great power', he warned, she should 'never turn the richest gem of nature's gifts to a purpose unworthy of them'.[17] In 1879, when her eldest brother, Archie, died of typhoid fever, Pattie stood by his bed with her father and a nurse as his spirit left his physical body. Writing to her grandmother in England she described dear Auntie Gracie and her little sister Ada bearing his spirit away. 'He has written a long communication to Mama and Papa and wishes them not to grieve,' she wrote. 'It is indeed the time when our religion is a great comfort to us, when we <u>know</u> that he can return and speak to us again.'[18]

Archie's funeral was huge, over a thousand people at the grave, for the Browne family was prominent in Melbourne's spiritualist circles. Browne was a wealthy man, a goldrush immigrant who had become a successful brewer, and he had made his home, Park House

in Wellington Parade, East Melbourne, a social centre for Melbourne's
well-to-do spiritualists. A confident, imposing man, he never wavered
from his spiritualist convictions and later published many accounts of
his experiences, including several descriptions of Pattie's mediumship.

Deakin became Pattie's class teacher at the Lyceum in July 1877,
when she was fourteen. As the rising star of Melbourne spiritualists,
he was a frequent guest at Park House and a regular participant in
the séances, later reminiscing to Pattie, 'Do you remember at Park
House when I held your hand in the circles and sometimes passed my
palms over your head.'[19] Sometime in the late 1870s, a medium told
Deakin that Pattie was his predestined mate and insisted that even
if he married another, she would be his wife.[20] This became his most
cherished prediction, despite a friend warning him that 'She will never
make a poor man's wife.'[21]

Deakin was in his element at the Lyceum. Free of the stain of
Original Sin, the Lyceum's children were innocent and full of potential.
Deakin led the children in a joyful exploration of their inner selves, with
music, marching, calisthenics and spiritual guidance. At the 1876 annual
Lyceum picnic at the Survey Paddock in Burnley, 120 children sang the
hymn 'O Let Us Be Happy', accompanied by a drum and fife band.[22]

When Deakin graduated to the position of conductor in 1876, he
compiled a guide for the Melbourne Lyceum based on the original
by the Lyceum movement's founder, the American A. J. Davis. In
the preface Deakin praised the Lyceum's commitment 'to Science
and Philosophy as its prophets, to Reason and Intuition as its guides,
to right thinking and right acting as its end, accepting Evolution as
the law to fulfil which all its energies are bent, and kneeling only to
Nature and the Divine in Humanity'.[23] In a question-and-answer item
published in the *Harbinger of Light* the following year, Deakin includes
the familiar virtues of the Victorian child: 'punctuality, order, attention,
diligence and earnestness; subordination and obedience, kindness and
self-restraint'; the difference is that spiritualists do not inculcate these
virtues through sanctions and appeals to authority but see them as
inherent in the child's nature. The glorious aim of the Lyceum is 'the
spiritual, moral and intellectual elevation of its members, and through

them the world at large'.[24] As conductor, he had ample opportunity to address the assembled children, and Pattie to gaze admiringly at him.

In 1876 Deakin joined a small committee of the Victorian Association of Progressive Spiritualists to investigate remarkable materialisations achieved by the medium Mrs Paton. Test séances were held in the semi-darkened first-floor room of Terry's Russell Street premises, and elaborate precautions were taken against fraud. The room was locked, and the grate and the gap under the door sealed. Mrs Paton was examined by the ladies and weighed before and after, as were the other participants. The results were astounding: a large lump of rock of the sort found between St Kilda and Brighton thumped onto the table, followed by a damp mass of seaweed, still smelling of the sea and inhabited by sea insects. Seven test sittings were held in all, and at the end the committee of investigation was sufficiently satisfied to send Mrs Paton a letter assuring her of its belief in 'the genuineness of her mediumship'.[25] Describing these events twenty years later, Deakin was still convinced of their authenticity. In other cases the same committee detected fraud, but this did not shake Deakin's faith in the genuineness of those spirit communications which survived careful testing. The detection of the fakes rather reinforced his confidence in spiritualism.

Sometime during 1876 Deakin's pen began to fly feverishly across the paper to the dictation of the spirit of John Bunyan and kept it up for forty-nine sessions. Week after week, in a semi-trance, 'the impressions came pouring in.'[26] In 1878 Terry published *A New Pilgrim's Progress, Purported to be Given by John Bunyan Through an Impressional Writing Medium*. Two hundred and fifty copies were available on subscription through the *Harbinger of Light*.[27] At the time Deakin believed it was authentic, but rereading it more than twenty years later he concluded that 'there is nothing Bunyanesque in the book except the title', nothing of his strong personality, none of his characterisation, his genius for narrative nor his homely style; 'the conclusion is particularly unlike him in its ultra-romantic sensationalism.' Deakin, however, remained fond of the book, and even entertained the idea that, had he the leisure, he could rewrite it.[28]

A New Pilgrim's Progress is the story of Restless who, driven by
an inner delirium, leaves his home and family in the City of Worldly
Content to seek his destiny as a great prophet. As an allegorical journey,
it draws on both Bunyan's original and on *Sartor Resartus*, although with
none of the latter's satire. Restless rambles across a confused landscape,
in which he meets helpers, tempters and spiritual advisers. His most
important encounters are with a young orphaned girl, Wilful, who
becomes his companion and eventually his wife, and with a Sage who
represents the spiritual wisdom of the East against the materialism
of the West. The Sage reveals that Wilful is a gifted medium, able to
perceive the oneness of the universe: 'there is no void in nature, no lapse
in time, no gulf in space, but what is filled with Life and overflowing
with Love...Spirit in its various conditions occupies all of existence.'[29]

There are also seven spirit guides, who conjure seven visions. With
the last, Restless descends into hell, 'the lowest depth to which it was
possible for humanity to sink', where it is revealed that his soul's mission
is to minister to other souls: 'the labour of charity, the service of God
is in it. Henceforth I renounce rest, enjoyment and honour unless in
its cause.'[30] This is a revealing conclusion. On descending into hell,
Restless does not learn how to avoid this fate himself, but instead how
to help others to avoid it. Deakin's unconscious mind displays no fear
of hell, no guilt, no consciousness of sin, no need for forgiveness. Unlike
Bunyan's Christian, who sought personal salvation, his mission is to
save others.

Midway through the journey, and after continuous spiritual development, Restless and Wilful are married and transformed into Redeemer
and Redemptress. Redeemer becomes a preacher, building the new, true
religion through miracles, teaching and example. The new religion is
persecuted and Redeemer endures periods in prison, but it also has
periods of triumph, with Redeemer as the inspirational preacher of
the new Philosophy of Spiritualism.

On one reading the novel is entirely about oratory, with many
descriptions of its hero's speechmaking, his uncanny mastery of his
audience and his receptivity to the direction of the spirit guardians,
who inspire his words.[31] On another, by the historian John Rickard,

with the love story of Restless and Wilful, Deakin was transforming his growing romantic interest in the young Pattie Browne into the wish fulfilment of marriage and a shared destiny.[32]

At the very end, Redeemer's mission takes on a political meaning and he becomes 'an orator who spoke to the oppressed of the errors of tyranny'. 'The spiritual wave of inquiry and reason which he had inaugurated had passed on into the political sphere of life.'[33] There follows a great political struggle, in which 'truth, liberty and spiritualism found themselves ranged against error, tyranny and materialism of gross sensuality.' Redeemer has become a liberal reformer. Finally, he and Redemptress are killed by agents of the tyrannical state in a political riot. Miraculously, however, their deaths lead to the overthrow of the tyrants and 'next morning the city rose free'. With this rather abrupt and unsatisfactory end, the spirit of Bunyan departed.

5

LIBERALS, CONSERVATIVES
AND DAVID SYME

THE POLITICAL SCENE in Victoria in the late 1870s was intense, divided
into two hostile camps. On one side were the squatters, bankers, large
merchants, the *Argus* newspaper, the Legislative Council (the upper
house of the Victorian parliament) and the Conservatives; on the other
were small farmers, shopkeepers, working men, the *Age*, the Legislative
Assembly (the lower house) and the Liberals. The divisions went back
to the 1850s, when the parliament of the new self-governing colony
had been established with two houses: a lower house elected on a wide
franchise, soon to include all men over twenty-one, and an upper house
with extensive powers and a very restricted franchise based on property
qualifications.

The Council's approval was needed for all legislation, including
money bills, which it could reject but not amend. It was also indissoluble, with its members facing the electorate on rotation, to protect
it, as the constitution so candidly put it, 'from any sudden impulse of
popular feelings'. Crucially, there was no mechanism to resolve disputes

between the two houses. Deadlock was the only possible outcome if
the Council persisted in rejecting the Assembly's legislation.[1] Popular
feeling against the Council was especially strong over its frustration of
the various land bills designed to break up the squatters' pastoral runs
into farms for the land-hungry goldrush immigrants.

The terms Liberal and Conservative are imprecise and confusing
as a guide to the politics of colonial Victoria. By English standards,
most colonists were Liberals. They opposed inherited privilege and an
established church, and supported equality of opportunity and political
democracy. But not all did, particularly those who had arrived early
and become wealthy, such as squatters and successful merchants. Their
representatives sat in the Legislative Council and believed that property,
no matter how recently acquired, conferred privileges on its owners.
They supported extra votes for property owners, and opposed payment
to members of parliament. Without this payment, most working men
could not contemplate standing for parliament. There were also some
unalloyed Tories among the churchmen and professionals who did not
share the colony's enthusiasm for equality, as well as merchants and
manufacturers who advocated the laissez-faire capitalism of neoclassical
economics and resisted any interference by the state with the workings
of the market. The historian Geoffrey Serle judges that about a sixth
of the members of the Assembly were Conservatives in these terms,
and most members of the Council.

Many more than this, however, were labelled Conservative by their
political opponents: some, who were also called Constitutionalists,
because they were cautious about moves to make the constitution more
democratic; others because they supported free trade. Free trade had
been an item of faith for English Liberals since the 1840s when they
fought against the Corn Laws, which protected farmers from imported
grain and pushed up the price of bread. In Victoria, though, many
Liberals had become convinced that the colony's future prosperity
would be enhanced by tariffs to protect its infant industries. These
would provide jobs for unemployed diggers and markets for farmers
as well as revenue for the government, which was fast running out of
land to sell and reluctant to impose direct taxation. Many free-traders

who regarded themselves as Liberals were pushed to the right by the popularity of protection and labelled pejoratively as Conservatives by protectionist Liberals.[2]

Putting aside protection, the terms left and right, radical and conservative, had some of their contemporary meaning as markers of attitudes to the role of government. As a new colony, Victoria's development depended on high levels of government investment in infrastructure such as roads, bridges and ports, which was sometimes called state socialism. There was pressure for government to control working conditions, especially of vulnerable women and children, and resistance to this from those who regarded contracts between employers and employees as none of the government's business.

After 1872, when the parliament passed an Education Act, a strong religious cross-current developed. The government took over from the churches the responsibility for elementary education, which was to be free, compulsory and secular. Catholics wanted to retain state aid for their own school system, as did some Anglicans; and many, both Protestants and Catholics, were worried by an elementary education with no religious content. The ensuing debate became a vehicle for the expression of mutual sectarian suspicions. Protestants did not want the state assisting in the spread of Catholic dogma and superstition, and Catholics saw the push for secular education as a Protestant ruse to diminish their faith. State aid for Catholic schools became a defining issue for many Catholics.

It's a confusing picture, particularly as the sort of stable organised parties we are familiar with scarcely existed. When people spoke of parties such as the Liberal Party they meant the groupings of men in parliament who caucused and voted together on key issues and generally supported either the leader of the government or the Opposition. But the votes of backbenchers, who prized their independence, were not locked in. Leaders put workable ministries together by calling on shared political values and past political alliances, but also by appealing to personal ambition and the self-interest of members needing to secure benefits for their electorates to ensure their re-election. There was no permanent party organisation outside the parliament, only electoral leagues which sprang to life during election campaigns to organise meetings and get out the vote, then faded away till next time. These leagues might identify themselves as Liberal, or with particular policies such as free trade or protection, or as supporters or opponents of the current government and its leading ministers.

From January 1865 to mid-1868, when Deakin was still a schoolboy, there was a prolonged crisis over the constitution and the powers of the upper house. Later, he would have a stake in its outcome through his idealisation of the scourge of the Council, the Anglo-Irish lawyer and member of the Assembly George Higinbotham. A proud, contradictory man of passionate high-mindedness, Higinbotham had nothing but contempt for those motivated by worldly and venal ambitions, especially that 'very dangerous class, the wealthy lower orders of the community' who controlled the Council.[3] And he insisted on the colony's rights of self-government in domestic affairs, without interference from the Colonial Office in London.

Higinbotham served in various ministries during the 1860s but in 1868, after the protracted struggle between the houses failed to establish any workable mechanism for resolving the regular deadlocks, he retired to the backbench and returned to the law. In 1876 he left parliament altogether. Famously, he refused a knighthood, describing it as 'a base, contemptible distinction', which merely gave a man 'a handle to his name'.[4] Deakin idealised him as 'The greatest of Australian orators and of Australian Liberals, the noblest nature and the most refined', 'who left the deepest impress upon public life and parliamentary traditions in Victoria'.[5] He set for Deakin standards of political conduct governed by selfless principle and unflinching independence, and provided him with an early model of a political life.

The next sustained conflict between the Council and the Assembly broke out in 1877 when Deakin was forming his political outlook. Liberal Premier Graham Berry had won a landslide victory. Berry, another self-made and self-educated goldrush immigrant, was a passionate protectionist with a radical's commitment to equality. From August to October 1875 he led a short-lived government which attempted to introduce a land tax stiff enough to break up the large pastoral estates. Inevitably the Council rejected it and the government fell. At the subsequent election in 1877, Berry was supported by the National Reform and Protection League, a broad alliance of manufacturers, trade unionists, miners and small farmers which represented a new level of political organisation in the colony. He won sixty of the eighty-six Assembly seats, an unprecedented victory which gave him a powerful sense of democratic legitimacy when the Council again proceeded to frustrate his legislation. At issue was a measure to continue payment of members of parliament which the Council opposed on the grounds that the government of the country should be reserved for men of means. Berry sought to bypass the Council by attaching the measure to an appropriation bill. The Council laid the bill aside, effectively denying the government supply and causing another constitutional crisis.

Berry called the Council's bluff. On 9 January 1878, many of the colony's public servants, along with the lesser judiciary and all the magistrates, were dismissed on the grounds that the government could no longer pay their salaries. The day was dubbed Black Wednesday. Departmental heads, senior surveyors, police magistrates, court officials and many others turned up to work to find themselves without position or salary. There was uproar: monster meetings, torchlight processions, furious editorials, marathon sittings of hysterical parliamentarians, rumours of further drastic actions by the government and mounting alarm as capital fled the colony to escape the 'Berry Blight'. Temporary compromises were reached to secure supply, but the fundamental question of the powers of the Council to veto popular legislation was left unresolved. Berry introduced legislation to amend the constitution to curtail the powers of the upper house. Predictably the Council rejected it.[6] Throughout these parliamentary manoeuvrings, class feeling ran high. Charles Pearson, who by education and background should have supported the Council, had already been forced out of the headmastership of the Presbyterian Ladies' College for speaking at a meeting of the National Reform and Protection League. He was now ostracised and his young wife, Edith, was dropped from the visiting rounds of former friends.[7] It was 'professional ruin for any barrister, doctor or school master in Melbourne to express sympathy with the Liberal Party'.[8]

As an ardent democrat, Deakin supported Berry in his fight with the Council, though he did not yet agree with protection. In June 1878 Charles Pearson was elected to the seat of Castlemaine for the Liberals. Deakin had qualified for the bar in 1877, and from his chambers at Temple Court he wrote to his old teacher to congratulate him. His election was 'a source of the greatest satisfaction to all Liberals throughout the Colonies, especially those like myself who sympathise with your free trade principles...I feel sure that with the exception of George Higinbotham no public leader possesses such confidence as you do.' He signed himself 'Alfred Deakin, Barrister at Law and formerly of the University Debating Club'.[9]

Pearson's election marked a conscious turning point in Deakin's political allegiance. With his already developed progressive sympathies and his rejection of dogma, Deakin would no doubt eventually have ended up in the Liberal camp, but Pearson's example hastened the move. 'The candidature of Professor Pearson for the Assembly satisfied me that the Liberal Party in the colony was entitled to the sympathy of one like myself who was saturated with the doctrines of Spencer, Mill, Buckle, superimposed upon an earlier and more durable foundation from Carlyle, Ruskin and Emerson.' He had been repelled from Berry's government by the caricatures of it in the *Argus*; 'If, however, a scholar and a gentleman, a historian and publicist like Pearson, was prepared to become their ally it was plain that I need have no hesitation in following the same flag.'[10]

When Pearson was elected Deakin was whiling away his days in his chambers off Collins Street writing a treatise on the History, Philosophy and Principles of Poetry. Briefs were hard to come by for a young man with few connections in a bar crowded with immigrant lawyers. At nights and on weekends he was busy with the affairs of the Victorian Association of Progressive Spiritualists. For one who believed his vocation was literary, he displayed surprisingly good organisational skills. Membership of the Lyceum increased when he was the conductor, and he oversaw its smooth transfer to new premises. As president of the Progressive Spiritualists for a year from September 1878 he improved the association's financial health. He also learned to chair meetings and handle difficult interpersonal interactions, and he got plenty of practice on the platform. Reports in the *Harbinger of Light* show him confidently warming up the crowd with a few facetious or self-deprecating remarks, before moving on to loftier matters.[11]

But none of this brought him any income. He was living at home and paying no board, though was expected to cover his personal expenses; and his law work earned him scarcely enough to pay the rent on his chambers. This was not viable. He explored the idea of becoming a preacher, discussing with Martha Turner, who led a small Unitarian congregation in East Melbourne, the possibility of succeeding her as she was planning to retire. Unitarianism rejected much of traditional Christian dogma, including the doctrine of the Trinity, for belief in a universal deity, but it did not subscribe to spiritualism's belief in communication from the dead and Miss Turner told Deakin that the congregation would not accept him.[12]

Looking elsewhere, 'naturally enough like most young men capable of nothing in particular and fond of reading, I began to turn to the Press.'[13] He sent off articles in the style of Ruskin on the pictures in the National Gallery to both the *Argus* and the *Age*, but received no reply. In May he approached David Syme, the proprietor of the *Age*, whose wife he knew through the Lyceum, about contributing to his paper. Syme said he could try, but pointed out that the *Age* was mostly interested in politics.[14]

Syme was at the height of his power, a tall, slim middle-aged man with iron-grey hair and beard, and a strong, resolute face who had turned the *Age* into the most popular and influential newspaper in the colony. Born in East Lothian to a stern Scottish schoolmaster and his wife, he had a miserable childhood in an austere household run according to Calvinism's joyless strictures. He had arrived in Victoria in 1852 via the Californian goldfields. An elder brother, Ebenezer, soon followed with his family and in 1856 he bought the struggling *Age*, which was already a radical broadsheet. David went in with him and on Ebenezer's death in 1860 he became the managing proprietor.

Under Syme the *Age* became a powerful force in shaping public opinion. It championed the working man, popular democracy and the rights of the Assembly, land reform, protection to foster local industry and an active state to develop the colony's potential. Its enemies were squatters, large merchants, free-traders, the Legislative Council, advocates of laissez-faire liberalism, pompous and dogmatic clerics, Catholics and the *Argus*, all of whom it lumped together as Conservatives and obstructionists, no matter how much free-traders might protest that they were the true Liberals. In 1868, when a hostile government and the large importers and merchants who supported free trade withdrew advertising from the *Age*, Syme defiantly dropped the paper's price to a penny. Circulation increased and brought greater influence for the paper, especially after Berry's election victory in 1877. In 1878 it was the most widely read Australian newspaper, its circulation four times that of its rival, the *Argus*. The *Age* projected a political world divided between the forces of progress and the obstructionists, the people of Victoria and their opponents, with itself as a crusader for progress and the masses.[15]

Syme gave Deakin an article in the *Fortnightly* paper to review. He 'rattled off' a sketch and left it at the office but was surprised when it failed to appear in print: 'Hitherto I had looked down upon press men and politicians as mere purveyors of news and superficial doctrines.' It was published some twelve days later, and Deakin was given further assignments, although some early pieces were rejected because they were more like a university essay than a newspaper article. At the end of July he became a regular contributor to the *Leader*, the weekly associated with the *Age* and edited by Syme's elder brother George, who was a hard taskmaster. Deakin was a quick learner and words were his métier, but more than thirty years later he described the few months when he worked under George Syme as 'the dreariest and most vexatious of my press life'. George Syme valued simplicity of style and plainness of expression, and he worked to rid Deakin's prose of its excesses and flights of fancy and to bring his emotional enthusiasm before the bench of hard facts. 'Never before nor since had I suffered such a grilling week after week until the situation becoming intolerable Mr. David Syme intervened…He knew me sufficiently to see that the best in me was being shackled—He had confidence enough in me to give me my head.'[16]

By the end of 1878 Deakin, now twenty-two, was 'out of leading strings', fully accepted as a member of staff at the *Age* and able to handle topics in his own way. As journalism was providing a modest income, he put aside the law. He was being given more and more work by Syme: a stint editing the *Leader*; monthly summaries for the *Illustrated News*; and writing much of the gossipy 'Under the Verandah' column after the bohemian novelist Marcus Clarke gave it up. 'There was hardly anything that at one time or another I did not write upon.' Critically for him he was not on a salary but paid only for what he had written. 'My position began and continued as one of complete independence…I could leave at any moment—my liberty of choice was secured.'[17] In his first serious position, Deakin needed the exit door left open.

Until he met Syme, Deakin had read only the conservative free-trade *Argus*, which his father took.[18] Writing for the *Age* completed the transformation of his political views begun by his admiration of Pearson. Now he began seriously to apply his mind to the political questions of the day.

> Of course they were treated from the standpoint of the paper, and championing its platform soon made it my own. My scruples as to state interference easily vanished…having the task of replying to the *Argus* continually thrown upon me, [I] became satisfied in the unsoundness of their arguments and the superiority of those by which I to my own satisfaction overthrew them.[19]

For a short time, however, Deakin did hold on to the free-trade convictions of his father and Pearson, until Syme

> showed me that while considering myself a Free Trader on the model of J.S. Mill I had at the same time developed his doctrine in my own way from other sources so as to have crossed the fiscal Rubicon without realizing how much I was at odds with fiscal or political laissez faire. It was as we crossed the old Princes Bridge one evening.

After that Syme made sure that 'gradually a full share of the articles expounding Protection came from my pen.'[20]

Given the importance of Deakin's support for protection in subsequent Australian history, it is worth probing his conversion. Although Deakin gives few details of the arguments Syme put to him, we can gather their gist from Syme's own writings. During the 1870s Syme published essays on political economy in the British quarterlies and in 1876 a book entitled *The Outlines of an Industrial Science*. In these he attacked the orthodox British classical-liberal economics of the David Ricardo and Adam Smith variety, with its faith in the self-regulating market which underpinned the doctrine of free trade. Influenced by German political economy, Syme argued that free trade meant monopoly for the British manufacturers and prevented the colony from developing its own economy and society. This was a nationalist argument that unsentimentally separated the colony's interests from those of Britain.

Syme also rejected classical-liberal economics' methodological assumption of an economic man motivated only by self-interest. Showing the influence of German idealism on his thinking, Syme argued that this was an untenable abstraction which excluded morality and the sense of duty. Nor, he argued, can it be assumed that the operations of self-interest are generally beneficial as postulated in Adam Smith's ideal market. Self-interest and individualism have their place, but need to be balanced by the interests of society as a whole, for which the state is the appropriate agent. Syme was happy to accept the description of his position as 'in the direction of State Socialism'.[21]

Deakin was already predisposed to such arguments from Carlyle's rejection of the dismal science of economics, with its mechanical operations of supply and demand leaving no room for the operations of the spirit. Syme gave these arguments a practical form in relation to the affairs of Victoria, turning Deakin's transcendental idealism towards the cause of colonial nationalism. For Syme the arguments over trade were about far more than economics, and his arguments for protection connected it to other aspects of Deakin's emerging political outlook: his optimistic faith in the state as an agent of a harmonised

and progressive common interest and his confident identification
with the colonial point of view.

When he began writing for the *Age*, Deakin was already a Liberal
by temperament and had a youthful eagerness to align himself with the
progressive forces of history. He was open-minded and against dogma
and superstition, but he had only the rudiments of a political outlook
and little detailed knowledge of the issues of the day. He learned his
politics with his pen as he took up the causes of his employer and in
persuading others he persuaded himself.

Learning about politics through working for the colony's one-man
political think tank and most able political lobbyist, Deakin was more
like many of today's parliamentarians, whose young adulthood is spent
in political work, than he was like his contemporaries, whose politics
were grounded in early hardship and grievance, or in defending their
wealth and social position. He was kind and humane by nature, but
he lacked the deep sense of personal obligation to the suffering or
achievements of others which animates most politicians whose politics
are intimately connected with their early experiences. Into this disconnect between politics and his self, Deakin's opponents would later pour
their accusations of his opportunism and chicanery.

Within six months of approaching Syme, Deakin had become his 'special
protégé', 'distinctly the pet of the proprietor having free access to him
and his private room at all times', invited for weekends to his country
house at Mount Macedon and a regular guest at his Melbourne residence.
The two tall, striking-looking men would walk together, and talk and
talk, Deakin with hands flying about, the young idealist and the dour
Scottish utilitarian thirty-five years his senior who regarded poetry as
nonsense and reading fiction as a vice. 'We argued continuously upon
religious, political, social and speculative subjects,' Deakin recalled.[22] Like
his brother George, David Syme brought facts and rational arguments
to the young man's enthusiasms, and it was under his influence that
Deakin, already practised in the debater's arts, learned to apply those
skills to all the leading issues of the day.

Deakin was well aware of the contrast between Syme's warmth

towards him and the aloof, rigid and remorselessly critical front he presented to others. He even allowed Deakin to tease him. Deakin later attributed Syme's cold severity to his miserable Calvinist childhood, driven by his schoolmaster father in a grim regimen of all work and no play. But 'underneath was an inner spring of warmth and tenderness very near the surface and quite easily set free.'[23] Or so the young Deakin found him. His affectionate relationship with his own father, William, had predisposed him to trust older men; he expected them to be interested in him and his ceaseless talk, or was at least not at all surprised when they were. Syme responded to the younger man's self-confidence and openness, to his playfulness and his enthusiastic, head-on rush into life. Perhaps in the young Deakin he was able enjoy something of the lost possibilities of his own joyless youth; perhaps he saw him as a harbinger of the young colony's confident future, unfettered by the dogmas and constraints of the old world. Whatever the attraction Deakin held for him, Syme was to provide him with extraordinary opportunities over the next decade, facilitating his entry into politics, supplying him with a steady stream of well-paid work, sponsoring his trip to India to investigate irrigation, and, after he returned to the bar in the 1890s, employing him on a major law case.

Straight after Christmas 1878, with the deadlock between the upper and lower houses still unresolved, Graham Berry and Charles Pearson sailed to London to press the British government to support their proposed constitutional reforms. The *Argus* sent its man too, F. W. Haddon, to put the case for retaining the Council as a check against the potential excesses of democracy. Parliament would not meet again till they returned.

Deakin spent New Year's Eve at the coming-out ball at Park House of Pattie Browne, who turned sixteen the next day. Among the brilliant company was a celebrated medium, and as the guests sat down for supper loud rapping was heard, said to come from his Indian spirit guide.[24] What Pattie thought of this intrusion on her party is not recorded. A graceful, translucent girl on the cusp of becoming a beautiful woman, she danced with Deakin, then twenty-two, for the first time. Pattie remembered,

He was a beautiful dancer and a great entertainer. He was very tall and slim, pale and suffering from weak eyes on account of over-strain—slight stoop which he was always battling against—terribly active and restless—never still—boys said 'he gave them the pip'—and with his eternal tongue—no one else was heard when he was about'.[25]

Pattie's mind's eye saw a bookish young man. A male friend remembered a much more physical Deakin, with 'wonderful powers as a swimmer' and 'an evening at Paddy's Market when you beat us all hands down at everything we tackled—shooting, swinging the hammer, shying at coconuts'.[26]

6

WEST BOURKE

IN FEBRUARY 1879 the death of the member for the electorate of West Bourke created a casual vacancy in the Legislative Assembly. West Bourke was to the north of Melbourne, fanning out from the suburbs of Flemington and Essendon into the rural hinterland between the roads to Ballarat and Bendigo, and taking in Gisborne, Romsey, Bacchus Marsh and Mount Macedon, where many of Melbourne's wealthy, including David Syme, had country houses. In the north-west corner lay the declining goldfields of Blackwood and Barry's Reef, where the miners could be relied on to support the Liberal cause.

The ensuing by-election would be held in the context of the Berry government's conflict with the Legislative Council and the desperation of its embassy to Westminster. The Conservative candidate was a well-known local councillor and businessman, Robert Harper, who had solid connections to the Presbyterian establishment. The Liberals did not expect to win, but they wanted to field a candidate. With nominations about to close, a local group of electors approached Richard Vale, a lawyer who shared chambers with Deakin, but he was not interested. Syme then suggested they ask Deakin, which they did; and once Syme had assured him of help with his election expenses, he accepted. He does not record discussing the invitation with his father, an indication perhaps that he was now beyond parental guidance.

Announcing Deakin as the ministerial candidate, the *Argus* declared that Harper had 'every prospect' of heading the poll.[1] Thus, wrote Deakin twenty years later, 'at the age of twenty-two I was suddenly whirled into politics to wage a desperate and hopeless conflict against an adversary of exceptional ability and claims upon this most difficult seat.'[2] He became a candidate on Friday, 7 February. Next morning his address, setting out his claims for election, appeared in the *Age*, written for him by the editor, Arthur Windsor. Deakin justified this easily, for 'Its substance was mine as it was his because at that time it expressed the policy of the paper in which we were both expounding it daily.'[3] His platform had four planks: reform of the Council, protection, defence of the land tax and the maintenance of the Education Act against Catholic claims.

Liberalism, with its commitment to individuals' freedom to exercise their own conscience and reason, had its foundations in the Protestant Reformation, and tended to see Catholics as backward and superstitious people who had given over their judgement to priests, and whose loyalty to the Pope potentially conflicted with their loyalty to king and country. Liberal hostility to Catholicism had surged in the wake of Pope Pius IX's 1864 Syllabus of Errors, which attempted to shore up the authority of 'the one true Church' against the heresies of a liberal and secular society. It had denounced the separation of church and state, along with a host of modern liberal beliefs, and the first Vatican Council in 1869–70 had proclaimed papal infallibility. In Australia, with its large numbers of Irish Catholic immigrants, Protestant hostility to Catholicism was reinforced by racist prejudice against the ignorant and feckless Irish and by growing Irish nationalism, which made their loyalty suspect.

Deakin was as scornful of the dogmas of Protestant clergy as he was of Catholic superstition. Nevertheless, the liberalism he was adopting had a Protestant foundation, and the *Age* for which he was writing was

overtly anti-Catholic. Secular state education was an article of his early
political faith and slipped easily in these early days into anti-Catholicism.
In an 1880 letter to Christopher Crisp, the editor of the *Bacchus Marsh
Express*, Deakin described the system of control of the Church of Rome
as 'the most repugnant that exists' in its invasion of individual rights
and liberties, 'the essentials of their creed as injurious to humanity and
antithetical to progress'. He was determined to keep 'priestcraft, dogma
and intolerance' out of schools.[4]

Armed with his four-plank platform, Deakin addressed his first
campaign meeting in the Town Hall at Flemington on the Saturday
evening. The small hall, which could accommodate around two hundred
and fifty people, was packed to hear the new Liberal recruit. 'Beginning
in an agony of nervousness…but soon attaining sufficient command
of myself to follow out the line of exposition determined upon, I flung
myself (so to speak) at my hearers with much enthusiasm.' His delivery
was rapid, over two hundred words a minute at the peak of his excitement, and 'there was a good deal of excitement in me then.' Familiar
with Liberal policies from writing about them, he was able 'to expound
his views with great readiness and fullness' and was well-pleased with
his reception. 'Ardent Liberals cheered at every pause; while in replies
to interjections and answers to questions I scored…off my adversaries.'

James Patterson, the minister for public works who was to share
the platform with him, was sceptical about the capacities of Syme's
recruit and waited in a nearby hotel until it was clear that Deakin
could command an audience.[5] Once the cheering had begun Patterson
entered the hall. He later told Syme, 'You were right, Syme, Deakin
is the man for us. He talks—by George he can talk!'[6] Reporting the
success of the meeting, the *Age* editorial remarked that the press is 'the
very best school for a politician to graduate from…a man who aspires
to form the opinions of others by writing leading articles is probably a
man who has tolerably matured opinions of his own.'[7]

On Monday, 10 February, just as reports of the Kelly Gang's hold-up
in Jerilderie were reaching Melbourne, Deakin set out on his campaign,
travelling by coach and rail from one meeting of Liberal supporters to
the next, through the small and large settlements of the electorate. As

the election was only eight days away, the pace was hectic. Between Monday and Friday, Deakin addressed ten meetings and travelled a couple of hundred miles. It was all a great novelty, 'to sleep in strange inns without friends or relations near, and much more to see for the first time rural life and manners'. Most of the time he had only the dimmest idea of where he was, 'launching himself after each meeting into space, going where I was told, finding someone who could show me the Hall and bring me to the active Liberals of the place, and so from strangers to strangers in an utterly unknown country, wandering in a perpetual whirl of mysterious and novel procedure'.[8]

Deakin was no longer a strict vegetarian, but he was still a teetotaller and he didn't smoke. Socialising with the local farmers and business men after the meetings was an unwelcome chore, and he generally excused himself as needing an early night. As the week proceeded, so did Deakin's grasp of the issues which concerned the electorate, and he began to develop his own views on matters such as Black Wednesday and the land tax. He now believed that all the dismissed public servants should be reinstated; he regarded the land tax as unscientific; and, though he had never thought about it before, when questioned by an advocate of temperance he announced himself opposed to hotels trading on Sundays. 'The constant discussion of public issues began to affect my mind, and so far as I could judge the addresses I delivered were improved as the contest proceeded.'[9]

Just as he had written himself into the Liberal political convictions of the *Age*, so he was now talking himself into more independent political views, refining his politics on the job and starting to make them his own. Some notes he made at the time show the sharply bifurcated foundations on which Deakin constructed his understanding of the difference between Liberals and Conservatives: 'Insist moral basis of Liberalism—immoral basis of Conservatism—Justice v. Selfishness and v. Greed...Evolution of policy and laws making for social growth... All such provisions point to larger and more effective Unions within the realm and then beyond it.'[10] It is an amalgam of Deakin's moral, scientific and religious thinking at this time, with liberalism as the agent of humanity's evolution towards higher unities, and it endured.

Contrary to the predictions of the *Argus*, Deakin won the seat, though with a reduced majority for the government candidate. The *Argus* claimed this indicated that the tide had turned against Berry and attributed Deakin's victory to two special factors: the very strong vote from the miners at Barry's Reef; and the intervention of the minister for railways, Mr Wood, who let it be known that the construction of the much-anticipated railway line to Lancefield depended on the return of Mr Deakin. It concluded, 'The seat is won but not with honour.' To the *Age*, of course, Deakin's victory was an endorsement of the government against the obstructionists.[11]

Although Deakin had won the seat of West Bourke with a clear majority, there was a problem. The polling booth at Newham had run out of ballot papers at 3 p.m. and the polling clerk had closed the booth early, depriving ten men of their vote. The losing side called for the reopening of the poll, which was deemed to be illegal by the attorney-general, Sir Bryan O'Loghlen. The 'unfortunate blunder' of the Newham returning officer and the unscrupulous attempts of the obstructionists to benefit from it by getting a second chance for the defeated conservative candidate were indignantly condemned by the *Age*: 'While the Liberals behaved with dignity and restraint, the conduct of the Conservatives was disgraceful'; 'A great poet has told us that to be weak is to be miserable, but in this case the weak were not only miserable, but discourteous, unjust and cowardly.'[12] These colourful editorials were largely written by Deakin himself.[13]

Deakin was convinced that the early closing of the poll had not affected the outcome; nevertheless, he found the doubt cast on his victory 'vexatious beyond expression'. He tendered his resignation to O'Loghlen, who refused it on the grounds that, as he had not yet been sworn in as a member of parliament, it was not possible for him to resign. 'The innocent cause of so much angry feeling', Deakin felt himself 'thrust into prominence before the whole Colony, enjoying notoriety of a not wholly pleasant character'. Deakin had spent a hundred and fifty pounds on the campaign, which was a substantial sum and more than an unskilled labourer could earn in a year.[14] Syme and Patterson each offered him cheques for fifty pounds, which he declined with thanks, 'preferring to maintain my independence of both Ministry and paper'.

After a few weeks the fuss over the poll died down. While waiting to be sworn in, Deakin set about learning the job of a local member in a new colony in which the government's coffers were seen as the solution to most problems, spending his time accompanying local deputations to government departments, representing constituents' interests to various ministers, interviewing 'aspirants for employment, relatives of deceased or dismissed civil servants, and a miscellaneous crowd of suitors associated with public movements or private ventures desiring patronage, subscriptions, introductions, and advice legal or constitutional but always gratis'.

Deakin was never entirely comfortable with the role of the local member of parliament as a broker between the government and his needy and aggrieved constituents, assisting them to access the public resources they believe are their due. More congenial were the social obligations, the round of district celebrations of shires, clubs, churches and institutes, and the picnics where he had use of a good horse and the opportunity for some delightful gallops. He was still president of the Victorian Association of Progressive Spiritualists and busy with its affairs, which had the added attraction of opportunities to socialise with Pattie Browne. In March 1879 they were both elected as leaders of the Lyceum. They would have seen each other every Sunday at least and Pattie would have had ample opportunity to observe his charms as he addressed the assembled children or chaired VAPS events.[15]

On the evening of 17 June 1879, Berry and Pearson returned from Britain. The Colonial Office had rebuffed them, declining to intervene in the internal affairs of the self-governing colony, particularly if it were to remove restraints on popular democracy. Unsuccessful though he may have been, to his supporters Berry was a hero, and he and Pearson were met by a huge, cheering crowd and accompanied from Spencer Street Station up Collins Street by a torchlight procession.[16] Deakin watched Berry address the crowd from a balcony next to the chief secretary's office in the Treasury Building, looking across Spring Street and down Collins. Deakin claimed that the journey to London had been valuable because 'it impressed on the minds of English statesmen the fact of the existence of the colony of Victoria'. A few days later he was introduced to Berry.[17]

Deakin was to be sworn in when the new parliamentary session opened on 8 July. Victoria's Parliament House stands on the ridge at the eastern end of the city, facing west down Bourke Street towards the docks on the Yarra. Designed in the 1850s as a massive colonnaded building with a noble dome, its grand neoclassical architecture displayed the colony's confident expectations of well-governed prosperity. It was built in stages, and the new Grand Hall (later renamed Queen's Hall) and spacious entrance vestibule which had just been completed were to be on public view for the first time. The dome, however, was never built.

Parliamentary ceremonies were occasions for spectacle, and the opening of this session in the early afternoon by a new governor arriving in a new state carriage drew a bigger than usual crowd. The vestibule and hall, as well as the galleries, were so full of spectators that the invited guests and the parliamentarians themselves had difficulty finding seats.[18] The Assembly met later that afternoon, at 4.30. With Ionic columns set into the wall, a gently sloping ceiling of mauve and gold, green carpets and leather upholstery, and a gallery each for the public and the press, it was an impressive chamber. Pattie Browne was in the public gallery that afternoon, as no doubt were William, Sarah and Catherine, looking down on the scene where Alfred was to make his dramatic entrance into Victoria's parliamentary life.[19]

Before the new members were introduced the problem of the early closing of the Newham polling booth was raised. A great deal of correspondence about this irregularity was read out to the Assembly, followed by debate as to whether or not the election of Alfred Deakin was valid and consequently whether or not he should be sworn in. In the midst of this the sergeant-at-arms announced the presence of the new members and escorted them into the chamber. Deakin sat through more doubts being cast on the propriety of his presence. He was to deliver the address in reply to the governor's speech, an honour generally given to a new member, and fidgeted nervously as the session dragged on through the preliminaries and then through tea. When the

Speaker finally called him, he spoke so rapidly that the parliamentary
reporters could barely keep up.

> Always highly nervous no matter how small the gathering to
> which I spoke, on this occasion my condition was so agoniz-
> ing as to threaten mental paralysis. This was mitigated by the
> circumstance that I gave little or no indication of the tremors that
> thrilled me, dried my palate and robbed me of control of my voice
> and knowledge of my movements.[20]

Like the professional actor he had once hoped to become, no matter
how great his inward agitation, Deakin's performative self would
carry him through. He had taken great pains with the speech and was
very proud of it. Quoting Spencer, Mill, Gladstone and a few lines of
Tennyson, he rehearsed the core beliefs of Victoria's colonial liberalism:
the radical possibilities open to those making a new nation; the superior
quality of Victoria's colonists; the absence of class in the colony compared
with Great Britain; the sacredness of the ballot box; and the key issue
of the day, the need to reform the powers of the Legislative Council,
and the advantages of a plebiscite to resolve deadlocks.

His speech showed the influence of Carlyle and the German idealists:

> With our boundless wealth and the opportunities of the illimitable
> future, it would be strange if the young Victoria did not look
> forward to something more than a mere aggregation of individuals
> gathered by accident or avarice—if we did not seek to establish
> a great people moved by large national aspirations, governed by
> wide national sympathies, and actuated by proudly loyal devotion
> to the State.

Then, suddenly, he changed tack, shifting to the more personal
matter of the difficulties of taking his seat. After some explanations of
the various moves he had made to resolve the issue before today, words
tumbling from his mouth, he announced his intention to resign—in
fact, he had the resignation letter in his pocket. He would recontest

the seat, but he requested no assistance from the government, and that no mention be made of a railway; 'in short there shall be no spot upon which any finger can rest.'[21]

Deakin's use of the word 'national' requires some comment, as it is one that has fallen out of usage. 'National' expressed an aspiration to unity of purpose and interest within the polity, rather than referring to an independent nation-state. It is not a synonym for Australian, and its opposites are not un- or non-Australian but sectional, partisan and parochial. Thus, although Victoria was a colony, it could establish a National Gallery, because the gallery was for all Victorians, not just for some.

In retrospect, Deakin judged the speech poor, too doctrinaire and dogmatic. Nevertheless, the house applauded wildly, 'for its manner, its fire and its conclusion'. Deakin always took great delight in recounting his capacity to win over his audience. The neophyte heard a more pragmatic judgement later that night, when he happened to ride home on the same omnibus as the premier, Graham Berry: 'It is all very well for you, it puts you on a pinnacle. But what of the party if you lose the seat at this juncture?'[22] Although Berry had a majority, it could not be relied on to support every legislative measure and his failure to resolve the conflict with the Council was eroding his support. Deakin declined to say anything about principle before party, but Berry was right: Deakin would never be entirely comfortable as a party man.

Twenty years later, when Deakin wrote an account of these events, their intensity for him was still palpable: a minor electoral irregularity had thrust him into the centre of the colony's politics; all eyes were on him as he made his maiden speech with its explosive climax; the situation was described as 'one of the most dramatic witnessed in the house'.[23] Just a few years earlier young Deakin had wondered if his future lay on the stage; now, in the chamber of the Victorian Legislative Assembly, he had found a theatre which suited his talents.

For a young man alert to signs, however, it was not an auspicious beginning. A new poll for West Bourke was scheduled for 22 August, six weeks later. Deakin entered the second poll with what he described as a sense of 'gay irresponsibility'. Sharing the same hotel on the campaign trail, his Conservative opponent, Harper, tried over breakfast to convince him that his qualifications for the position were so wanting that he should withdraw from the contest. Deakin demurred on the grounds of party, but his sporting instincts were roused. He proceeded throughout the campaign to play tricks on his opponent, mimicking his set-piece speech when he appeared first, so that Harper 'found himself everywhere being charged with stealing my speech and repeating my figures'.[24]

Country election meetings were occasions of public entertainment as much as political enlightenment and horseplay of all kinds was toler-ated. Deakin exploited his powers of repartee to the full, ridiculing his opponents for the amusement of his supporters, his wit matched easily to the 'very imperfectly informed storekeeper or farmer' who challenged him. In one incident he reduced a pompous local Conservative to 'a trembling, tongue-tied picture of helpless imbecility'.[25] It was always possible, though, for these rowdy meetings of men to become violent, and Deakin recounts several incidents of scuffles and punch-ups at the back of the hall while he held the platform.

A far more disturbing incident occurred at Barry's Reef during one of his early campaigns, when he was addressing a meeting of miners. He had observed in the audience a jaunty well-dressed man who took his seat with a swagger and was in the district with a pocket full of money to entice votes away from the Liberals. Deakin launched into his speech, 'as usual speaking with great impetuosity and fire, followed as always here with a growing accompaniment of cheers and stamping as the audience became more and more excited'. Without warning he switched his attention to the natty election agent, contrasting his underhand ways with those of the simple upright elector relying upon his reason and his vote to secure just laws and protect his rights. The man cowered as the applause thundered and Deakin, extemporising, pursued his line of attack, 'asking what cause it was which found it necessary to bribe to secure votes and what kind of creature destitute of manliness, conscience and patriotism' would stoop to such degrading and treacherous work.

I was quivering with excitement myself and the whole crowd appeared to be quivering too as they answered my appeals, no longer with applause but with a low, threatening, increasing and ominous growl. Then my breath almost stopped. Scores of gleaming eyes and vengeful faces were fixed upon mine and turning angrily towards the man in the midst who crouched lower and lower before the approaching storm about to burst upon his devoted head. There was no more jauntiness or impudence now. He was as white as a sheet and trembling as a sail does when a boat is going about. It needed only a few more words and a gesture and what would have been left of him when he had escaped those sinewy arms would probably have been unrecognizable. When my heart beat again, as it seemed after a pause as long as eternity, I realized for the first time what I was doing, that I must not stop but lead the lightning generated to strike elsewhere. Without a perceptible halt therefore I continued in the same vein a furious denunciation of the classes who employed such agents, their past history, their present plans, their financial hold upon the country and how it might be saved from their grasp; so gradually winding away from the man and his mission until they were occupied with other questions and forgot him. Never have I passed so dreadful a quarter of an hour.[26]

Later that night the victim came to Deakin's room to thank him for saving his life. Deakin never repeated the dangerous experiment. Just as the teenage Deakin had stepped back from his hypnotic power over a susceptible young man, so he now drew back from oratory's potential to meld individuals into a crowd which becomes a pliant instrument of the speaker's will. The incident revealed to Deakin his demagogic power, and it frightened him. He was exhilarated by the roar of the crowd and by his own power to arouse a response, but he recoiled from working with the crowd's darker emotions.

In these early election campaigns Deakin revealed his extraordinary gift for oratory, both to his political mentors and to himself. He could sway an election meeting, carried away by his own feverish excitement and the crowd's response. In the middle decades of the nineteenth century, when a widened franchise required more public means of political communication, political language left parliament for the platform, where the speaker's task was to get out the vote by arousing electors' passions.

Evangelical preaching had trained people in the art of listening to long, rousing sermons and preaching was good practice for political oratory.[27] When Deakin spoke to the Progressive Spiritualists in lofty rolling phrases repudiating dogma and singing the beauty of a divine universe, he was also learning how to engage an audience, to win them over with humour and appeal to their better natures. His transition from religious to political oratory had already been prefigured by Restless in *The New Pilgrim's Progress*. He became an orator for the Liberals when 'the spiritual wave of enquiry and reason which he had inaugurated had passed on into the political sphere of life.'[28]

Deakin left a record of his extraordinary capacities for extemporised oral performances:

> Up till 1909 I practically did not know what it meant to hesitate for a word…As a rule I only referred to a few rough notes… my speeches emerged while my mental eye was roaming among fresh springing suggestions over an often very prolific and always fruitful area. I was improvising, making retorts, or quotations, or outlining new departures, these being presented as are the features of a country to an observer in a train who uses them in an argument with his fellow passengers.[29]

The visual metaphor is striking. His daughter Vera White recalled her father telling her that when making a speech before a cheering crowd, as he approached the climax he would 'see a row of synonyms and pick out the most apt'.[30]

Deakin's oratorical powers drew in part on his phenomenal memory and in part on the internalisation of the rhythms of English from his wide reading, particularly of poetry and verse drama. But his success as an orator also drew on his physical presence and capacities, his height, dark good looks and physical stamina. The exhilaration of oratory is one of the reasons Deakin stayed with politics. Subject to occasional depressive moods, and often feeling a disconnect between his inner and outer self, on his feet on the platform all self-consciousness fell away and he was fully present in the moment.

7

'I AM THE BOY'

SHOCKED TO BE defeated by a parvenu, the Conservatives had worked assiduously to register electors and this time Robert Harper won the poll by fifteen votes. Deakin was not overly concerned by this close defeat. Liberals, who had rallied around a young man with such a high sense of honour, had met his electoral expenses and he was well content, spared 'a tedious tariff session in which I should have been most unhappy'. He would also have missed out on 'the delightful trip to Fiji'.[1]

Ever since he had seriously put his mind to divining his life's path, Deakin had sought assistance from various specialists in character and the future: astrologers, phrenologists and above all mediums, whom he consulted very frequently between 1876 and 1882. Mostly their advice was too general to be of much assistance, an outcome he accepted 'with composure, being of the opinion that such purely personal issues were not worthy of the attention of visitors from higher spheres'. He did, however, keep records of such prophecies as were given, believing that this was 'a way of testing the veracity of spirit communication'. In the mid-1890s Deakin used these records to recount a series of prophecies which had been fulfilled by subsequent events, mainly in his political career, but also in his personal life. Looking back on the notes he found 'inexplicably accurate forecasts of the future'. 'What has materialism to say about such "coincidences"?' he asked.[2]

Among the predictions were travels. The first, received in 1876, was vague as to time and destination. The prophecies gradually acquired more detail, including, in January 1878, that his companion would be a white-haired man and it would be at no expense to himself. So when, just after his election defeat in August 1879, an elderly white-haired gentleman of his acquaintance suddenly stopped him in Collins Street and invited him to accompany him to Fiji, Deakin took this 'remarkable coincidence' to be the fulfilment of the earlier prediction.[3]

The white-haired man was Sydney Watson, a wealthy squatter and an active spiritualist. He was a good friend of Hugh Browne, who later dedicated one of his pamphlets to him.[4] Three of his daughters were pupils at the Lyceum and his sister-in-law, Miss Elizabeth Armstrong, was a prominent Melbourne trance medium who may well have known of Watson's intentions. She may even have been the source of the prediction.[5]

Apart from their shared interest in spiritualism, Watson was an unlikely congenial companion for a young liberal reformer, and a very different sort of man from the self-improving goldrush immigrants among whom Deakin had grown up. He was a squatter with a run, Walwa, on the Upper Murray, and firmly in the Conservative camp. When the Land Acts of the 1860s, weak enough as they were, opened his holdings to selectors, he, along with many Victorian squatters, looked north for fresh pastures. He sent two of his sons to the Gulf country in Queensland and himself travelled to Fiji, where he purchased three sizable holdings.[6] Watson was part of the expansion of Victorian pastoralists into New South Wales, Queensland and Fiji, which confirmed Melbourne's position at the time as the country's principal financial centre.

Deakin and Watson sailed from Melbourne on 18 October 1879 and arrived in Suva eleven days later. Deakin spent the evening before his departure at Park House, where Pattie sang for the guests, including the song 'Waiting'. Deakin took it as a secret message: 'Come, for my arms are empty! Come for the day was long!' she sang. 'All my soul responsive answers and tells me he is here.'[7] After a couple of days of wretched seasickness, Deakin occupied himself reading, and arguing about political, religious and social questions with Watson and the captain.

His letters to Catherine from Fiji abound with enthusiasm for all he sees: the grand scenery, the strange vegetation, the gigantic flowers, the old capital of Levuka 'situated between the sea and a precipitous range of grandly rugged hills, the hospitality of the villagers, the wild dances of the natives'. Fiji was exotic, but also familiar, as he quickly established a routine centred on the British colonists' club, pursuing a regimen of vigorous exercise in the early morning, reading after break-fast, attending to business with Watson during the day and socialising on the club verandah in the evening with capital chaps. Here he heard of the wonderful prospect for investors in the new British colony. 'Tell Papa,' he wrote to his sister, 'that I have an idea that he might come here when he leaves the office and do well...At present I am half inclined to come myself. What is wanted is capital, though large sums are needed to get quick returns.' 'The land question is being rapidly settled and anyone with £5,000, energy and knowledge of coffee, sugar or cotton planting is sure to do well.'[8]

Deakin slipped easily into the assumptions of British colonial rule in a potential new land of settlement. But surely in all that talk on the verandah he heard things to trouble his optimistic liberal assumptions. The land question, for a start. In the 1860s, when the price of cotton was high because of the American Civil War, Australian investors had acquired large areas of land on Fiji for plantations. But the legality of these acquisitions was shaky and, when Fiji became a British crown colony in 1874, a Land Claims Commission was established by the first governor, Arthur Gordon, who was sympathetic to the indigenous inhabitants. Many investors lost a lot of money, and Watson was presum-ably visiting Fiji on business to do with his titles.

Then there was the question of native labour. Britain had abolished slave-trading in 1808 but not the appetite for coloured workers. By mid-century a vigorous labour trade had sprung up in the Pacific, including with the colony of Queensland. The labour was indentured, not owned, and so technically not slavery, but kidnapping, or blackbirding, was rife.

Watson's eldest son, Archie, arrived in Fiji in 1872, sent by his father to manage his newly acquired land holdings. Archie failed to rise to the challenge and fell in with chancers on a notorious blackbirding brig, the *Carl*, which was caught bringing Solomon Islanders to Fiji to work on the plantations. Archie was charged with kidnapping and murder. The charges were never brought to court, and he hightailed out of the Pacific, ending up in Germany, where he studied anatomy before going on to a respectable career as the Elder Professor of Anatomy at the University of Adelaide.[9]

British officials closely involved with the case were still in Fiji when Deakin visited with the miscreant's father and he met them: the governor, Arthur Gordon, and the colonial secretary, John Thurston, who was instrumental in organising Archie's bail. Could Deakin have been unaware of Archie's fall from grace, particularly as it cost Watson a good deal of money to keep him out of jail and avoid a public scandal? And what did he make of evidence of sexual relations between Europeans and native women? Perhaps he failed to notice, though this is unlikely in a lively twenty-three-year-old man.

Deakin dined out with the British elite in Fiji. A select dinner given by the governor was 'first class', the table surrounded by 'a ring of native servants'. After dinner Deakin had a long chat with the governor, who in fact 'spoke to no one else that evening', and followed up with an invitation to lunch, 'tete-a-tete'. 'I fancy that will be pleasant,' he writes offhandedly to Catherine, as if an invitation to dine with a colonial governor was an everyday occurrence for him.[10]

Gordon was the first member of the British imperial elite Deakin had seen up close. He does not record what they discussed, but it is likely that, as usual, he did most of the talking. He must, however, have known of the tense relations between Gordon and the Australian settlers in Fiji, whom Gordon described as made up of 'those who simply desire the extermination of the natives and those who desire to utilize them as serfs or slaves'.[11]

Deakin arrived back in Melbourne in mid-December 1879. A general election was due in late February of the following year. Before he left for Fiji the local Reform Leagues had made clear that they were keen for him to contest West Bourke again and would meet his expenses. Deakin declined, setting out his reasons in a letter to the secretary of the Bacchus Marsh Reform League which was published in the *Bacchus March Express* on Christmas Eve. He had, he wrote, no desire to enter a political life. As well as already having sufficient occupation and employment and no special desire to become a parliamentarian, he had a number of serious misgivings about contemporary politics: the 'thick and turbid' atmosphere of parliament, in which the decencies of debate are entirely neglected; his inability to support either the government or the Opposition, which would force him to occupy an independent position when the crisis demands party men; and the political patronage for civil-service posts, which makes the duties of a representative 'if not humiliating then at least distasteful'.[12]

By the time the next issue of the *Bacchus Marsh Express* was published, on 3 January 1880, Deakin was well on the way to changing his mind. Demurring all the while about his lack of desire to re-enter political life and grateful to the electors for the kindness shown him, he agreed to stand if no other suitable candidate was forthcoming, and if the Reform League was happy with those of his views which differed from Berry's government.[13] In later recollections he added another motive: the personal rivalry between himself and Robert Harper, whom he was anxious to fight to the finish. He believed, though, that were he to reject the opportunity to stand for West Bourke, another seat would soon be forthcoming if he desired it.[14]

To assist with this decision, and going by the pseudonym of Wilson Esquire, on 9 January, Deakin consulted the phrenologist Professor A. S. Hamilton, who provided him with a set of phrenological measurements and a full written study of his character. The use of the pseudonym was no doubt a precaution lest Hamilton's advice be corrupted by the recognition of his name after the publicity of the Newham electoral blunder. Hamilton, though, was active in Melbourne's small intellectual world and likely knew the identity of the young man seeking his guidance. He had over thirty years' experience as a phrenologist, and his character study of Deakin is a shrewd amalgam of generalised description of the occupational aptitudes needed for professional life and kindly advice of an older man to a younger. Head measurements revealed Mr Wilson to be a man of quick observation, penetrating intelligence, lively wit, good language and logical acumen, and hence well suited to his position at the bar. He is public-spirited and after a few years of study may well make his way successfully as a member of parliament.

In pointing him towards politics, Professor Hamilton missed Deakin's extraordinary powers of oratory. He gave no encouragement to his literary and philosophical aspirations: 'You are not an original nor profound thinker and have not <u>great</u> force of character. Yours is an intellect of ability not <u>genious</u> [sic].' This must have been a disappointing judgement for Deakin to read. He had just added a final section to an ambitious aesthetic treatise on Poets and Poetry, mostly written during 1878 under the twin influences of Ruskin and Spencer.

Professor Hamilton gave him two further pieces of advice: to learn patience; and to marry. 'Morally speaking you cannot afford to trifle with your own soaring and ardently affectionate nature, therefore the sooner the better you see your way to a happy matrimonial alliance… as you are very strong in conjugal desire.'[15] Later that year Hamilton also read the head of Ned Kelly. The chief secretary refused his request for Kelly's skull, so he based his phrenological study of Kelly's criminal character on the death mask which he helped the waxworks owner Maximilian Kreitmayer to prepare.[16]

Deakin decided to run. His previous two election campaigns were for by-elections, but this third was for a general election. West Bourke returned two members to the Assembly, so Deakin had a running mate, Donald Cameron, who had a somewhat questionable reputation. One elector, while attacking Cameron's character, had 'not a word to say against Mr. Deakin, except that his opinions were not the same as they were yesterday'.[17] The two Liberal candidates were both defeated, along with Berry's government. Deakin was more disappointed with this defeat than the earlier one; but he took it philosophically and returned to his thriving press work, for which he was now being paid at the highest rate.

Shortly after the election, on 10 May 1880 one of his regular mediums casually told him that he would be in parliament within six months. As the parliament had been elected for three years, this was, he declared, impossible.[18] The Liberal free-trader James Service had formed a government with support from a Catholic grouping led by the former premier John O'Shanassy, which was focussed on the single issue of state aid for Catholic schools. Service took up the unfinished business of reforming the Council, proposing a reform bill which widened the franchise and provided for a double dissolution if Council twice rejected a bill from the Assembly—to be followed by a joint sitting. This was the very mechanism which would later be incorporated into the federal constitution. Deakin, still wedded to the idea of a plebiscite to resolve deadlocks, returned to the hustings to oppose Service's reform bill.

On 28 May the Reform and Protection League held a mass meeting at the Princess Theatre. Deakin was the first speaker. His task was to explain the bill to the audience. He had had only a few hours to study it, 'and in a state of pitiable nervousness crept to the Princess Theatre where a sight met my astonished eyes that fairly took my breath away. A packed crowd of 2500 strong, obviously in a high state of emotional tension, crammed every corner of the old building.' The *Argus* put the crowd at only fifteen hundred, but even so it was much larger than the three or four hundred Deakin was used to and he 'was almost paralyzed into speechlessness'.[19] Nevertheless, he mustered his platform skills. First he outlined the critical features of the bill and then moved to attack, the audience following eagerly with rounds of applause; when he concluded they gave him 'an immense ovation'. 'My position as a public speaker was at once established.'[20]

In the early hours of Friday, 25 June, James Service's reform bill was defeated in the Assembly by two votes, amid great excitement. Party allegiances were loose in nineteenth-century parliaments and the outcome was unclear until the last moment. Deakin was in the gallery, no doubt covering the parliamentary drama for the *Age*, which carried a detailed report in that day's paper. As the house did not break till

3 a.m., skilled and rapid writing was required to make the morning edition.[21] A few days later, the four-month-old parliament was dissolved and the way cleared for the medium's prophecy to be fulfilled. The electorate of West Bourke thus faced another campaign, its fourth in eighteen months, and Deakin was yet again on the hustings. This time his running mate was the Irish baronet Bryan O'Loghlen, with whom the Liberals hoped to win the Catholic vote.

The campaign was bitter and Deakin was personally attacked in the conservative *Daily Telegraph* for his unorthodox religious views. He was a 'Spiritist and a Comtist and moreover an advocate of free love and an enemy of Christian marriage'. It was alleged that Deakin was behind the circulation in the electorate of Auguste Comte's humanist calendar, in which the months of the year were named after great men of history, and that this was a blasphemous attack on the Catholic calendar of saints. Readers were also informed that Deakin was the president of the Victorian Association of Progressive Spiritualists and the author of *The New Pilgrim's Progress*, 'a vile catchpenny publication', 'the record of the delirious dreams of an illiterate, ignorant and impure mind'.[22] Deakin survived the ridicule to top the poll, which was held on 14 July 1880. He was now, again, the member for West Bourke, but he had learned that his spiritualism was a political handicap.

The Catholic vote had switched allegiance from Service to Berry, bringing Berry within reach of a majority; only within reach, however, so some sort of coalition seemed inevitable. In Deakin's subsequent account of the formation of the ministry, the first steps he took as a member of parliament 'sought to bring about an honorable union of parties'. Both on his own initiative and with Berry's consent, he became the Liberals' chief negotiator, 'Berry treating me from the outset as of the first rank'. The Liberals, urged on by the *Age*, preferred not to have to rely on the Catholics, who commanded nine votes in the Assembly and demanded state grants for their schools as their unconditional price. Deakin visited the upright Conservative Henry Wrixon in his Kew mansion Raheen, where Daniel Mannix later lived, but was not able to persuade him into a coalition with Berry. In the Liberal caucus, Deakin opposed any concessions to the Catholics.

In the end there was no formal coalition with the Conservatives and Berry relied on support from the Catholic faction to form a ministry, which he put together in a room at the old White Hart Hotel in Spring Street next to the Grand, now the Windsor. Deakin was one of the few Liberal caucus members Berry invited to accompany him, and during the negotiations Berry offered him the position of attorney-general, saying: 'I like you and can work with you.' Deakin, aware of his inexperience, had the good sense to refuse, but this is another indication of his extraordinary capacity to win the confidence of older men.[23]

The student of American presidents James Barber argues that a politician's first independent political success lays down much of his subsequent political style: remembering his early victory, he repeats the style that delivered it.[24] Although we only have Deakin's word for the part he played in the negotiations, the role of go-between, the facilitator of compromise and co-operation, is one he was to play again and again in his political career, as he positioned himself between conflicting forces and sought the harmonious middle ground.

On Sunday, 1 August 1880, just two days before his twenty-fourth birthday and in the midst of the negotiations over the ministry as a newly minted MP, Deakin began a Spiritual Diary and kept it up until early 1882. It is an extraordinary document, recording in great detail Deakin's regular attendance at séances: the 'shades' who appeared, the questions he asked them and the advice they gave. Because he decided only to record communications from the spirits about his personal and everyday life, omitting those on abstract, philosophic and purely spiritual affairs, it is of great autobiographical interest. Most of the séances took place in the parlour of a Mrs Stirling in her small cottage off Swan Street in Richmond, though some were conducted by a Mrs Cohen, who predicted that within three years Deakin would hold the reins of office. This prediction is only recorded in his summary diary for 1880 and not in the detailed séance diary.[25]

Deakin periodically rewrote accounts of his life based on earlier notes and diaries which have since disappeared. Inevitably the older man smoothed away much that was embarrassing and silly. In the manuscript 'Personal Experiences of Spiritism', which was written in the 1890s, he suggests that his keen interest in spiritualism was driven primarily by metaphysical and ontological questions. The diary, contemporaneous with the events it records, brings us much closer to its psychological drivers, the anxieties of a young man eager to make his way in the world and hungry for reassurance. It reads like a dream diary, as Deakin sits in a darkened room straining to hear the messages of the spirits through the often ambiguous words of the medium.

The diary record begins with a séance held the day before, on 31 July 1880. Perhaps it was the remarkable political salience of this séance which prompted his decision to begin a record. The shade of the popular Victorian Liberal premier Richard Heales, who had died in 1864, predicts that the negotiations with Henry Wrixon will be unsuccessful and the ministry formed weak and short-lived. The next ministry will be stronger and include him. Heales' shade, 'my political father', then delivers an apocalyptic warning of a great struggle between church and state over the Bible in state schools, in which 'I should be an object of peculiar hatred of the priests—my life would be attempted by the RCs—must not leave political meetings at night alone, or go alone.' This is straight-out projection. As Deakin works to prevent Catholics from achieving their political ends, he fears their revenge. Warnings of threats appear regularly in the diary. Mostly Deakin is the particular target of vague enemies, but on occasions the threat is more global, as in an approaching geological cataclysm in which parts of Great Britain and the Netherlands will be inundated by the ocean.

In his first few months as an MLA, Deakin visits Mrs Stirling most weeks, generally on a Saturday, and sometimes more often. The shades of John Knox, Thomas Macaulay, John Bunyan and John Stuart Mill, among others, appear and all are keen to help him. The spirits urge him not to yield to depression but to trust all to them; they advise him on reading and on his health. At the first séance recorded he learns that 'A grand spirit—will lend my words weight—so that I shall convince and conquer in spite of opposition—shall be great Reformer.' In September he is instructed to rest, eat fruit and avoid stimulants. That same month, as Berry is attempting yet another bill to reform the Upper House, Macaulay urges him to read his history of the reign of Charles II for precedents on the rights of the Assembly. And in November he promises to be with him when he delivers a lecture, 'to fill his mind with the results of his knowledge'.

The diary returns again and again to the question of Deakin's life's purpose. He will be a great reformer—but whether in law, politics or the work of the spirit was not yet clear. Predictions about future successes in law indicate that Deakin still considered a legal career to be an option. Mostly, though, the choice was between politics and religion: 'Am inspired to be a Reformer both in Church and State—have done something in the first—now do more in the State—almost too spiritual for politics.' But whatever the field, 'I am the boy.'[26]

On the morning of Friday 17 December the usual parade in Mrs Stirling's parlour was joined by Archibald McIntosh, a financial guide from Ballarat, who had died five years earlier. Macaulay vouched for him as 'a good and reliable spirit'. Along with an astrologer, another regular séance visitor, McIntosh became a source of financial advice for the new member of parliament on the purchase of shares in various mining ventures in Gippsland and in a speculative gas company, Dixon Gas, which claimed to have discovered an easy and practicable method of decomposing water.[27] The spirits were giving him this financial advice 'to free and strengthen me for their higher work'.[28]

As the diary moves into 1881 the focus of Deakin's anxiety shifts from his political career to his financial speculations. He was now seriously courting the eighteen-year-old Pattie Browne and money would lend weight to his suit in the eyes of her wealthy father. He sent greeting cards to 'Miss Browne' for Christmas 1880 and her birthday on 1 January 1881.[29] Later that month he consulted a Madame Siecle, who assured him that the gas shares were certain to succeed ultimately and predicted that he would become more successful, 'always rising upwards'. Her most exciting prediction was that he would be married 'to a dark lady—brownish' and be very happy.[30]

By the end of 1881 Deakin's feet were on his life's path, but it seemed to him accidental, the result of circumstance and the absence of a compelling alternative. Almost two decades later, in 1900, Deakin wrote an autobiographical narrative called *The Crisis in Victorian Politics* in which he rehearsed the options and false starts of his youth: the literary life, the theatre, religious preacher, teaching, bookkeeping, journalism. He had insufficient talent or originality for the theatre, for poetry or for literary prose, and these were unlikely to return the annual income of three to five hundred pounds to which he aspired. His attempt to become a Unitarian preacher had been rebuffed. He did not want commercial employment because it was directly involved with making money, which seemed to him 'as to the ancient Greeks unworthy of a free man and inconsistent with independence'. Teaching was drudgery, with its endless repetitions. Journalism was too concerned with the transient and superficial, a mechanical mode of earning one's living which reduced 'the mind to a machine and one's pen to that of a press hack'. As he runs through his options, he does not even mention the law, for which he had qualified, and concludes that he became a politician 'by sheer force of circumstance rather than by independent choice'.[31] Deakin is remembering here his youthful reluctance to knuckle down, to put on the yoke of adult responsibility and routine, but he is also revealing his need for variety and action, for work which will pick him up and carry him along, in which his own excitable, restless energies could be aligned with the movements of the cosmos.

He would, he writes, 'have been content with a life without public appearances, public speaking or public notice under a veil of anonymity and largely in communion with Nature', earning 'a small sufficiency by the publishing of the very best that thought, observation and study should enable my mind to yield to the cause of culture'. This is the life of Wordsworth, a romantic idyll for countless aspiring young writers, but Deakin never seriously attempted to live it, nor would it have held his restless nature. Intermittently, when politics proved wearisome, in moments of despondency at the transience and futility of it all, Deakin rekindled these literary aspirations, and in his private hours he wrote and wrote. But politics had opened up to him another more dramatic mode of living the life of the word, and he was brilliant at it.

8

MP AND LOVER

THE PARLIAMENT DEAKIN joined on 14 July 1880 a few weeks before his twenty-fourth birthday was filled with stout, grey-whiskered men of the goldrushes. Slim, his curling beard dark and his skin fresh and clear, Deakin was conspicuously young. And he was unworldly, a temperance man, unmarried and living at home, with a high-minded view of the role of the legislator. In one of his first comments to the house he argued that some means were needed to prevent members from being besieged by the petty, personal matters of their constituents: it was derogatory to the standing of the member, and it took him away from 'matters of a purely public nature'.[1] But pressure from constituents was constant. Patrick Malone, who was tendering for the New Gisborne and Macedon mail run, asked Deakin to put in a good word for him with the postmaster-general, adding that if his tender was accepted Deakin would find a ten-pound note on his desk.[2]

As Richard Heales' shade had predicted, what was to be Berry's final government was weak and short-lived, lasting just short of twelve

months until 9 July 1881. Towards the end, Berry did finally achieve
some reform of the Council, but it was touch-and-go. The electorate
and most parliamentarians were heartily sick of the issue and wanted
the government's attention back on practical matters, such as railways
and irrigation schemes.

In Deakin's account of the final act in this long-running drama,
he again played the crucial role. Negotiations over a compromise bill
dragged on through the first half of 1881. Syme and the *Age* were
insisting on 'No Surrender' and Berry was ready to abandon the bill
altogether. Some Opposition members were open to compromise,
and for others it was a chance to destabilise the ministry and open up
opportunities for personal advancement. According to Deakin, 'The
consequence of all these conflicting elements was that the situation
as it developed was in the hands of two men—Fincham and myself.'

When the Liberal caucus majority voted for the abandonment of the
bill, George Fincham, the member for Ballarat West, declared he could
not accept the vote as binding and must take an independent course.
'To the surprise of everyone I followed with a similar declaration of
independence, for although my ideas were well known it was thought
my relation with the *Age* would have fettered my action.' For two days
Deakin was cold-shouldered by his caucus colleagues and courted by the
Conservatives, who assured him and Fincham that the Council would
negotiate. So evenly balanced were the numbers in the Assembly that
with two defections there was majority support for another conference
with the Council. 'The dice was cast. The Bill was saved…My vote
had been the last and perhaps least, but most decisive factor in this all
important achievement.'[3]

Again Deakin believed himself to be the pivot on which the outcome
depended; again he resisted seeing a political situation in terms of
competing parties; again he asserted his independence and freedom
of action. A pattern was emerging, in which no one could ever be
completely sure what the enigmatic Mr Deakin would do.

The resulting bill expanded the Council's membership and extended
its franchise, but it contained no mechanism to resolve deadlocks, thus
increasing the Council's democratic legitimacy while failing to curb its

powers.[4] After the expenditure of so much political time and capital, it was not much of a result. Two weeks later, on 1 July 1881, Berry's government lost a no-confidence motion. Deakin found the whole experience disillusioning, as he saw men vote for 'mere party ends and party action in defiance of personal judgement and conscience'.

The new ministry was a scratch team of the opportunistic and inexperienced, led by Deakin's Catholic running mate in West Bourke, Bryan O'Loghlen. Deakin regarded him as weak and lazy, but the real villain in his eyes was Thomas Bent, commonly known as Tommy, 'the most brazen, untrustworthy, intriguer whom the Victorian Assembly has ever known', and it was to his mastery of the art of snaring men that Deakin attributed the ministry's survival beyond a few weeks. In fact, it survived until January 1883.[5] Bent was a Conservative who viewed Berry as a dangerous radical, but his greatest loyalty was to his electorate, centred on the seaside suburb of Brighton, and he worked hard to direct government spending its way. A tenacious fighter, he was, wrote Deakin, a master of lobbying, log-rolling and obstruction.[6]

During sitting weeks, parliament convened on Tuesday, Wednesday, Thursday and occasionally on Friday, commencing at 4.30 p.m., with a break for dinner from 6.30 till 8. Business often continued till midnight and beyond. As Deakin was regularly writing both the overview of the week and the 'Verandah' column for the *Leader*, as well as items for the *Age*, time sitting on the Assembly's benches earned him a double income. Inevitably his independence was questioned, particularly when anonymous paragraphs appeared in the *Age* strikingly similar to his and Syme's known views.

Deakin, though quick to question the integrity of others, always bridled at doubts cast on his own: he was on no one's lead string, under no obligation to any single individual for being in the house; he never consulted anyone on how to vote or speak, or whom to blame or praise. To prove his independence, he pointed to the two occasions on which he had severed himself from his party: his 1879 resignation, and his voting against the party on the reform bill.[7] Such piety drove Bent to distraction. To one of Deakin's accusations of jobbery, for which he had scant evidence, Bent retorted, 'The honourable member for West

Bourke must have had a spiritual manifestation on this subject.'[8]

In September 1881 Deakin introduced his first piece of legislation: a bill for the protection of animals, with the second-reading speech on 5 October. Deakin had been elected to the committee of the Victorian Society for the Prevention of Cruelty to Animals in January and the society had approved the bill, which aimed to clarify the meanings of cruelty to animals, already illegal under the Police Offences Act.[9] It specifically prohibited tying a second horse and dray to the back of the first, a practice which risked injuring the second horse. Deakin told the house that the question of cruelty to animals 'was one about which every humane person must share the same feelings…it was the duty of the Legislature to seek to afford every protection to poor creatures who could not protect themselves or tell of the injuries they received.'[10] Concern for the welfare of animals was another bond he shared with Pattie Browne, a good horse-woman and fiercely protective of animals.

Deakin's diary for 1881 is sparse. Brief notes on the political drama are interspersed with milestones in his courtship of Pattie: 'Learn 3 rejected—P'; 'back late train—others asleep—but P'; 'Revelation with P. Town Hall ball.'[11] The day after the revelation, on 7 July, and a week after Berry's government had fallen, Deakin asked Hugh Browne for Pattie's hand. Pattie was now eighteen. She had been educated at home by governesses and then at a fashionable ladies' college, Grantown House, patronised by the Anglican establishment, where she learned to sing and to sketch, and studied to matriculation, but did not take the exams. The now dilapidated three-storey, wedding-cake terrace still stands in Nicholson Street, Fitzroy, opposite the Royal Exhibition Building.

Pattie grew up in a boisterous family of ten. When she was very small the family lived in the country, where her brothers caught a cockatoo for her which lived with her until her old age. Pattie remembered several incidents from her youth when her quick-thinking and resourcefulness saved the day: rescuing her mother from drowning at the St Kilda baths, her sisters from a fire in a hotel at Healesville and a child from convulsions.[12] Browne thought his eldest daughter strong-willed and gave Deakin only qualified approval of the engagement, asking that it not yet be made public till they had tested each other a little further.[13]

Deakin left Melbourne next day for his first trip to Sydney and the Blue Mountains, from which he wrote her long, artless letters.

> My dearest child though I am delighted to hear you say how sure you are that you really know your feelings towards me…If ever you waver or weaken or have other attractions that instant you must speak to me and the next instant no matter how bitter it might be—you should be free. I do not fear such a contingency.
>
> I loved you but was determined to try to make you love me…I stood aside to leave the field free for your other suitors.
>
> I am not the least afraid of your will—Have I not done all I could to develop it. Your father said hopefully that I might break it—I fancy he would have stared if I'd told him I didn't intend to try… I don't want a wax doll for a wife.

Neither he did, but there is a Pygmalion fantasy here, as Deakin vows 'to make you a woman worthy of any man's affection' and asks, 'Are you tired of being taught…I trust not—Indeed my teaching is just about to begin.' Deakin frequently addressed Pattie, who he had first met when she was eleven, as 'my dearest child', as he poured out his aspirations for her development: 'I am always so glad to see you developing intellectual tastes and turning from follies and common places to real thought and genuine affection—I want to see you well read—well spoken, refined and cultured'; and he urges her to the self-sacrifices and labour of 'the higher life'. Pattie's letters have not survived, so we don't know what she thought of her lover's patronising enthusiasm for her continual improvement, or whether she was irritated when he requested an amnesty on 'Bulletins on her haberdashery'.[14]

The Brownes were not pleased with the engagement. They held higher hopes for their beautiful eldest daughter than this talkative young man who, though clearly gifted and ambitious, was only the son of a clerk and could not yet keep their daughter in the manner to which she was accustomed. Attempting to dissuade her, they suggested that the couple were temperamentally unsuited, she too strong-willed and he too masterful for a happy life together. They even suggested her suitor's health was too delicate.[15]

Pattie fought hard with her parents for her choice. No doubt she knew from her lover of the medium's repeated prediction that she was his predestined mate; and though we know little of Pattie's other suitors they are unlikely to have been as physically attractive as Deakin, 190 centimetres to her 178, with his intense brown eyes and soft mouth. One suitor, a baronet, bought for her the hand-embroidered Kashmir shawl that Queen Victoria had sent out for the 1880 International Exhibition, evidence both of his means and his expectations, which were almost certainly encouraged by the Brownes. But he was much older, forty at least, and she only eighteen.[16]

True to his promise, Deakin set about continuing her education. The first time they were permitted to walk out together unchaperoned, they sat in the Fitzroy Gardens while he read to her from *Sartor Resartus*. On another occasion he read to her from *Pilgrim's Progress*.[17] They rode together and went on very long walks through the sparsely settled fringes of Melbourne to Red Bluff on the bay, or to Burwood in the east, he talking about Ruskin, Tennyson, Emerson and poetry in general. He wrote to her often, ardent letters from the parliamentary library or the house during debates, arranging to meet on the corner of Spring and Collins streets, urging her to write 'as I do without the least restraint…just let your thoughts take shape on paper without thinking about them', and continuing his instructions 'to make you the admiration and envy of all who know you'.[18]

At the beginning of 1882, on the brink of married life and with the contours of his future as a public man before him, Deakin announced to himself a new beginning to his spiritual life: instead of the arrant nonsense of his séance diary, he will put the remaining pages of the notebook to better use and henceforth record thought rather than superstition. There is a new heading, 'Memoranda 1882'. The first entry, 'Ideal Satisfaction', poses Carlyle's question from *Sartor Resartus*, 'Is there anything that can fill up the essence of desire?' After some meandering,

Deakin concludes, 'It is well doing—the consciousness of having done right is a blessedness that never wanes or fades but remains rock like for us to rest upon forever.'[19]

The previous northern-hemisphere spring James Froude had published his edition of Carlyle's explosive *Reminiscences*, which included a section based on the private journals and letters of Carlyle's wife, whose unhappiness Froude largely blamed on Carlyle's egotistical self-absorption and, he hinted, his sexual inadequacy. Carlyle had been dead less than two years and the public was shocked by this intrusion into the secrets of a man's home and marriage bed. Deakin had a copy by January 1882 and read it avidly, reflecting on his hero's loveless, dyspeptic nature.[20]

Still, the teacher of his youth was not to be discarded for his all too human failings and a few days later he wrote, 'Canst thou by searching find not God? Yes! Yes, after long watching and long weariness the dawn is coming to me—the knowledge for which I have waited several years—have felt the need of—for myself and all mankind.' He notes a recent change in the temper of his mind, due to experience and the inevitable mental ripening, 'So much so that I could almost believe looking back that my guidance has been from the most providential to this end.'[21] And so he embraced the Everlasting Yea.

The beginning of his life with Pattie, however, seemed to be retreating as the Brownes attempted to delay the marriage. The Brownes were themselves in no position to be arguing against hasty marriage. They had eloped when Elizabeth was only sixteen and Hugh twenty-three, and Elizabeth's clergyman father was no doubt not particularly taken with his future son-in-law either. Browne was forceful and used to getting his way. But Pattie refused to bend to his will. Deakin wrote to her in February that 'The situation at your house is getting more and more serious. I am anxious to find a speedy way out of it.'[22] Soon after, she moved to Adams Street.

In mid-March, after 'storms and struggles at Park House', the Brownes finally relented and the wedding date was set for 3 April.[23] Pattie was defying her parents, and as a consequence there was no dowry, although it is not clear whether this was the parents' punishment or the daughter's angry assertion of her independence. For Deakin it became another strand in their romance: 'She came without dower, peerless and priceless—we owed them nothing.'[24]

The couple was married by the registrar-general in a quiet wedding at Park House, with neither church nor society in attendance. Pattie was radiant on her father's arm, with daphne in her hair and Catherine as her bridesmaid. On their wedding night at Adams Street, 'beyond control, beyond recall, Lip flew to lip, love all in all.'[25] Deakin never allowed the thrill of that night to fade, and he evoked its memory often in his annual anniversary poems to Pattie. He wore the watch chain she gave him as a wedding present for the rest of his life.

Catherine had vacated her own bed for the bridal couple and stayed the night with friends. Returning for breakfast the next day, she felt awkward before the young flushed faces and wished she had stayed away. Next morning the new Mr and Mrs Deakin took the steamer to Launceston for their honeymoon. Pattie remembered that they walked for miles and miles. Fortunately she was strong, as he made her slide down the Cataract Gorge at Launceston, and together they undertook 'a terrific climb' up Mount Wellington in Hobart to enjoy the 'transcendental' views. He talked all the time: 'He never relaxed, he was always reading or discussing the deepest subjects…such an old mind for such a young man.' He was also always thinking about his health, 'what he should eat and what he should do to become stronger'. To Catherine he wrote with extraordinary obtuseness, 'We often wish you were with us.'[26] It is unlikely that Pattie shared this wish.

On returning, the newlyweds moved into Catherine's vacated bedroom, and then into a new room the ever-accommodating William added to the house. They lived at Adams Street for two years. Pattie, who had been untroubled by household duties at Park Street, learned the rudiments of cooking and housekeeping from Sarah, and Deakin continued his public life. Pattie was able to observe the family dynamics at close quarters, how William read aloud to them for hours on end, and the intense discussions between brother and sister.

These first two years must have been difficult for the young couple in the first rush of their sexual life, constrained by shyness and convention from public displays of affection. As the ardent young husband explained, if he could not express himself openly with kisses and caresses and a thousand delicate endearments of delight, he shrank back into himself and expressed nothing at all.[27] Pattie was alone for much of the day with her mother-in-law and much older sister-in-law, particularly after the amiable William left for his one and only trip Home in February 1883. Pattie and Catherine were close at the time, but this was not to last. Whenever Alfred was away he would send his 'darling girl' passionate letters declaring his love.

They did not plan to live at Adams Street forever. Deakin's diary for 1882 records a land purchase in January, but it is not clear where this was.[28] In April, soon after their wedding day, William bought a block of land in Walsh Street, South Yarra, on which Pattie and Alfred were to build their family home. The block was subdivided from six acres of crown land bought by the developer Francis Beaver. William was the first purchaser, buying a choice double block with a clear view west across the Botanic Gardens to Port Phillip Bay.

In 1886 William transferred the title to Alfred. Blocks in the new subdivision sold slowly over the next few years, including five to Alfred's school friend Theodore Fink, who was already doing well.[29] Entries in a small leather notebook of William's indicate that, like the rest of Melbourne in the 1880s, he was raising mortgages and buying and selling land, including in 1884 half of the Adams Street block to the Melbourne Tramway and Omnibus Company, which was introducing cable trams to the inner suburbs. In 1888 he bought land in Lilydale. He was closely involved in Alfred's financial affairs, paying bills for him, transferring money to and fro, and in 1886 lending him two hundred pounds at 10 per cent per annum.[30] It is not clear whether the Walsh Street block was a wedding gift, or whether Alfred paid it off to William, but either way it shows William's continuing generous and practical support for his only son.

Over the Christmas–New Year period at the end of 1882 Pattie and Alfred holidayed at Phillip Island and then with the Symes at Mount Macedon, where Deakin enjoyed long horse rides. It is unlikely that

Pattie, a keen rider herself, joined him, as she was by now three months pregnant. Towards the end of January 1883, perhaps prompted by his impending fatherhood and a year after he had embraced the Everlasting Yea, Deakin contemplated the costs of Carlyle's stern admonitions to find and follow one's duty, as he renounced youth's open-ended sense of life's possibilities: 'The whole world is necessary to a man,' but 'he has only a single cranny open to him.'

In a reflection called 'A Complaint', Deakin confronted a dilemma to which he would return again and again, between 'The social man—the man of duties, of relations, of the mart and the ballot box, of newspapers and the home' and 'the individual man of travel and knowledge and adventure who walks face to face with nature and sees with an undimmed vision the greatest and most solemn verities of the universe glow upon him from every morning's sun'. The latter murders duty and starves affection; the former, knitted into the social order, is hemmed in, and his love for wife and children 'does not fill his soul. He also has a hunger for nature, solitude, wandering communication with the infinite face of his mother earth.'[31]

9

JAMES SERVICE, ANNEXATION

AND FEDERATION

DEAKIN WAS SOON busy again with the ballot box. O'Loghlen's unproductive ministry had collapsed after bungling an overseas loan and a new election was held in February 1883. James Service led the Conservatives to a slight majority over the Liberals and negotiated a coalition government with Berry, with himself as premier and treasurer. A sober, hardworking Scottish merchant, Service was already politically active as a Chartist when he arrived in Victoria in 1853 aged thirty. Almost immediately he became involved in municipal politics and soon after entered the Legislative Assembly. When he became premier he was sixty and had a great deal of political experience. Although labelled a conservative because of his support for free trade and the powers of the Legislative Council to check the Assembly, and his opposition to payment of members, he was as firmly against entrenched privilege as any colonial liberal and, like his close friend George Higinbotham, he refused a knighthood.[1] In forming a coalition with Berry, however, he was flexible and pragmatic, meeting him on the emerging common ground of Victorian politics and accepting the tariff and payment of members.

Charles Pearson wrote to his wife that the Conservatives had completely adopted the Liberal programme, and with all the decent men of the two parties fused into one strong following, he was hopeful the coalition would last. Disappointingly, he was not a member of the new ministry. Service told him that, in the face of unrelenting opposition from the *Argus*, he could not include him.[2] The *Argus* also tried to veto Deakin but it was too late, as Service had already accepted Berry's nomination of him. When, in early March 1883, aged twenty-six, Deakin was sworn in as commissioner for public works and minister for water supply, Mrs Cohen's prophecy of August 1880 that he would be holding the reins of office in three years was fulfilled. More mundanely, his elevation increased his backbencher's allowance of three hundred pounds a year to a minister's salary of fifteen hundred.[3]

Even so, he hesitated before accepting Service's offer. On 4 March, four days before he put on the yoke of ministerial responsibility, he returned to the dichotomy of 'A Complaint', though in the political form of the choice between 'the two great paths' of reforming society from within or from without, between those who accept the limitations of the social order and are entrusted to some extent with its powers, and those who, refusing to put on its livery, gain freedom but lose influence. It is the political idealist's core dilemma and Deakin came down firmly for the chance to do limited good.[4] Deakin's first three years as a minister were served under a competent chief in an effective and confident government in a booming colony. Victoria was prosperous and becoming more so. Melbourne was the financial capital of Australia and one of the largest cities in the British empire, its growing population creating demand for housing, public buildings and infrastructure.

In April, with the rest of the ministry Deakin visited Ballarat for the celebrations of the hundredth locomotive engine built by the Phoenix engineering works. It was a grand occasion. A public holiday had been declared and fifteen thousand people assembled to watch the engine roll forward. It was festooned with flowers and flags, the ministers hung from the doors, and the band played 'See the Conquering Hero Comes'. The festivities were somewhat marred when scalding water spurted from the funnels and showered the politicians, but nevertheless it was a stirring celebration of Victorian industry, of its skilled workforce and of the benefits of government support for heavy manufacturing.[5]

If Deakin had felt beleaguered by the continual requests from his constituents for assistance with personal matters, his position as commissioner for public works was far worse in a fast-growing colony where government was the major provider of infrastructure. Together with the minister for railways and the postmaster-general, as commissioner for public works he disbursed the funds needed to develop Victoria's suburbs, towns and hamlets, to open up new districts and to establish Melbourne as a modern metropolis.

Every Wednesday, Deakin received up to a dozen delegations from shires and councils. The Bairnsdale Shire wanted a bridge over the Mitchell River, Apollo Bay wanted a jetty, Kew property owners wanted the deferment of payment to a bridge builder who had illegally lowered the road, Mansfield wanted assistance with a track to the new goldfields, St Arnaud needed funds to complete the town drainage, Geelong wanted a new dredge for Corio Bay, and so on, from the Murray to the sea. Deakin's response was invariably that he was favourably disposed to the request, particularly if the shire or council offered to meet half the costs, and that he would consider it when the next budget estimates were being prepared.[6]

To parliament he complained that he did not have sufficient information to determine an equitable distribution of grants for improvements, and was thus 'placed in a degrading position'.[7] Deakin disliked anything that smacked of the exercise of personal power and recoiled from building a political base through patronage. Instead he looked for impersonal rules and procedures, or at least clearly articulated and transparent priorities, to guide decisions and determine the allocation of resources. He thus welcomed the new government's early establishment of the Public Service Board to oversee recruitment, appointments and advancement, and so put an end to ministerial patronage and jobbery.

On 14 July 1883 Deakin became a father. Ivy was born at Adams Street after a long labour, noted in his diary as 'P's agony'. Pattie later complained of the rough medical treatment she received at Ivy's birth, and blamed it for some of her subsequent ill health.[8] Her mother seems to have provided little support, leaving her to depend on her mother- and sister-in-law as she coped with a new baby. As with other rites of passage, Deakin marked Ivy's birth with poems, these filled with wonder at her 'sweet fairy form', 'her purity and perfect loveliness'.[9]

With his new responsibilities as a father and a minister of the crown, Deakin pruned his commitments. He gave up the 'Verandah' column, later offering the post to Theodore Fink, and in November 1884 he resigned his membership of the bohemian Yorick Club, which he had most likely joined in 1879 when he and Fink were companionable young men about town. Melbourne's bohemia held few attractions for Deakin, the married man, new father and teetotaller.

When not at official functions or out of town, he dined at home or with his parents and sister at Adams Street. He withdrew from official duties with the Victorian Association of Progressive Spiritualists, though his intellectual interest and belief in messages from beyond continued, and he still gave occasional lectures on spiritualism. Through all this, he continued to read obsessively. The pages where he summarises his activities for 1883 are shared between brief dated notes of events, trips and meetings, and a numbered list of more than a hundred books he read that year, as he crammed reading into the spaces of his day.[10]

As a boy Deakin had used reading as an escape and he took the habit into his adult life. Even at his busiest in politics he still found time to read, before and after breakfast, on Sundays, when travelling, thirty to forty hours a week in the summer months, and even in the house during tedious or meaningless debates.[11] Lists of each year's voluminous reading in his notebooks and diaries are not so much accounts of time spent worthily on self-improvement, but evidence of another life and another self. If no book was to hand, or it was too dark to read, 'in sleepless nights, in long journeys and weary waitings' he would recite some of the thousands of lines of English verse stored in his remarkable memory—Wordsworth, Tennyson, Shakespeare's plays and much else.[12] It was as if he dreaded a silent mind.

•

James Service was a good premier to be serving under while Deakin learnt the ropes of government administration. Sound and well organised, he ran an efficient cabinet and had a clear political agenda. After David Syme, Service was the major influence on Deakin's developing political outlook and style, far greater than Berry. These two lowland Scots drew Deakin into their own enthusiasms and encouraged his capacity for sustained, methodical work. Syme convinced him of the benefits of protection and of an active state to lead national development; Service bequeathed to him his unrealised dreams of federation and an Australian Pacific empire.

Service's election platform had, like most of the other candidates', included the commitment to work for federation of the Australian colonies. On a clear sunny day in June 1883, celebrating the meeting of the Victorian and New South Wales railway lines at Albury, to rousing cheers Service expressed the hope that the colonies now 'looped together with bands of iron' would achieve federation in his lifetime.[13] He had recently returned from Europe, where he had sensed the new imperial energies, and he regarded federation as an urgent strategic necessity if Australia was to forestall European incursion into its region.

Africa was being carved up by European powers, and French and German interests were active in Australia's north and east. In the late 1870s Berry had proposed that all the islands in Australia's part of the world should be held by the Anglo-Saxon race.[14] The Dutch had controlled the western half of New Guinea since 1828; France had annexed New Caledonia in 1853 and Britain, Fiji in 1874. The other islands to Australia's north, including the eastern half of New Guinea, were as yet unclaimed by a European power, although planters, traders and missionaries had an active presence, and the Australians wanted Britain to act. But the Liberal government of Gladstone had no interest in claiming new territory in the Pacific.

Service regarded foreign affairs as so important that he created the first premier's department for foreign affairs. He believed that a federated Australia would not only be better able to persuade Britain to its point of view, but that it would also have the financial capacity to contribute to the administrative costs of the imperial possessions, which

Britain was sure to demand.[15] Service lifted Deakin's eyes from purely domestic issues to Australia's external environment, and the dreams of federation and of an Australian imperial presence in the Pacific became entwined for him as they were for Service.

In April 1883 the Queensland premier, Thomas McIlwraith, frustrated by British inaction, took possession of the eastern half of New Guinea and its offshore islands in the name of Queen Victoria. He was responding to calls in the German press for the colonisation of New Guinea and did not wait for permission from Britain. His motives were partly strategic and partly the need to ensure supplies of labour for the growing sugar industry in North Queensland. Although initially agreeable, the British government officially disallowed the annexation. Gladstone's friend Arthur Gordon, with whom Deakin had dined when he visited Fiji, persuaded Gladstone that, given their record with the Aborigines and their appetite for native labour, the Australians were unfit for such responsibility.

All the Australian premiers supported McIlwraith, but Service was the most enthusiastic. The *Age*, rejecting the timorous British policy, could see no reason why 'the great colonising race of Englishmen should be debarred from replenishing this magnificent wilderness.'[16] There were howls of protest when the annexation was disallowed. The colonists also wanted Britain to curtail the French presence in the Pacific. Since the late 1870s, Australians had been irritated by the presence of French convicts in New Caledonia, both because it reminded them of Australia's convict origins and because some of them escaped to Australia. As well, Presbyterian missionaries were active in the New Hebrides, where they had campaigned against blackbirding. Their Victorian supporters lobbied hard for an end to French control. The solution in Service's eyes was for Britain to annex New Guinea and the islands to the east of it, including the New Hebrides. Introducing his annexation policy to parliament in July 1883, Service claimed that 'The islands of Australasia ought to belong to the people of Australasia.'[17]

Britain was not prepared to jeopardise its delicate diplomatic negotiations with France over possessions in North Africa for the sake of a few islands in the Pacific, which it regarded as of little value. The colonial secretary, Edward Stanley, suggested that a federation of the colonies should precede any steps for annexation.[18] No doubt this was a stalling move, but it cemented the link between annexation and federation in colonists' minds and raised the question of the priority of the Australian colonies in Britain's strategic thinking. The colonies did not expect to manage their own foreign relations, but they did expect to be consulted on matters in which they had a direct material and strategic interest.

Public support for annexation was strongest in Victoria, reaching fever pitch in September 1883 when news filtered through that the French government was proposing to transport five thousand criminals a year to the Pacific, including the New Hebrides, where they would be freed on the condition that they did not return to France. Service concluded that France was clearly planning to annex the New Hebrides and turn it into a 'cesspool for convicts' on Australia's doorstep. Escaped convicts would make for Australia, and Australia's convict stain would be darkened anew. Public meetings, resolutions and newspaper editorials all called for Britain to take pre-emptive action.[19]

To a meeting of six hundred people at Castlemaine's Theatre Royal at the end of September, Deakin stressed the undesirability of a convict colony so close to Australia's shores—a sentiment, he believed, that was felt strongly by free immigrants and their children. Escaped convicts, he asserted, could never become good colonists and good citizens, and nor could their children, who would inherit their parents' criminal proclivities. Referring to his brief personal experience of islands similar to the New Hebrides, he asked if these beautiful islands were to be turned into a 'prison sink' with the natives at the mercy of the worst sort of white man.

There was, however, one merit to the present danger: 'it had sent a thrill of sentiment from one end of the continent to the other...a desire for a United Australia. Instead of provincial it had made us feel national.'[20] This is not one of Deakin's best speeches, but it shows him starting to direct his oratorical gifts towards the goal of a federated Australian nation, which was fast becoming a Victorian cause.

If the colonies were federated, Deakin told the parliament the following year, then Britain would have to take them more seriously. The lesson of the failure to persuade Britain to annex the New Hebrides and New Guinea was the complete powerlessness of any of these great and populous communities by itself to gain a hearing with a foreign power, or even in the Imperial Parliament...The colonies appear to be so many separate, small communities scattered around the sparsely inhabited shores of a great continent and therefore are scarcely entitled to speak with the authority of a united people.[21]

At the end of 1884 Germany formally annexed the top half of eastern New Guinea. In response, Britain did finally establish a protectorate in the south-eastern part, but swifter, more resolute action would have forestalled Germany's move.[22]

One result of the annexation crisis was the transformation of the Victorian-based Australian Natives Association from a traditional friendly society into a political pressure group. All friendly societies had exclusive membership based on place of birth, ancestry or sometimes religion. When the ANA formed, in 1871, it was for the Australian-born only and added to the usual insurance benefits the provision of activities to enhance the moral, social and intellectual capacities of its members, including debates on the topics of the day. It grew only slowly in the 1870s, but after it took up the twin causes of federation and annexation its membership exploded, from 430 members in 1881 to more than eight thousand in 1891, by which time it was a powerful and effective pressure group.

In 1884 Deakin joined the Prahran branch.[23] These sons of the soil regarded themselves as having a special responsibility for national questions, and for the next two decades the ANA gave Deakin's political life a representative base. He had entered politics because of David Syme's encouragement and his own aptitude, and in so far as he represented any general social experience or interest it was that of the native born. In 1883 there were only twelve native-born men in the eighty-six-member Assembly.[24] Deakin became the most celebrated, speaking on behalf of those, like himself, who knew no other land and must find their destiny here or nowhere.

Early in 1884 Deakin started another series of reflections, called Clues, which he began with Carlyle's 'Blessed is he who has found his work; let him ask no other blessedness.' Numbered, dated, of varying length and on miscellaneous topics, the clues are written for an imaginary reader because Deakin felt the lack of conversation with those who shared his interests.[25] Reading alone was not enough, he reflected: he needed discussion to assimilate what he read. It was becoming evident to him that Pattie would not be his intellectual companion. For her twenty-first birthday, on New Year's Day, 1884, he gave her a copy of Ralph Cudworth's *The True Intellectual System of the Universe*, 'a work of which I have long promised myself the perusal, tho' which she never opened having no taste for that kind of literature'.[26] No doubt as the nursing mother of a six-month-old she would have preferred something more diverting than this seventeenth-century philosophical treatise on religion, ethics and free will. Despite his kindness, and his love for his wife, Deakin's intense self-absorption often made him obtuse.

The Brownes were spending the summer in Hobart. Pattie, baby Ivy and Sarah Deakin joined them to enjoy the cooler weather. Deakin missed Pattie and wrote often, complaining that he sent nine letters to her four. He also complained that she had not told him that her father was giving lectures on spiritualism while in Tasmania. 'Because I would not like to hear it is no reason why you should not have told me,' he wrote. 'He is certainly to be commended for his energy and zeal in the cause of what he believes to be the truth.'[27] Browne had become a fanatical spiritualist, publishing long accounts of his experiences and writing many pamphlets for the Society for the Propagation of the Truth.[28] By now Deakin was not much involved with spiritualism, despite continuing to believe in the possibility of spirit communication. It was, he had learned, an invitation to political ridicule. Pattie too had distanced herself. When she tried with the planchette board in her own home, her 'powers were nil'.[29]

Deakin was turning to more conventional religious practices. In August 1884, on the Sunday of his twenty-eighth birthday, he began yet another series of intimate reflections, a prayer diary to which he gave the mock archaic title 'The Boke of Praer and Praes'. He was to maintain this diary until 1913, writing over four hundred prayers in these twenty-nine years.[30] The diary began with a preface:

> Almost always I realise the existence of God. Always I believe in him with my intellect & turn to him with my heart. But I am anxious for a closer and more permanent relationship. Almost always I believe in the spiritual efficacy of prayer, & and often I am inclined to pray. Sometimes, the power to put my cry into words will come, sometimes it will not come. I will write these prayers so as to open the channel wider.

The prayer diary reveals Deakin's deeply felt need for an intimate interlocutor from whom he could seek reassurance about his worth and the rightness of his life's path. The prayers' most common forms were praise of God and thanks for His mercies, confessions of unworthiness and deficiency of character, and petitions for enlightenment and certitude. Most common was the plea 'O Lord show me the way.'

With his increased salary, Deakin could now provide a home for his family. In 1884 he, Pattie and baby Ivy moved from Adams Street into rented accommodation in St Kilda, South Melbourne and finally South Yarra. Pattie, described by a friend who visited them at this time as 'the beautiful queenly girl with the great brown eyes', could now manage her own household.[31] Alfred could also afford to test his destiny with more adventurous investments. Likely on the advice of fellow member of parliament Fred Derham, he invested a thousand pounds in a Queensland sugar plantation, Pyramid, eighteen miles north of Cairns and named after the shape of a local mountain. Twelve years older than Deakin, Derham was a successful businessman who had married into the thriving Swallow & Ariell biscuit-manufacturing business. He shared Deakin's love of books and for the next decade or so they were close friends, despite Derham's more conservative political views.[32]

Notwithstanding his later commitment to a White Australia, Deakin had no qualms about investing in an enterprise which employed coloured labour. In 1884 eighty-four Pacific Islanders, ninety Chinese and twenty

white men worked on the Pyramid estate, and Deakin would likely
have agreed with the judgement of the anonymous Vagabond in the
Argus that 'the imported Kanaka boy has a better time of it than the
agricultural labour of Great Britain or on the Continent.'[33]

Deakin was acutely financially embarrassed when calls were made
on Pyramid investors for a further thousand pounds. Dreading 'further
monetary responsibilities as a blow to my independence, social and
political', on 30 May 1884 he wrote to Derham requesting his assistance,
which was immediately forthcoming.[34] Between 1880 and 1884 Victorians
invested massively in the Queensland sugar industry, most of which
was lost when the world price slumped.[35] Pyramid did worse than most.
Poorly managed and situated, by 1887 it was in the hands of the Bank of
Australasia and investors lost more than a hundred thousand pounds.[36]

His independence was always a touchy issue for Deakin. In June he initiated an exchange of insults with the member for Ballarat West, William
Collard Smith. Despite his avowed preference for discussing measures
not men, Deakin was not above turning his tongue on opponents, and
he variously accused Collard Smith of laziness, greed, drunkenness,
dereliction of duty and self-serving fawning, when 'the honourable
member trailed his sword and his trumpet at the heels of the Chief
Secretary from one end of the colony to the other'. The innuendo was
too much for one of Collard Smith's colleagues, David Gaunson, the
lawyer who had represented Ned Kelly at his pre-trial. He interjected:
'Trailed his what?' Deakin dismissed Gaunson as 'the publican's puppet,
he must move as the wires are pulled'. Gaunson responded:

> When the late Mrs Anna Bishop was here she had a little dog,
> whose collar bore the inscription—'I am Anna Bishop's dog, whose
> dog are you?' I see no necessity for the honourable member to
> have a collar, but if he had one it ought to have engraved on it—'I
> am David Syme's puppy; whose dog are you?'[37]

10

IRRIGATION AND
THE FACTORY ACTS

IN 1883 DEAKIN resigned as minister for water supply, claiming that water was of such importance that it deserved its own portfolio, but he continued to take carriage of the government's water policy. A 'water famine' in the early 1880s had devastated farmers and settlements in the north and north-west, with the government having to run emergency water trains to some towns. Water trusts were established, and reservoirs, weirs and channels constructed to ensure water supply for domestic use and for stock.

In October he introduced an Amendment to the Water Conservation Act to enable trusts to also be formed for irrigation.[1] Water could thus become an agent of development, enabling agriculture in areas of precarious rainfall and hence closer settlement of the land. Deakin had no direct experience of the travails of the drought-stricken districts. His ideas about irrigation came in the main from Hugh McColl, a nuggetty Scotsman sometimes unkindly called 'water on the brain McColl' for his ceaseless promotion of the benefits of irrigation for northern Victoria.[2] Deakin was a convert and for the next decade or so believed that irrigation had the force of progressive destiny behind it.

The *Age*, the *Argus* and most parliamentarians supported irrigation. In 1883 the colony's leading newspapers had sent their respective agricultural editors to California to study its methods of irrigation. Curiously they were brothers, John and Thomas Dow, sons of a Scottish stock breeder and overseer near Geelong, now working for the rival papers. John Dow was also the member for the electorate of Kara Kara, in north-west Victoria. The brothers' reports excited a great deal of interest and at the end of 1884 the government announced the establishment of the Royal Commission on Water Supply and Irrigation, with Deakin as its chairman. He was to embark immediately on an investigative visit to America, accompanied by John Dow, who would report for the *Age*; E. S. Cunningham, for the *Argus*; and J. D. Derry, a state engineer with experience of irrigation in India.[3] In his diary Deakin notes that the idea of the California trip was raised on 29 November 1884 and announced on 12 December.[4] They were to leave Melbourne for Sydney on Christmas Eve, and Pattie and Ivy would go with him.

A week before the planned departure two of Pattie's younger brothers, Willie and Hugh, drowned in Port Phillip Bay, having taken out their yacht, *Iolanthe*, against their mother's remonstrance. Hugh Browne visited a medium to investigate the details, and, he hoped, to receive a message of remorse from his drowned sons for disobeying their mother. Here he learned that a sudden squall had toppled the yacht at 9 a.m. and a shark had torn off their limbs. Some weeks later, the same medium communicated to Browne that he should go immediately to Frankston Pier, where he arrived just as a large shark was being hauled ashore. Inside the stomach was one son's right arm up to the elbow, with keys, pipe, twelve shillings in silver and a gold watch stopped at 9.[5]

Pattie and Alfred left for Sydney on the day of the inquest, but before the grisly discoveries in the shark. They were to spend a few days in Sydney and surrounds with Fred Derham and his wife, Frances, before boarding the steamer for San Francisco. Walking in the Blue Mountains, Alfred carried Ivy in his arms.[6]

In a farewell letter to Derham written the day before he and Pattie embarked, Deakin wrote, 'my hopes are *not* more buoyant but I mean to do my best…I shall learn much if it be only of my own littleness…but shall not have pleasanter recollections than those of our past hours and I shall find no such friend.' He concluded the letter with an extravagant declaration: 'In all friendship then and in fidelity to the highest in us touching even upon that love which passeth the love of women. Goodbye dear old fellow.'[7] Today this Biblical reference to the love between David and Jonathan would raise erotic possibilities, but for Victorian men it was regarded as a stronger bond precisely because it was not erotic—rather, a companionship of souls and minds in which the pleasures of the body played no part.[8] Deakin yearned for a soulmate and Pattie remembered that at this time of his life he had a number of men friends, far more than later.[9]

This was Deakin's second trip overseas, and Pattie's first, and they were looking forward to the journey. But Pattie discovered she was not a good sailor and was seasick every day. She was miserable, grieving for her brothers and receiving only the most perfunctory of birthday greetings from her family, as she complained in an affectionate letter to Catherine. Deakin, though, was the life of the party, entertaining the ship with his stories and boyish antics.[10]

They sailed via Auckland, Samoa and Hawaii, reaching San Francisco Bay on 29 January 1885. Deakin wrote long diary-like letters home, which were later edited by Catherine into a travel diary, as well as being the basis for articles in the *Age*. In keeping with the travel genre, they are mainly descriptions of landscape and topography, tourist sites and first impressions of the people, with occasional pompous reflections. Comparisons with Australia are frequent, but this is as much to help the home folk as to steady himself amid the unknown.

Like many Australians on their first visit to the United States, Deakin's early impressions were the largeness of it all: San Francisco Bay, which could contain all the navies of the world in safety; the seven-storey Palace Hotel; the mirrored dining room at their hotel, which could seat two hundred; and the size of the people and the meals. 'Most people are stout here. Meals are enormous and very rich.' To his and Pattie's taste, the women were over-dressed and nearly all were painted; the mostly clean-shaven men met with more approval, well-dressed and 'with the brightness of eyes and quiet assurance which seems to say American'. He also noted approvingly in a letter to Derham that it was possible to do business in America without drinking.[11]

While Pattie and Ivy remained in Los Angeles, the men investigated the irrigation works of California, observing the orangeries, vineyards and orchards, oases of life and abundance in the arid landscape. In Los Angeles they met the irrigation engineer George Chaffey who, with his brother William, had established an estate of ten thousand acres of irrigated land at their own expense, which they were in the process of selling to settlers. Named Ontaria, this temperance settlement, planted with blue gums and silky oaks, later became the template for Mildura.[12]

The travellers worked hard, rising at 6, travelling long distances in Pullman sleeping cars, jolting along rough roads to investigate channels and head works. But they also had great fun, playing poker on the long journeys and swapping yarns with the men they met along the way. Dow remembers that the Americans boasted of the size of their farms and their flocks, and that when Deakin told them Australia's biggest sheep station shore a million sheep per year, they took it as a tall story.[13]

The party made a quick trip south of the border to investigate the irrigation schemes and floating gardens of Mexico City. Mexico was the first place Deakin visited which was entirely outside the orbit of the English-speaking world. In Fiji he had stayed at the club and mixed with English and Australians. Mexico was very different, a Catholic country built on the ruins of Aztec civilisation and the bones of human sacrifice. English speakers were scarce, and the party relied on their Spanish-speaking Pullman conductor as a guide.

Deakin's letters from Mexico lack his usual easy self-assurance. To maintain his voice of confident narration, he frames his Mexican experience with the conceit of 'the land of mystery and imagination, of wonder and of contradictions, that together make it a land of dreams'. The history is of peoples who were 'at once civilised and savage, amiable and bloody'. He was out of his depth, and he knew it: 'I am incapable of grasping its meaning or its features which as soon as I regard them seem to dissipate into thin air and leave me musing instead of observing. And yet I am here.'

Still, he tried to describe in vivid detail what he could see from the street: the exotically dressed people, the bargaining rituals, the buildings and streetscapes, the sweeping views, the evening promenade in the plaza, the beggars, the ubiquity of the intoxicating drink pulque, the seclusion of the women, and so on. One evening he and his companions fell in with a band of carousing students, a musical club dressed in knee breeches and black velvet doublets, singing and playing tambourines, guitars, castanets and violins.

Deakin admired the grand architecture and the rich decoration of the Catholic churches and cathedrals, but standing in the courtyard of the Church of San Domingo in which the bones of victims of the Inquisition were buried he reflected: 'It makes me proud to belong to the Liberal Party to learn that whenever the Church has been robbed of its ill-gotten jewels and plate, it has been by the incursion of the great Liberal Party, here as elsewhere always short of cash when it has to carry on the government.' He pondered too, the benefits that the Anglo-Saxon would bring to the despotism and poverty of the country, and doubted if the Mexicans would be able to do much for themselves 'until the Anglo-Saxon invasion comes. This may not be for a century, but come it must.'

Such reflections, though, seem staged and self-conscious in comparison with his raw and agitated response to a bullfight. He can scarcely look or contain his indignation as gored horses are stitched up and returned to the arena, and as the bull staggers and bellows to its death. 'All this too on a Sunday under a cloudless sky, with women and children looking on. My faith in humanity was badly shaken that day. The dresses were brilliant but the moral atmosphere was black as hell.' In the end, Mexico was too foreign for Deakin to assimilate. Leaving Mexico City, back in his snug Pullman car, 'The veil has dropped. The vision has faded. The dream has become a memory.'[14]

Back in the United States, Deakin's confidence returns. As the party travels up through the snow-covered prairies to a wintry Chicago he has plenty of time to write his travel diary and work on his notes on irrigation. Then across to New York, via Buffalo, where they visit Niagara Falls, which occasions extended description. From New York, Deakin made a personal literary pilgrimage to Concord, the village of the Transcendentalists Emerson and Thoreau and the novelist Nathaniel Hawthorne, and to the Sleepy Hollow Cemetery, where their bones rest. He also spent a day in Boston, visiting the main sites of the War of Independence and the campaign against slavery, before rushing to catch the sleeping car back to New York.

Deakin the traveller was indefatigable. He rose early, crammed his days with sightseeing, only resting his legs when he visited the theatre, sometimes taking in both a matinee and an evening show. Henry Irving's Lyceum Company was playing in New York, with the beautiful Ellen Terry, and Deakin went three times, relishing this opportunity to see the best of British theatre.[15]

Returning west, somewhere between Denver and Fort Collins, gazing out at the foothills of the Rockies from his Pullman car, Deakin recorded in a small leather notebook a change in his sense of self, a decentring in which he realised that

> Religion and many of my beliefs are hereditary, not immediately from my parents perhaps…but rooted in me by the influence of race and the bias of disposition. I had my hour of freedom in which I scoffed and flouted at the confirmed credulity of doctrine, as if Reason and knowledge were created by myself, but it was a short time.

Recognition that he is not the author of himself follows close on his visit to Boston and Concord, his first to one of the sources of the liberal thought and culture which had shaped him, making him 'conscious of the strong current of inherited belief sweeping away the little system I had built up of my own'.[16]

Meanwhile, in Los Angeles, Pattie was spending five miserable, lonely weeks in a boarding house with Ivy. 'I sit and think of home and of poor Hughie and Willie and cry for hours,' she wrote to Catherine, and wished she were there with her for company. She filled her time sewing, reading and tripping about with Ivy, who 'causes no little interest in her red jersey and woollen bonnet'. Pattie was a proud young mother engrossed in the wonder of her first child, but she missed Alfred dreadfully. When he said goodbye to her to travel south, she felt as if her heart would break, and her days hung on the arrival of his often disappointingly short letters. She dwelt too on a rift with her family which compounded her loneliness:

> I pray and long that we shall all be united and fond of one another once again. I can't help loving them but can never forget the wrong they have done me...I should be happy if on my return they were eager to see me and to ask our forgiveness and be once more the fond father and mother of days gone by when no one was to be compared with me and nothing was too good for me.[17]

Deakin returned to Los Angeles on 28 March 1885, in time for their third wedding anniversary, which he marked, as he was to do for their rest of their marriage, with a poem: 'whirled upon the mighty pulse of steam' he had come home, 'not to its roof and wall / But to its soul—thyself—and our child.'[18] He was, however, surprisingly insensitive to Pattie's situation, grieving for her brothers and alone with a small child in a strange city, not just for a few days but for more than five weeks. In letters to both Derham and Berry, Deakin expressed the hope that the break would do Pattie good. He worried about the effect of the heated rooms and rich food on her health, but he never mentioned her grief.[19]

They arrived back in Melbourne on 9 May and by mid-June Deakin had his report ready to present.[20] It is a model of succinct, persuasive and informative prose. Deakin was later to praise Service for 'his skill in marshalling masses of facts or figures, in grouping and grasping, in interpreting, classifying and contrasting them; summing up the argument or situation by homely metaphors and terse epigrammatic phrases'.[21] Here he showed himself similarly able to present complex technical information in accessible form.

The main import of the report was to argue that Victoria was just as suitable for irrigation as the western states of America, with similar soil, climate, rainfall patterns, products and costs of labour. Both are new countries, 'settled by the pick of the Anglo-Saxon race', gold-seekers who remained to build a new nation under free institutions.[22] But there was one big difference: attitudes to the state and its role in the provision of utilities, including irrigation works which were nearly all in private hands. Most of America's state governments did not even collect data on irrigation, and the committee had to rely on information from private persons.

Deakin's trip to the United States was to have long-lasting conse-quences for Australia's water policy. He was already disposed to an active state, and the trip convinced him that the government needed to take control of water rights before vested interests became too deeply involved. The report's first recommendation was that 'the State should exercise the supreme control of ownership over all rivers, lakes, streams and sources of water supply, except springs arising upon private lands.'[23] The second was that the state should disperse the water for irrigation purposes on the basis of judgements by its own professional and quali-fied officers. These recommendations were the basis for the legislation Deakin framed the following year.

The report was well received, but once it was finished Deakin seems to have experienced a crisis about his vocation. A period of illness had followed his 'excess of application' during and after the trip, and he occasionally noted sleepless nights in his diary. On 3 August he wrote: 'Birthday 29 and nothing done.'[24] A mood of futility and depression pervades Deakin's prayers and private writing in the last months of 1885. Usually his prayers are in the formal archaic language of the Anglican prayer book, but on 11 October, 'in the hours of dullness and stoneness of soul', there was a second prayer in a different voice, direct, staccato and self-flagellating:

Me afflicted at last with sense of wasted life...unearned ease, undeserved blessings & unmerited response. Me shallow & poor

& frail in spirit, in mind & in flesh. Me selfish & barren, even to
bitterness & blackness of soul. Me the mere creature of other
wills, though closed to Thine. Me the mere counter of the ideas
of others, producing none, Me the figure upon the stage of life
letting all power slip past me, without use or benefit. Me sunk in
dreamy sloth & wayward idleness. Me humiliated—me shamed.[25]

In September 1885 he had introduced the government's Factory,
Workroom and Shops Bill, but it was not going well. In 1882, as a
backbencher during O'Loghlen's government, Deakin had been a
member of a commission to investigate trading hours, which heard
from shop assistants of their long hours behind the counter. In 1883
he and Berry had urged the widening of the Shops Commission's
scope to include working conditions in factories. The commission
gathered evidence of children working who should have been at school,
of unhealthy and dangerous conditions in unsanitary factories, of
extraordinarily long hours for very low pay for women in the garment
industry, and similarly long hours for many shop assistants, with some
young girls working ten to fifteen hours a day.

Deakin left no record of his reaction to this report, but it must have
shocked the sheltered young man, exposing him to the realities of life for
many of his peers, working since twelve or thirteen while he pursued
his intellectual and spiritual development. In the debates on the 1885
legislation, he described the lot of small shopkeepers and their assistants,
confined behind counters in ill-ventilated and uncomfortable premises,
their daily work 'a round of monotonous drudgery, the effect of which
was made worse by the want of exercise both of body and mind', and
the strain imposed on their nervous and digestive systems.[26]

In framing a legislative response to the commission's report in
1883, Deakin had included only the least controversial of its thirty-nine
recommendations: on factory sanitary conditions, employment of women
and children, and early closing of shops. But opposition to even this
moderate legislation was fierce, opponents claiming it interfered with
the natural rights of employers, and he dropped it. After consultation
with the Chamber of Manufacturers and the newly formed Employers'

Union on one side, and with the Trades Hall on the other, he was now introducing an even weaker version, which he hoped would satisfy the critics. But he was being forced to make more concessions and must truly have felt that power was slipping past him, 'without use or benefit'. The bill was yet to face the Council, which could be expected to weaken it further still—which it did.

Progressive Liberals in the Assembly such as Charles Pearson argued hard for a stronger bill, and a number of strengthening amendments were moved, but Deakin declined to accept them. And when the Council weakened the bill still further, Deakin accepted it without a fight, unleashing none of his oratorical powers on the obstructionists in the upper house.[27] A decade later, in 1896, when another amendment was before the Assembly, he attacked the Council bitterly for its emasculation of the bill.[28] But in 1885 he bridled his tongue.

There is a puzzle here. Everything in Deakin's past predisposed him to take the workers' side: his humanitarian sympathies; his identification with progressive reform; his belief in each individual's capacity for intellectual and spiritual development; his kindly, sentimental nature; the example of his mentors, Higinbotham, Berry and Syme. In 1882 he had supported the first attempt to amend the 1873 Factories Act and been a member of the Commission of Enquiry into shop opening hours. He knew the evidence and the suffering. In March 1884 he had attended the opening of the new Council Chamber at the Trades Hall, where Berry and Higinbotham both gave 'splendid speeches', and he spoke at supper.[29] That year he also introduced a bill, based on the British act, to legalise trade unions, which, though weakened by Council amendment, provided them with some protection.[30]

Deakin's later Labor opponents found the solution to the puzzle easy, in his middle-class origins and identifications—and this is partly true. With his comfortable early life Deakin lacked the grievance-based anger that can be such a powerful driver of reform. But Deakin was always open to compromise, and the 1885 legislation did make significant gains. Child labour was virtually eliminated in factories (though much survived in domestic settings), and an inspectorate was created which, though weaker than it might have been, did lead to substantial improvements in working conditions. With the energies gathered against him so strong, he may well have felt deserted by the spirit of reform which he had entered politics to serve.

Mid-October, around the time of his bleak prayer of despair, anxious about his work and considering whether 'politics is my best field', he decided to consult the Sibyls, the prophetesses of Ancient Greece who helped men divine their destinies. First he opened Chapman's translation of Homer at random, his finger landing on the following lines from the *Iliad*:

> And that far-seeing god grants some the wisdom of the mind,
> <u>Which no man can keep to himself: that, though but few can find,</u>
> Doth profit many, that preserves the public weal and state,
> And that, who hath, he best can prize.

This was encouraging, and he underscored the lines which indicated both the rarity of his insights and the responsibility to share them.[31] His second approach to the Sibyls was to reread Carlyle's *Past and Present*, which he had first read in 1873.[32] The copy he almost certainly read on this occasion is still in the family's hands, a cheap American paperback edition published in January 1885, with Pattie's name on it.[33] Carlyle points him firmly to the duty which lies nearest him, the many opportunities awaiting the reformer.

Thick blue proofreader's pencil underlines sections on democracy and the art of government; the injustices of laissez faire and the spiritual poverty of the market economy; sanitation and education reform; the lives of the working poor; and, above all, the importance of work. As well as his favourite quotation, 'Blessed is he who has found his work,' three on idleness are marked: 'One monster there is in the world: the idle man'; 'In idleness alone is the perpetual despair'; and the last line of Goethe's poem 'The Mason Lodge', 'Work, and despair not.' These two trials of the Sibyls were marvellously congruent. Homer reminded Deakin of his responsibilities to his Creator for the use of his gifts, Carlyle of their application in the world.

Whatever the needs of his inner life or the result of the trials, there

were also family considerations. Pattie was pregnant again, with the baby
expected in the middle of 1886. Deakin's trials of the Sibyls confirmed
his political vocation but the trip to the United States and Mexico had
unsettled his confidence. In November he wrote:

> Everything is shaken...we have pulled down the roof on our head
> and live in thought this hour in one century, the next in another
> age—in a medley of countries, a contest of creeds and forms of
> creeds—a wrestle of philosophies and an expansion of the actual
> known world corresponding to that of the ideal so that all peoples,
> places, events pour in upon us & we are everywhere losing our
> identity and gaining chaos.[34]

Deakin lived in a dualistic universe in which the material world
was shadowed by a spiritual world, where ultimate meaning lay. But
this meaning was never easy to discern. His reading, his writing, his
prayers were all quests for certainty: for a stable metaphysical framework
to incorporate his intuitions of the mysterious divinity of the universe
and to ground his life's purpose. He found the certainties offered by
conventional religions neither intellectually nor spiritually convincing; and as he began to disengage from spiritualism, he pursued an
increasingly private quest, shared with neither Pattie nor, except very
rarely, with other men. Regularly in his private writings, he reflected
on his aloneness.

In the last months of 1885 new political opportunities were opening
up. Service, Berry and a senior Conservative, George Kerferd, were all
planning to retire from parliament at the end of the year. What would
happen to the leadership of the government? Berry favoured Deakin to
succeed him as leader of the Liberals; and as premier Service was looking
to Duncan Gillies, another Scot who had been in the Assembly almost
continuously since 1859. The *Argus* broke the news of the retirements
on Boxing Day, ahead of the official announcement.[35] The Conservative
parliamentarians supported continuing the coalition, but there were
voices urging the Liberals to fight the coming election alone: David
Syme and the *Age*, the Liberal newspapers in Ballarat and Bendigo,

Charles Pearson and other radical Liberals. The Liberal caucus had to decide; and it had to elect a new leader.

Deakin spent the Christmas week at Phillip Island with Pattie and Ivy, bathing, strolling on the beach, and thinking about his future. He was communicating by telegraph with the *Age*, and scanning his inner and outer world for signs as to the way ahead. On New Year's Eve he returned to Melbourne, where telegrams and letters awaited him. He had been nominated leader of the Liberal Party, but he was unsure: 'is it worth taking—is this not all leading me farther & farther from my goal—In God I trust.'[36]

The Liberal caucus was evenly divided on whether to stay in the coalition or go it alone. Deakin supported a coalition but, he told Christopher Crisp, editor of the *Bacchus March Express*, if the party were to decide against it loyalty to his party would override loyalty to his coalition colleagues in the ministry: 'poor as party spirit often is it is still something that pertains to principles which operate as a guide to electors and prevents the House from degenerating in to a mere collection of self-seeking individuals.' He also told Crisp that 'I do not want to be leader and have not yet decided whether even if selected I could accept.'[37]

On 19 January 1886 the Liberal caucus decided to continue with the coalition and unanimously elected Deakin its leader. Gillies became premier and treasurer, and Deakin chief secretary, which was at this time the second ministerial position. It was something of an omnibus portfolio, with responsibility for the colony's internal affairs, including policing and law enforcement.[38] Deakin brought into the ministry his old teacher Charles Pearson as minister for education and his American travelling companion John Dow as minister for lands and agriculture.

Although a week later he noted the 'Idea of resignation' in his diary, he was soon in the thick of another election campaign.[39] At the election, held on 5 March, Deakin won his seat with a majority of a thousand and when parliament met the coalition could rely on a comfortable majority.[40] The Opposition, which included experienced men from both sides who missed out on ministries, was led by Tommy Bent.[41]

Service and Berry had left the government's finances in good shape.

Deakin reported that his and Gillies' first budget in July achieved a
'cheering' surplus of three hundred thousand pounds. By the end of the
decade this surplus had turned to debt, as the government borrowed
and spent to please all askers, especially on the ever-expanding railway
network. In 1886 Deakin, however, was confident that 'with gold below
the soil and water on the surface, and the bright sky above, there will
be prosperity from one end to the other.'[42]

As chief secretary, Deakin was responsible for the administration
of the weakened Factory and Shops Act. The act allowed local options
to municipalities to vary shop closing hours from the specified 7 p.m.
weekdays and 10 p.m. Saturdays, and so was largely ineffective. Country
towns generally accepted early closing, but it was very different in
Melbourne where many municipalities opted out and some traders defied
the law. Angry shop assistants demonstrated for months in premier
shopping streets such as Bourke Street, Bridge Road, Brunswick Street
and Smith Street, with local larrikins joining in to create mayhem. The
chief secretary was also responsible for maintaining law and order on
the streets. Mounted police were deployed against the rioters, and many
shop assistants continued to work sixty and more hours per week.[43] In
this conflict between law and order and his private sympathy with the
shop assistants' cause, Deakin sided with law and order.

Deakin's primary legislative preoccupation during 1886 was the
Irrigation Act, and complementary legislation to enable the Chaffey
brothers to establish an irrigation colony on the Murray at Mildura. His
second-reading speech on the bill on 24 June lasted for four hours. The
crown would acquire the primary right to use and control the water in
every watercourse in the state. The aim was to encourage investment
in irrigation schemes, with provisions for easement of aqueducts over
private land and the extending of government loans to self-governing
locally based trusts which would construct works for storage, diversion
and distribution.

Deakin stressed that successful irrigation depended not on the
government alone but on the energy and joint actions of the farmers
wanting to invest their capital and labour. It also depended on skill
and experience in growing fruit trees and drying and canning fruit,

and on the latest technology for pumping large volumes of water from rivers. All of this the Chaffey brothers would bring to Victoria.[44] An agent of the Chaffey brothers had visited Deakin in October 1885 to sound out possibilities, and in February 1886 George Chaffey arrived.[45] Deakin met with him regularly during that year as they negotiated an agreement acceptable to both sides. This was not easy, as the Chaffey brothers wanted a large grant of freehold land in return for their knowledge and capital.

Debate on the bill to enable the Chaffey brothers' scheme ran alongside the debate on the Irrigation Bill in the second half of the year. Tommy Bent, commonly described as 'Bent by name and bent by nature', led the charge against 'the Yankee Land Grab', claiming there was something behind this bill 'which was hardly straight'.[46] The government was forced to put the scheme out to public tender, but the Chaffey brothers were the only applicants and the enabling bill finally passed in mid-December 1886.[47]

Deakin's other significant legislative initiative during 1886 was to sponsor the Aboriginal Protection Amendment Act, requested by the Board for the Protection of Aborigines. The 1869 Aboriginal Protection Act, which gave the board wide-ranging powers over the lives of Aboriginal people, defined Aborigines in terms of community affiliation rather than race. The 1886 amendment differentiated between the treatment of people of full and mixed Aboriginal descent, and was the first piece of Australian legislation to use race as its operative criterion. Known as the Half-Caste Act, it removed people of mixed descent from the reserves with the intention, he told the parliament, 'of making the half-castes useful members of society, and gradually relieving the State of the cost of their maintenance'.[48]

This had terrible consequences for Victoria's indigenous people, breaking up families and kinship groups on racial criteria that they themselves did not observe, and was the beginning of child abductions by the state. It also deprived the reserves of the workers they needed to become self-sufficient farming communities. A deputation from Coranderrk, a reserve for Aborigines near Healesville, led by the remarkable Aboriginal elder William Barak, persuaded Deakin to take out some of the more punitive clauses, but he did not abolish the board's authority over the reserves' inhabitants as they requested.[49]

Deakin was not unsympathetic to the claims of the remnant of Victoria's Aboriginal population. As premier, Graham Berry had always given a sympathetic hearing to their grievances against the board's petty tyranny, and Deakin followed suit. In 1882 he asked questions in parliament about the severity of a sentence on the Coranderrk resident Thomas Bamfield, whom the board regarded as a troublemaker.[50] Later, when he was chief secretary and the board, supported by the local settlers, proposed to give the Framlingham reserve near Warrnambool to the Council of Agricultural Education, Deakin granted a request from the local member, John Murray, that 'out of the millions of acres that had been taken from the blacks of the western districts—including some of the best land in Australia—the remaining blacks should be allowed some 500 or 600 of very inferior land.'[51]

But Deakin was not a fighter, and he had no emotional capacity for lost causes, no matter how just. Nor did he ever question the legitimacy of the land grab on which white settlement was based. Along with the other goldrush immigrants, William and Sarah Deakin had arrived in Victoria after the pastoral invasion. The land was already taken and the chief imperative was its productive development.

Deakin accepted the consensus view that Aborigines were doomed to extinction as a separate race. The key issue for the Half-Caste Act was government expenditure. It would, Deakin told the parliament, enable the state to 'get rid of the maintenance of the half-castes and quarter castes'. Asked if they were to merge into the general population, Deakin replied: 'That was the intention.'[52] The legislation was rushed through in the last sitting days of 1886 and Deakin made no mention of it in his notes on the year's events. As the historian Patrick Wolfe has observed, 'White people's intentions did not need to be consciously hostile for their actions to have devastating consequences.'[53]

Deakin turned thirty in August 1886 and marked the occasion with an elegiac poem whose theme was to be repeated many times in the years to come:

My youth has gone and with my youth much more
Glances & dreams & visions—there were stars
Crowning the world of night—beyond life's bars
Souls set sail on a sea without a shore.[54]

It is hard to know how to read this mood, though he may well have been feeling the weight of his family responsibilities. His second child, Stella, was born on 3 June 1886, and Deakin's cousin William Bill was building the growing family a fine free-standing, two-storey house on the block in South Yarra that Deakin's father had purchased in 1882. Deakin was always conscious of the material sacrifice Pattie had made in marrying him, and the house was much more like the Brownes' handsome house in Wellington Parade than his own parents' single-storey dwelling. They called the Walsh Street house Llanarth, after Sarah Deakin's birthplace. The Deakin coat of arms was in the stained-glass window above the front door, and a window of ivy and stars on the main stairs celebrated their two daughters.

Choices had limited his life's horizons—they always do—but they had also brought achievements. On New Year's Eve he summed up 1886 as 'a successful year publicly—still rising higher and higher'. Contemplating the inevitability of a public fall, he warned himself not to become too attached to success and assured himself that its loss would not bother him: 'Secure in my confidence in my principles I shall not be subject to suffering or injured by apparent failure and misfortune.' As the entry goes on, it becomes a rambling prayer of gratitude to the Light for his success and dedication to its continuing service: 'to realise the Light to see clearly by it, to walk by it, trust it and spread its radiance through my life and thought.'[55]

11

TRIUMPH IN LONDON

IN THE SECOND week of 1887 Deakin took another step in his political ascent. Cabinet selected him to attend the Colonial Conference in London being held in conjunction with Queen Victoria's golden-jubilee year. He learned of his selection on 11 January and was to leave seventeen days later. Dignitaries did not travel light, and the opening pages of his diary for the year are filled with lists for the extensive wardrobe he hurriedly assembled for the journey and for the various official functions in London: a summer suit and helmet for the tropics, a dress suit, frock coats, tennis trousers, overcoat, nineteen shirts, twenty-three collars, gloves, studs and cufflinks, a felt hat, a bell topper and much else. He also took a hammock and chair for the ship, French novels to help him brush up his schoolboy French, and four Baedekers.[1]

With this journey, as he recorded later, the last of the prophecies from 1878 to 1880 was fulfilled, that:

before long I should be officially sent to London to appear for

Victoria before a tribunal which was not a court of law but a gathering like a court, that would deal with the interests of Victoria, of Australia & of the whole empire—I was to attend, to belong to, & to address a tribunal which she described as the highest in the land—It was to sit in London & its consequences were to be very great.[2]

Although this was occurring a little later than the medium had envisaged, for Deakin it became another of the otherwise inexplicable occurrences supporting his continuing faith in spiritualism and reassuring him of the providential direction of his life. It is likely that both the governor, Sir Henry Loch, and Charles Pearson pressed the case for Deakin to be sent.[3] Handsome, well-educated and astonishingly articulate, this native son could represent the promise and confidence of the colony to those in London who feared that the British race might be degenerating in the Antipodes.

After an unbearably sad breakfast at home, Deakin farewelled Pattie, Ivy and baby Stella. Parting from Ivy, who was now three and a half, 'nearly conquered me', he wrote to Catherine. 'All my few pearls hang on a single thread—one mother, one sister, one wife, one father. Two children. I am blessed.'[4] Emotion almost overcame him again when he parted from his friend Derham: 'hated to say goodbye to you so coldly in a crowd, but perhaps it was better so. Men must not seem women but believe me it is a pull on my heart strings to say goodbye to you for so long.'[5]

Prior to leaving, Deakin had repaid some of his financial debt to Derham, thus partially offsetting 'the most unfortunate sacrifice of yourself to save me'. From on board he asked Derham for a further favour: in the case of a sudden election, could he send the nomination forms to London. He then added a request which shows a scheming Deakin of which little evidence has survived. He had heard that one of the parliamentarians was on the brink of insolvency and suggested that the government through friends buy up his bills cheaply, so that he could be made insolvent and the seat secured for another fellow. This would have to be done 'with the most elaborate caution and circumspection, so that it could not be traced to any of us under any circumstances… You and Gillies could arrange it without any other member of the Cabinet ever knowing of it.'[6] Clearly, at least when young, Deakin had an appetite for intrigue that belies his reputation for moral rectitude.

Deakin's long travel letters home were lovingly transcribed by Catherine and are the basis for his account of the conference in *The Federal Story*. Like his letters from Mexico and the United States, they are full of lively detail. He travelled by steamship via Ceylon and Aden, and through the Suez Canal to the Mediterranean. Until the 1970s, when airline travel became affordable, this was the route most Australians took to Europe. In Egypt, Deakin visited the Pyramids—which, he told Derham, 'remind me of that accursed company on which so much of your money was recklessly thrown to save me'.[7]

Deakin left the ship at Brindisi to travel overland through Italy, Switzerland and France, visiting Naples, Rome, Florence, Venice, Turin and Paris, dashing about the galleries and cathedrals to see the art and architecture of the great masters. An intrepid traveller with little fear of physical danger, he climbed the slopes of Vesuvius near Naples, first on horseback and then on foot and the shoulders of bearers, right to the rim of the crater. In Rome he visited the graves of Shelley and Keats in the Protestant cemetery, the old part 'separated by a moat so that heretical ashes may not mingle with the sacred earth of Rome'.[8]

Deakin arrived in London on 17 March with a bad cold and spent the first week writing, resting, and catching up with friends and colleagues from home. Graham Berry, in London as Victoria's agent-general, was a member of the delegation, as was James Service, who was interrupting his retirement tour of the Continent. David Syme was also in London on one of his regular trips abroad. Deakin met too with his friend from university Richard Hodgson, who had studied moral philosophy at Cambridge with Henry Sidgwick and was achieving fame as a psychic researcher: he had just exposed Madame Blavatsky, the Russian medium and one of the founders of the Theosophical Society.

An associate from his spiritualist days, the photographer and painter

Henry James Johnstone, took Deakin on tours of the galleries, where he marvelled at London's visual riches. He also began to receive invitations from various leading politicians to whom Charles Pearson had recommended him, such as the Liberal reformer Charles Dilke and the Scottish Liberal colonial administrator Grant Duff. And, as did other colonial delegates, he visited Mr Poole, tailor to the Prince of Wales.[9] Apart from fashionable new clothes, he would need a court uniform for the Prince of Wales' levee and the presentation to Queen Victoria at Windsor.

With so many friends to show him round, Deakin felt immediately at home in the great metropolis, which he judged to be just a vastly scaled-up Melbourne: 'Put only one story on the houses, have the streets not quite so clean and a good deal older and twist and tangle all the straight ways and you have London.'[10] Society too was familiar: dinners, At Homes, balls and banquets. Deakin's debut in London society was at a dinner at Sir Henry Holland's, the colonial secretary, followed by an At Home for three hundred or so, which 'consists of a great crush *in*, spasmodic small talk in breaks of about five minutes each with a few of your neighbours, and then a great crush *out* again'. For an outsider looking in on the glittering crowd, with no friends to greet, no political business to transact, the titled men and women were but 'faces in a gallery of pictures and talk a tinkling cymbal…Titles don't grow out of a man or a woman—they are stuck on from the outside, and are always artificial and often ridiculous.' 'Even a pallid aesthete with fringed hair, a despairing expression, and a crimson velvet gown did not move me.'[11]

There is perhaps a little too much protesting in these early impressions as Deakin steadied himself in London's aristocratic society. At the Holland dinner he had flirted with the married twenty-two-year-old daughter of the Earl of Carnarvon, who was astonished by his knowledge of books. 'We were very lively, to the surprise I think of some others, she invited me to her house—do not mean to accept.' In his hotel he had a photo of Pattie, Ivy and Stella on one side of his dressing table and of Katy and Mama on the other, anchoring his commitments.[12] A handsome, engaging man, Deakin attracted the attention of women as well as men. The garden designer Marie Theresa Earle, who was twenty years his senior, asked if she could write to him sometimes, as she had had 'the feeling of being understood' in their conversations, which included discussion of the Carlyles' marital difficulties.[13]

The conference between the Colonial Office and the self-governing settler colonies was the result of lobbying by the Imperial Federation League, which was formed in 1884 to promote closer union in the empire.[14] In spite of its official title, the Australians insisted on calling it the Imperial Conference. The rapid growth of the settler colonies, together with improved transport and communication, was putting pressure on the institutions of imperial governance. This would be the first time members of the British government would meet with representatives of the self-governing colonies to discuss their mutual problems. The crown colonies were excluded, as was the jewel in the imperial crown, British India. The British government's intention was to keep the conference narrowly focussed on practical matters, namely the organisation and financing of imperial defence and postal and telegraphic communications. Although participants could raise other issues, they were discouraged from discussing imperial federation.[15]

The conference took place against the background of a new competitive phase in European imperialism spurred by the determination of the recently united Germany to establish an overseas empire. France, Italy and even Belgium followed suit. As a naval power Britain had the jump on its land-based European rivals. It already had an empire on which the sun never set, made stronger by the mid-century outpouring of British migrants to the settler societies of Australasia, Canada and the Cape Colony.

Mid-century, imperial enthusiasm among Britain's political elite had been sluggish, but this was changing as overseas possessions became a potential strategic advantage in the competition for power in Europe, a case the Victorians were keen to push. On the way over, Deakin had read James Froude's *Oceana, or, England and Her Colonies*, published just the year before and based on Froude's travels through England's colonies, where he found 'the race is thriving in all its ancient characteristics.'[16]

Froude's was but the most recent in a series of books on the English diaspora. The young Charles Dilke included the United States in his travels through English-speaking lands to discover 'the grandeur of our race already girdling the earth'. The idea of the Anglo-Saxon race became a popular way of uniting Britain and the United States, ascribing to both a shared love of liberty, a resourceful independence and restless energy. Because of its exclusion of the Celtic Irish and Scots, a unifying Anglo-Saxon race was never universally accepted, and its obvious German origin was unsettling in the face of Germany's growing militarism. Nor was it at all clear how Anglo-Saxon unity would be expressed politically.

In 1883 John Seeley published *The Expansion of England*, in which he argued that 'Canada and Australia should be considered no differently from the English counties of Kent and Cornwall. We must cease to think that emigrants when they go to colonies leave England.'[17] This fanciful political geography retained its attractions for imperial loyalists until well into the twentieth century. In 1948, seeking to keep the idea of empire alive in the changed post-war world, on the boat from Australia to war-ravaged England Robert Menzies echoed Seeley, writing that 'the boundaries of Great Britain are not on the Kentish coast but at Cape York and Invercargill.'[18]

In the nineteenth century the words 'race' and 'nation' were used interchangeably and ambiguously. Race described both observable differences in physical type and different levels of cultural achievement linked by loose notions of biological determinism. The cultural critic Robert Young argues that this idea of race predated scientific racism, and that after scientific racism was discredited these meanings were transferred into modern ideas about ethnicity.[19] Nation too was ambiguous, shifting during the nineteenth century from the meaning it had for the French revolutionaries of a political association to a cultural association, a fusion of people and culture in which shared history and language created a distinctive character. When to this was added the claim that people who shared a culture should be self-governing, it became a revolutionary idea, fuelling nationalist uprisings and challenging the legitimacy of dynastic monarchies and multiracial empires.

The ideal of one nation, one race, one state raised difficult questions for the British across the globe, especially as belief in the inevitability of competition between the races developed towards the end of the nineteenth century. How was the union of race and political purpose to be maintained in an empire that included self-governing British colonies as well as crown colonies of non-British peoples? How were the inevitable differences of interest and perspective of these geographically dispersed polities to be negotiated? And if the shores of the empire were indeed dispersed across the globe, how were they to be defended, and who was to pay?

Questions of defence were uppermost in the minds of the Victorian delegation to London, together with Britain's continuing refusal to annex the New Hebrides. Deakin had come determined to put Victoria's views, and was well aware that he was himself one of the arguments in support of the Victorians' claims. As the only native-born Australian delegate he was on display, the primary exhibit of the type of man the colonies could contribute to the empire. The main occasions for his display were a series of speeches, each one bolder than the last, in which, in the name of a fervent imperial loyalty, Deakin challenged the assumptions of Britain's elites about the subservience of the colonies to British interests.

The first was at the welcome banquet given by the Imperial Federation League at the Freemasons' Tavern in Great Queen Street. Such banquets and dinners followed a set form of a series of toasts accompanied by short speeches between the many courses. By a stroke of good fortune for Deakin, the nominated proposer of the toast to 'the Navies, the Armies and the Civil Service' had a cold, and he was called on. 'There was a time when the colonies were looked upon as a source of weakness to the naval and military strength of the empire,' he told the two hundred and fifty assembled lords and gentlemen. 'But such was not the case now, for even the smallest of the self-governing colonies was proud to do something towards its own defence.' The Australian colonies desired an Australian naval fleet, provided by the imperial government but maintained by the colonies, he said. Referring obliquely to the Victorians' differences with Britain over the New Hebrides, he added that although 'we are a remarkably pacific people, we intend to be masters of the Pacific'.[20]

While he had not been as well prepared as he would have liked, he judged the speech 'not altogether a failure. Some thought it the speech of the evening.' Edward Arnold from *Murray Magazine* told him: 'You represent in the highest sense the best and most intelligent sentiments of Victoria.' That night too he met John Bright, the champion of the Anti-Corn Law League and the hero of free trade. Now an old man, he told Deakin,

> we might cut the painter, and when I told him we were attached to the mother country, rejoined that we proved this by taxing our parents' goods, to which in my turn I answered that this was because instead of treating us as children she only put us on the same footing in her own markets as her enemies and rivals.[21]

Britain's commitment to free trade and its repudiation of a territorially exclusive empire sat uneasily with the calls for closer imperial union which, some thought, could be advanced through preferential trade agreements.

Deakin's second display of his independent colonial thinking and oratorical talents was at the opening session of the conference on 4 April. Sir Henry Holland had asked the Conservative prime minister, Lord Salisbury, to dignify the opening with a brief appearance. Salisbury had been prime minister since June 1885, when Gladstone lost power because of his support for Irish Home Rule. Tall and heavy-set, Salisbury was the last British prime minister to govern from the House of Lords and had been a trenchant opponent of parliamentary reform. He represented all the prerogatives of wealth and privilege that were anathema to Australian Liberals. As a young man he had toured the settler colonies and was in Victoria in 1852 at the height of gold mania. While appalled at the vulgarity of many diggers, he was also impressed by the high degree of civil order and obedience, concluding that this was because 'the government was that of the Queen, not the mob; from above not from below.'[22] Since then he had accommodated himself to colonial self-government and democracy, but he resisted the expansion of the empire.

Holland asked Salisbury for 'a few words of welcome' which would give him the chance to point out to the colonies that 'cases might arise in which strict colonial views might clash with the necessities of Imperial policy, and that in such cases H. M. Government, with every desire to uphold Colonial interests, has a right to expect concessions from the Colonial Governments.'[23] Holland knew that the Australian colonists would raise the New Hebrides and hoped Salisbury might encourage them to see things from Britain's perspective. Salisbury did not tackle the issue directly, but he did stress the need for the colonies 'to take part in the defence of Empire in all its portions'.[24]

Salisbury left soon after his welcoming remarks, so was not present when Deakin took his turn. The people of Victoria, he said, were loyal imperialists, who agreed with the need for a common defence and for improved sea and cable communication, but there were other great issues not yet referred to: 'the preservation of our shores from the terrible taint of foreign convictism, and the extension of the boundaries of the empire'. The lords and gentlemen were warned that the Victorians would continue to push for the annexation of the New Hebrides. He went on to describe the difficulties the colonies had in communicating their concerns to the British government, their relations mediated first by the Colonial Office and then the Foreign Office, 'and behind the Foreign Office again lies that mysterious entity, the Cabinet, which is not only paved, but walled and roofed with good intentions unfulfilled.'

Deakin contrasted the spirited enthusiasm of the French and German governments for imperial expansion in the south-west Pacific with the disdainful indifference of the Colonial Office, and stressed the indissolubility of colonial and imperial interests.

> We cannot imagine any description of circumstances by which the Colonies should be humiliated or weakened, or their power lessened, under which the Empire would not be itself humili- ated, weakened and lessened. And we are unable to conceive any circumstances under which the wealth or status of the Colonies

could be increased, which would not increase in the same degree the wealth and status of the Empire.

He concluded with the hope that 'Colonial policy will be considered Imperial policy, that Colonial interests will be considered and felt to be Imperial interests.'[25]

Deakin was thrilled with himself. Victoria 'had got away with the lead and kept it', he told Derham, and he marked the date in his diary with a large asterisk.[26] With this speech, reported verbatim in the press, he had made his dramatic entrance to imperial politics. The next day he was offered and declined a knighthood, writing to Pattie: 'your chance of being Lady Deakin has been thrown away by your loving husband...To have declined the honour at thirty years of age is not so remarkable, but having the offer of it so early is another instance of my marvellous good fortune in public affairs.'[27] To Charles Pearson he wrote that when Holland asked him for recommendations for knighthoods, he recommended him, Pearson, but they did not want to go outside the conference representatives.[28] He then hoped his declined honour would go to Service, 'for he has been more truly Australian and Imperial than any', but it went to one of the other Victorian delegates, James Lorimer.[29]

Deakin's refusal was perhaps in part motivated by consciousness of his own youth, but its effect on his public reputation for selfless modesty made it a precedent never to be broken. As one welcome-home address said, 'though the proffered honour was well-deserved, you have, by your refusal of it earned a higher niche in the temple of fame than any that could have been bestowed upon you.'[30] Had he tried he could not have wished for better publicity.

A few days later the conference broke for Easter, and Deakin travelled to Edinburgh for a brief visit with Pattie's relatives—Hugh Browne's sister and her clergyman husband, the Reverend Masson. Back in London he was inundated with invitations to breakfast, luncheon, dinner, the theatre and the political clubs around Westminster which had given conference delegates temporary membership. He visited the

House of Commons, and observed Parnell and Gladstone arguing for Irish Home Rule.

Whenever he could he visited the art galleries—the National Gallery, the Royal Academy and private galleries like the Grosvenor and Dore. Along with Carlyle, Ruskin was another of the teachers of Deakin's youth. Seeing art through Ruskin's eyes, as a moral, spiritual and aesthetic meeting of artist and viewer, Deakin was primed for strong emotional responses to the works of the masters he knew only from engravings. Colonials could easily keep abreast of literature but art was another matter, and his letters home are full of detailed descriptions of paintings and his responses to them.

The practical business of the conference was conducted in committees. For the Australian colonies, the main result was finally to achieve an agreement in which the British government provided new naval vessels for Australasian waters and the colonies paid running costs and maintenance.[31] Intercolonial rivalries were a constant undercurrent, particularly between Victoria and New South Wales, with Deakin boasting frequently of Victoria's primacy and prosperity. This was about more than native pride. British capital was pouring into Victoria. At the start of the year the government had raised a loan of three million pounds, the third instalment of an eight-million-pound loan, paying interest at 4 per cent.[32] Investors were being reassured that their money was safe, and their appetites kept sharp for future capital raisings, both by the government and the much riskier private sector.

By mid-May Deakin's prominence among the colonial delegates was such that he was invited to respond to the Duke of Cambridge's toast to the Prosperity and Advancement of our Colonies at the banquet of the St George's Club, Hanover Square. He opened blandly enough, sharing the hope of His Royal Highness for closer union, and said that the delegates had been overwhelmed by kindness, but he was now confident enough to deliver a few home truths to the rulers of the empire:

> [As] far as any real knowledge of the aspirations of the colonies were concerned an absolute and innocent ignorance seemed to prevail...

> while in the newspapers of the colonies full information was given
> of every political and social movement in the mother country, the
> Press of this country give little else than cricket matches of what
> occurred in the great Australian colonies…for the realization of
> many of the ideals which were cherished by the politicians in this
> country it was only necessary to look to Australia. Education was
> free and they had satisfactorily settled the Ecclesiastical question.

After this stern admonition to the rulers of England for their
parochialism, Deakin moved on to a soothing invocation of 'the unity
of the Empire, of which the colonies were proud to be considered
members'.[33] Writing home, he reported the speech to be 'a great sensation…nearly every speaker afterwards referred to my remarks…and
all the papers that I've seen give me the best place when they give the
colonial speeches at all.'[34]

The culmination of Deakin's London performances came a week
later at the closed meeting on the Pacific Islands, when he 'faced' Lord
Salisbury with all his oratorical powers at the ready.[35] The press was not
present, though a report leaked out almost immediately, and Deakin
later gave a detailed account in *The Federal Story*. Holland had asked
Salisbury to speak as foreign secretary. He hoped Salisbury would tell
the colonists that they 'must not try to claim all the Pacific Islands for
Britain'. Salisbury replied, 'I will do my best to keep my temper but
the *outrecuidance* of your Greater Britain is sometimes trying.' The
French word means impertinence, or presumption.[36]

According to Deakin, Salisbury spoke carelessly, even cynically. 'His
tone breathed the aristocratic condescension of a Minister addressing a
deputation of visitors from the antipodes whom it became his duty to
instruct in current foreign politics for their own sake.' Salisbury told
the colonials why Britain would not annex the islands and suggested
instead the acceptance of the French proposal that France have the
islands in exchange for stopping convict transportation to the south-west
Pacific. Service and Berry both made spirited defences of Victoria's
position; then it was Deakin's turn. Here is his account, written in the
third person, as if by a fly on the wall:

Deakin followed almost last, because, though official head of the Victorian representatives, he wished to pay all deference to his late Chiefs who preceded him at his request. He broke quite new ground not only with unrestrained vigour and enthusiasm on the general question but because he did so in a more spirited manner, challenging Lord Salisbury's arguments one by one and mercilessly analyzing the inconsistencies of his speech. They were asked to surrender the New Hebrides as of little commercial value and in the next breath were told that the French set the greatest store by them for commercial development. For us to attempt to negotiate a great power like France out of her place in the joint protectorate was presumption, and yet an even greater power, the British Empire, was asked to consent to be negotiated out of her place without even a protest...It was admitted now that the Republic had not kept faith with us, but urged that their chaotic political conditions explained the lapse...We were reminded that the French were a high spirited and powerful nation, perfectly prepared to defend their rights by war if necessary. Had then the colonists come thousands of miles to learn that Great Britain was no longer proud nor high spirited and was not prepared to defend the rights of her people or to resist unjust demands? If so, it was a most unfortunate but very impressive manner of teaching the lesson. Deakin went on to declare in an impassioned manner that the people of Victoria would never consent to any cession of the islands on any terms and the Australian-born who had made this question their own would forever resent the humiliation of a surrender which would immensely weaken their confidence in an Empire to which hitherto they had been proud to belong.

The effect of such a protest was electrical. Lord Salisbury several times stared at the speaker, as well he might, in considerable amazement at his plain speaking and in some discomfort at the stern debating retorts to his inharmonious contentions.[37]

Deakin knew he had been bold, but lacking the ingrained habits of class deference of the British-born he did not realise quite how bold. He wrote to Derham that he had given Lord Salisbury 'a good shaking and some plain language…he needs educating re the colonies.'[38] Salisbury could say the same of Deakin re England. He was having diplomatic difficulties with the French government on a range of issues much closer to home and wrote to Holland next day that the Australians were

> the most unreasonable people I have ever heard or dreamt of. They want us to incur all the bloodshed and the danger, and the stupendous cost of war with France of which almost the exclusive burden will fall on us, for a group of islands which are to us as valueless as the South Pole—and to which they are only attached by a debating club sentiment.[39]

Salisbury was half right. Deakin's speech was a debater's systematic rebuttal, as if this was an exchange between equals. But Salisbury missed the symbolic significance of the issue as a focus for growing national feeling.[40] He had more mighty matters on his mind than the affairs of a small colony in the Southern Ocean, no matter how significant it felt itself to be.

Deakin was relieved when a few days later Salisbury pushed through a crowded room at Lady Holland's At Home to tell him that instructions had been given to the British ambassador in Paris not to yield any of the British interests in the islands, and 'afterwards went out of his way to speak to him privately and publicly in the warmest way as belonging to the type of men to whom the destinies of Australia might safely be entrusted'.[41]

Deakin was always sensitive to the impression he made as he smiled into another man's eyes and shook him firmly by the hand. As in Melbourne, these older English men were charmed. Sir Henry Holland was an early conquest. Deakin noted that Service told him, 'he has fallen in love with me as other elders have done.' Leading literary and political men were also 'attracted' or 'took greatly' to him: James Knowles, founder of the influential monthly the *Nineteenth Century*; Frank Harris, the new young editor of the even more influential *Fortnightly*; Liberal politician Lord Edmund Fitzmaurice, Charles Dilke's oldest friend; and Dilke himself, with whom he dined several times.[42] He even charmed the

Prince of Wales, who accepted the presidency of Victoria's forthcoming
Centennial International Exhibition. The prince had refused so many
invitations that 'Everyone, even Sir Henry Holland, declared it would
be impossible. It was only my insistence and effort that led to him being
pressed so that he consented,' Deakin boasted to Derham.[43]

It was all very gratifying and, as London warmed to Deakin, so he
warmed to the great imperial city. He remained, though, a provincial:
London's size made one feel 'lost, isolated, overlooked, overwhelmed
until personality itself seems in danger', and he thought one could
only work here 'by deadening oneself to the life that crowds around'.[44]
In his letters home, Deakin said little about the visible urban poverty
which affronted most Australians visiting England for the first time,
though this became a theme in his account of his later trip in 1900 in
The Federal Story. In 1887 he was fully engaged keeping himself steady
amid the glamour of the imperial elite, holding on to the worth of his
own small life before the weight of history.

Buoyed by the belief that it was his destiny to speak for Victoria, and
finding that no matter how audacious he was he continued to find favour,
Deakin was everywhere. His eagerness seems to have been somewhat
indulged by the older members of the conference, who 'one and all seem
rather pleased at the way in which the young Victorian is acting on the
motto "Advance Australia".'[45] Characteristically, Deakin affected a
certain detachment towards his success, telling Derham that although
in the debate on the New Hebrides he was more self-assertive than ever,
'it is the Chief Secretary who does this, and not the private person who
thinks he dislikes it. I only hope I have not trodden on too many toes.'

He was pleased with the recognition he was getting, 'because it
was evidence that I am at the level of the other representatives of the
other colonies and evidence that Victoria has now got the first place,
and I hope to have been a little means of achieving this.'[46] This transfer
of personal motives and gratification to larger themes is a familiar
move of politicians as they hitch the star of their own ambitions to
broader causes; it is, if you like, the sine qua non of political action,
what gives the private motive its public face. It also helps those like

Deakin, uneasy about self-serving ambition, to enjoy the pleasures of
their success.

By the beginning of May, Deakin's sense of his prime audience was
shifting as he began 'to speculate as to the light my conduct will be
regarded in Victoria'.[47] His London speeches and their reception had
been well covered in the Victorian press. The *Age* claimed that he was
seen in London as 'the chief personal success of the conference—partly
due to his facile oratory and excellent personal appearance, but more
still to his being regarded as the representative of "young Australia"
and his fearless championing on all occasions of colonial ideas whether
calculated or not to find favour in official eyes.'[48]

A week before leaving he made a whirlwind tour of Oxford, where
his father had started his working life, seeing all the landmarks in a
single morning. That afternoon he took tea with his father's sister and
his cousins in Witney, and visited his paternal grandparents' graves. This
seems to have been the only contact he made with his parents' families,
and it was very brief. He wrote to Catherine that he was sorry to see
none of Mama's relations; had he known of any she especially cared
about he would have made a point of seeing them, but he had not time
to go in search of them, nor to visit Llanarth as he had so much desired.[49]

By the time he left London on 11 May, Deakin was exhausted. He
was no longer a total abstainer, but to survive the heavy social demands
he had observed 'the utmost care and abstemiousness, eating little,
drinking less and only claret and smoking not once since I left home'.[50]
Still, at a dinner in the Ironmongers Hall he enjoyed 'Real turtle soup
with green fat on it, and a square of lemon, delicious!'[51]

As he reflected on the boat home, through 'sudden changes of scene
& life & fashion' he had remained 'faithful to principle of conduct &
undisturbed—most go mad—you have learned the lesson'.[52] Amid the
pleasures and temptations of Vanity Fair, he had kept his head and his
sense of who he was. 'This much I can say my own dearest', he wrote
to the 'wife of my heart', 'that I know myself better and I know my
love better than I did before, I know that...it survives an absence and
that I am yours so truly that no beauty and no temptation has power
to win my heart from you.'[53]

12

NATIVE SON

DEAKIN LEFT THE P&O steamer *Parramatta* at Adelaide on 16 June 1887 to catch the overnight train to Melbourne. He was exhausted, suffering from poor sleep and a bad cold. But there was to be no sleep that night. At Serviceton, Dimboola, Horsham, Murtoa, Stawell, Ararat, Beaufort, Ballarat and Geelong, the train was met by crowds of cheering men, mostly young members of the ANA, who had turned out in the small hours of the morning to welcome their hero home and to present him with addresses praising his conduct in London: his refusal of the knighthood, 'his bold and fearless advocacy of the right of Australia to control the Pacific', his successful representation of 'the true feelings, sympathies, and aspirations of Australian nationality'. At the end of a late-night parliamentary sitting a large contingent of ministers and parliamentarians, including his friends Derham, Pearson and Dow, travelled by special train to meet him at Ballarat.

There were more crowds when his train finally pulled into Spencer Street, just before ten o'clock on Friday morning, yet another address and a reply to be made, his voice weak from fatigue and illness.[1] The leader in the *Age* that morning began, 'Mr Deakin returns to his Ithaca today,' and went on to an extravagant comparison of the temptations and triumphs of his London visit with Ulysses' epic voyage, including his refusal of the bribe of immortality with a knighthood, 'one of the few really original things of permanent value and interest to come out of the conference'.[2]

By late morning he was in the carriage to his new home in Walsh Street.[3] Pattie had overseen its completion while he was away. But in this 'coldest, dampest and bleakest winter', their reunion was marred by illness.[4] She was suffering from winter ills, with ear abscesses and rheumatic fever.

His first week back was Jubilee Week, an empire-wide celebration of Queen Victoria's fifty years on the throne. The parliament declared a two-day holiday so loyal citizens of the colony that bore the monarch's name could enjoy celebratory dinners, banquets, balls, concerts and tournaments. On Tuesday morning Deakin attended the governor's levee, in his new court uniform with feathered hat and sword. Later that day he spoke at the Lord Mayor's jubilee banquet where he received a tremendous ovation, with men waving handkerchiefs and calling 'Deakin, Deakin'. He spoke mostly about the enthusiasm in London for the upcoming Centennial Exhibition and the great honour of the Prince of Wales' acceptance of the presidency.[5]

That night, despite the rain, he and Pattie, along with two hundred thousand Victorians, turned out to admire the Illuminations. The city was brightly lit and decorated: stars, crowns and mottoes in brilliant flames, public buildings outlined in electric lights, banks and the best shops lit with coloured lamps. It was barely fifty years since Melbourne had been founded, and Victorians congratulated themselves that the contrast between the glades of silent gums and the glittering new city was a marvel 'never yet produced on any spot of mortal soil'.[6]

Over the next few weeks Deakin was feted at a series of welcome-home banquets, but when on 5 July he rose to make his report to the Victorian parliament he was met with a point of order from Tommy Bent: he had not attended the Colonial Conference as a delegate of the parliament, so what exactly was the parliamentary status of this report?[7] By the next day this was sorted out, but it took some wind from Deakin's billowing sails. He was at pains to point out to a house jealous of the prerogatives of self-government that none of the discussions at the conference committed the parliament in any way.

A week later Deakin received the most enthusiastic of his homecoming receptions at an ANA banquet at the Athenaeum in Collins Street. Deakin's handsome half-profile surrounded by a wreath of wattles graced the front of the programme and on the back was the Deakin family crest. Deakin was now with his own. Introducing him, Jefferson Connelly, president of the ANA and a Bendigo lawyer, said that Australians regarded his success at the Imperial Conference as their success.

Deakin rose to speak, to hearty and long continued cheering. The conference, he said, marked a turning point. Whereas previously the colonies' relations with the government of Great Britain were 'through the intervening veil of irresponsible officials' often unable to distinguish between a crown colony and one enjoying self-government, the colonies had now met the ministers of Great Britain 'face to face'. But the colonies could never be truly self-governing and truly independent in foreign policy while they were dependent on the mother country for defence, and for this they needed a navy. The path to the colonies' greater independence was neither separation, nor imperial federation, but establishing their own prosperity based on protection, and federating among themselves. Only then would they be able to afford to defend themselves; only then would they be taken seriously. George Higinbotham then proposed a toast to the watchword of the ANA, 'Australia and Australian Federation'.[8]

In three cryptic entries at the back of his travel diary, Deakin reflected on the private, inner meaning of his trip. In the first two, he again went over the evidence for the spirit world, and referred to his conversation in London with his friend Richard Hodgson, now a professional sceptic of psychic phenomena. The third reads: 'Athens after Delos, Rome after 2nd Punic—natives—opinion—awaken them.'[9] Deakin was pondering the relationship between the prophecies of his youth, his recent triumphs and the path ahead.

'Athens after Delos' refers to a confederation of fifth-century Greek city states, formed under Athens' leadership to fight the Persians. 'Rome after 2nd Punic' refers to the victory over Hannibal of Carthage, which laid the foundations for Rome's imperial ambition. A federal project makes sense, but an imperial one? Was Deakin's commitment to an Australian-governed Pacific this grandiose? The last few words, though, are clear, with their reference to the national 'awakeners' of the multiracial Habsburg empire: he was to be the awakener of the native Australians' national sentiment.[10]

The day after the banquet he visited Mrs Stirling for the first time in six years, hoping no doubt for another prophetic message from beyond. From the summary in his diary, he heard nothing conclusive about his own future: 'Min. not last long—Great change in world outside in 2 years—Health—struggle soon.'[11] She was wrong about the ministry, which lasted until the end of 1890, and the rest is vague enough to allow for any number of confirmations.

Deakin's legislative achievements for the remainder of 1887 were a bill for neglected children, which was a response to growing public concerns about larrikin street gangs, and a licensing bill which resolved the conflict between publicans and temperance advocates by expanding the scope for local options to restrict hotel licences. A motion to provide a government pension to the impoverished widow of Marcus Clarke, however, was defeated. Clarke had died in 1881 aged thirty-five, leaving his wife with six children to raise. While Deakin and others praised Clarke's literary genius and the lasting significance of his monumental 1874 novel of the convict system in early Tasmania, *For the Term of his Natural Life*, opponents denounced Clarke for publicising the 'diabolical and outrageous affairs which took place in Tasmania many years ago…a story of things they did not want to hear much about these days', and which could damage modern Australia's reputation.[12]

On his way to London, Deakin had observed irrigation works in Egypt and Italy, and after his return he wrote a report for the Royal Commission on Water Supply which located irrigation in the context of the competition between the races.[13] Indian wheat and Chinese rice raised by irrigation were underselling the products of the European irrigator, and he argued that 'to succeed in his struggle for existence with coloured labour and its low price, the white farmer of the future must bring his superior qualities into full play,' supported by the best agricultural science and most up-to-date technology.[14] In modern terms, sophisticated irrigation was a way of adding value to Australian labour to enable its products to compete with those of low-waged countries, but in late-nineteenth-century thinking this argument was couched in terms of racial differences.

Deakin had been impressed by the irrigation co-operatives of north Italy. (The American political scientist Robert Putnam was later to observe the same traditions of co-operation and use them to formulate his enormously influential concept of social capital.[15]) Deakin praised the north Italians as 'an active race, ingenious and energetic, as well as frugal and patient'.[16] The Egyptians could never have achieved the same results, he said. In this pre-sociological thinking, observable physical differences in skin colour and physiognomy became the explanation for observable social, cultural and economic differences between peoples and the competition between them for the world's resources.

Deakin had returned from abroad with a heightened sense of the competitiveness of world trade and its impact on national economies, as well as of escalating military competition. With the great powers armed to the teeth, war appeared inevitable. Europe, he reflected, was gathering itself for a plunge.[17] No doubt he discussed the world's shifting power alignments with his friend Charles Pearson, whose understanding of world history was far deeper than his own. A few years later Pearson published *National Life and Character*, in which he dared to question the inevitable historical supremacy of the British race. In a direct reference to the young Dilke's pride in 'the grandeur of our race girdling the earth', Pearson predicted a very different global future:

> the day will come, and perhaps it is not far distant, when the European observer will look around and see the globe girdled by a continuous zone of the black and yellow races, no longer too

weak for aggression or under tutelage, but independent…invited
to international conferences, and welcomed as allies in the quarrels
of the civilised world. The citizens of these countries will then be
taken up into the social relations of the white races, will throng
the English turf, or the salons of Paris, and will be admitted to
intermarriage…we will be humiliated.[18]

Such changes he concluded were inevitable, 'Yet in some of us the feeling
of caste is so strong that we are not sorry to think we shall have passed
away before that day arrives.'

Today's widespread revulsion at the accepted racial hierarchies
of the late nineteenth and first half of the twentieth centuries and
embrace of multiracial nations, makes the place of race in the thinking
of humane liberals such as Pearson and Deakin hard to fathom. Pearson
was a much more careful and subtle thinker than Deakin, and he was
not a political orator, shaping his phrases in response to the mood and
views of his audience. His book is now mainly read for evidence of
late-nineteenth-century colonial thinking about racial hierarchies and
global racial competition, but it deserves fuller attention. At home in
the *longue durée* and with a nascent sociological imagination, Pearson
canvassed other fading certainties as the scope for individualism shrank,
the power of the church declined and the state replaced the family in
raising children. Reading Pearson's thinking about race in the context
of his other arguments helps us to understand the place of race in
the thinking of liberals like Deakin as nationalism took on some of the
cultural and psychological work once done by religion.

The mid-century crises of faith had weakened the intellectual
authority of the church. Pearson welcomed aspects of this, arguing that
in the treatment of women, children and dumb animals, the morality
of the state is higher. But the decline of the church and of religious
authority also risked a crisis in motivation and raised the spectre of
nihilism for public moralists like Pearson.[19] With the death of God,
what was to stop people lapsing into cynical ennui, and society into
amoral anarchy? Would moral progress, which was a liberal article
of faith, continue without the belief in a divine purpose in creation?

What would motivate the development of character and inspire selfless, idealistic and noble actions?

The answer was the nation. The future of society, Pearson argued, depended on enhanced national feeling, with patriotism a high form of altruism. But it was necessarily a particularistic altruism, and Pearson also predicted that the immigration of aliens in large numbers was likely to be restricted everywhere.[20]

The problem for us today, only too aware of the horrors to which nationalism was to lead, is to balance nationalism's history of violent conflict and exclusion with its capacity to inspire pride and selfless service, and to answer basic existential questions for people by locating them in generational time and imbuing their limited lives with larger meanings. For social liberals like Pearson and Deakin the nation underpinned their faith in the capacities of an active state to improve the moral and material lives of ordinary people, and gave meaning to their life's work.

13

HIGH BOOM

DEAKIN'S PUBLIC LIFE during 1886 and 1887 was the most satisfying
it was ever to be, and he had less need for prayer and the recuperative
solaces of his inner world. But by early 1888 politics was deadening his
spirit with 'the weariness of one who in an endless maze of inexhaustible
mystery feels and finds the steady dropping of details like drops of water
from a perennial spring petrifying my heart and mind'.[1] In April he met
with Duncan Gillies and Charles Pearson and offered to resign.[2] He was
succumbing to one of his periodic depressions when meaning drained
from his world and conviction from his political vocation. As his hold
on the events of the day loosened, he slipped into a dissociated lassitude:

The outward scene and the current of affairs pass by me as if I were
in a dream. I can only with effort compel myself even languidly to
protect myself in purse and in prospects or position. The keenest
interest in a struggle dies in me almost as soon as the struggle
is over. On the other hand I see those around me eager, hard,

tenacious, ambitious, jealous of their rights and prosperity, fierce
to resent attack, the same today as yesterday, forgetting nothing,
demanding all…I feel myself by comparison weak, dilettante,
fatalistic, a dreamer.[3]

This was in May 1888, and two weeks later the *Argus* reported that,
due to illness, Mr Deakin had relinquished all public duties. It was
just a year since his London triumph. His sense of disorientation and
detachment from his public self at this time is a captured in a gothic
tale, 'The Theatre', that he wrote a few days after seeing Edward
Bulwer-Lytton's romantic melodrama *The Lady of Lyons* at the Princess
Theatre.[4] Attending this same play, musing on the illusions of the stage,
the narrator finds himself looking through the flesh and grease paint
of the actors till actors and audience alike become automata, and he,
with 'a choking sensation of terror', passes through the phantom walls
to rise into 'lampless, glowless spheres in which there were neither sun
nor stars nor planet nor mind, except my own, & this was driven out
trackless and beaconless upon the vast & everlasting void'.[5]

This crisis had some obvious outer causes. Parliament was exceed-
ingly frustrating, with the rowdy Opposition, led by Tommy Bent,
nothing but 'a bunch of brawlers', stonewalling and moving procedural
points and motions of no-confidence for hour after acrimonious hour.[6]
Although Deakin was an aggressive debater who could muster his
sporting instincts to trade points on the floor, he did not draw his psychic
energy from the thrill of winning but from the belief that his efforts
were aligned with history's moral progress. He loathed obstructionists,
particularly when they were fat and venal like Bent.

His spirits were restored by a new friend, the young American
philosopher Josiah Royce. Royce, on a Pacific voyage for his health,
bore a letter of introduction from Richard Hodgson, who was now in
Boston as secretary of the American Society for Psychical Research,
which had been founded by William James just a few years before.
Royce had worked with James at Harvard and shared his sceptical
interest in the paranormal. In June, Deakin was due to attend a colonial
conference in Sydney. He invited Royce to travel to Sydney with him,

and they spent six days together in the Blue Mountains.

It was a friendship made in heaven. They were the same age, born to English immigrants in goldrush colonies—in Royce's case, California. Copiously read and sharply intelligent, they inhabited a shared intellectual world and were both embarked on the search for metaphysical justifications of a divine universe. They talked and talked, on the long train trip from Melbourne to Sydney, and as they walked with eyes trained by Wordsworth through the sublime landscape of the Blue Mountains' gorges, valleys and plateaus, discovering mirrors in each other for the recesses of their souls.

Royce was successfully traversing the literary life path of Deakin's youthful dreaming. He had already published a philosophical treatise, *Religious Aspects of Philosophy*, which offered new proof for the existence of God and the divinity of the universe, a novel, essays of literary criticism and a history of California. For a few days and nights, Deakin experienced the pleasures of unrestrained conversation with a man who matched his own intellectual capacities and verbal fluency, 'the best trained and informed mind in metaphysics and kindred topics that I have ever had the opportunity of enjoying'. They ranged together across questions 'from the Moral Order to the conduct of Melbourne newspapers, and from telepathy to the Chinese problem'.[7]

Royce wrote for *Scribner's Magazine* about the days spent together with his unnamed friend, 'A young man, nervously active in temperament, cheerful, inquiring, speculative, unprejudiced—unless it were in favour of the political tendencies of the country where he is a Cabinet Minister—an admirer of America and good scenery, a lover of life, of metaphysics, and of power'.[8] Deakin represented the energy and democratic possibilities of the young Australian civilisation, and Royce described his friend's 'frank and intelligent confidence in the power of the State'. He predicted that 'Australia will show us some of the most remarkable experiments in State Socialism that have ever yet been seen.' He described too his friend's impatience with the amount of time a minister in a parliamentary system must spend on politics, rather than on administration and legislation. 'Day after day he must sit in the House, gibing at the Opposition. A colleague makes some parliamentary blunder. Well, then, the minister is bound to support this colleague through thick and thin and to repair the blunder in debate.'[9]

The occasion for Deakin's trip to Sydney was a renewed popular crisis over Chinese immigration. After the influx of Chinese gold-seekers in the 1850s, the numbers of Chinese in the colonies had been in steady decline. Most Chinese people lived harmoniously within the community, and undertook a far greater range of occupations than the market gardeners and cooks of popular literature.[10] Nevertheless, there were pockets of strong anti-Chinese feeling. In Victoria, these centred on the furniture trade, where Chinese dominated the manufacture of cheap furniture, and in 1887 an Anti-Chinese League was formed. Because of the difficulties of enforcing the Factory Act in Chinese furniture workshops, particularly the sanitation requirements, the matter came within Deakin's purview as chief secretary. Resentment was strongest against unskilled labourers who were willing to work long hours for meagre pay, and Deakin was receiving frequent delegations from the Anti-Chinese League.[11]

Much of Deakin's response to the issue is unremarkable from today's perspective: that the Chinese should be required to conform to Victorian laws and customs, and so compete under the same conditions as applied to the Europeans. But he also spoke easily of the dangers of 'the invasion of this country by Chinamen' and supported the labelling of furniture to 'prevent Chinese made furniture being palmed off on those who preferred goods made by their own countrymen'. Appealing again to the competition between the races, he claimed that 'If we save one conquered trade, and prevent the Chinese from conquering others, we shall have accomplished a great good.'[12]

The issue was a difficult one for the colonists. Once again, colonial aspirations conflicted with imperial priorities. Treaties between Britain and China, from whom Britain had forced extensive trade concessions, allowed for the freedom of movement of Chinese people throughout the British empire, an agreement which the Australian colonies, with their various restrictions on the Chinese, clearly disregarded. In 1887 the Chinese imperial government had sent two commissioners to investigate the Australian colonies' treatment of the emperor's subjects and they heard many complaints of unequal treatment. The British government was uncomfortable with any legislation that singled out the Chinese, yet it was well aware of colonial feeling that might spill over into more general colonial assertions of independence.

On 27 April 1888 the *Afghan* sailed into Port Melbourne carrying more than two hundred and fifty Chinese men, far in excess of the fourteen new immigrants it was permitted to carry. As well, forty-eight passengers had fraudulent documents. The Trades Hall and the ANA staged protests, and Victorian officials negotiated a settlement in which the *Afghan* sailed on to Sydney without landing any passengers.

In Sydney the coincidental arrival of the *Afghan* with several more ships carrying Chinese immigrants was met by huge protesting crowds which demanded that the premier, Henry Parkes, prevent the Chinese from disembarking. Parkes rushed through exclusionary legislation. Subsequent legal challenges, which ended up in the Privy Council, confirmed that colonial governments did possess a general prerogative to exclude aliens. Victoria had hoped that the question could be settled by diplomatic negotiation between Britain and China, rather than by colonial legislation. But if the colonies were to legislate, it had to be uniform.[13]

The June intercolonial conference in Sydney was to seek agreement on uniform immigration laws. Deakin and Gillies were the delegates for Victoria. Henry Holland, now Lord Knutsford, wrote to the delegates that he recognised their strong desire to restrict Chinese migration, but he urged them to draft a law that put immigrants from all foreign nations on an equal footing and so avoid offending the Chinese. This, he hoped, would pave the way for a diplomatic agreement with China to restrict the emigration of Chinese labourers.[14]

Deakin drafted the conference's response to Knutsford, which asked the British government to negotiate a treaty with China that would exclude all Chinese from Australia, except for students, officials, travellers and merchants.[15] The colonies agreed to uniform legislation, with the machinery of exclusion the already familiar one of limiting Chinese ship passengers by the ship's tonnage.[16] The issues and the mechanisms of exclusion canvassed at this conference shaped Deakin's future thinking on immigration. He accepted as axiomatic that it was impossible for white and coloured people to live civilly side by side, that Australia was a white man's land and that it must be kept that way. Its temperate zones, Charles Pearson wrote a few years later, were perhaps 'the last part of the world, in which the higher races can live and increase freely'.[17]

After the conference Deakin returned to the mountains, 'solus', taking long, solitary walks and writing a rambling fantasy, 'Autumn Has Come'.[18] The scenery and conversations with Royce had reawakened his youthful dreams of a literary life and returned him to thoughts he had recorded as his train carried him though the foothills of the Rocky Mountains four years before: he was not the author of himself. 'We are what others have made us…individuality is a cautious compound of other lives.' A man must accommodate himself to the times in which he lives, as 'those that belong by affinity to another age or race must share the destiny of the community in which they are numbered.'

The idea of race helped Deakin to answer deep existential questions about the balance between contingency and necessity in any life. The political historian Benedict Anderson was later to argue that nationalism performed the same function by locating individuals' lives in generational time, and giving us objects of loyalty and service beyond our selves.[19] Race was never a complete answer to Deakin's quest for his destiny, but the idea of a race-based community did provide a psychological hook for him into what was becoming the leading concept of his age.

His few days with Royce had left him lonely. Back in Melbourne he bemoaned his 'lack of conversation with those who read what I read or care to discuss the subjects that most interest me'. Reading good books required conversation and discussion to assimilate them, and this he lacked. It is not entirely clear why he missed 'the safety valve of speech'.[20] He certainly did not lack male companionship. His friendship with Derham was still strong, with regular visits and games of tennis, and he could discuss social and political questions with Pearson and Syme.

On the day he returned from Sydney after the intercolonial conference, Deakin made this entry in his prayer diary:

After again a long silence something has been wakened in me by the burning iron of remorse. Aid me O God to atone for the past and if it be possible to undo or even remove the evil done to others. After this enable me to conquer the evil which it has done to myself and to kill the root of that evil within me.[21]

What had he done? Or thought? Or felt? Both La Nauze and Rickard speculate that his remorse may have been over his interference in his sister's marriage prospects when he diverted one of her suitors whom, he later learned, Catherine would have accepted. This would indeed have been a matter for deep regret, but it is not an act of evil, and there is no direct evidence for it. The historian Diane Langmore, in an essay on Pattie, ponders the possibility of infidelity.[22] I am inclined to Langmore's interpretation, with the proviso that for a man like Deakin even to lust after another woman would have felt like a betrayal and there is no evidence he ever succumbed to temptation. Temptations there would have been, of that we can be sure, particularly on his long trips from home.

At the beginning of 1888, Australia's centennial year, Deakin had written to Charles Dilke, 'We are still in the full tide of material prosperity and progress.'[23] The year began with a wild speculative boom in shares in Broken Hill's silver mines and ended with Melbourne's extravagant Centennial Exhibition, which spared no expense to display the achievements of the Australian colonies to the world and bring pleasure to the people. London's 1851 Great Exhibition at the Crystal Palace had transformed the humble trade fair into an international event. Philadelphia held a World Fair in 1876 to celebrate a century of American independence, and in 1878 France held the Paris Exposition to display the remarkable revitalisation of its culture and industry since it lost the Franco-Prussian War just eight years earlier. International exhibitions were what prosperous, liberal nations did to show the world and themselves that they were at the forefront of progress. Sydney had one in 1879, as did Melbourne in 1880 at the magnificent new Exhibition Building. Melbourne's was hugely successful, with crowds of visitors, including the Deakin family. Government revenue was boosted, new markets opened and capital poured into the colony.[24]

With the centenary of British settlement coming up, why not another international exhibition to display the astonishing achievements of Australia's colonists in building civilisation in a continent which just one hundred years ago was 'thinly populated by tribes of savages'?[25] It fell under Deakin's responsibility as chief secretary, and he had introduced the matter to cabinet at the end of 1886. He had also promoted it at every opportunity during his 1887 visit abroad, including his coup in securing the Prince of Wales as the honorary president. It would mark Melbourne, 'the Queen of the South', as a global city, and no expense was to be spared. George Higinbotham resigned as president of the organising committee because of the wanton extravagance.

On 1 August 1888, two days before Deakin's thirty-second birthday, ten thousand guests celebrated one hundred years of European settlement beneath a laurel wreath extended over the crowd by the colossal figure of Victory.[26] Was this a subliminal reference to the vanquishing of the land's original inhabitants? Or just a general sculptural boast in a city filled with boasters rushing headlong into a speculative land boom?

A myriad of land banks and finance companies were forming to redevelop city blocks and finance suburban subdivisions and housing developments. The land boom had been building since the mid-1880s, as an expanding population and the now adult children of the goldrush migrants pushed demand for housing. During the boom decade of the 1880s the population of Melbourne grew by around two hundred thousand, a massive increase of about 75 per cent.[27] The boom was further boosted when the new hydraulic lifts set city buildings soaring up to nine floors, contributing to the tripling of city land values.[28]

It was also fuelled by speculative fever, as the pace of subdivision outstripped realistic assessments of potential population growth. According to *Table Talk*, the daring weekly paper which displayed an insiders' knowledge of Melbourne's interconnected business and political elites, 'The previous summer about 100,000 allotments were sold. Melbourne's population stands at about 65,000 households. So if every household moved out if its existing dwelling right now, there would still be 35,000 allotments to spare.'[29] It was a land bubble waiting to burst.

Neither Gillies nor Deakin had Service's experience with public finance and it is unlikely they could have reined in the boom's reckless animal spirits had they wanted to. But they did not see the need. The budget they delivered in 1888 had the largest surplus ever. Ominously, government debt was also the highest ever, after a loan of eight million pounds to expand Melbourne's network of suburban railways. Private debt was also growing, as leading land developers spent the profits of their speculations on grand homes and luxurious living.

Some cautious voices pointed to the declining value of exports against imports, the lack of growth in production, the inevitability of a depression, but no one listened. The 1888 *Banking Record* summed up the general belief that interest payments would be easily met, 'as we believe that the capital has been outlaid on increasing the productive capacity of the country'. Deakin was to repeat this argument many times in the years ahead, but it had little foundation. The fifty million pounds of British capital which flowed into Victoria between 1885 and 1890 was mostly spent on land speculation, conspicuous consumption and rebuilding Melbourne, rather than on expanding productive capacity.[30]

The land boom hit a bump in October 1888, when the Associated Banks decided to stop lending money for land purchases and raised interest rates by 1 per cent. An early casualty was James Mirams, whose Premier Building Land and Investment Association was forced into liquidation. Mirams, a former Liberal politician, was found guilty of issuing a false balance sheet with intent to defraud and sentenced to a year's imprisonment.[31] Deakin lost some hundreds of pounds, ruefully telling Berry that he 'got into the land boom just as it closed'.[32]

More losses were to come, but he also made a lucrative investment when Theodore Fink arranged for him to become a secret shareholder in the Herald and Sportsman Newspaper Company. According to Fink, 'this turned out of very considerable value,'[33] though it is not recorded in any of Deakin's autobiographical reminiscences. In his prayers he expressed misgivings that in his pursuit of wealth and power he had 'entered into perilous ways' and reminded himself of their justifications: wealth 'for the sake of those dependent on me', and power for its usefulness, 'that I may follow and persuade others to follow the path which shall lead to the elevation of national life and thought and permanence of well-earned prosperity'.[34]

Federation was starting to take shape as the guiding purpose of Deakin's political life, but it was floundering politically. Protectionist feelings were strong among Victoria's farmers, who wanted to increase the tariff on livestock and agricultural products entering Victoria from New South Wales. Gillies and Deakin resisted on federalist grounds and began moves to reduce other intercolonial tariffs, but intercolonial free trade was not yet politically feasible.

With typical overstatement, in August 1888 Deakin claimed that the stock tax was 'the parting of the ways...we either join hands and go together or we separate and dig between one colony and the other a gulf, the bridging of which we cannot foresee.' He deplored that Victoria's parochial interests were put ahead of the question of the larger Australia—but, as he was reminded by opponents, members of parliament had a duty to the interests of those who voted for them, and they were Victorians.[35] Deakin wrote to Dilke that he was 'prepared to go out of public life altogether rather than be responsible for an internecine war of tariffs throughout Australia'.[36]

Gillies and Deakin fought off an Opposition motion of no-confidence on the stock tax, but the issue continued to fester and in September parliament rose with an election called for the following March. West Bourke was divided in two for the 1889 election, and Deakin chose to stand in the newly created urban electorate of Essendon and Flemington. The government was easily returned, and Deakin would hold this seat for the rest of the century.

He was under pressure from the *Age* and from some in the Liberal caucus to break with Gillies and form a ministry of Liberals, but he wasn't interested. He wrote to Berry in April that 'after the land boom people of all classes deprecated any fierce party struggle. Besides the trouble is where to find a *casus belli* if we wanted one.'[37] Deakin's interest in politics was flagging once more, as another year of cabinet meetings, budget preparation, parliamentary debates, deputations and official visits stretched out before him with no grand purpose to lift them above the mundane.

Perhaps he took some comfort from his first official visit to Mildura in June 1889, steaming down the Murray from Swan Hill and on to the irrigation colonies of Wentworth in New South Wales and Renmark in South Australia.[38] The progress of Mildura was astonishing: twenty-five miles of channels completed, thirty more miles under way, the great pump installed. Running through the middle of the new town was Deakin Avenue. Writing his name across the once arid Mallee scrub, this grand arterial boulevard was five miles long and two hundred feet wide, planted with Moreton Bay figs and sugar gums and with a reserve in the centre for a tram.[39]

On 7 July 1889 Deakin began a 'Gospel According to Swedenborg', which he worked on over the next nine months, finishing it in early April 1890. Al Gabay suggests that the date was deliberately chosen, the seventh day of the seventh month in Deakin's thirty-third year, the age which has special significance to Christian mystics, as Jesus was believed to be thirty-three at the time of his crucifixion.[40] The day before Deakin had prayed that in the writings of the eighteenth-century Swedish philosopher and theologian Emanuel Swedenborg he might find the 'guidance and inspiration' to become 'a vehicle for the diffusion of goodness and truth'.[41]

When Swedenborg was fifty-three and a successful scientist, engineer and politician, he began to experience dreams and visions in which the Lord instructed him to bear witness to the objective existence of the spiritual world and the immortality of the soul, and to explain the spiritual sense of the scriptures. This he did in theological writings which were widely read by those seeking new foundations for their Christian faith, such as Blake, Coleridge, Carlyle, Emerson, Thoreau, and William and Henry James. It is likely that Deakin first read Swedenborg in the early 1870s.[42]

Deakin's unconventional religious life is difficult fare for twenty-first-century secularists. His spiritualism was but an early stage in his quest for spiritual knowledge and for an ethical basis for his political work. Spiritualism was focussed on communication beyond the grave, rather than on the Christian life in this world, and its ethics, though generally progressive, were shallow. For the past few years Deakin had been systematically reading the Bible. His prayer diary shows him moving towards a more conventionally Christian religious life, with a belief in a supreme, divine being to whom he owed a life of duty and goodness.

In Swedenborg, Deakin found a thinker who combined a seer's witness to a greater reality with a practical ethics. Swedenborg confirmed his belief in spiritual revelation, and put the Ideal of Unselfish Love at the heart of the religious life. For Deakin, the spiritual and ethical aspects of religious truth formed intertwined nets across the void of a meaningless universe and a purposeless life. A few years later he would advise his daughters that life without God is selfish and sensual, 'narrow, hard, harsh and discordant'; that without God eternal life, self-sacrifice, self-control and devotion to the Ideal are rendered ridiculous.[43]

Swedenborg kept a 'Spiritual Diary', the same name Deakin used for his record of the revelations in the séances of the early 1880s. But Deakin's early spiritual diary had negligible ethical content, concerned as it was with predictions about his political future and advice on his share purchases. His 'Gospel According to Swedenborg' shows the deepening of his religious life, as its focus moves away from prophecy and supernatural marvels to a conception of the Ideal concerned with how to live in this world.

Swedenborg taught that the ideals of love and wisdom only become real in use, in the actions of people and the choices they make; and he believed they were increasingly present in human affairs as humanity's understanding and compassion evolved. It was an optimistic creed, with providence clearly on the side of progress, but Deakin did not always find it easy to discern the Divine in his messy everyday world.[44]

14

1890—FEDERATION AND

THE MARITIME STRIKE

IN 1883, IN the immediate aftermath of Queensland's attempt to annexe New Guinea, an intercolonial convention was held in Sydney to discuss federation. A Federal Council was created to further the cause, but not all colonies joined. Henry Parkes, although long a supporter of national union, kept New South Wales out, and South Australia was equivocal. Thus weakened, the council was, Deakin said, 'little more than a debating society'.[1] Until New South Wales was in, no progress could be made.

In the face of Victoria's glamorous prosperity, Parkes was jealous of New South Wales' status as the mother colony. In 1887 he had even put forward a bill to mark the centenary of the First Fleet by renaming New South Wales 'Australia', and he did not join the other colonial statesmen for the opening of the Centennial International Exhibition in Melbourne. The turning point was his Tenterfield address in October 1889. The New South Wales governor, Lord Carrington, persuaded the ageing leader with his eye on posterity's judgement to throw his energy into the confederation of the colonies; it would be a 'glorious finish' to his life's work.[2] So Sir Henry Parkes turned his prodigious political talents to becoming the Father of Federation and strode majestically onto the federal stage.

The metaphor is Deakin's. Politics and theatre lay close in his imagination. Deakin did not regard all the world as a stage, but the idea of himself as an actor captured the distance he liked to hold between his inner self and his public work, and to remind him of the transience of worldly achievement. In Parkes he saw a master of the craft:

> First and foremost of course in every eye was the commanding figure of Sir Henry Parkes, than whom no actor ever more fully posed for effect. His huge figure, slow step, deliberate glance and carefully brushed-out aureole of white hair combined to present the spectator with a picturesque whole which was not detracted from on closer acquaintance...His studied attitudes expressed either distinguished humility or imperious command. His manner was invariably dignified, his speech slow, and his pronunciation precise, offending only by the occasional omission or misplacing of aspirates...He had always in his mind's eye his own portrait of a great man, and constantly adjusted himself to it...Movements, gestures, inflexions, attitude harmonized, not simply because they were intentionally adopted but because there was in him the substance of the man he dressed himself to appear. The real strength and depth of his capacity were such that it was always a problem with Parkes as with Disraeli where the actor, posture-maker and would-be sphinx ended or where the actual man underneath began...
>
> It was not a rich nor a versatile personality, but it was massive, durable and imposing, resting upon elementary qualities of human nature elevated by a strong mind. He was cast in the mould of a great man and though he suffered from numerous pettinesses, spites and failings, he was in himself a full-blooded, large-brained self-educated Titan whose natural field was found in Parliament and whose resources of character and intellect enabled him in his later years to overshadow all his contemporaries.[3]

Deakin's portrait of the seventy-four-year-old Parkes is a tour de force of sharp-eyed perception and sympathetic admiration for the grand old man of New South Wales. If this were a morality play, Parkes is undoubtedly Vanity, but Deakin also recognised the breadth of vision, the capacity to inspire and the deeply held liberal principles of the man who had started life as the seventh child of a poor tenant farmer and wanted to be remembered as the Father of Federation.

In 1890, during one of Melbourne's February heatwaves, thirteen representative public men, including two delegates from New Zealand, met to discuss federation. At the grand welcoming banquet in Queen's Hall, before four hundred cheering, handkerchief-waving men, Parkes replied to the toast to 'A United Australia'. He followed the sober James Service, who had described colonial tariffs as the 'lion in the path' to federation.

As the premier of a free-trade state, Parkes was fully aware of the difficulties of bearding this particular lion. Knowing that getting strong and stable support for federation from free-trade New South Wales was unlikely, Parkes' solution was to postpone the settlement of the tariff question until after Federation had been achieved, leaving it to the future federal parliament to sort out.[4] He spoke instead of what the colonies shared:

> The crimson thread of kinship runs through us all. Even the native born Australians are Britons, as much as the men born in the cities of London and Glasgow. We know the value of their British origin. We know that we represent a race…for the purposes of settling new colonies, which never had its equal on the face of the earth. We know, too, that conquering wild territory, and planting civilised communities therein, is a far nobler, a far more immortalizing achievement than conquest by feats of arms.[5]

The conference adopted a resolution, moved by Parkes, that the best interests and prosperity of the Australian colonies would be promoted by an early union under the crown and agreed to meet a year hence to start the arduous work of drafting a constitution.

The collapse of a few land-finance companies at the end of 1888 had not spoiled Melburnians' appetite for speculation, and early in 1889 the boom resumed, with land banks, finance companies and some building societies successfully wooing British investors for funds to invest. And the Victorian and municipal governments continued to borrow. The 1889 budget was a 'prosperity budget', with a declared surplus of £1.7 million available for government spending, supplemented by another London loan of four million pounds.[6]

Deakin looked forward to passing a health bill, a bill to establish the Metropolitan Board of Works to sewer Melbourne and perhaps a large railways bill. 'If we pass these,' he wrote to Dilke, 'we shall indeed have done well and earned a recess.' In London a strike had broken out on the docks, and he told Dilke that there was 'a ferment of sympathy' in Australia, and in Melbourne in particular, for the striking workers, with substantial funds raised. 'The entire interest,' he wrote, 'is humanitarian and unselfish.'[7]

For all his faith in prophecy, Deakin's idealist optimism made him a poor reader of the times, and generally blind to the way material interests rather than providence were shaping the colony's future. Not only would prosperity be over when export prices fell or overseas investment faltered, but workers were becoming more organised and militant. In mid-August 1890, a year after the London dock strike, members of the Maritime Officers Association started to walk off their ships as they docked in Melbourne. Wanting closed shops, the Maritime Officers Association had affiliated with the Melbourne Trades Hall Council, and the employers demanded they disaffiliate. The officers were joined in a sympathy strike by seamen, and the maritime strike quickly spread to the other colonies and other unions, including the rapidly growing shearers' union and the coal miners, who refused to produce coal for ships. Other industries were soon paralysed.

The conflict with the ship owners was as much about employers' attempts to halt the growing solidarity of the labour movement as it was about wages and conditions. Employers had been watching with mounting alarm as the local craft unions, with their inward-focussed guild consciousness, gave way to the new unions of unskilled and semi-skilled workers, which were building nationwide organisations and whose leaders talked of class struggle.[8]

The strike unnerved Chief Secretary Deakin. It disrupted the unloading of coal, as well as the stoking of the gasworks which supplied most of Melbourne's lighting. The police feared that dark, unlit nights would provide cover for criminals to rob and burgle respectable citizens, even for riot and plunder. A mass rally of unionists was to be held in Flinders Park on the Yarra Bank on the last Sunday in August. The night before, Deakin prayed:

> God grant thy spirit to us. Let it be poured abroad and awaken all men to their better selves so that in these hours of strife and industrial conflict peace may be preserved...Grant me O God Thy grace and wisdom to discern the needs of each hour that I may act with power and promptitude to suppress violence and with mildness and moderation so that all possible suffering may be avoided.[9]

On the preceding Friday cabinet had decided that 'order must be obtained at all hazards.' The decision was not Deakin's alone and he was supported by James Bell, the minister for defence, and by Premier Duncan Gillies. In New South Wales, Premier Henry Parkes made the same call, as did the new premier of Queensland, Samuel Griffith. The police had the primary responsibility for civil order, and as soon as the strike began the Victorian chief commissioner, Hussey Malone Chomley, began calling in extra ammunition from country police stations and arranging for reinforcements. Six hundred and fifty special constables were sworn in, mostly city merchants and residents wanting to protect their property from mob violence.

The police felt they were dealing with something potentially more violent than the familiar agitations of the unemployed, which had no organisation behind them.[10] Much more controversial than the special constables was the bringing to Melbourne of a hundred members of the Mounted Rifles under the command of Colonel Tom Price. This was a voluntary militia, but it was the military, and a provocative escalation of the government's response. The government also issued a proclamation, posted all over the city, warning that if those on strike violated the law they would be vigorously punished.[11]

There were no riots. Friday was a clear moonlit night, and kerosene lamps and electricity provided adequate substitutes for much of the gas light. The crowds at the Sunday rally were orderly and the Mounted Rifles stayed in the St Kilda Road barracks. It was rumoured, however, that Price had instructed the troops that, if ordered to fire, they should 'fire low and lay the disturbers of law and order out.' In the unionists' suspicion of the way the powers of the state were gathering against them, this became 'fire low and lay the bastards out.'

Belief in official authority's propensity to violence was made more plausible by the fact that Tom Price was the son of John Giles Price, the cruel and arrogant disciplinarian commandant of Norfolk Island, on whom Marcus Clarke based the appalling Maurice Frere in *For the Term of His Natural Life*. In 1857 John Price was killed by convicts when investigating conditions in the prison hulks at Williamstown, an event well within the memory of older Melburnians.[12] Vengeful violence was to be expected from the son of such a father; and a man whose father had died at the hands of the mob had good cause to fear its violence.

Price later claimed that firing low was standard orders, to aim for the knees not the body, but the unionists thought he and his men should not have been anywhere near their peaceful rally in the first place.[13] Why, asked Billy Trenwith, the only unionist in parliament, were men who had bravely volunteered to defend the people against an invader being called to array themselves against the people?[14]

It was a massive overreaction on the part of the government, and Deakin had pushed for it. Perhaps his schoolboy fantasy of saving the city from the Irish had been reactivated. Great struggles and impending crises were recurrent events in his imaginative life and this may have influenced his evaluation of the risks of disorder. The government had prepared for the worst rather than hoped for the best.

In parliament the following week Deakin was at pains to distinguish the law-abiding unionists from the threat posed by the criminal class.

The government was bound to preserve order, he said, 'and not to leave the city at the mercies of mob law and roughs and rascals'. He had received intelligence that men 'known to police' were making their way to Melbourne. Crowds of unruly men were gathering at the wharves, attempting to prevent non-union labour from unloading the ships; non-union stokers at the gasworks had been harried and booed.

No written record of this intelligence has survived, and constables on the beat generally reported nothing untoward. Chomley's memoranda, however, are more alarmist.[15] Perhaps Chomley was embellishing the risk to justify his military-style preparations. Deakin also insisted that the government could not tolerate aggression against non-union men who were willing to work when union men would not.[16]

Labour was becoming more organised and, in response, so was capital. Where did this leave the state? In a debate on a private member's bill to establish courts of conciliation, Deakin struggled to think it through. Imagining capital and labour as two great armies ranged against each other, 'organised to fight with courage and desperation', the state and its representative institutions 'might be crushed like an egg shell'. But if the executive was forced to choose, 'The sympathies of the State and of its Ministers must necessarily be with its citizens.'[17] How, though, would this sympathy be manifested? During the maritime strike the state had been unable to force the warring parties to compromise and it had helped employers use strike-breakers.

The maritime strike was the first of the great strikes of the early 1890s. All failed, but they had two transformative consequences. The union movement concluded that it must form a political wing to elect working men to parliament, and began forming labour parties. And the progressive middle class concluded that the state should have the power to intervene in strikes, which led to the development of Australia's distinctive system of conciliation and arbitration courts.

The strike added to the government's woes as it fought off repeated no-confidence motions from the Opposition about the state of the government's finances. The Centennial International Exhibition had made a loss of almost a quarter of a million pounds, in part because

of the huge cost of the electric lighting, and in part because too few
Melburnians were interested in the high cultural fare on offer.[18] Again
the 1890 budget was expansionist. Every country hamlet wanted a
branch line and another extravagant railways bill was put forward at
an estimated cost of eight million pounds.[19]

Deakin's defence of this bill shows the weakness of his understanding of government finances. His parliamentary adversary was William
Shiels, who had been a fellow member of Charles Pearson's University
Debating Club. Shiels, a free-trade Liberal with progressive achievements in advancing the rights of women, warned of the fearful risk
the state was running with its unrestrained spending: 'the outlook is
dark and troubled, a cloud of danger overhanging us, a menace to our
national and financial stability.'[20]

Shiels was not alone in his warnings, and articles had started to
appear in the London financial press questioning the Victorian government's financial competence. In November, London's Barings Bank,
which had lent heavily to Argentina, almost collapsed. The Bank of
England orchestrated the bailout, thus avoiding a global financial crisis,
but the Baring crisis made British investors even more concerned about
the financial soundness of the heavily indebted Australian colonies.

Deakin would have none of it: the colony was not like Argentina,
which had no assets to show for its borrowed money. Victoria had an
asset for every borrowed pound, he claimed; all borrowing had been
spent on development.

> Are we to lose heart and courage—we the generation who have
> grown up in this favoured land, who have seen the enormous
> capital of Melbourne, the fourth city in the British empire, spring
> into being in the short space of a life time—are we to turn our
> backs on our fathers and ourselves, to say all achievement is over?[21]

Deakin accused Shiels of listening to the pessimists. To Deakin,
pessimism was a moral failing, 'a frost which threatens religious morality and society', while optimism fostered the generous and good and
repressed the narrow and selfish.[22] Optimism for Deakin was not an

aspect of temperament, but a moral, even a spiritual, duty. From his first entry into politics he had abhorred the obstructionists, those who were negative, who raised doubts about the possibilities of progress, whose vacillations and carping doubts threatened the realisation of the Ideal.

Nevertheless, the government did agree to establish a Public Works Committee to assess the benefits of the various railway proposals. This concession to the government's critics, wrote Timotheus of the *Argus*, needed a man who could make it gracefully: 'The right man was available in Mr. Deakin who has a happy knack—an exceptionally happy knack—of explaining away an awkward situation, and few qualities are more important in the political world than this.'[23]

15

ALFRED, PATTIE AND CATHERINE

BY APRIL 1889 Alfred and Pattie had been married for seven years. They had two healthy young daughters, an elegant home, and sufficient income for a cook and a maid, though they did not keep a carriage. Pattie was a practical person. She enjoyed creating a comfortable home for her busy husband and caring for their children, and she was a good gardener and a capable nurse who regularly helped out neighbours when children were sick.[1] When time permitted she would sketch and paint, but she was not much interested in the metaphysical and abstract political questions which filled Alfred's leisure; she was not even particularly interested in the practical political questions that filled his days, except as a loyal supporter. She was the companion of his bed and hearth and the mother of his children, and every wedding anniversary and every birthday he wrote her a poem.

Since Ivy's birth, Pattie had been frequently unwell and confined to bed. She had been suffering from a long and painful illness, which, Deakin told Berry in 1889, prevented him from entertaining. Pattie believed that some of her troubles were caused by poor treatment during the birth, and she seems also to have experienced excessive and painful menstrual periods, which left her debilitated and weak. The family referred to it as her 'complaint'.[2] In 1888 she consulted Alfred's old spiritualist mentor, the herbalist and bookseller William Terry; and in 1889 she was examined under chloroform.[3] But she was not cured. She also experienced two miscarriages. The dates of these are not recorded, but they may have occurred between the births of Stella on 3 June 1886 and Vera on Christmas Day 1891.[4]

Alfred was not unhappy with Pattie. Whenever not officially engaged he dined at home, and when they were separated he wrote her letters full of endearments and concern for her health. He enjoyed domestic life: gardening, reading to the children, playing with them and the family pets, strolling with Pattie, visiting his parents and sister on Sundays. But marriage is, he was learning, a compromise. Tension was growing between Pattie and his beloved older sister, Catherine, who was in her late thirties and still living with their parents at Adams Street, where she would live for the rest of her long life.

Catherine was a clever woman, a gifted musician with keen intellectual and literary interests. Pattie recalls that she and William would discuss literature for hours on end.[5] In 1875, when Charles Pearson became the founding headmaster of the new Presbyterian Ladies' College, and when Catherine was twenty-five, she studied for the matriculation as a mature-age student. She passed, but women were not yet admitted to the university, so she took a position on Pearson's staff. Two years later, when he was forced out as headmaster because of his liberal views, she too left. Her diary shows how upset she was by the conflict and the loss of her position.

Small, serious and shy, Catherine did not have her brother's charm or his good looks. She had hoped to marry, but it didn't happen. Perhaps her brother had discouraged a suitor, though the evidence for this is thin. As likely, she was too retiring and modest, an earnest bluestocking in the days when women wanting a husband were expected to flirt. Music was a possible alternative. She obtained a certificate in Piano, Harmony and Teaching at the Melbourne School of Music, and briefly considered a career as a concert pianist. Her close friend Ada Gresham advised her against it, given the strain it would cause to her nervous temperament: 'I have always thought music ought to be a source of greater contentment and happiness to you than it is.'[6] Catherine was thirty-three when Ivy was born, and almost thirty-six when Stella came along. By then it was very unlikely she would have her own children, and she fell in love with them, a willing child minder and aunt, eager to help bring them up. Adams Street became their second home.

On 3 August 1890, Alfred's thirty-fourth birthday, just before the maritime strike, the family made a sentimental trip to their first family homes in George and Gore streets, Fitzroy. Pattie had neuralgia and likely did not accompany them. That night, as his year turned, Deakin prayed, 'Youth is past and manhood unfolded to its full but I find myself still feeble, still doubting, still uncertain of my life and part,' and he concluded with his recurrent plea to 'serve Thee and if possible to know that I am serving'.[7] It was a Saturday, and that night he wrote fourteen of his Clues, wrapped in his woollen dressing gown in his cold study while Pattie slept. He reflected on how few friends are made for life; and on the unselfishness of marriage, when men and women renounce access to easy sexual pleasure.

> The impulse of the male is gratification and that is always best obtained from the young and attractive unencumbered by the cares of maternity. If the female were purely self-regarding the same would be true of her. Nature has however implanted in most of them a maternal instinct which leads them to unreasonably and in a selfish sense unnaturally sacrifice themselves and their pleasure.[8]

Monogamy, he concluded, is the most unnatural and hence the most unselfish of relationships, an illustration of our higher nature and a test of our morality. So he redeemed his sexual frustration.

In mid-July 1890, the day after Ivy's seventh birthday, he had a 'long talk with P about future preparations', and a few days later he prayed that he may be qualified for 'the discharge of my duties to my darling little ones and may make them earnest and sincere in their lives and

in their knowledge and love of thee'.[9] On 7 September, the Saturday
after the mass meeting of strikers, Alfred completed a 'Testament for
the guidance of his daughters in the event of his death'. It is a long,
ponderous document which had been some months in the making,
written by a man weighed down by responsibilities.

His first desire for his daughters was that they be brought up
religiously, but as far as possible apart from sectarianism, for without
belief in God and in immortality 'there can be no true or efficient
morality from generation to generation, no task for the race, no goal
for it to attain.' Life without God is selfish and sensual; nothing is more
horrible than 'the selfish, their cruelty, their licentiousness and their
falsehood...it is to save my children from these horrors and these terrible
sufferings that I plead with my children to conquer their selfishness
and seek to lead a life of purity and self-sacrifice in the interests of
others.' The Testament's emphasis on the vice of selfishness shows the
influence of Swedenborg, but his repeated references to his daughters'
purity show he also feared other vices.

Dark fears lurk in this strange, obsessive document about the fates
that could befall fashionable, pleasure-seeking women abroad in the
world. Vigorous debates on the 'woman question' and the 'marriage
question' were underway, challenging the mid-Victorian ideal of the
Angel in the Home, contented helpmeet to her husband, raising his
children in the moral and spiritual virtues which were her specialty.
Women were agitating for the vote, and for the law to recognise that
for many of them marriage was anything but heaven on earth, and
rather a degrading tyranny of drunken husbands and unwanted sex
and pregnancies. Other women worked as prostitutes in the thriving
sex industries of British and Australian cities.

In 1888 and 1889, shortly before the Testament was written, Britain
and Australia had been gripped by moral panic when translations of
Zola's novels were published in editions cheap enough for any shop
girl to buy and read about prostitutes and the adulterous French. The
publisher, Henry Vizetelly, was convicted of obscenity in two trials
in Britain, and Deakin asked the police commissioner to hunt out
copies of Zola translations in Melbourne with a view to prosecuting

the booksellers. Chomley advised Deakin that they were insufficiently obscene to warrant seizure, as did the attorney-general. But Deakin persisted, and turned to Customs to prevent the importation of the offending editions, initiating the Australian use of Customs to restrict obscene publications.[10]

Deakin's two young daughters were his hostages to fortune in this dangerous world, and his solution was seclusion. They would not be sent to boarding school, and as far as possible would be educated together at home until old enough to attend college or university. Although not spelt out, the implication was that Catherine would have a large hand in their formal education while they were 'taught all household duties and economies by their mother'. They were to exercise regularly; be taught tennis, horse riding and dancing; eat a plain wholesome diet (he recommends vegetarianism as serving many women best); and be total abstainers, except in medical crises. 'I desire my children neither to be athletes nor blue stockings, and least of all fashionable.'

As he tries to imagine his daughters' futures, Deakin swings confusedly back and forth between the lives of the two women he loves, his wife and his sister, recoiling from regarding his sister's spinsterhood as a second-rate life—which is where many of his arguments seem to be heading. After claiming that woman's noblest function is to bear healthy children inside a blessed marriage, he counters that virginity is precious and far better than a hasty marriage to 'the gross, the selfish, or the silly and weak'. He sees financial independence as more important to a woman than a man, and runs through the possible professions: medicine is noble, teaching is arduous and poorly paid, art and music are not to be encouraged, perhaps a business such as that of a milliner could be acquired. It is all rather unconvincing, as what he clearly wants is for his daughters to be safely tucked up at home with a good man.

Deakin supported the rights of women, but he was not a prominent advocate. He voted for the successive private members' bills which unsuccessfully attempted to enfranchise Victoria's women, he supported legislation to ease divorce, he welcomed women's greater educational opportunities. But he did not take the lead on these reforms. His wishes for his daughters show a degree of ambivalence about women's emancipation. Not for them the life of the New Woman, out and about in the world. Rather, he imagined their future lives, whether married or single, to be home-centred, 'lives of secluded study, domestic duty, quiet cheerfulness, intellectual in cast and unselfish in end such as shall ensure happiness to you and to all connected with you if undertaken with religious zeal, humility and consistency'.[11] Are lives lived within such straitjackets of self-control and parental expectation what he would have imagined for his sons?

On 15 October 1890 Deakin underlined in his diary the enigmatic note 'P & K controversy', and three days later he recorded 'discuss with P'.[12] We don't know exactly what precipitated the discord between Pattie and Catherine, but Pattie was increasingly resentful of the role Catherine was assuming in the girls' education and her own relegation to the domestic sphere. Catherine saw herself as helping out, but to Pattie she was assuming too much control. She felt sidelined as a mother, expected only to feed, clothe and nurse the children, and she did not share Deakin's desire to seclude them from the world.

> The aunt was to train and educate and advise the family, to discuss with her brother all the details of which I was not even made aware…I was not allowed to bring them up as I would if I had been free as a mother should be. Their childhood would have been more normal. They would have had children to play with.

Pattie believed her sister-in-law debarred her children 'from the pleasures and joys of youth', expecting too much self-denial, and that this was harmful, especially to Ivy. We know from Catherine's diary that the blow-up was serious, 'a horrible misunderstanding', and it left her feeling dreadfully lonely. She took a trip to New Zealand in January 1891, and on her return Pattie's coldness made her feel like a stranger at Llanarth. Pointedly, she was not invited to a dinner Pattie and Alfred gave for the Symes. All Pattie's married life, Catherine had been there. She had accompanied them to every important event and been invited to every formal dinner they had given, and was her husband's chief confidante on financial matters. Pattie was finding it very hard to bear.[13]

16

TANGLED TIMES

THE GILLIES–DEAKIN government was defeated on 30 October 1890, after its overreaction to the strike propelled enough extra votes across the floor for Opposition leader James Munro to win a no-confidence motion. The main issue, however, was the ministry's financial extravagance and the mountain of public debt. The agreement with the Chaffey brothers came in for special attack as an example of gross maladministration. Deakin vigorously defended it and talked up the prospects for Mildura, but the signs were that the spirit of progress was ebbing there too.

Accepting the inevitability of defeat, Deakin made a gracious farewell to office. He had been a member of the government since 1883 and chief secretary for almost five years. He was proud of the government's achievements. Departments of Health, Water Supply and Agriculture had all been established; relations with neighbouring colonies were more cordial; and the recognition obtained from the British government in regard to imperial questions 'entitles us to feel that the colony is attaining its manhood'. He repeated his familiar claim that government debt was not a problem when it was balanced by assets. Deakin's was a generous nature, and on the brink of losing office he stepped outside his partisan role to express warm feelings towards the men whose measures he opposed and to thank them all for 'the kindnesses universally extended to one who was young and inexperienced seven years ago', when he first became a minister.[1]

The next day, Friday, 31 October, Syme wrote to him, offering him a holiday after his years of office: 'What do you say to a trip to Egypt to report on irrigation there?'[2] By Tuesday he and Syme had agreed that the trip would be to India; on Wednesday he started his reading about the subcontinent; and three weeks later he was on the boat, with Syme's son Herbert as a last-minute travelling companion.[3] Deakin could not put the cares of office behind him quickly enough, and the tensions at home, for the excitement and surprises of travel and the pleasures of again taking up his journalist's pen. Leaving the boat at Colombo for a strange and brilliantly coloured new world, with 'groves of magnificent palms, long stretches of native vegetation, and teeming brown nudities', it seemed 'like the sudden realization of long forgotten visions which maturity has unwillingly and sadly obliterated'.[4]

Deakin was the first politician to see Australia's proximity to Asia as an opportunity as well as a threat.[5] To be sure, the strategic threat was there. Russia was already pressing on the north-west frontier of India, which was of central significance to Britain's eastern empire. Should India fall into foreign hands, Australia would need a navy to defend its access to the seaways. But he also saw opportunity, and lamented Australia's small trade with India. Australia had no comparative advantage in wheat, but Deakin saw possible markets for dairy, fruit and vegetables, the very products that irrigation was designed to foster. With enthusiastic practicality, he packed three tins of butter to test how their quality survived the journey. The two opened at the end of the sea voyage were very fine, but the third, after a three-thousand-mile train trip to Calcutta, had spoiled and turned to ghee. The market he had in mind was the British pining for butter for their bread, not the natives frying vegetables for their curries.

India didn't unsettle Deakin as Mexico had. The British Raj was

familiar, and he was far more at ease with the mysticism of Hinduism and
Buddhism than with the superstitions of Latin-American Catholicism.
In an intense two months he visited all the major irrigation works of
the subcontinent, including the extensive canal systems of the Ganges
and the Punjab and the city water works of Bombay and Calcutta. He
believed he was the first white man, other than officials, to travel up
the Sirhind Canal in Lahore, on a boat pulled by natives, sleeping on
a hinged ledge with his boots for a pillow.[6]

Deakin saw invasion as India's repeated fate, with the British but
one of a long line of conquerors. He admired the grandeur of the
Moguls' temples, monuments and palaces, but considered they did
not compare 'for an instant…with the great engineering works of the
white invader…the splendid railways, roads, telegraphs…knitting the
distances and diversities of India into a national whole', nor with the
irrigation schemes which secured the country against famine.[7] Deakin's
heroes of empire were the men of the trowel rather than the sword,
the 'gallant company of engineers' who built the great canals carrying
water to the dry plains and food to the half-starved ryots.[8]

Deakin's articles on India were published in the *Age,* but also in
Sydney's *Daily Telegraph* and Adelaide's *Advertiser*, which helped to
make his name known beyond Victoria.[9] They were subsequently
collected into two books: *Irrigated India* and *Temple and Tomb*, the first
substantial works by an Australian on the subcontinent, and for a long
time the only ones, which has made Deakin something of a hero to
Australia's India-wallahs. Deakin went to considerable lengths to have
these books published. The India Office in London did not think them
of sufficient interest, even if they were 'in the voice of the charmer', so
he turned to Philip Mennell, a fellow *Age* journalist now working in
its London office.[10]

Mennell was to prove a very useful London contact for Deakin. On
this occasion he agreed to arrange for the publication of an anthology
of the articles on irrigation, putting up fifty pounds himself if Deakin
would match it, for a print run of a thousand hardbacks.[11] Deakin had
interspersed his detailed technical articles on irrigation with essays
on history, architecture and religion, pitched 'in another key', with

more richly decorative language to capture India's exotic marvels and complex history.[12] These were anthologised in a paperback, *Temple and Tomb*, published in Melbourne, and it is likely that Deakin bore the entire printing costs.

Deakin's writings on India show a flexibility in his thinking about race when he was unconstrained by public office. Always attuned to the possibilities of opposites coming together into higher unities, he mused about the benefits of 'half-breeds', Eurasians who might be able 'to transfuse the Caucasian capacity for self-government into a new native caste, or carry into European families a sufficient strain of Hindu blood to render them climate proof and capable of permanent residence'.[13] Like all other British visitors to India, he praised the benefits Britain brought to the subcontinent, particularly when compared with the Moguls, but he also recognised the aspirations of educated Indians for self-government, and the humiliation of being ruled by an alien race.[14]

Deakin talked to fellow passengers on his long train journeys, and *Irrigated India* includes the voices of some of them: a Brahmin railway clerk taking his son to see the wonders of Jaipur who supported the demands of the native Congress for representative institutions, and quizzed him about Australia's experience of self-government; a wealthy and refined Muhammadan landowner in the north-west, dressed in western style, who was sceptical of the benefits of granting democratic rights to the Hindu; and a Bengali clerk who spoke passionately about the social and cultural destruction wrought by the British, and the hopeless, helpless poverty of the masses.[15]

On 17 February 1891 Deakin arrived back in Melbourne. Ten days later, he, Pattie and the children left for Sydney, where the 1891 Federal Convention was to meet: 'in quantity and in task, by far the most important representative gathering which had ever met in Australia'.[16] The new Victorian premier, James Munro, headed the delegation which had been chosen before the Gillies–Deakin government fell the previous October, and included them both. Deakin was the youngest delegate.

The task of the convention was to hammer out a draft federal constitution, which would then be endorsed by the colonial parliaments.

The constitution needed to balance the sovereignty of the smaller colonies against the democratic rights of the majority of the population in Victoria and New South Wales. The European populations of the colonies were unequal: Western Australia had around forty-eight thousand white people, against well over a million in each of New South Wales and Victoria. Compromises would be needed and these representative men were prepared to make them.

The institutional framework they agreed on, with a popularly elected lower house and an upper house with equal representation of the states and equal powers except for money bills, has endured, though it had hurdles to clear before all the colonies accepted it. Deakin and his fellow Victorians were uncomfortable about the upper house having any powers over money bills at all. There was as yet no agreed means of resolving deadlocks between the houses, and the unequal representation in the Senate rankled with majoritarian democrats' commitment to votes of equal value, as did its indirect election by state parliaments.

Debating the powers between the houses, Deakin evoked the new Australia they were forming as 'a young giant' entitled to absolute enfranchisement. 'We can wear no constitutional garb capable of cramping a muscle or confining an artery of national life,' he argued, and must establish a constitution 'broad-based upon the people's will'.[17] If federation was to be achieved, however, majoritarian democrats would have to give way, as he well knew. The question was, how much?

The draft constitution was largely the work of Queensland's Samuel Griffith, Tasmania's Andrew Inglis Clark, South Australia's Charles Kingston and New South Wales' Edmund (Toby) Barton. The last two were to become Deakin's comrades-in-arms as they led the federation cause in their respective states. Both were some years older than Deakin, but native-born lawyers like himself with around a decade of parliamentary experience each. In temperament, though, they were very different from him. Kingston was quarrelsome and could be vindictive, whereas Toby Barton was a genial club man with a warm and generous nature.

Though both were protectionists, Kingston's politics were far more radical. He had been the South Australian premier, with Labor's support,

for most of the 1890s, leading a progressive government which granted
women the vote and pioneered legislation for arbitration and conciliation.
He was also a hot-headed fellow who had been arrested for planning
a duel in Adelaide's Victoria Square with a conservative member of
the Legislative Council who had denounced him as a disgrace to the
legal profession.[18]

The convention settled the name of the federation: the Commonwealth of Australia. This was Henry Parkes' choice, but Deakin seconded
it and lobbied energetically for it against those suspicious of its republican
overtones. It sounded well, he argued, it was free from party, it was
distinctive and it was Anglo-Saxon, the words 'common' and 'weal'
going back to the beginning of the English language.[19] The appeal to
the Anglo-Saxons shows the influence of the Oxford Regius Professor
of Modern History E. A. Freeman, who argued that the institutions of
self-government originated with the Anglo-Saxons, the original English
free men. Anglo-Saxonism was especially attractive to the Australians
because it included the United States as well as Britain, and they were
looking to both to help them model their new institutions.[20]

Deakin judged the convention to have been 'fairly successful', but was
not sure there would be much public interest in the future of the nation,
as the deepening economic depression kept people's attention fixed on
the miserable here-and-now.[21] After returning to life on the backbench
in the middle of April 1891, he had more time to read, write and garden,
and to contemplate his future, but the path ahead was unclear, with the
malign star in the ascendant and all 'cross grained and out of joint'.
Like weather at sea, such times 'have to be endured, if possible steamed
through but even then the storm may travel with us', he wrote.[22]

The shearers' strike in Queensland, which ran from January to
June, was bitter, with a real threat of violence as the state used armed
men to protect non-union labour, and arrested and gaoled the leaders.
In a public lecture at the Melbourne University Union, Deakin referred
obliquely to the sharpening conflict between capital and labour, and
the challenge from 'the communal demand for an equal share of the
earth, sky and water and for fixed obligations on every man of wealth

and power'. But he offered no practical solutions, instead putting his faith in 'evolution'. The lecture was, he judged, 'a great success'.[23]

In 'the tangle of the time' he prayed for clues as to his main task, for glimpses of the Light, the eternal truths that transcend the vicissitudes of daily material life. 'Let me but see—but see.' By the second half of 1891 he was struggling again with depression, and named it as such.

> O God, once more the waters have gone over me, I am drowned... as I sink inward to the coreless emptiness of things almost without a struggle or a sensation except that I know my loss and my loneliness...Strip my lethargy, scorch my wavering faith so that I may accept my part and perform it without the endless questioning and weary round of iterated unrealities. Make me real.[24]

Two séances with Mrs Cohen provided no answers, despite the spirits' reassurance that the economic depression would soon pass. Federation was predicted, but with free trade, which would be a terrible blow to Victoria and could lead to an uprising. The spirit of Dr Motherwell, who had died in 1886, advised him to rest on his oars as there would soon be a change of government, which he would be called suddenly to lead, and there would be a far greater struggle than anyone expected.[25]

Lines run through these entries, dismissing them as nonsense at some unspecified later date. Deakin was in fact planning to return to the law, a scheme on which the spirits made no comment, and in November announced that he would resume his practice as a barrister the following January.[26] The year ended with the birth of his and Pattie's third daughter, on Christmas night. No doubt they were hoping for a son as a fortnight later she was still unnamed.[27] Vera was their last child.

The late 1880s, when Deakin's colonial career was at its peak, were the last days of Australia Felix and the goldrush immigrants' dreams of a prosperous society free from the entrenched class differences and constrained opportunities of the Britain they had left. It was also the midpoint in Deakin's life, when a man realises he has stopped growing up and started to grow old. Opportunities remain for achievement and success, but the limitless horizons of a fortunate youth are gone, and with them youth's reckless energies. As the colony's prosperity plummeted over the next few years, so did Deakin's spirits.

All through 1891 the storm clouds William Shiels had predicted were gathering over Victoria's economy. The value of land at the peak of the boom was far in excess of any realistic assessment of demand, but companies and individuals had borrowed against it nevertheless. With prices falling fast and loans difficult to raise since the Baring crisis, many were careering towards bankruptcy. The decline in the price of wool in the later 1880s savaged the terms of trade and the maritime strike added to the woes. Unemployment was rising, and a financially straitened government was unable to resort to the usual remedy of public works to tide the unemployed over till things picked up. People began to leave Victoria to find work elsewhere, increasing Melbourne's rental vacancies and placing further downward pressure on property prices.

Worried banks began to call in overdrafts. Panicky depositors withdrew their funds or failed to renew when their term deposits matured. Building societies were especially exposed. They took in short-term deposits but lent to home buyers long-term and did not have sufficient cash reserves to withstand a run. George Meudell, who worked for various land-boom financial institutions and had a keen sense of the dangers ahead, kept a reserve of a thousand sovereigns in a safe deposit box against the day when the banks would close their doors. Foreshadowing Donald Horne seventy years later, he described Australia as 'a good country badly managed'.[28]

It is difficult to trace the labyrinthine financial dealings of these years, as finance companies, banks and building societies were formed and liquidated, assets and liabilities shifted among them, and bankruptcy courts avoided by secret compositions with debtors. And it was meant to be difficult, as a close-knit group of rich and powerful men kept each other afloat until times improved, as they fervently believed they soon would. If the public knew how shaky some of the grandly named institutions were, they told each other, it would only make things worse. Parliamentarians were prominent on the boards of directors, and most politicians speculated in land. Liberals, with their optimistic enthusiasm for development, were the most energetic.

After Deakin returned from London in 1887 as Australia's most
celebrated native son, he was invited to join the boards of various
companies. Not all were directly implicated in the land boom: namely
an engineering works in South Melbourne, Robison Bros., Campbell
& Sloss Ltd, which built locomotive engines, and the Union Trustee
Company, whose main business was the administration of deceased
estates. But four others proved to be short-lived boom-time companies
whose fortunes depended on the inflated value of real estate. All went
into voluntary liquidation in 1892 and 1893, two with Deakin still a
director.

Deakin skimmed lightly over his involvement in the land boom
and bust, with only this brief comment in his autobiographical notes:

> When with the rest I plunged into the boom losing all the money
> my father had available which he had confidingly placed at my
> disposal and having to face the long and bitter experience to repay
> it as I at last succeeded in doing to my mother and sister after his
> decease.[29]

The historian Geoffrey Serle declared him an innocent abroad, led
astray by his worldly friends Theodore Fink and Fred Derham; and
his commitment to repaying his debts has been taken as evidence of his
integrity and moral rectitude.[30] But Deakin was not just one of the herd.
He was the colony's former chief secretary, and a leading member of the
ministry whose investment in railways had fuelled the boom; he was
on the boards of four companies that went bust, taking many people's
savings besides his own and his father's; and when the prosecutions for
fraud started, he was back at the bar, working for the defence in some
of the pivotal prosecutions.

Confidence as much as credit was the currency of the boom, and
Deakin's prodigious capacity to inspire it was a valuable asset for companies touting for investments and deposits in Melbourne's crowded
financial sector. His name appeared on prospectuses and advertisements,
and his skills were used to chair meetings. And it worked. In 1893 Daniel

Jenkin, a Parkville cordial manufacturer, refused to pay calls on his thousand shares in the Australian City and Suburban Investment and Banking Company, of which Deakin was an inaugural chair, claiming that the original prospectus was fraudulent. The company brought an action against him. Asked in court what information he had relied on when deciding to invest, Jenkin replied, 'the guarantee of 8% for three years and the names on the prospectus, especially Mr. Deakin and Mr. Bell. They were then at the head of affairs, and I thought I may place my money with them.'[31]

Deakin was likely recommended onto the board by Theo Fink and his brother Benjamin, who was perhaps the biggest land-boomer of them all. Benjamin Fink went spectacularly bust in 1892, with debts of more than a million and a half pounds, and departed Melbourne for permanent self-imposed exile in London. In 1888 he and Deakin had gone together to see the fashionable new opera *Esmerelda*, about the heroine of Victor Hugo's *The Hunchback of Notre-Dame*, with a happy ending to suit the times.[32]

In 1886 Fred Derham had persuaded Deakin onto the inaugural board of the Australian Property and Investment Company. Derham was the chair, but the company lasted less than two years before being amalgamated with the Real Estate Bank, chaired by the premier, James Munro.[33] Deakin was also an inaugural director of the Union Finance Guarantee and Investment Company, invited by Robert Reid and William McLean, big men from the top end of Melbourne's commercial world. That company lasted till May 1892, when it went into voluntary liquidation, with Deakin still on the board. Shareholders raised questions about misleading balance sheets and special treatment of the director, the same Robert Reid.

At an acrimonious liquidation meeting shareholders learned they faced a call of £3.10s per share, a severe financial blow to the Deakin family. Alfred had three hundred shares, William two hundred and Catherine three hundred, which made for a combined liability of £2,800. This is likely one of the family debts Deakin repaid, taking responsibility for the calls as well as refunding the initial capital. Syme and Pearson, no doubt also persuaded into the company by Deakin, were also shareholders. Further calls followed: five shillings at the end of 1892, and fifteen in April 1893.[34]

Deakin's most direct involvement with the boom's crash landing was as chairman of the City of Melbourne Building Society. The society was founded in 1877 by Matthew Davies, fellow parliamentarian and since 1887 Speaker of the Assembly. When Deakin became chairman, it was just about to move into a new building on the corner of Elizabeth Street and Little Collins Street. The building is still there, at 112–118 Elizabeth Street, with its turrets and balconies and steeply pitched slate roof, the name of the once proud owner high on the side. It was a handsome building, but modest compared with the commercial palaces being built by other institutions, such as the Mercantile Bank of Australia in Collins Street, with its massive entrance arch and richly decorated banking chamber.[35]

By the end of 1891 the City of Melbourne Building Society was bleeding. Unlike many other financial institutions it was relatively well managed, with a very small amount of non-income-producing property, but it could not withstand a run and was headed for voluntary liquidation.[36] The directors decided to suspend payments on Saturday, 28 November, with Deakin to address a meeting of shareholders and depositors on the Monday. That night he prayed:

> Disaster has overtaken me at last O God! And upon me lies in some degree the responsibility for disaster to many others. Grant that it may be mitigated for them. It seems idle to pray for individuals or masses carried down in the sweep of events, and it seems selfish to pray for oneself.

Nevertheless, his mind raced ahead to personal implications: 'My capacity for public usefulness is diminished and my possibilities of literary work limited by this failure which appears to push me back into private life and professional drudgery…If I could understand I should be encouraged.'[37]

At the Monday meeting Deakin needed to maintain confidence, in order to buy time for the society to trade out of its difficulties. He summoned all his oratorical powers for the task and judged the meeting a 'Great Success'. So did the short-lived weekly *Bohemia*, which reported his astonishing feat of transforming panicked shareholders and depositors 'from a den of roaring lions to a nest of sucking doves', noting with heavy sarcasm that 'If we ever start a building society, and there is a possibility of it going bung, we will secure the services of Alfred Deakin as chairman.'

> Before the meeting began, the room was a seething sea of red-hot indignation, in which the wrath came up in bubbles. Deakin stood at the door, silent and possessed, as though he were the least important figure in the business. People who would have gladly shaken his hand a week ago…now walked past with head averted…When the chairman entered the room to take his place with the other directors, one or two endeavored to applaud, but a general scowl put an end to any demonstration of this sort. These people had come to wail and curse, not to applaud.
>
> Deakin got up and the hum ceased. His speech was a masterpiece. In a twinkle every man in the room was in possession of every fact relating to the society, and the appeal to their manhood. Nothing more stirring has ever been heard from a Melbourne platform. The look of anger passed away from clouded faces; men found themselves cheering where they expected to be hissing; women beat their parasols and squealed their approval. At that moment had Deakin asked for 20 years to realise, he would have got it. About a dozen wealthy men jumped up in different parts of the room and literally threw their deposits at his head…The directors had scored; the frightened bulls had been taken by the horns; mind had once more been victorious over matter.[38]

Liquidation was averted, but the society was still obliged to close its doors while a committee formulated a plan to restore liquidity. Depositors were urged to forgo their rights to withdraw when their terms ended. Deakin prayed for 'the wisdom and courage to temper the blow to those upon whom it is falling', and for calmness and confidence among all, 'so that our country may reap only good and useful lessons from its privations'.[39] But by April 1892 the society had still not reopened and in September it went into voluntary liquidation.

Deakin was mortified. He offered to resign from his directorship of the Union Trustee Company. His resignation was not accepted, the chairman replying that it rather 'increased that confidence and trust which has always been reposed in you'.[40] Adding to his personal humiliation, his father-in-law offered him a thousand pounds.[41] Pattie and Alfred were on better terms with the Brownes at this time, but still too proud to accept direct help. Advice was a different matter, and Deakin dined often with Browne at the Grand Hotel (now the Windsor) and talked money.[42]

From November 1891 till March 1892 building societies, land banks and finance companies tumbled like ninepins, taking with them the fortunes and reputations of some of Melbourne's leading citizens. Throughout the 1890s Maurice Brodzky's weekly *Table Talk* carried regular stories about company manipulations and irregularities. Deakin was not implicated in any frauds, and his investment losses were small beer: thousands, not hundreds of thousands, of pounds. He was never at risk of bankruptcy and he paid his calls. But men he knew well were involved in some of the boom's worst excesses: the Fink brothers and Fred Derham, for a start, and many of his parliamentary colleagues, including James Bell. The financial empires of the Speaker, Sir Matthew Davies, and of the premier, James Munro, both collapsed amid allegations of fraud.

Deakin later described Munro as 'a speculative plunger, at that time thought to be a sound financier'.[43] But the conduct of this staunch Sabbatarian, elder of the Toorak Presbyterian Church and fierce foe of the liquor trade, was far worse than Deakin's mild description acknowledged. When his companies were wound up it was found that to pay for his investments he had borrowed from the financial institutions he controlled, lent hundreds of thousands of investors' money with little security to his friends and family, and indulged in accounting tricks to make his companies appear solvent.

As financial disasters loomed, Munro's ministry moved to limit the damage to company directors. Late in 1891, just a few days after Deakin's

eloquence had gained the City of Melbourne Building Society some
time, the government rushed the Voluntary Liquidation Act through
both houses in a single day. The act's ostensible purpose was to protect
companies temporarily unable to pay their debts by preventing minority
shareholders from forcing a company into compulsory liquidation. But
it had other desired effects in Melbourne's financial house of cards, as it
became extremely difficult for creditors to wrest control of a company
from those who had wrecked it and force them into the courts where
their management could be scrutinised.[44] Munro took advantage of the
new act the day after it was passed. In February 1892 he handed the
premiership to Shiels and appointed himself Victoria's agent-general
in London, but a public outcry forced him to return to Melbourne to
face accusations of fraud.[45]

The Voluntary Liquidation Act enabled companies to wind up
their affairs quietly. Early in 1892 the ever-resourceful Theodore Fink
discovered a way for individuals to do the same. Fink was facing
bankruptcy, which would ruin his legal reputation and practice. An
obscure clause in the Victorian Insolvency Act provided a legal escape
hatch, allowing debtors to come to private arrangements with their
creditors in order to continue trading and preserve their reputations. So
long as three-quarters of the creditors present at a meeting agreed, the
meeting could force a composition onto the other creditors, no matter
what the conduct of the insolvent might have been.

All sorts of tricks were used to ensure compliant meetings, which
would enable the insolvent to avoid public exposure through the courts
and to walk away from his obligations, including calls on shares in other
companies. This uncalled capital simply vanished, hastening the collapse
of further companies into the maelstrom. Secret compositions, as they
became known, were widely used by the leading boomers, including
the Fink brothers and Fred Derham. A new verb was coined, 'to fink
it', and it became impossible for a bewildered public to know who was
solvent and who was not.[46]

During 1892 the law firm Fink, Phillips and Best organised most
of Melbourne's secret compositions: Theo Fink had discovered them,
was the first to make use of them and was now restoring his finances by

providing the legal services for others to do the same. For his partner
P. D. Phillips it caused such 'distress of mind…to be acting with Fink
whose want of all moral sense is particularly apparent in the present
time' that he dissolved the partnership. If Deakin had any qualms about
his old school friend's behaviour he did not record them. How much
he knew about the secret compositions of his associates is unclear, but
Fink's financial difficulties would have been obvious when in September
1892 he relinquished his house in Walsh Street to its mortgager.[47]

In March 1891 Syme had urged Deakin to return to office and join
Munro's ministry, but he was not interested.[48] Later that year Deakin
told Dilke that, although he could have organised a strong Liberal Party,
there would be little stability for some time to come. The bitterness
left by the strike, the stock tax and the depression had all combined
'to create a cross-sea which would be hard for anyone to weather', so
he would stand aside 'until the elements of the situation have resolved
themselves'. Should he take office again it would be 'on his own terms
and when there was a reasonable expectation of giving legislative effect
to his principles'.[49] A year later, in December 1892, he repeated these
sentiments to Charles Pearson, who had returned with his family to
London. He was 'determined not to accept office in this house until a
straight Liberal majority is secured, pledged to do work that will last
or that promises to last. On this rock I have built my resolve.'[50]

At the election in April 1892 Deakin had recontested and won his
seat. As a presage of things to come, however, he was opposed by a Trades
Hall candidate—a bootmaker, William Morris—who polled 1,040
votes to Deakin's 2,212. Indignant at the government's heavy-handed
response to the maritime strike, in 1891 the Trades Hall had organised
the Progressive Political League to support its candidates. The league
expressed an emerging working-class consciousness but as yet had
few policies to distinguish its candidates from the Liberals. Despite his
actions during the strike, Deakin was still viewed as an ally by some
at Trades Hall. He was invited to join the South Yarra branch of the
league, and he and Berry were both approached as potential candidates
for the April election, though both declined. Deakin endured some

rowdy election meetings, and was heckled about the maritime strike.[51] He wrote to Dilke that he was opposed by both the Labour League and the Conservatives, and thus had 'to fight for my seat against enemies from both extremes'.[52]

The election confirmed William Shiels as premier and Graham Berry returned to the ministry as treasurer. During 1892 Shiels struggled to reduce government expenditure and to find new sources of revenue. Dogged by the unfolding evidence of Munro's profligacy and fraud, he was only too happy in early 1893 to lose a no-confidence motion to James Patterson, the tough sixty-year-old ex-butcher who had been in the Assembly and the real-estate business for the past twenty years and had given Syme his favourable judgement on young Deakin's first appearance on the public platform. Patterson was completely out of his depth.[53]

In June 1892 Deakin had to front yet another failing enterprise, the irrigation settlement at Mildura. The market for fruit, then a luxury item, had shrunk with the depression; credit was hard to get; and channels were leaking over the settlers' land as yabbies riddled them with burrows. Aggrieved settlers who felt they had been lured to the settlement with false promises were refusing to pay the water rates due to the Chaffeys, hoping that if the brothers could be driven out the government would take over the settlement and give them free water.

Deakin was invited to visit and revive the settlers' optimism. He tried, addressing them for ninety minutes on the history of the scheme, talking up its prospects, and asking them to settle their differences 'in a reasonable English way'.[54] But, in what he later described as 'a situation of civil war', he failed. Acrimony increased and in 1893 the Chaffeys put their company into liquidation. Deakin's dream of a thriving irrigation settlement in the colony's north-west corner seemed doomed.

17

THE DEATH OF WILLIAM
AND RETURN TO THE LAW

BY THE WINTER of 1892 it was clear that William Deakin was dying. He was seventy-two, with the savings he had made to secure his and Sarah's old age sadly depleted by his faith in his son's advice. In October he transferred the title of the house in Adams Street and all his assets in the Mercantile Bank to Catherine, on the understanding that she would look after Sarah 'for the rest of her natural life'.[1] Caring for aged parents was the spinster's fate, and Catherine accepted it willingly.

William was cared for at home by Sarah and Catherine, with the assistance of a nurse, his pain eased with chloroform. Alfred prayed for him and called daily. On 21 December 1892 William said, 'it will not be long now'; and, later that day, 'Katie come and finish your job. Stupefy me.' Alfred arrived minutes after his father's last breath, and together the sister and brother 'made him ready for his last journey'.

Pattie was not well, and she and the children were at Flinders on Western Port Bay, staying with the Brownes. She did not attend the funeral, which was a quiet affair, with Sarah, Catherine, Alfred and

Dr Charles Strong of the Australian Church, who officiated. After the funeral Alfred had a long talk with Catherine about the future. Given the financial pressure Deakin was under, an amalgamation of the two households was an obvious economy, and Adams Street could be rented out to provide an income for Catherine and Sarah. Deakin told Catherine that Pattie was willing for her and Sarah to share their home. Catherine could scarcely believe it. She was right.

When she and Sarah went to Flinders a week or so later, although Pattie received them kindly she was vexed and out of sorts. Soon after they arrived, Alfred had to tell Catherine that, contrary to his assurances, Pattie did not want them at Llanarth. In fact, she had issued Deakin with an ultimatum: if Catherine came to live in their home, she, Pattie, would leave 'that day and forever'. The only cross words she ever had with Alfred were over Catherine.[2]

'So that is settled,' wrote Catherine. 'I suppose someday I will realise how thoroughly she dislikes me and my ways and has misunderstood my interest in herself and the children. All my life seems wasted and in the wrong.'[3] Poor Catherine. Exhausted from nursing her father, grieving his death, she was now subjected to a rejection she felt bitterly and that could have been avoided had her brother had more insight into the feelings of his wife and discussed his plans with her beforehand. But Deakin disliked conflict and was not prone to dwell on its causes. His diary entry for the day he broke Catherine's heart records only that he shot twenty-six rabbits.[4]

By the end of January 1893 he was ill. In February he prayed for mercy 'in failure, in backsliding, in coldness, in neglect, in surrender to evil, in selfishness, in sloth'. More prosaically, he told Josiah Royce: 'My health at present is indifferent and my purse low—below zero considerably.'[5] Catherine too was in poor health and turning to séances for comfort. On a stormy Sunday afternoon in April, Pattie and Alfred attended a séance at Adams Street with the medium Mrs Cohen, who was also a family friend and so well acquainted with the details of William's death.

Catherine recorded that Papa came, coughing and wheezing and asking for just 'a little sniff' to relieve his pain. He said he was happy, though would not feel quite at home till Mama joined him, and was pleased they were still in the old house so he had somewhere to visit; he had travelled a good deal and joined a club to study astronomy and visit the other planets. Various other relatives also appeared. Deakin does not mention this séance in his subsequent writings about spiritualism. The lonely Catherine attended a number of séances that year at which her father appeared, and on the night of her forty-third birthday she heard him tapping on her pillow.[6]

At the beginning of 1892 Deakin had returned to the law and set about the urgent task of repairing his finances. It was a reluctant acceptance of professional drudgery, compelled by his family obligations. A clichéd, sentimental story he wrote in May about a struggling artist 'compelled to sell himself…just to buy bread for his little ones' reveals its psychological costs. The story also reveals the disappointments of his marriage. The artist, Hans, had once been bright and full of prospects, and had he remained a bachelor he might still have been living 'the life to which he was born'. Coming home from work to his meagre supper and poor lodgings, he contemplates escape from the fetters of his life, and from his wife, Gretchen. After the passion of their courtship and the haze of the first year of love, he is now only too aware of her limited horizons.

There are parallels between Gretchen and Pattie which suggest some autobiographical pressure in this fantasy. Both knew little of housekeeping when first married, but applied themselves diligently and were now thoughtful and competent mothers and housekeepers; both were unintellectual, absorbed in home and children, and with little interest in metaphysical questions. Hans imagines another woman, wealth and fame in another life, the realisation of his true self, but when he faces up to the life to which he was consigning Gretchen and the children floods of tears wash the temptation away. Deakin first conceived this story early in 1891.[7] For more than a year, Hans' predicament was a melodramatic accompaniment to the burdens of domestic duty and the compromises of marriage.

Unlike Hans, however, Deakin prospered from his drudgery. Compared with his young days as a briefless barrister, he now had reputation and contacts. In 1892, his first year, he earned £674, double what he had hoped. It was mostly probate work, but there were a few opinions and a couple of trials.[8] With three hundred pounds from his backbencher's salary and some director's fees, his annual income was soon back in four figures; his taxable income for 1894 was £1,527.[9]

In April 1892 he defended the notorious serial murderer Frederick William Deeming, who was going by the name of Baron Swanston when he was arrested in Perth for the murder of his wife, whose decomposing body was found entombed in a rented house in the Melbourne suburb of Windsor. After the bodies of another wife and their four children were found similarly entombed in Liverpool, England, Deeming became a transnational sensation.

The public was transfixed, particularly after Deeming claimed to be Jack the Ripper, a claim that was almost certainly false. He also claimed to be insane, and Deakin argued this as best he could in his unsuccessful defence. Deeming was hanged on 23 May and a death mask made for the phrenologists. This was just a week after the Union Finance company had gone into liquidation, taking almost three thousand pounds of Deakin family capital with it.[10]

Over the next few years, the financial scandals created plenty of work for lawyers, and some of it flowed Deakin's way. Although the governments of both Munro and Shiels were reluctant to initiate proceedings against those involved, public outrage sometimes demanded action. In October 1892 an elderly Pentridge prison warder, John Hogan, wrote to William Shiels, who was now premier, to complain that he had deposited his life savings of nine hundred pounds with the Anglo-Australian Bank on the basis of misleading statements in the bank's balance sheets and lost it all. Shiels did nothing so Hogan went to the press, which published the allegations and forced the government's hand. Eighteen people associated with the bank were arrested and tried for issuing false reports and balance sheets.

Deakin defended the bank's chairman, Charles Staples, at his trial in March 1893, asking the jury, 'Who should go free in the city of Melbourne if rash and even reckless speculation were considered criminal? Who should escape gaol?' Who indeed? But speculation was not the crime—it was fraud—and Staples was given the maximum sentence of five years.[11] Despite the result the case did him good, Deakin told Pearson, launching him at the bar, where he was enjoying unprecedented success. He had been engaged for the two major cases of the year: the prosecution of directors of the Mercantile Bank, and the libel case of Speight versus Syme in which Richard Speight, the chairman of the Railways Commission who oversaw the expansion of the railways under the Gillies–Deakin government, sued David Syme and the *Age*. Deakin was to appear for Syme. 'Were it not for my load of debt,' he wrote to Pearson, 'I would feel quite easy now.'[12]

The Mercantile Bank trial brought the former Speaker Matthew Davies to the dock, defended by none other than Theodore Fink. Deakin defended another of the directors, his former ministerial colleague James Bell. Fraudulent practices had been revealed during the liquidation process in the second half of 1892. These had been courageously pursued by an outraged honest accountant, William Simpson, who had been appointed by the liquidators to a committee to examine the bank's affairs.

If not friends, Bell and Deakin were close associates. They had been fellow directors in the failed Australian City and Suburban Investment Company, and Bell had been minister for defence during the maritime strike. When proceedings against the directors began, Deakin raised a laugh by protesting that his client could not afford a long trial: 'The crown does not care, for it has the inexhaustible purse of an almost insolvent colony.'[13] The directors had not laid their heads together, said Deakin, but had accepted the word of their manager.

> What more could Mr Bell have done? Would any director in the world question a statement of others after receiving such an assurance from his officers and receiving the certificate of the auditors?…It was scarcely plausible that a man with a career behind him like Mr Bell was the sort of man likely to join in a conspiracy to deceive and defraud the public.[14]

Despite the conventions governing a barrister's role, there is something unsettling about Deakin's capacity to slough off the consequences of his previous roles and move on. It must have crossed his mind that, given his own financial naivety and the fate of the companies of which he had been a director, he could well have been in Bell's place. He too had trusted the managers and auditors. What more could he have done?

Deakin's defence of Bell succeeded and Bell was not committed to trial. Nor were the other defendants, except for Davies and the manager Millidge, and this only after a division of opinion among the magistrates. The case dragged on, despite heroic efforts by the solicitor-general, Isaac Isaacs, to see justice done, which saw him defy the premier, James Patterson. Outraged public opinion was on Isaacs' side, but his political colleagues were furious and the government did everything it could to prevent the trial. In his pen portrait of Isaacs in *The Federal Story* Deakin reports that he 'was not trusted or liked in the House,' but omits to mention Isaacs' efforts to bring Davies and Millidge to trial, as the colony's leaders closed ranks to save each other's reputations. Again he is expunging the scandals of the early 1890s from political memory.

For decades to come Melbourne's society was scarred by the scandals of these years, as stories of unpaid debts, undeserved ruin and lost wealth were passed down the generations of middle-class Melbourne. The early 1890s changed Melbourne from a flashy young metropolis of new money and grand buildings into the staid provincial town of the first half of the twentieth century.[15] Not until the 1980s and a new boom were the grand houses of the 1880s again filled with ostentatiously wealthy Melburnians. It too was followed by a bust, though nothing as severe as that of the early 1890s.

With so many parliamentarians also practising lawyers, and with backbenchers requiring other sources of income to support a middle-class life, conflicts of interest were barely perceptible in the winding-up of failed companies and the court cases that followed. Directors and managers became liquidators, and lawyer-parliamentarians who had themselves been directors of failed financial institutions defended their colleagues. It was like a game of musical chairs, and with the legal work flowing his way Deakin profited from it with no apparent qualms. The case in which this was most remarkable was Speight versus Syme. In the late 1880s and early 1890s the *Age* published a series of investigative articles into the management of the Railways Commission, revealing the influence of land-booming parliamentarians on its decisions and accusing Richard Speight of incompetence, extravagance and deceit.

Although David Syme could never pin down any actual corruption on Speight's part, he believed he had mismanaged the railways, and from early 1891 he campaigned to get rid of him. William Shiels, the minister for railways in the new Munro government and a critic of the extravagance of the publicly funded railways, began to rein in the power of the commissioners. In February 1892, when he became premier on Munro's resignation, he suspended the commissioners, who then resigned. They also issued writs for libel against the *Age*, each claiming twenty-five thousand pounds in damages. In his defence, Syme pleaded fair comment as a public journalist.

Syme's legal team was headed by James Purves QC, who was the acknowledged leader of the Victorian bar and a founding member of the ANA. Deakin was Purves's junior. The Great Railways Case, as it was known, ran from June 1893 until November 1895, when costs were decided and Speight's appeal for a retrial dismissed. After the first trial of ninety-eight days the jury awarded Speight damages of one hundred pounds; the second, after an appeal by Syme, awarded him a derisory farthing. Deakin worked hard on the case, collecting and making sense of masses of technical information. The *Argus* backed Speight, hoping no doubt to damage Syme. This gave Deakin an excuse to quiet whatever unease he may have had about Speight becoming a scapegoat for the profligacy of his and Gillies' government.

When the case finally ended Purves gave a dinner at the Athenaeum Club to celebrate David Syme's heroic stance against the mania of the boom and his epic fight for press freedom. Deakin also spoke at the dinner. The *Age*, he said, gave him his first insight into the condition of the railways and the abyss towards which the colony was heading. One wonders what he was doing when he was the minister for public works, or chairman of the engineering company Robison Bros., Campbell & Sloss Ltd when it won a contract to build locomotive engines for the

Victorian Railways. Presumably, as he had done with the various land companies, he believed what he was told and was in his political interest.

Further, he told the dining men, the contest was not as it might first appear, between a private citizen and a powerful newspaper proprietor, for behind Speight was 'every enemy of the *Age* and its policy and every enemy of Liberalism' who saw the case as a chance to ruin Syme.[16] This was rationalisation devoid of Deakin's usual moral scruples. The only doubts he expressed were to Charles Pearson, that the exposure of the mismanagement and reckless extravagance 'might risk the reputation of our Railways with English investors'.[17] The evening ended around midnight with the assembled men singing 'Auld Lang Syne'.

A month before the start of the Syme defence, on 1 May 1893, Deakin was defending James Bell in the large white room of Melbourne's Second Civil Court in Queen Street. The rest of the city was practically at a standstill after the government's surprise declaration of a five-day bank holiday. The rolling financial crises of the previous three years had finally reached the large trading banks, which shared the government's banking business. Six of the city's major trading banks had suspended operations in the previous two weeks and more suspensions were on the way.

Although these banks had not speculated in land themselves, they were exposed to individuals and financial institutions which had. British deposit holders were particularly shaken and were withdrawing their money. Rumours about which bank was safe swirled through the city as runs shifted from one institution to another and branch managers called for more sovereigns to pay those demanding their deposits in gold.

It was the worst financial crisis in Australia's history. The new premier, James Patterson, hoped the bank holiday would break the panic and give the banks time to restructure. Over six weeks, from early April to mid-May 1893, thirteen of Victoria's banks closed their doors. All but one had reopened by the end of August, but the damage was immense. Deposits were locked up and banks became extremely cautious about extending credit, which added to the general economic stagnation. Public confidence in the financial system was shattered and Australia's reputation abroad as a safe place to invest badly damaged.

An inexperienced government had panicked and made the crisis worse.

The New South Wales government took a different course, backing the banks and stopping the panic. Geoffrey Blainey argues that Victoria's bank crashes were far from inevitable. Personal insolvencies, liquidations, loss and hardship were unavoidable, but 'public confidence was the fickle goddess that ruled the situation' and panic turned depression into disaster.[18]

In early 1892 Charles Pearson had bemoaned Victoria's lack of capable leaders, noting that since Deakin refused to take office there was none but the old men to fall back on, the younger native-born parliamentarians being not yet of much standing.[19] Had Deakin been in government rather than on the backbench, had he agreed to lead the Liberals, would he have made a difference? Would his leadership have restored confidence more quickly and so lessened the length of the depression and softened the hardship? Could he have stilled the panic, as he had eighteen months previously with the City of Melbourne Building Society? We cannot know.

The more interesting biographical question is why, given the public's confidence in him, he didn't try. A psychological rather than a moral question, it suggests Deakin's floundering faith in his own capacities. To both Dilke and Pearson he wrote that he was staying out of office until he could be sure he could realise his liberal principles; to his God he confessed, 'I even dread the influence I seem to possess because uncertain of it being exercised for good and still more dread to increase my responsibilities, blind as I am how should I lead the blind.'[20]

Deakin did not take the leadership at this time because he did not have a clue about what could be done to restore the colony to financial and economic health, beyond the usual measures of public-service retrenchments and increased taxes. He was a champion of the spirit of progress when times were good, but he was not the man for a crisis. Like most other Victorians he saw the crisis as well-deserved punishment for greed and indulgence. Of the Day of Humiliation and Prayer called by the churches for 17 May 1893, he recorded the trite observation, 'humiliation at failing to make money & prayer to be able to make it in the future, when it ought to have been humiliation at the descent into selfish conscienceless greed and the prayer for higher ideals and pure living'.[21]

Deakin's solution to the gross failures of the material realm was to turn his attention away from the Real to the Ideal, which seemed to him manifest in the revival of interest in federation underway in 1893. Perhaps federation was the answer to his prayers to be shown the way ahead. Still, it was to be neither a straightforward nor well-lit path, and Deakin continued to be haunted by the events of the early 1890s.

At the end of 1893, holidaying with the Brownes in Flinders, he had a vision in the early dawn:

> It seemed as if I had died or my spirit been set free and soared up…a trumpet tongue pronounced my name and I stood erect for judgment, my eyes dazzled, my heart bowed but my head high and with courage in my shame. There was no need for speech but an irresistible tide of interrogation swept through me—the me of all my past—and in an instant I lived all my life again from childhood onward, followed with inconceivable rapidity into every crevice of desire, every turn of thought and every secret deed by the awful searchlight of an unfathomable flood of purity and trust. It was terrible in its revelations of pettiness, grossness and guilt and atom as I was I shrivelled like a dead leaf in a furnace of flame and crushed by an awful sense of failure, weakness and wickedness. But this was met by a reacting ebb of self-assertion that was almost pride…with tears of humility gushing from my eyes I suggested as in an unspoken reply that circumstances had made me what I was. Then from the height above me descended an ineffable pity…What wonder that as drifting down to my body I awoke my eyes and cheeks were wet.[22]

18

MIDLIFE

AT THE BEGINNING of 1893, as Melbourne struggled with the aftermath of the boom, the movement for federation was stuck, mired in parliamentarians' caution, intercolonial rivalries and popular indifference. At the 1891 convention in Sydney it had been agreed that the participating governments, which included New Zealand, would submit the draft constitution to their parliaments for endorsement. But New Zealand had withdrawn; Western Australia, South Australia and Tasmania were waiting to see what the big colonies would do; Queensland was waiting on decisive action from New South Wales; and New South Wales, where many had serious misgivings about federation, was dithering through the dying days of Henry Parkes' last premiership. And Deakin's judgement that 'Victoria alone and as usual fulfilled her obligations' somewhat overstated the colony's commitment.[1]

The draft constitution bill was debated and amended in both Victoria's houses, but the legislative process remained unfinished as cascading financial disasters overwhelmed the colony and discredited the parliament. The *Age* and the Trades Hall attacked the bill as undemocratic, demanding that it enshrine the principle of one-man-one-vote, which meant rejecting the proposed equal representation of all states in the Senate. Radicals were especially alarmed at a nominee upper house, with members chosen by state governments, as happened in the United States at the time.

In February 1893, at the inaugural meeting of the South Yarra branch of the ANA, Purves argued that federation was a chance to redeem the reputation of the Australian colonies in the eyes of London. This appeal to mundane material interests spurred Deakin to oratorical overreach when his turn came to rise to his feet and rouse the crowd. Federation was not just a practical arrangement, but 'the one ideal worth living, working and if necessary dying for'. As his local paper wryly observed, 'We don't know that he is doing anything extraordinary to prove that it is worth living for, to say nothing of going into heroics and dying for it.'[2] Oratory alone would not move things forward. Organisation was needed, and a plan.

In Victoria the young men of the ANA were the drivers of federation, organising public meetings to build enthusiasm. They were Deakin's special constituency, the group he represented not just in his policies and values but in his very being. He was their man in public life, who reflected back to them the special destiny of the native born for the nation's future and whom he could always rely on for a rapturous welcome. Every political leader who becomes iconic has such a special group: Robert Menzies' forgotten people, Gough Whitlam's baby boomers, John Howard's battlers. Identification with the experience of the group nurtures the leader's sense of purpose, and its support secures his place in history.

Victoria was the ANA's base, but for federation to succeed New South Wales had to come on board and support be built beyond the ranks of the native born. At the banquet at the annual conference at Kyneton in March, Deakin urged the ANA to establish a federal organisation open to all.[3] Similar moves were afoot in New South Wales. Edmund Barton had taken over the leadership of the federation movement in the colony from the ailing and aged Parkes. And federation leagues were forming in the towns along the Murray River, where bridges with customs houses at both ends were constant reminders of the need for action.

At the end of July a conference was convened at Corowa, a small New South Wales town west of Albury in rich pastoral country where, just a few years before, Tom Roberts had painted *Shearing the Rams*. The Corowa conference was an unofficial gathering of supporters of federation from Victoria and New South Wales, together with a few more sceptical delegates from the new labour parties. Deakin did not attend, as he and Purves were engaged in their other double act of Speight versus Syme. It was the only crucial moment in the progress towards federation that Deakin missed.

John Quick from the Bendigo ANA had come to Corowa with a plan that would shift the federation movement from the parliaments to the people. Voters in each colony would elect representatives to a convention, which would determine a federal constitution bill, which would then be submitted to referenda. To make sure that all this actually happened, Quick proposed that each colony map out the whole process in legislation. This was a stroke of practical political genius, creating a clear and manageable path to the final judgement of the people.[4] Federationists could now start mobilising support for the forthcoming popular votes. The conference also called for the formation of a central federation league in Melbourne to bring together the various groups working towards federation and provide a forum for discussions of the draft constitution.[5]

Deakin had two great political gifts: his oratory and his charm. He could bring a public meeting to its feet, and in private he could talk away doubts and negotiate a compromise. Both were acts of persuasion, the one exercised on halls full of people, the other face to face; one to excite enthusiasm, the other to find common ground. He brought both these gifts to the hard work of achieving federation. He also brought himself, the brilliant native-born man whose upright and independent public persona embodied the spirit of the emerging nation. The bush legend was still in the making: the sun-bronzed, laconic, unruly shearers and drovers had not yet captured the national imagination. Deakin was the harbinger of a different Australia that was metropolitan, urbane and sophisticated, and he could hold his own on the world stage.

Although Victoria was the colony keenest for federation, there was much to settle. Business groups wanted a customs union to precede political union. The Trades Hall would only support a federation based on one-man-one-vote, which would be unacceptable to the smaller colonies. Republicans hoped federation would be a prelude to separation from Britain, which was unthinkable to loyal colonists aspiring to unity under the crown. And people with no work and little money had more pressing concerns. Victoria in 1893 was, Deakin told Pearson, sunk deep in the Slough of Despond.[6]

In mid-December 1893 Deakin chaired a meeting in the supper room of the Melbourne Town Hall convened by the ANA. He asked speakers to reflect on the obstacles to federation and how to overcome them. For himself, 'long ago he had made up his own mind that no question should be put second to federation. From either the local or national standpoint…the best remedy that could be applied to all the ills, political, social and financial, from which Australia was suffering would be immediate federation.'[7]

In June the following year the ANA convened another meeting, this time in the main body of the Town Hall, with Deakin again in the chair. The proposal to form a federation league was the main agenda item and most of Melbourne's opinion leaders were present, together with representatives from thirty-four political organisations: trade, commerce, labour, agriculture, professional associations, and the full gamut of political clubs and leagues. The only exclusions, Deakin told the meeting, were organisations 'of a religious character', to prevent sectarian discord from disrupting a league for all classes and creeds.

But there was another exclusion—women. No representatives had been invited from the vigorous Women's Christian Temperance Union, the recently formed United Council for Women's Suffrage, nor from the professional associations of women teachers and public servants. It is not an absence Deakin ever commented on. Although he supported women getting the vote, he never really saw them as political agents, or imagined them on the public stage.

The meeting was a great success. The league was formed and Deakin became chair of its constitutional committee, which took on the task of seeking out and overcoming the obstacles to federation, and devising compromises between antagonistic parties and interests.[8] For the next six years, his main political goal was the achievement of federation.

Early in June 1894 Deakin learned that Charles Pearson had died in London of pneumonia. Pearson had returned to London with his family in August 1892 to take up the position of secretary to the Victorian agent-general. It was a well-paid post and Pearson needed the money after his losses in the crash. He thought it was permanent but in January, James Patterson, an old political rival, gave him notice. The doctor had advised Pearson, who had weak lungs, to winter in the Riviera, but this was now out of the question. He could not afford it. Pearson's wife, Edith, was understandably bitter, writing to Deakin that the way he was treated 'in the end literally killed him'.[9] I can find no record of Deakin's response, but for his friend and colleague to have been so pettily and vengefully discarded after his long and dedicated service to Victoria would surely have confirmed his decision to stand aside from the struggles for office.

In August 1894 the Patterson ministry lost a no-confidence motion. Munro, Shiels and Patterson had all been premiers of coalition ministries, with a revolving door of Liberals and Conservatives in the key portfolios. Their most urgent task was to restore the government's finances, and they pursued various measures such as public-service retrenchments and salary cuts, and increases in customs duties and the price of postage, none of which really worked. Patterson's budget in July was a disaster. The *Age* delivered its judgement: he was a nincompoop and had to go.[10]

The no-confidence motion was moved by the Liberal George Turner, who had just replaced Shiels as leader of the Opposition. Patterson called an election and was thrashed, thirty seats to the Liberals' sixty-five, with fourteen new Labor members. Deakin was returned comfortably, but the rise of Labor's vote was an ominous warning to middle-class Liberals in working-class seats that their days were numbered.

In this election, however, Deakin's main opponent was a young conservative, a local man from a well-known brewing firm and a retired Essendon footballer. People wanted new blood, he said, criticising Deakin for inaction. Deakin's policy speech to his electors was strong on condemnation of the government's 'reckless, frivolous, criminal indolence', of 'the blunder budget' of 1893 and 'the burlesque budget' of 1894, but it had few remedies for the problems overwhelming the colony and said nothing about unemployment and little about federation.[11] According to one political journalist, his public reputation was losing its shine: 'It is impossible to disguise the fact that the honourable Alfred has, to a large extent, lost caste with former supporters. Brilliant oratorical critic as he is, people fail to find in his address anything that will help the colony out of her troubles.'[12]

The most telling criticism of him was his failure to take the helm of the ship of state, when everyone knew he could have been the one to lead the electoral campaign against the government, and could now be premier, instead of the dull and workmanlike Turner. As premier he would have led Victoria in the negotiations with the other colonies over federation. The short-lived bohemian weekly the *Free Lance*, under the heading 'The Decadent Deakin', observed:

Since Turner has taken the position that should have been occupied by Deakin if he had fulfilled the promise of his youth and his sponsor the *Age*...Deakin has been little more than the echo of his own promised future...He has let I dare not wait upon I would. He has been all things to all men. He has very nearly missed the bus.[13]

The election had returned a Liberal majority, the best since 1877, so a coalition would not be necessary, but Deakin would not even join the ministry. Why not? To some he pleaded 'the opinion of his medical advisers'. The *Argus* reported that he was reluctant to relinquish his position at the bar, the same reason he had given for declining the leadership of the Opposition some weeks earlier. *Table Talk* suggested it was 'the chagrin of having refused the Premiership. As Chief Secretary or Attorney General his abilities would have served the country, though his ambition might have been disappointed.'[13] The only area of public service Deakin seemed committed to was federation, and his continual refusal of office raised his personal stake in the outcome, for if federation failed he would have little to show for the decade apart from the restoration of his family's finances.

The next step towards federation was to be the premiers' conference in late January 1895, to discuss giving effect to the Corowa plan. This was the initiative of the new free-trade premier of New South Wales, George Reid, who later claimed that he had picked federation out of the gutter and set it on the path to success.[15] Reid called the conference to coincide with a meeting in Hobart of the largely ineffectual Federal Council, of which Deakin was still a member. The initiative was now with the premiers, so although Deakin addressed the Hobart ANA and met with various public men he had ample time for sightseeing and sea bathing.[15]

Apart from John Forrest of Western Australia, the premiers all agreed to push ahead with the Corowa plan and put enabling bills to their parliaments to authorise its key steps: the popular election of delegates to the constitutional convention and the referenda on the draft constitution. And the premiers added another step. Before it was put to the people, the draft constitution bill was to be referred to the parliaments to give them a chance to propose amendments.

Victoria's new premier, George Turner, was native born, a member of the ANA and committed to federation, so the path ahead was to be relatively smooth in Victoria. Deakin, who might himself have been Victoria's first native-born premier, was sidelined by a hard-working suburban solicitor, described by an *Age* journalist as a quiet 'little man in the shabby brown suit and cheap spectacles', whose commitment to consensus was to restore the government's finances and the colony's confidence.[17]

But if Deakin would not govern, he could write, and his portrait of Turner in *The Federal Story* drips with snobbish condescension: 'Turner was the ideal bourgeois who married early and who was in dress, manner and habits exactly on the same level as the shopkeepers and prosperous artisans who were his ratepayers and constituents.' He went on, as a speaker Turner was plain, commonplace, with no oratorical flights or polished rhetoric. He had no hobbies, no amusements, no diversions, no enthusiasms and no vices. He never read a book and his politics were expedient, with no theoretical basis.[18]

Deakin did not feel sidelined. At the end of his manuscript on 'The Crisis in Victorian Politics', which he wrote in 1900, Deakin left a brief note: had he continued the manuscript, it would have shown 'How I helped defeat the Shiels government [1892–93] and more than anyone did defeat the Patterson Government [1893–94], and made and sustained that of Turner [1894–99]'. Most contemporaries thought that if anyone was pulling the strings of these governments it was David Syme; in a claim to rival Deakin's, Syme boasted to his first biographer, Ambrose Pratt, that, had he kept a diary, it would have shown how every ministry was made and 'been a complete secret inner history of Victoria'.[19]

Deakin was devoted to the federal cause throughout the 1890s, but it only needed him some of the time. He spent the middle years of the decade at his legal practice and pursuing his lifelong search for spiritual enlightenment. Around 1895 he wrote a long manuscript on his personal experiences of spiritualism in which he reviewed the evidence and considered possible explanations for various paranormal phenomena. He was now sceptical about the authenticity of his own experiences of mediumistic speaking and writing which, he judged, were 'just such as I would have delivered myself had I possessed the courage to speak upon such subjects without nervousness and without special preparation'.[20]

On many other remarkable phenomena he kept an open mind. As with his séance diary, this manuscript shows just how seriously Deakin took the paranormal and his abiding interest in the fate of the soul at death. He never completely repudiated the spiritualism of his youth. He continued to attended lectures given by visiting spiritualists, as well as the occasional séance, and he was always alert to mysterious noises about the house.[21] He concluded, however, that as a religion spiritualism was no longer making progress. It had created 'the mood of respectful critical expectant attention of the scientific study of the occult...with a view to the spiritual unfoldment of the spiritual forms lying latent in humanity…Beyond that it appears unable to go.'[22]

So he was looking elsewhere, including to theosophy, which had been founded in 1875 in New York by dissatisfied spiritualists. Theosophy accepted as genuine many spiritualist phenomena, but put forward different explanations derived from the ancient religions of the East. Its first treatise, Madame Blavatsky's *Isis Unveiled: A Master-Key to the Mysteries of Ancient and Modern Science and Theology*, appeared in 1877. William Terry stocked it in his bookshop and Deakin read it in 1878.[23]

Deakin's fascination with the wisdom of the East was already evident in 1877 in *The New Pilgrim's Progress* and he developed an abiding interest in eastern religions, giving occasional public lectures on Hinduism, Buddhism and the Koran.[24] In 1891 Madame Blavatsky's offsider, Colonel Henry Steel Olcott, visited Australia from India, where the theosophists were now based. Deakin met with him privately and chaired his lecture on Buddhism as a rational religion for free thinkers.[25]

The Australian colonies were on the international circuit for religious speakers, and in 1894 the celebrated orator Annie Besant visited. Besant had moved from her earlier socialism to theosophy. In a flowing white satin gown she spoke for an hour without a note, calmly, clearly and sincerely, of the spiritual malaise of a morally enfeebled and materialist age. Although he was in the middle of the election campaign which ended the Patterson government, Deakin managed to hear one of her five Melbourne lectures and to have a private audience. He also hosted the founding meeting of a new theosophical lodge at Llanarth and became its first secretary. His membership of the Theosophical Society only lasted a year, and the day he resigned in 1896 he formally joined the congregation of Charles Strong's Australian Church in Flinders Street.[26]

Deakin was already attending regularly, often with Ivy, sometimes with Catherine and occasionally with Pattie. He was an active member for the rest of the decade. Apart from his year with the Theosophical Society, this was Deakin's only membership of a religious congregation since the Victorian Association of Progressive Spiritualists in his youth and it shows the maturing of his religious life. It is not clear when Deakin first met Strong, who had officiated at his father's funeral at the end of

1892, but he would certainly have known of him long before. Strong was a liberal martyr, the centre of a religious *cause célèbre* who had been driven from his pulpit by accusations of heresy. Deakin may well have first met him in spiritualist circles, as Strong occasionally attended séances and was interested in psychical research. In a curious coincidence, in January 1880 they both sought advice from the phrenologist Professor Hamilton, who advised Strong that he needed to be more combative.

Strong had come from Glasgow with his family in 1875 to take up the ministry of the Scots Church, where the pride of Melbourne's Presbyterian elect worshipped. His liberal theological views soon attracted a broad congregation to his Sunday sermons, but they gravely offended his orthodox clerical colleagues, causing much friction. Eventually the hard men of the Westminster Confession accused him of heresy and forced him from the ministry. The press, the public and many Presbyterians regarded Strong's treatment as a travesty of justice. A new congregation of religious liberals gathered around him, forming the Australian Church in November 1885 and inviting him to be its minister. They built him a large new church in neoclassical style with seating for twelve hundred and a magnificent organ, now in Melbourne University's Wilson Hall.[27]

The Australian Church was non-dogmatic, committed to the worship of God, the preaching of the gospel of Jesus Christ, and the religious life of Faith, Hope and Love, but free from creeds and legislated ecclesiastical forms. There was no trinity, no virgin birth, no predestination, no salvation of the elect, no hell and eternal punishment, no original sin, no atonement and redemption, no seven-day Creation, none of the obstacles to faith which stood between many progressive nineteenth-century people and the God they longed for. Spiritualism, unitarianism, theosophy, transcendentalism and Swedenborgianism all sought to salvage and protect what each regarded as the core truths of Christianity from the battering waves of materialism and secularism.[28] Deakin sampled them all. For a time he found in the Australian Church a congenial spiritual home, more theologically orthodox than his notorious spiritualism, and with stronger links to his political life.

For Strong, the essence of Christianity was to be found in the Jesus of the Sermon on the Mount and his commandment to 'love thy neighbour as thyself', rather than in the drama of sin and redemption of Jesus on the cross. The focus of the Christian life was not salvation in the next world but the creation of the Kingdom of God on earth in a society based on freedom, justice, compassion, charity and reconciliation. Social, economic and political reform, Strong preached, was thus proper work for Christians.[29]

As the depression of the early 1890s deepened, Strong denounced capitalist greed and supported various schemes to alleviate the suffering of the poor. With the Reverend Horace Tucker of Christ Church, South Yarra (father of Father Gerard Tucker, who founded the Brotherhood of St Laurence) he promoted a scheme to settle the unemployed in the country. They solicited support from Deakin who, despite his general sympathy, had grave doubts about its practicality, which turned out to be well founded as the settlements were undercapitalised and soon collapsed.[30]

Strong provided Deakin with a far more productive and less self-focussed bridge between his spiritual and political lives than the mediums' prophecies of political destiny, grounding his response to the emerging class politics in charitable humanitarian sympathy. During these middle years of the 1890s Deakin gave a number of public talks on the issues of the day which show his political thinking increasingly moving to religious rhythms. 'Am I my brother's keeper?' was the title of a Sunday-afternoon address at the Malvern Congregational Church in June 1894. It posited the development of the individual consciences that make up society as the key to progressive social change. Melbourne *Punch* published a cartoon on 'The Evolution of Deakin from Pressman to Politician to Preacher'.[31]

Under the influence of Carlyle, Deakin had already rejected the soulless individuals of utilitarianism and classical political economy. This rejection was being given vigorous life in the 1890s by the writings of the late T. H. Green, the Oxford moral philosopher whose think-ing shaped the new social liberalism of the late nineteenth and early twentieth centuries. Green challenged classical laissez-faire liberalism's preoccupation with protecting individuals from interference from the state. All citizens deserved the opportunity to develop their God-given potential, he argued, and where they were unable to do this the state should assist; and Christianity should focus on the problems of this world rather than salvation in the next. Strong had been taught at Glasgow University by a close associate of Green, the theologian John Caird.[32]

Social liberalism found fertile ground in Australia, where colonial liberals already embraced a far wider role for the state than in Britain. With the depression bringing old-world poverty and suffering to Australia, colonial liberals were looking for new directions. In March 1895 Deakin gave a talk to the Hawthorn Liberal Association titled 'What is Liberalism?' He outlined the usual genealogy of the fight for civil, legal and political rights, from the Magna Carta to the extension of the franchise, noting that female suffrage and one-man-one-vote were still to be achieved. The future of liberalism, however, was in what he called its 'reconstructive element':

> Liberalism would now inculcate a new teaching with regard to the poorest in the community, that all should have what was their due. By fixing a minimum rate of wages and wise factory legislation, wealth would be prevented from taking unfair advantage of the needy, and the latter would be saved from leading wretched and imperfect lives.[33]

In the middle of 1895 Deakin became the treasurer of the newly formed Anti-Sweating League, which aimed to awaken the public conscience to the evils of long hours of work in poor conditions for pitiful pay, and convince of the need for the state to protect the helpless workers. The league's immediate object was to strengthen the 1885 Factory Act, and its main focus was on women working in the garment industry in sweatshops and as outworkers. A secondary target was Chinese-run factories, particularly furniture makers.

The league's sentimental slogan, 'The union of all who love in the service of all who suffer', shows its origins in middle-class pity and shame. It was a thoroughly Protestant affair. The president was a Congregational minister; Charles Strong was a vice-president; and the secretary, Samuel Mauger, a devout and teetotal hatter, was also a Congregationalist. Although Trades Hall was supportive, it was more interested in achieving conciliation and arbitration for union members than improving the pay and working conditions of non-unionised women and Chinese.[34]

Arousing the public conscience was Deakin's metier and he spoke passionately in parliament and at public meetings about the sacrifices of the many enabling the few to live in ease: 'Let them see that the clothes they wore and the bread they ate did not come to them stained with the blood from the martyrdom of the toiling masses.'[35] His audience was always the beneficiaries of sweating as customers or employers, never the exploited workers themselves. Change would come from awakened middle-class conscience, not aroused working-class anger, as he called for the state to protect the 'thousands of helpless, honest, hopeless, half-starved women' from being thrust further into misery by human harpies.

This alliterative litany was delivered to a packed meeting at the Melbourne Town Hall in April 1896. The Legislative Assembly had passed a revised Factory Bill the previous December and sent it to the Council, which, true to form, had returned it with amendments to weaken its impact. Deakin called for the original legislation to be passed unamended: 'a living thing, into which the breath of life has been breathed by the people of Victoria', it will not die at the hands of the Council, he said.

This was rhetorical overreach, even for Deakin. When, midway through his address, Deakin made some mildly favourable remarks about Sir Frederick Sargood, the Conservative leader of the Council, there were loud cries of disagreement. Then, according to the observer from the *Free Lance*, he changed tack, working himself

> into a red hot fury against the Council with an excited pantomime of arms and legs. He did this once without drawing cheer. Then he did it again, this time with the help of a book that he shied at the water bottle on the Chairman's table. Then he sat down amidst the cheers.[36]

Just as long ago at Barry's Reef, when he changed course to protect the natty electoral agent, we glimpse here Deakin's extemporary oratory, adjusting itself to the response of the crowd, and we glimpse too his dependence on its cheers. Deakin excelled at the emotional peroration, the climax to which he built with argument and image, capturing his listeners with the grace of his eloquence, then carrying them to the heights with the irresistible onrush of his words. This was the goal of the performance, the merging of orator and audience in a standing ovation that took both out of themselves in their dedication to a higher purpose.

Deakin's performative self had a manic energy. Observing him during the campaign for federation in Queensland, where anti-federal feeling was strong, the Liberal politician Anthony St Ledger remembers his first impression: 'There was a nervous feverish pulse in his manner, which was reflected in his speech. "That man never rests," I said to myself, "nor ever will rest!"'[37] Until he hears the crowd's cheers, and quietly leaves the platform.

The meeting's indignant response to his defence of Sargood had hit a nerve. Sargood claimed that one of the amendments had in fact been suggested by Deakin while they were lunching. Deakin defended himself vigorously, as he always did when his version of events was challenged, but whoever was right, as the *Colac Herald* noted, 'Common people ask why Deakin was lunching with Sargood. Vacillation and compromise have dogged Deakin too long.'[38] Sargood defended the actions of the Legislative Council in a long letter to the *Argus*, to which Deakin in turn responded in a bitter speech to the Assembly in which he denounced the Council for mutilating the bill, as it had previous factory bills.[39]

Deakin's was the sole voice urging the Assembly to send the original bill back to the Council. The Council had accepted a great deal, and the resulting act, which established wages boards in key industries, was an international landmark in the regulation of wages and conditions of work. The impulse of the legislation was to protect minors and helpless women, but in a world first it was extended to adult men. Deakin was out of step and his speech was uncharacteristically bad-tempered.[40] Alexander Peacock was the chief secretary; George Turner was the

premier. However much Deakin might have itched to take on the
Council, it was not his call. Perhaps, too, he was protesting his sympathy
for the workers a little too loudly in order to deflect long-standing doubts
about his vacillating sympathies with the big end of town.

Almost certainly, he was tired and feeling beleaguered. His speech
on the Factory Bill was made late at night after a very long day, and
his health was troubling him, as was Pattie's. He was making weekly
visits to Mr J. C. Eugen, a magnetic healer and clairvoyant, and having
frequent 'bad nights'.[41] As well, the problems at Mildura were again in
the public eye. The Chaffey brothers' company was bankrupt and the
liquidator's report revealed that it had been seriously undercapitalised
from the outset.

The *Argus* blamed Deakin as the minister responsible for the
establishment of the settlement: 'his lack of business acumen', 'his
crass ignorance of the ways of the world', 'his aerated oratory' and
'the gush, the glamour and the cheap enthusiasm with which he had
deceived himself and then others', especially trusting settlers lured from
England with their small capital and high hopes. Deakin was stung by
'the vindictive assertions with which you have freely bespattered me',
and complained that the field of combat had been enlarged to include
the Factory Bill and his dispute with Sargood. He defended himself
in three letters to the editor on consecutive days. 'For years you have
pursued me in my public career with bitter hostility,' he wrote, and
offered to testify at the royal commission into the Mildura settlement
which was about to begin.[42]

The commission ran through the middle months of 1896, and
Deakin appeared in July. He argued in his defence that problems had
only emerged after 1890 when he was no longer in government, and
that the Chaffeys had overstretched themselves by taking on a scheme
at Renmark for the South Australian government. Defending the
government's initial decision, he remained optimistic about the future
of the Mildura settlement, particularly if a railway could be built to get
the settlers' fruit to market. He also believed that although the settlers
had no legal claim on the government, they did have a moral claim, as
the government had encouraged their settlement.[43] As W. K. Hancock

wrote of the origins of Australian paternalism, 'the settlers, remembering that the government had put them there, not infrequently imagine that it has in some way or other accepted an obligation to keep them there.'[44]

Deakin's testimony to the commission and that of the American Stephen Cureton, who undertook much of the original negotiation for the Chaffeys, cleared Deakin's name of any suggestion that he had been soft on the Chaffeys. Quite the contrary, said Cureton: the terms were far less favourable than they had expected and Mr Deakin was 'as firm as the base of the Rock of Ages' in protecting the colony's interests.[45] Still, Cureton's testimony did not really address the effect of Deakin's 'aerated oratory' in promoting a scheme that had lured many into financial hardship. Nor did it assuage Deakin's profound inner disappointment at the scheme's failure.

Deakin liked to begin his day with something to open up the lungs and get the blood racing—chopping wood, skipping backwards, playing hockey with the children. If he was in the country, he would cut scrub or go for a bracing horse ride. Most weekday mornings he would walk the four kilometres or so from Llanarth into town. After the cycling craze hit in the mid-1890s he would cycle.

The inventions of the chain-driven safety bicycle, the pneumatic tyre and the diamond-shaped frame had transformed bicycles from dangerous and uncomfortable bone-shakers into serviceable means of personal transport. Deakin took lessons, bought a bicycle and rode it at every opportunity: to parliament, to Adams Street, to St Kilda and Port Melbourne, to the cemetery on Sundays to visit William's grave. As he became more confident he would go on long excursions down the bay. He also bought a bicycle for Ivy, and most Sundays she rode with him. Bicycles gave unprecedented mobility to women, and Catherine was soon cycling too, but not Pattie.[46] Cycling became another of Deakin's activities that she did not share and it replaced their Sunday strolls.

Deakin made few diary entries about Pattie in the 1890s. Mostly he recorded her poor health, but did note her occasional sketching trips to Melbourne's outskirts. She rarely accompanied him to social events, and only occasionally on his visits to his sister and mother in Adams

Street. Relations between the households were cool and a startling poem written in May 1894, when he was relinquishing the leadership of the Opposition to William Shiels, suggests that his marriage was causing Deakin a good deal of silent pain. The poem came to him while he was in a condition of emptiness, prompted he thought by Coleridge's lines on estrangement 'like cliffs which had been rent asunder'.

> We stood together, yet apart,
> Blood warmth the only warmth remaining,
> A million leagues from heart to heart
> While lip to lip kept closely straining.
> O my first love that this should be
> The crown of our sad Calvary
> Since nailed to wedlock's wooden cross
> The gain of all our lives is—loss.[47]

Pattie was spending a good deal of time in bed. In July, after his own sixth visit to the clairvoyant and magnetic healer Mr Eugen, Deakin took Pattie and they went together, twice a week, for a further seven visits. Eugen promised to cure all chronic and constitutional diseases without the use of any medicine, to give clairvoyant diagnoses, and to answer any question while under control of a spirit. Nothing was gained and Deakin did not pay for the last two visits. Pattie's health continued to be poor, with Deakin praying often for 'my dearest wife's recovery of health'.[48]

A few months earlier, in February 1896, Pattie's parents had moved into the property a few doors down Walsh Street once owned by Theodore Fink and now called Ventnor. Deakin's diary records frequent comings and goings between the households, but there was also tension. In mid-August there was a 'storm and settlement' with the Brownes.[49] In the continuing conflict between Pattie and her parents, Deakin was loyal to his wife. Two years later he wrote to Catherine of a new bout of strife. 'HJB came up last night and interviewed me in bed with the familiar explanation that it has all been a misunderstanding. I refuse to have this put upon Pattie's shoulders—further attempts at

understanding with them is hopeless—so just have to let the breach
pass like its predecessors.'[50]

In these difficult middle years of the 1890s Deakin and Pattie discovered Point Lonsdale, the small settlement on the western head of Port
Phillip Bay overlooking the narrow entrance known as the Rip. Rather
than staying with the Brownes at Flinders, they began to spend the
summer on the other side of the bay, with Deakin going up and down
to town on the Queenscliff steamer and Pattie and the children staying
until well into February. The first cottage they rented, Utopia, a small
double-fronted weatherboard house, is still there, in Cheshunt Street.
Later, they built a house of their own, Ballara, which also still stands.

For Pattie and Alfred, Point Lonsdale became a special family place
where they could spend time with each other and their children and
Deakin could relax. For him it provided the peace to read and write,
but also opportunities to swim and ride, indulge his boyish sense of fun
and enjoy the children's amateur theatricals.

19

'THE TIMES THAT TRY MEN'S SOULS'

THE COROWA PLAN was for popular elections of candidates to a convention which would design the constitution. The enabling bill passed the
Victorian parliament early in 1896, though only after vigorous lobbying
to get it through the Council in which Deakin's conciliatory skills were
deployed to the full. The election for delegates was held early in March
1897 on the principle of one-man-one-vote.

Deakin stood on a ticket supported by the *Age* and won third spot
out of the ten, after George Turner and John Quick. The *Age* held
such sway in the colony that all ten candidates on its suggested ticket
were elected, Liberals and democrats to a man, with no one to speak
for conservative Victorians' distrust of the powers of lower houses. Five
delegates—Deakin, Turner, Quick, Isaac Isaacs and Henry Bournes
Higgins—were active members of the ANA. Only one, Billy Trenwith,
was a labour man and trade unionist.

Deakin was the only Victorian who had been at the 1891 convention
in Sydney and before that at the 1890 Melbourne conference. He knew

well the arguments and sensitivities that would shape the debates, and had already tested the mettle of many of the delegates from the other colonies. His staunchest ally was Edmund Barton, who now led the cause in New South Wales. At the end of March 1897 Deakin packed his new bicycle on the train to Adelaide, where the conference delegates were to meet, ten from each colony except for Queensland, where commitment to federation was weak and a vigorous movement to create a new colony in North Queensland was preoccupying the Brisbane-based government. For much of the time Deakin stayed at the seaside resort of Largs Bay, so he could begin each day with a sea bath and either cycle the fourteen kilometres into the South Australian parliament, where the convention sat, or catch the train.

With a break at Easter, the convention lasted till early May, when deliberations were halted so that the premiers could visit London for the jubilee of Queen Victoria. As the premier of the host colony, Charles Kingston was the president, but in Deakin's eyes Barton was the leader. He chaired the committee drafting the constitutional machinery and the distribution of powers and functions, and so had to steer its various clauses through the convention, negotiating the amendments, anticipating stand-offs and seeking resolutions which would survive the referenda. Deakin was filled with admiration for Barton's tact and skill and his gift for conciliation.

Determined to do everything in his power to achieve federation, in his first speech to the convention Deakin declared:

> Were it a question today…of accepting the Commonwealth Bill or postponing Federation even for a few years, I should, without hesitation, accept the Commonwealth Bill…It is perhaps possible for us to fail altogether in our high aim, and we may easily fall short of its final achievement; yet it is certain to be long before such another opportunity can present itself…Political opportunities of this sort if missed rarely return again in the same generation.

The speech concluded with one of Deakin's classic perorations:

> The Constitution we seek to prepare is worthy of any and every sacrifice, for it is no ordinary measure, and must exercise no short-lived influence, since it preludes the advent of a nation. Awed as I feel by the fact that we come from, that we speak to, and that we act for a great constituency, awed as I feel in the presence of those who sent us here, I am more awed by the thought of the constituency which is not visible, but which awaits the results of our labours—we are the trustees for posterity for the unborn millions, unknown and unnumbered—whose aspirations we may help them to fulfil and whose destinies we may assist to determine.[1]

The public gallery erupted in applause, prompting Kingston to call for order to be maintained, 'however eloquent the provocation'. A few days later Deakin prayed, 'Subordinate the personal, the selfish, the aggressive, the obstinate in us that we may fulfil thy larger purpose. For myself O God obliterate me thoroughly, shut myself and my interests from my sight, or consciousness, in my surrender to Thy Will as thine instrument.'[2] Deakin had come to the convention not as a representative of Victorian interests, nor even as an advocate of democracy, but as a facilitator of destiny.

The big problem was how to resolve the democratic demand for majority rule, being assertively pushed by George Reid, with the small states' fears of being swamped by New South Wales and Victoria. As the constitution would go to referenda in both the most and the least populous states, a resolution acceptable to all was necessary. The conflict centred on the role of the Senate, which would have an equal number of delegates from each state. Democrats had already won a great victory in that the Senate would be elected by popular vote rather than by the state parliaments, but its powers were contentious. New South Wales would not accept a Senate that could veto majority decisions of the House of Representatives and the Victorians too were wary, given the long history of conflict between their two houses.

Further, Reid argued that as two-thirds of the future Commonwealth's revenue would come from Victoria and New South Wales, the lower house must control the government's finances. South Australia,

Tasmania and Western Australia would not accept a toothless Senate, and if they voted together would win every time. If the Senate won control over money bills, New South Wales would withdraw and the federation would be doomed for the foreseeable future.

So Deakin turned his persuasive powers on federationists from the small colonies. On a trip to Broken Hill he, along with two other Victorians, persuaded three Tasmanians to support a compromise, 'that they must be content to allow the Senate to make suggestions and not amendments in money bills unless they wished to shipwreck the whole Bill'. The limitation of the Senate's money powers passed by a single vote and the bill was saved—though, Deakin noted grudgingly, it was without the slightest effort from Mr Reid and his ministerial colleagues.[3]

Time and again during the debates Deakin argued that the fears of the small states were unfounded. The lines of division in the Senate would not be between the less and more populous states, but between two parties, which would be

> divided by the line of 'More progress and faster' and 'Less progress and slower', in other words Liberals and Conservatives...We shall have party government and party contests...alliances will be among men of similar opinions, and will be in no way influenced by their residency in one State or another.

Deakin also argued that the endurance of state sovereignty did not depend on the Senate's approval of federal laws but on the division of powers in the constitution. It was, he said, the constitution and the High Court rather than the Senate which would be the real, effective guarantors of states' rights, with most of the federal government's actions having no effect on state interests.[4]

Deakin's first prediction was prescient, but the second was to prove overly optimistic. Optimism was one of Deakin's great gifts which he urged the delegates to share. When the convention reconvened in Sydney in September 1897, Deakin warned during the debate on how to resolve deadlocks that by continually dwelling on what is likely to be a very rare occurrence 'we are apt to overload our imaginations, to overcharge our apprehensions, and to arouse an unnecessary amount of heat.'[5]

In October, Deakin had to pause in his work for federation to fight the Victorian election. Many members were returned unopposed. With his prominence in the convention Deakin might have expected to be too, but he was challenged by Cornelius Bishop, a glassmaker and former president of the Trades Hall Council, who campaigned hard against him as both a traitor and an absentee member: 'no man could represent the working class who was not a worker…nor could any man represent a labour district properly who lived elsewhere, say, in some fashionable suburb.' Bishop wondered how many electors ever saw their member between election campaigns. Deakin's majority was slashed to fewer than four hundred votes.[6]

The coincidence of the birth of the new Commonwealth of Australia with the start of a new century can invest federation with retrospective inevitability. But this is not how it looked to Deakin as federation's fortunes ebbed and flowed on the 'cross currents of provincialism'. When it was all over and the Australian constitution an act of the British parliament, he reflected that 'if ever anything ought to be styled providential, it is the extraordinary combination of circumstances, persons and most intricate interrelations' which led to federation. To those who followed its fortunes 'as if their own, and lived the life of devotion to it day by day, its actual accomplishment must always appear to have been secured by a series of miracles'.[7]

These are the concluding words of Deakin's own account of this series of miracles. On Saturday, 12 March 1898, at the close of the third session of the convention, in Melbourne, when 'under conditions of great nervous exhaustion and irritability, we [had] practically completed the draft bill', he began to write what he called 'The Inner History of the Federal Cause: 1880–1900'. This was published posthumously in 1944, when most of its protagonists were dead and unable to argue with Deakin's vivid prose.

The outer history, he wrote, would be covered by the official documents and records of debates; his inner history would tell of the way 'individual idiosyncrasies, attractions and repulsions' shaped the constitution that was offered to the Australian people. Written in the third person, the narrative distances Deakin the political actor from its author. Nevertheless, some of Deakin's own prejudices break through, in particular his loathing of George Reid. Here is how he describes him:

> Even caricature has been unable to travesty his extraordinary appearance, his immense, unwieldly, jelly-like stomach, always threatening to break his waistband, his little legs apparently bowed under the weight to the verge of their endurance, his thick neck rising behind his ears rounding to his many folded chin. His protuberant blue eyes were expressionless until roused or half hidden in cunning, a blond complexion and infantile breadth of baldness gave him an air of insolent juvenility. He walked with a staggering roll like that of a sailor, helping himself as he went by resting on the backs of chairs as if he were reminiscent of some far-off arboreal ancestor…He never slept in a public gathering more than a moment or two, being quickly awakened by his own snore…His extreme fatness appeared to induce this state and for that his self-indulgence was chiefly responsible since he denied himself nothing that he fancied, sucking ice or sweetmeats between meals and eating and drinking according to his fancy.[8]

Deakin also wrote memorably about Henry Parkes constantly adjusting himself to his own idea of the great man, but, for all Parkes' faults, in the end Deakin allowed him a visionary nobility. Deakin gave Reid no saving graces and no excuses. Reid was the antithesis of the abstemious Deakin, who kept himself fit and trim and never ate between meals. The animal imagery is the giveaway: arms swinging like an ape, or rollicking 'as a hippopotamus might if he had climbed into a ferry boat and was determined to upset it unless given his own way'.[9]

Allowing his physical repulsion to blind him to the political difficulties Reid faced in winning support for federation in New South Wales, Deakin slid far too easily from Reid's physical to his moral turpitude. There was widespread opposition in New South Wales to the equal representation of the smaller colonies in the Senate, as it departed from both the conventions of responsible government and the commitment to majority rule; hence Reid's determination to limit the Senate's powers over money bills. If the equal representation of minnows like Tasmania and Western Australia was the price of federation, many in New South Wales thought it was too high. Did federation have to include the entire continent? Perhaps Tasmania could be merged with Victoria?[10]

And always there was the question of trade, with the free-traders fearing that the new federal parliament would be protectionist. The historian John Hirst gives a very different assessment of Reid's contribution to federation from Deakin. It was 'a magnificent political achievement', for which he could take much credit as the leader of a colony divided on the issue who ultimately carried federation against considerable opposition from his party.[11]

Deakin's federation hero was Edmund Barton, 'solid, sober, studious…heart and soul devoted to his task, always at his post, and treated with the most marked respect and admiration by all his colleagues', with 'the laurels of leadership' upon his brow.[12] When Barton and Deakin had first met, at the 1891 convention, Deakin had thought him a little weak. He contrasted his fine forehead, intellectual, well-balanced head and 'eyes of remarkable beauty and expression, glowing like jewels in the ardour of his inspiration', with his fish-like mouth and large jaw, 'pointing not only to strength of will but love of ease and indulgence'.[13]

Barton was too fond of good living for Deakin, but his portrait of him is affectionate compared with his grotesque caricature of Reid. By 1897 Barton had proven himself a true federationist. His leadership of the federation leagues and his speeches up and down the country had kept the federal flame alight in New South Wales, and he had chaired the three sessions of the 1897–98 convention with skill and tact. 'Than ourselves there are no two public men in Australia who have been drawn together by a stronger bond of sympathy in the cause of Australian union,' Barton wrote to Deakin as they congratulated each other on their service to the cause.[14] At the celebratory banquet after the successful second referendum, Deakin singled out the sacrifices Edmund Barton had made for Australia as dwarfing all others.[15]

The final session of the convention was held in Melbourne over six searingly hot summer weeks early in 1898. South Gippsland was on fire, with 1 February dubbed Red Tuesday for its unprecedented ferocity. Smoke hung over the city and invaded the chamber of the Legislative Assembly, testing the tempers of the weary, sweating men. Still unresolved was the question of money. The draft constitution gave the Commonwealth the power to collect customs and excise, which was an important source of revenue for state treasuries, and electors feared the costs of another layer of government. Already the vertical fiscal imbalance that still dogs Commonwealth–state financial relations was apparent.

A solution was suggested by the premier of Tasmania, Edward Braddon: that the Commonwealth return three-quarters of the customs and excise revenue to the states, which was agreed to. Deakin had earlier argued for a similar guarantee of fixed revenue to the states, which appalled the free-traders from New South Wales, who feared the upward pressure this would put on customs revenue. They dubbed it the Braddon Blot and it was later limited to the first ten years after federation.[16]

Prospects for success at the forthcoming referenda did not look good. The premiers of the two major colonies were not yet prepared to endorse the constitution, Western Australia would not vote on the bill until it had been adopted in the east, and Queensland was not yet part of the process. Only the South Australian and Tasmanian delegations were united in support, as these small colonies had more to gain than lose.[17]

Deakin could not do much about the situation in New South Wales, but he could try to save the bill in Victoria. The Age was poised to oppose it as undemocratic, injurious to Victorian interests and likely to lead to lower tariffs. Deakin believed that parochial self-interest was also at play and that the paper feared its loss of influence in the new Commonwealth. Deakin judged that if the Age opposed the bill, then Turner would follow. He was not an ardent federationist, and depended heavily on the support of the Age to retain office. There were also other voices arguing for delay. Isaac Isaacs, the attorney-general, and the radical Liberal Henry Bournes Higgins both opposed it on democratic grounds, as did Victoria's labour representative at the convention, Billy Trenwith.

A powerful countervailing force was needed. The ANA annual conference was meeting in Bendigo in the final days of the convention, and Deakin was due to speak at its banquet on Tuesday, 15 March 1898. The day before, he was called to a meeting at the *Age* with David Syme and his senior editors, Arthur Windsor and Benjamin Hoare. Syme told him that the *Age* was against the bill, and tried to persuade him to 'use his influence to moderate the ANA's enthusiasm'. The *Age* did not support 'federation at any cost', but it suspected Deakin did. By the time Deakin arrived at Bendigo's Shamrock Hotel for the banquet, the ANA had already declared for the bill with three rousing cheers. He spoke last, after Higgins and Isaacs, whose arguments for delay had met a hostile reception.[18]

Delivered without notes, this was the supreme oratorical feat of Deakin's life, his gift used not to prop up a failing building society or win an election, but to create a nation.

> MEMBERS OF THE A.N.A.—We have heard much tonight of politicians and a good deal from them. We have also heard something of the Federal Convention and addresses from some of my fellow-members; but it is in neither capacity that I propose to speak, because I recognise that the united Australia yet to be can only come to be with the consent of and by the efforts of the Australian-born. I propose to speak to Australians simply as an Australian.
>
> You are entitled to reckon among the greatest of all your achievements the Federal Convention just closing. The idea of such a Convention may be said to have sprung up among you, and it is by your efforts that it must be brought to fruition. One-half of the representatives constituting that Convention are Australian-born. The President of the Convention, the Leader of the Convention, the Chairman of Committees and the whole of the drafting committee are Australians. It remains for their fellow-countrymen to secure the adoption of their work.

We should find no difficulty in apprehending the somewhat dubious mood of many of our critics. A federal constitution is the last and final product of political intellect and constructive ingenuity; it represents the highest development of the possibilities of self-government among peoples scattered over a large area. To frame such a constitution is a great task for any body of men. Yet I venture to submit that among all the federal constitutions of the world you will look in vain for one as broad in its popular base, as liberal in its working principles, as generous in its aim, as this measure. So far as I am concerned, that suffices me. Like my friends, I would if I could have secured something still nearer to my own ideals. But for the present, as we must choose, let us gladly accept it.

I fail to share the optimistic views of those to whom the early adoption of union is a matter of indifference. Our work is not that of an individual artist aiming at his life's achievement, which he would rather destroy than accept while it seemed imperfect. What we have to ask ourselves is whether we can afford indefinite delay. Do we lose nothing by a continuance of the separation between state and state? Do not every year and every month exact from us the toll of severance? Do not we find ourselves hampered in commerce, restricted in influence, weakened in prestige, because we are jarring atoms instead of a united organism? Is it because we are so supremely satisfied with our local constitutions and present powers of development that we hesitate to make any change?

...At a time like the present this association cannot forget its watchword—Federation—or its character, which has never been provincial. It has never been a Victorian, but always an Australian Association. Its hour has now come. Still, recognising the quarter from which attacks have already begun, and other quarters from which they are threatening, we must admit that the prospects of union are gloomier now in Victoria than for years past. The number actually against us is probably greater than ever; the timorous and passive will be induced to fall away; the forces against us are arrayed under capable chiefs. But few as we may be, and weak by comparison, it will be the greater glory, whether we succeed or fail. 'These are the times that try men's souls.' The classes may resist us; the masses may be inert; politicians may falter; our leaders may sound the retreat. But it is not a time to surrender. Let us nail our standard to the mast. Let us stand shoulder to shoulder in defence of the enlightened liberalism of the constitution. Let us recognise that we live in an unstable era, and that, if we fail in the hour of crisis, we may never be able to recall our lost national opportunities. At no period during the past hundred years has the situation of the great empire to which we belong been more serious. From the far east and the far west alike we behold menaces and antagonisms. We cannot evade, we must meet them. Hypercriticism cannot help us to outface the future, nor can we hope to if we remain disunited. Happily, your voice is for immediate and absolute union.

One word more. This after all is only the beginning of our labours. The 150 delegates who leave this Conference, returning to their homes in all parts of this colony to report its proceedings, will, I trust, go back each of them filled with zeal and bearing the fiery-cross of Federation. Every branch should be stimulated into action, until, without resorting to any but legitimate means, without any attempt at intimidation, without taking advantage of sectionalism, but in the purest and broadest spirit of Australian unity, all your members unite to awaken this colony to its duty, thus making Victoria move from end to end with the warm life blood of Federation. You must realise that upon you, and perhaps upon you alone, will rest the responsibility of organising and carrying on this campaign. The greater the odds the greater the honour.

This cause dignifies every one of its servants and all efforts that are made in its behalf. The contest in which you are about to engage is one in which it is a privilege to be enrolled. It lifts your labours to the loftiest political levels, where they may be inspired with the purest patriotic passion for national life and being. Remember the stirring appeal of the young poet of genius, so recently lost to us in Bendigo, and whose grave is not yet green in your midst. His dying lips warned us of our present need and future duty, and pointed us to the true Australian goal—

> Our country's garment
> With hands unfilial we have basely rent,
> With petty variance our souls are spent,
> And ancient kinship under foot is trod:
> O let us rise, united, penitent,
> And be one people—mighty, serving God![19]

As one body, the natives rose to their feet, yelling and cheering and waving their handkerchiefs. Deakin was the mirror for their idealism. In him they saw their best and noblest selves; together they would stare down the doubters and prevaricators and make history.

The pathos of the closing poem was a masterstroke. Its author, thirty-two-year-old William Gay, whom Deakin knew through the Australian Church, had died of tuberculosis just months before in Bendigo.[20] Gay could not be said to have died for the cause, but with his poem Deakin invited death to the banquet table, reminding all there of the transience of life and rousing them to embrace their historic moment which might never come again.

The result was as the *Age* had feared. The ANA conference had been like 'a new baptism when the disciples of Jesus were filled with the holy spirit', and the natives went back to their branches enthusiastic to mobilise the Yes campaign.[21] With operating branches across the colony, in all the major regional towns and suburbs, the ANA had a formidable organisational base.

The weeks between the end of the convention and the Victorian referendum in early June were frenetic. Deakin was inundated with invitations from ANA branches to address meetings, and he accepted as many as was physically possible, often four or five a week. He hoped popular enthusiasm would scare Turner and the *Age* away from a campaign against the bill, but he was also active behind the scenes bringing pressure to bear. The first to be converted was Turner. Several MPs, including Theodore Fink, were members of the ANA and they let Turner know that for them the bill was a test question. Should he come out against it, they would withdraw their support for his government.

In April, on a public platform shared with Deakin, Turner declared that he would support the bill. The *Age* took longer, but in late May, after Deakin had met with Syme and been invited to draft a leader, it too declared for the bill.[22] There was a No campaign, not arguing against federation in principle, but urging delay to get a more democratic deal. Higgins persisted stubbornly with his opposition, though Isaacs swung into line behind the government.

Polling day was Friday, 3 June 1898. That night Deakin stood in the cold with the crowd outside the *Argus* office in Collins Street watching the results come in. People sang 'God Save the Queen' and cheered as Victoria embraced the bill: Ballarat, 3,350 Yes and 116 No; Geelong, which Higgins represented, 2,306 Yes, 491 No; Hawthorn, 2,047 Yes, 237 No; and so on.

It was a different story in New South Wales, where the majority of parliamentarians opposed the bill and Reid had prevaricated. In his infamous 'Yes–No' speech, Reid had cogently set out all the arguments against, only to conclude: 'I consider my duty to Australia demands me to record a vote in favour of the Bill.' The speech was delivered on 28 March, just after the conclusion of the convention, to a packed Sydney Town Hall. Barton felt betrayed and Deakin saw further evidence of Reid's cunning and self-interest. The New South Wales Legislative Council had insisted on eighty thousand Yes votes for the referendum to succeed, which was more than a simple majority, but there were only 71,595, so the bill was lost.

The game was not yet over, however. Next day Reid sent the other premiers a telegram suggesting a conference of premiers to amend the bill to make it more acceptable to New South Wales. Federationists were furious with Reid, whom they regarded as a saboteur. They were reluctant to allow him to become the saviour of the bill, but they could not easily oppose him when he was offering a way forward. Reid hoped to have his amendments agreed to before the New South Wales election, at the end of July, but not all the premiers would agree to meet. Such was Barton's distrust of Reid that during his consultation with Deakin over Reid's invitation, he provided him with a code for their telegrams, 'to obfuscate any spy Reid may have in the telegraph office'.[23]

Barton was in a difficult position. If he supported the current draft constitution at the forthcoming election while Reid put forward an amended bill, such was the ambivalence in New South Wales about federation that Reid would undoubtedly prevail. Reluctantly, Barton negotiated amendments with Reid that both could support: the abolition of the Braddon Blot, two-fifths majority at a joint sitting and the capital in New South Wales. Reid won the election narrowly, leaving him reliant on Labor for support. Barton failed to gain a seat, though he subsequently won a by-election when a member resigned in his favour. He became the leader of the Opposition.[24]

The premiers' conference to discuss Reid's amendments was held in Melbourne in closed meetings from 29 January to 3 February 1899. Deakin urged Turner to co-operate with Reid, suggesting to him a compromise on the location of the capital, that although in New South Wales it be at least a hundred square miles in size and a hundred miles from Sydney. The premiers agreed to an amended bill to be put to the people at a second referendum. Queensland was now on board, though not yet Western Australia.[25]

Once again Deakin took to the campaign trail, and this time the referendum succeeded in all the participating colonies, with Victoria returning an even larger majority. Deakin believed that the risks to the bill had increased patriotic feeling. On the eve of the second vote, in late July 1899, as torchlight processions marched down Swanston Street and up Bourke Street to Fitzroy and Collingwood, Deakin addressed a final meeting in the Melbourne Town Hall. As usual he spoke last, delivering a federation oration, which in the opinion of the *Argus* had never been equalled for fervour and eloquence:

> When Australia raises its flag it would be the flag of a united nation and not even a Colonial Secretary in Her Majesty's Imperial Government would venture to pull it down...The swinging of this globe is bringing us nearer to tomorrow's dawn. When its sunlight silvers the vast panorama of this continent and the richly jewelled islands that lie within its seas, it shall shine upon a territory by which the act you will then perform and the solemn compact in

to which you will then enter will be bound once and forever in a united Commonwealth, an indissoluble union, everlasting and strong—into an Australia—one and indivisible.[26]

Deakin's special gift was to create the future Australian Commonwealth as an object worthy of sacrifice and devotion, elevating it above sectional and parochial interests, and appealing to the idea of the nation which had captured the nineteenth-century western political imagination: that a people united by territory, history, religion, race and culture should be joined under a political rule to which they consented. Barton's catchcry, 'A nation for a continent', had unfurled the territory, and Deakin's final images of the swinging globe and the sun silvering the land imbued the coming federation with cosmic significance.

Liberal nationalism has an inherent contradiction. It speaks of the universal values of liberty and brotherhood, but it applies them to particular populations. Deakin was well aware of the contradiction: his prayer would be 'wide as thy Universe…it would embrace all living things', 'were not this to render it pointless and featureless', and so he narrowed his focus 'to my kind, to my race, to my nation, to my blood, and to myself, last and least'.[27] A couple of years later he prayed for blessings 'for my wife and children, family, country, nation, race and universe'.[28]

Nations are inherently limited. Without invisible bonds of sympathy, they could not exist, Deakin told a Pleasant Sunday Afternoon at Malvern's Independent Church, pointing to the dissolution of the great Chinese empire. With those in different parts of the country strangers to each other, 'the Chinese are not and never have been a nation.'[29] Deakin knew that the nation was, in Benedict Anderson's memorable phrase, 'an imagined community', and the task of his oratory was to lift his listeners from the petty and provincial to feel part of something higher, greater and more unified, even though this fell well short of universal brotherhood.

The butchery of World War One and the horrors of fascism had not yet fully revealed nationalism's capacity to mobilise people for evil. It was axiomatic to Deakin that more unified was morally superior to less, and closer to the Ideal. Under Strong's influence, the religious sensibility which saturated Deakin's political thinking had become more overtly Christian, as in this prayer on the night of the first referendum, in June 1898:

> Aid us to purify ourselves by our labours for the general weal and to invoke spiritual and moral principles so as to link us with our brothers on the highest plane to which we can at present attain… Thy blessing has rested on us here yesterday and we pray that it may be the means of creating and fostering throughout Australia a Christlike citizenship.[30]

20

LONDON, 1900

IN AUGUST 1899 Herbert Brookes, the bereaved son-in-law of Charles Strong, came to Deakin for help. A fair young man of thirty-one, he had been married to Strong's daughter Jenny for less than a year when she died suddenly, and he was lost in the blackest grief: 'the heart of Life is taken clear away from me and my interest is in the other world where my angel lover shines like a star,' he wrote in a letter to his dead wife to be sealed in a tin box with a piece of their wedding cake.[1] Deakin already knew Brookes a little through Strong and the Australian Church, and Strong now asked Deakin to try to ease his son-in-law's distress.[2]

Deakin, eleven years older than Herbert, responded immediately. Since he and Fred Derham had drifted apart in the early 1890s, Deakin had no male friend whom he loved, and he took Brookes immediately into his heart:

> I have no son and the difference in age is not great enough to justify the feeling but when I did lay my hands upon your shoulders it

was with just such an overwhelming feeling with and for you as
I should have had if you had been my son—If you will come to
me on that footing my home is always open to you and I shall
welcome you as sincerely as a father or elder brother...I even
hope that I have found a friend—a very rare experience for me.[3]

A comment in Brookes' first letter suggests that, in their first meeting,
Deakin too bared a little of his soul: 'If ever you think of things you
have done that you are sorry for (and I take it you do from the visions
you told me of), first think too of the friendly human hand you pressed
on a poor weak being's shoulder.'[4]

Deakin was a man of sentiment, very different from Brookes' father,
who had never known his own father nor made a pal of his sons. William
Brookes had come to the goldfields as an eighteen-year-old, making his
fortune through inventiveness and shrewd investments. By the 1890s
he was wealthy and enjoying the life of a gentleman, with a mansion
in Queens Road opposite the Albert Park Lake, and several pastoral
properties. His youngest son, Norman, who learned tennis on the family
court, became the first non-British player to win at Wimbledon and an
Australian sporting hero. Herbert, the eldest surviving son, recoiled
from his father's leisured life and his conservative politics. He was an
earnest young man whose desire to serve God in the world had drawn
him to the social gospel work of Charles Strong.[5] He was working as
an assistant mine manager at an alluvial goldmine near Creswick when
his beloved Jenny died. His grief nearly sent him mad.

The two men exchanged letters over the next weeks and months.
Deakin advised him on remedies for his 'soul paralysis' and Brookes
reported on the slow progress of his return to life. They also exchanged
books. Deakin sent him *Sartor Resartus*, and addressed him playfully as
Dr Teufelsdröckh Junior. Brookes sent him his annotated copy of the
sermons of the renowned American preacher Phillips Brooks.

The intimacy of the notes made Deakin 'shrink, as if I were intruding
on a soliloquy...How enraptured she must be to realise the depths of
your tenderness and fidelity—but grieved to see you so pained.' Brookes
must now accept his destiny, and not let his gifts lie idle, 'for His sake,

for hers and for your own'.[6] Deakin developed such a strong sense of
Jenny that he felt she was talking through him.

> I am not superstitious nor am I what is called 'a medium'—but I
> have an impressionable inner sensitiveness which is a great stay
> to my faith at times. Recently in connection with yourself I have
> been feeling like a man using the telephone for his own purposes
> [who] is…compelled to overhear…a message which is being sent
> at the same time from someone else to some other person along the
> line. Some invisible voice full of love tenderness pity and courage
> has been calling you in my hearing. I can only surmise it is your
> wife, or someone speaking for her. Whoever it is does not speak
> to or through me but is trying very earnestly and devotedly to
> speak to you.[7]

One could read this passage as evidence of Deakin's continuing belief in
communication from beyond the grave, or as revealing his extraordinary
capacity for sympathetic introjection as he takes another man's pain
into his heart.

The letters to Brookes also reveal Deakin's own strategies for tackling
inner adversity. Deakin had not known the despair of black grief, but he
did know the sense of futility which drains life of its purposeful energy:
'you must take hold of yourself with both hands and live according to
your conscience. You have duties to your wife, your family, your country
and yourself—and in that order.' Deakin chides him, too, for the touches
of black humour in his letters because it is 'the bitter fruit of pessimistic
doubt written in the Mephistophelean vein…by the spirit that denies
and in denying withers.' Faith was the recommended antidote: 'Faith
is no gift from the gods—it is a growth of oneself, only to be secured
by patient cultivation—such as has cost me twenty years labour.'[8]

Under Deakin's guidance Brookes was soon reading *Sartor Resartus*
and skipping in the fresh air of a morning. When in town he was visiting
Llanarth. Before his first visit, Deakin advised him what to expect of
his daughters: 'They see very few visitors, and make very few calls and
friendships, I hope they will retain their simplicity.' Their upbringing

was following the pattern Deakin laid down in his 1890 Testament of a serious, wholesome, home-centred life.

The girls' day started with vigorous exercise, and a breakfast of oatmeal porridge (without sugar), fruit, toast and the occasional raw egg yolk. Then they went to Adams Street, where Catherine taught them every morning until their early teens, when they went to school. Their father, Vera remembered, was 'a strict disciplinarian'. He never slapped or spanked them, but nor did he praise them. He asked Brookes to refrain from implying 'admiration of anything they say or do that appeals to you and talk to them as if they are sensible pupils and point out their errors to them as a matter of course'.[9]

When Brookes first met the girls, whom he called the 'Trinity', Ivy was sixteen and at a nearby private school, Stella was thirteen, and Vera almost eight.[10] Ivy was Deakin's favourite. Except when ill, neither Stella nor Vera appear in his diary. Ivy is there often, cycling with him to Port Melbourne or the cemetery, accompanying him to the Australian Church on Sundays. He taught her to shoot, recording her first rabbit with a father's pride, as well as her first musical evening and her first party.[11]

Stella is the greatest favourite with visitors, he told Brookes, but she suffers in some respects in comparison with her sisters.[12] Likely she was chafing at the restrictions of the secluded life Deakin had imposed on his daughters. A city of refuge for men could become a cage for women. Even as a young child, she had resented it. Deakin wrote to Catherine from Sydney in 1891 that 'Stella says she wishes she was a man, for then she would leave Pattie at home with the children and go out and enjoy herself. She gets brighter and more audacious as she grows.'[13] But as she grew, she came to be perceived as the difficult one of the three, particularly later when she wanted to pursue a career.[14]

Early in 1900, while the family was holidaying at Dromana, Deakin received news that the new premier, Allan McLean, wanted him to go to London as Victoria's representative while the constitution bill was being debated in the British parliament. McLean had been premier only a few months, following Turner's loss of a no-confidence motion, and he lasted only till the election at the end of the year. It was quickly decided that they would all go, Pattie, the girls and Catherine, leaving late January for a four-month trip. The Brownes, who were keen for Pattie to see Europe, paid the fares for her and the girls.[15] Deakin invited Brookes to come with them, as he thought it would do him good.

Pattie, who was a bad sailor, spent the journey in her cabin, and Brookes was sunk in depression. The girls played deck cricket and quoits with their father, and Ivy played at a ship-board concert. The party left the ship in Italy and travelled up through France to London, with Brookes as the 'baggage man', their route repeating Deakin's grand tour of 1887: Naples, Pompeii, Rome, Florence, Marseilles, Paris, London.

In London they stayed at a private hotel in South Kensington, with a flat roof so that Deakin could skip in the early morning before disappearing into his day of meetings, luncheons, dinners and banquets. Pattie was too unwell to accompany him on most social engagements, even to the official reception at Windsor Castle for the delegates and their wives, though a private visit for the family was later arranged. As well, Vera remembered that 'Father believed in her being with her children.' While in London, they sought specialist medical advice from the gynaecologist Arthur Lewers on Pattie's condition and an operation was advised, most likely a hysterectomy, which, to her later regret, they decided against. The family hardly saw Alfred, though he planned their itinerary, which included all the main sites and plenty of theatre and opera.[16]

In this city of theatres, wrote Deakin, was to be played out 'the last scene of the last act which closed the contests of ten years with a last wrestle against no less antagonists than the British Government in general and its most capable negotiator, Mr Chamberlain, in particular'. For him it was a return to the stage of his 1887 triumph, and something of a repeat performance. The colonies regarded the bill they had brought to London as final, approved by the people and not to be amended. The colonial secretary, Joseph Chamberlain, once the radical Liberal mayor of Birmingham, wanted amendments. Salisbury was still the prime minister, now leading a coalition government after the Liberal

Party had split over Home Rule for Ireland and Liberal Unionists had allied themselves with the Conservatives to oppose it.

In *The Federal Story* Deakin presents the negotiations as a contest between Chamberlain on the one hand and three staunch federationist delegates—himself, Barton and Charles Kingston from South Australia. Deakin judged that Kingston would not be easily manipulated by Chamberlain, unlike James Dickson from Queensland and Philip Fysh from Tasmania, who were 'vacillating and self-interested'. For Deakin the central dramatic conflict was between national independence and imperial overlordship. Whatever the merits of Chamberlain's various amendments, Deakin believed he was 'resolved to demonstrate the supremacy of the Imperial Parliament and his own too by insisting upon some alteration however small.'[17]

Negotiations were complex, and the delegates had to consult with their premiers back home, but the federationists fought hard. Deakin's account of the toing and froing is extremely detailed, showing just how closely he was watching each player's moves and weighing up the options for action. As in his confrontation with Salisbury, so in standing up to Chamberlain Deakin presents himself as speaking truth to power, plainly warning Chamberlain to back off lest he be responsible for delaying federation by causing a third referendum.

Chamberlain had not anticipated that the amended constitution would need to go back to the people and dropped most of his proposed amendments, except for keeping open a path for appeals from Australia's High Court to the Privy Council in London on constitutional matters. At issue was whether the High Court or the Privy Council would be the final arbiter of constitutional disputes. Chamberlain had support from the London press, as well as from Australia, where the Boer War was heightening imperial sentiment. This was Chamberlain's war, forced on an initially reluctant Britain to strengthen the empire's control over southern Africa and bring the Boer republics to heel. The colonies had sent troops, and Australia's bushmen soldiers were winning praise for their fighting skills. The war weakened the federationists' hand back home, as many thought that severing an imperial tie, however slight, was disloyal when the empire was at war.

The three federationists fought on, seeking to win over English public opinion.

> Putting their backs against the wall they accepted every one of the public invitations to dine showered upon them by Clubs, Guilds and public bodies and constituting themselves missionaries preached the gospel of the Bill without amendment, no matter what toast they proposed or replied to or what the nature of the gathering might be.[18]

The bill, the whole bill and nothing but the bill, backed by the voices and the vote of the overwhelming majority of the Australian people: this was the message. When Chamberlain introduced the bill to the House of Commons without the clause limiting appeals, there was some protest on behalf of the colonies from the Liberal Opposition and Chamberlain decided to seek a compromise. Right of appeal to the Privy Council in matters pertaining to relations between states, or between the Commonwealth and a state, would be allowed if the governments concerned consented. According to Deakin, Chamberlain believed on the basis of a similar arrangement with Canada that the Australians would always prefer the higher tribunal; the three federationists thought otherwise. With the bill now satisfactory to them, they 'danced hand in hand in a ring around the room to express their jubilation'.[19]

Deakin's diary for the three months in London is crammed with appointments—dinners, luncheons, banquets and private chats. With sightseeing excursions and outings with the family, there was little let-up. By the time the family left London, on 1 June, he was exhausted, with a painful outbreak of boils on his neck. Brookes did not return with them, staying on to continue his grand tour. They spent three weeks travelling through France and picked up the boat home at Marseille. Pattie was seasick again, and Deakin spent a good many nights sleeping in the Smoking Room.

When Deakin arrived in Adelaide the governor of South Australia, Lord Tennyson, sought a private audience in which he conveyed that 'the highest authorities in the Colonial Office…were perfectly aware of what they owed to his conciliatory efforts. They wished him to understand that to him more than any of his colleagues they attributed the finally satisfying compromise which had been secured.' Deakin is the source for this pleasing confirmation of his view of himself as the great conciliator.[20]

As in 1887, he received another hero's return, deputations meeting his train from Adelaide at Ballarat and Bacchus Marsh, a crowd at Spencer Street, and a Citizens' Welcome at the Town Hall for 'one of Victoria's most brilliant sons'. The mission in London, he told them, was 'the most important of his life'.[21]

The Victorian government had made a thousand pounds available to Deakin for his expenses on the trip, of which he returned four hundred and fifty. In his budget speech William Shiels, now the treasurer, praised his 'example of economy and refinement of feeling'. Deakin was acutely embarrassed. Barton was in Melbourne that day. He had been toasted and dined in Queen's Hall, but 'as all Australia knew Mr Barton and Mr Kingston had not only spent the whole of their allowance, but cabled for more', running through at least fifteen hundred pounds each.[22]

Deakin was already solicitous of Barton's financial situation. During the two referenda campaigns Barton had neglected his professional business, and was 'in desperate financial straits', according to his New South Wales campaign colleague Bernhard Wise: 'At least £5,000 must be raised to clear him and enable him to give attention to the election of the federal parliament.'[23] Deakin wrote to both the *Argus* and the *Age* defending Barton and Kingston: they had each sacrificed over six months of professional income and given six months' arduous service to their country; he had stayed in London a month less than they had; and because he was a member of parliament, he had 'allowed myself only a share of the cost incurred'.[24] It was not a very convincing defence, and served to heighten the contrast between Deakin's concern for the public purse and his companions' profligacy.

The incident is revealing of Deakin's touchy independence, his wariness of being beholden. He praised Barton's service to the cause of federation as outweighing all others and minimised his own. Prima facie, this can seem humble; but is it really, with the implied contrast between himself and a man like Barton, who deserves our praise and needs our help? It is of a piece with his repeated refusal to accept official honours. Arising from this trip, he declined an honorary doctorate of Civil Law from the University of Oxford, as well as a Privy Councillorship, though the Queen did not court another rebuff by repeating her offer of a knighthood.[25]

It may be that Deakin felt his refusal of honours was by now part of his public persona and could not be compromised, or that an innate egalitarianism made imperial honours distasteful, though he never criticised others for accepting them. But the rejection of worldly honours is also a withholding of the self from society's judgements. I am not as other men, it seems to say, men who care for the world's praise; it means little to me as I test my achievements at the bars of my soul and my God, and go my own way according to my own convictions.

Early in the trip to London Deakin was introduced to the editor of the *Morning Post*, James Nicol Dunn, by the Australian-born journalist and author of sensationalist novels H. B. Marriott Watson.[26] Now that the colonies were federated, the proprietor, Algernon Borthwick, was considering a regular letter from Australia, and Deakin was being sounded out. The *Post* was an independent conservative paper, with an interest in the emergent nationalism of the self-governing colonies and opposed to free trade.[27]

In late November 1900 Deakin received an offer: five hundred pounds annually for a weekly letter and cables on important items not covered by Reuters. His friend Philip Mennell, who had been in Melbourne earlier in the year, was the go-between. Deakin accepted immediately. He would adopt a Sydney persona and write as 'the Australian correspondent'. His first letter was in the mail the next day. Deakin went to great pains to guard his anonymity. He used the name Andrew Oliver for telegraph communications, and occasionally sent them in code. He even had his daughters address the letters, lest his handwriting be recognised at the post office.[28]

Deakin's motives in accepting this assignment were complex. In

1887 he had complained to London's clubmen about how little attention outside cricket the English press gave to the affairs of the colonies, and consequently how ignorant the English were of colonial conditions and aspirations. His weekly letters could make good some of this lack, enabling 'Englishmen to follow political, material and social developments all over Australia so as gradually to bring them in touch with that part of the Empire'.[29] The five hundred pounds a year was a welcome supplement to his anticipated ministerial salary and provided something to fall back on should he resign, an option Deakin always liked to keep open. He also enjoyed the secrecy and boyish intrigue, later telling the English journalist Richard Jebb that 'The situation is fit for fiction rather than real life and that is one of its attractions though its responsibilities are hazardous in the extreme.'[30] Less consciously admitted perhaps, the anonymity enabled him to drop his public veil of courteous affability and express himself more directly, even as he maintained his preferred detached stance of the onlooker towards his own motives and actions.

It was not uncommon for politician journalists to write anonymous articles on the affairs of the day for the press. Lord Salisbury himself had done so for both the *Saturday Review* and the *Quarterly Review*, though not when he held high office. When Deakin became the Australian correspondent, the parliament was not yet inaugurated, he held no official position, and the initial agreement was for a year's trial. He had, however, decided to stand for a federal seat, and he and Barton were already discussing the future ministry.

The day that he accepted the offer from the *Morning Post*, Deakin was farewelled by his old constituents at a 'smoke concert' at the Moonee Ponds Town Hall. Those who had commended the Commonwealth to their fellow countrymen, he said, had incurred an obligation to make all the advantages they had promised come true. That night his prayer was of thanksgiving 'for present release under happy political circumstances, for rest, and for further freedom from financial anxiety'.[31]

21

THE HOPETOUN BLUNDER

IN SEPTEMBER 1900 Deakin was invited to stand for the new federal constituency of Ballarat.[1] At a ceremony at the City Hall on 22 September he was presented with a petition of two thousand signatures requesting that he allow himself to be nominated. He accepted and was, he told the assembled citizens, gratified that the immense petition was 'thoroughly federal', signed by all classes and with miners well represented.[2]

Deakin was wise to accept. The class politics that was squeezing inner-city Liberals and would transform Melbourne's electoral landscape over the next decade had not yet gripped the gold towns. In Ballarat, which had the strongest ANA branch in the country, the optimistic, self-improving, radical-liberal political culture of the goldrush immigrants which had nurtured the younger Deakin was still very much alive. And Ballarat had voted almost unanimously for federation, with a 96.7 per cent Yes vote compared with 81.6 per cent in Victoria overall.[3]

The city was proud to be represented in the first federal parliament by Australia's best-known native son, whereas in the new federal

MAYPOLE HOUSE
HIGH ST.
· SOUTHEND ·

Alfred L. Shepherd

DAY & ELECTRIC LIGHT STUDIOS.

Clockwise from top:

1. The Deakin family, 1857. From left: Catherine, Sarah, William and baby Alfred.

2. Destined for each other: image constructed for Pattie and Alfred's twenty-fifth wedding anniversary, 3 April 1907.

3. Alfred Deakin's birthplace, 90 George Street, Fitzroy.

JOHNSTONE O'SHANNESSY & Cº
Next Post Office.   Melbourne.

JOHNSTONE O'SHANNESSY & Cº
Next Post Office.   Melbourne.

Clockwise from top left; late 1870s:

4. Catherine Deakin.

5. Sarah Deakin.

6. William Deakin.

7. The young barrister.

7, Collins St East   I. W. Lindt.   Melbourne

Clockwise from above:

8. Hugh Junor Browne.

9. An intense young man, 1879.

10. Alfred's first birthday card
to Pattie, 1 January 1880.

11. Park House, Wellington
Parade, East Melbourne.

Clockwise from top left:

12. Pattie Deakin, San Francisco, 1885.

13. The 1885 Victorian irrigation delegation to the United States. From left: J. D. Derry, Deakin, John Dow and E. S. Cunningham.

14. Pattie's copy of Carlyle's *Past and Present*, bought in the United States, with Alfred's blue pencil markings.

THE REV. CHARLES STRONG, SCOTS' CHURCH, COLLINS-STREET.

Clockwise from top left:
15. Charles Henry Pearson.
16. Charles Strong.
17. David Syme.
18. James Service.

19. Top right: Program for the ANA's banquet welcoming Deakin home from London, 11 July 1887.

20. Above: Deakin in his Windsor uniform.

21. Above: 'The Arriv[al] of Mr Alfred Deakin', *Illustrated Australian News*, 25 June 1887.

22. Left: Llanarth, Walsh Street, South Yarra.

Clockwise from above left:

23. 'Striking the Rock', Melbourne *Punch*, 3 June 1886.

24. 'The Evolution of Deakin', Melbourne *Punch*, 14 June 1894.

25. 1897 Victorian election ephemera.

26. On the backbench, 1896: Deakin left side, back row, second from end.

27. Federation Conference, Melbourne, 1890: Henry Parkes at centre;
Duncan Gillies wearing top hat; Deakin in back row, third from right.

28. Deakin's photo was subsequently inserted into this garland of women,
from the late 1890s. From left: Ivy, Stella, Sarah, Vera, Catherine and Pattie.

29. Federation comrades: Edmund Barton and Deakin, 1898.

30. The Barton ministry, 1902–03. Standing, from left: James Drake, Richard O'Connor, Philip Fysh, Charles Kingston, John Forrest. Seated: William Lyne, Edmund Barton, Governor-General Lord Tennyson, Deakin, George Turner.

Clockwise from left:

31. Home handyman.

32. 'Where is my "Sartor"? Oh, here it is', Melbourne *Punch*, 1 October 1903.

33. Prime Minister Deakin, 1905.

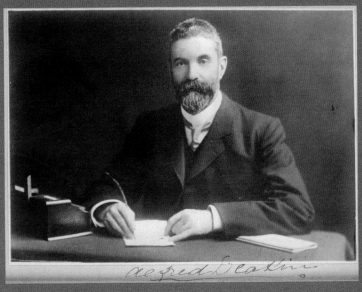

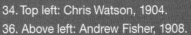

34. Top left: Chris Watson, 1904.

35. Top right: George Reid, 1903.

36. Above left: Andrew Fisher, 1908.

37. Above right: Billy Hughes, 1902.

38. Above: Watercolour of spider orchid by Pattie Deakin, 1913.

39. Left: Pattie at her writing desk.

40. Right: Ballara, Point Lonsdale.

41. Below right: In the garden at Llanarth.

42. Below: Alfred's 1908 birthday poem for Pattie.

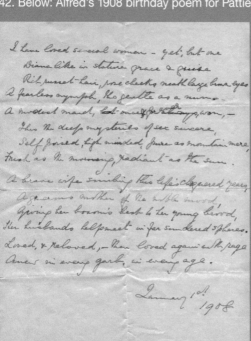

Clockwise from left:

43. 'Advance Australia' postcard, London.

44. Deakin the orator, London, 1907.

45. In England, 1907.

"Australia"

(The Hon. Alfred Deakin.)

46. Above: Joseph Cooke visiting Ballara, January 1909.

47. Left: 'Married to the Family' *Worker*, Sydney, 7 April 1910.

Clockwise from top left:

48. Deakin leaves Parliament House on his retirement, January 1913.

49. Portrait by Arthur Woodward, 1913.

50. The Deakin, Brookes and Rivett families in the garden at Llanarth, circa 1912. Back, from left: Pattie, Vera, Alfred, Ivy and Herbert. Front: Wilfred, David and Stella.

The last photo
taken with my
Dear One.

August 1919.

51. Top: Deakin with Pattie and Vera on
the verandah at Llanarth; left, the caption
on the back of the photograph.

52. Above left: Deakin with his two-year-
old grandson Rohan Rivett and Catherine
at The Elms, 10 September 1919.

53. Above: Alfred and Pattie's gravestone,
St Kilda Cemetery.

electorate of Bourke, which incorporated much of Deakin's previous electorate of Essendon and Flemington, the Labor vote was on the rise. At the elections in November 1900 for what would be Victoria's first state government, Essendon and Flemington was won for Labor by Edward Warde, a wood turner from Abbotsford, after four candidates splintered the Liberal vote.[4]

A few days later Barton was in Melbourne, and invited Deakin to join him should he, Barton, be asked to form the first federal government.[5] In the last months of 1900 the two men were in regular contact, discussing the make-up of the first ministry. Deakin did the design work, suggesting the number of portfolios, their names, and the split between the House of Representatives and the Senate; and he argued very strongly that External Affairs should be taken by the prime minister.[6]

They also discussed who might get which portfolio and how to balance representatives from the different colonies. Western Australia had now voted to join the federation, largely on the votes of Victorians in the goldmining areas. Barton wanted a congenial ministry of protectionists and committed federalists. After Deakin, Richard O'Connor, a Sydney lawyer and parliamentarian, was his second choice. O'Connor had been Barton's comrade in arms in the struggle for federation in New South Wales, and a member of the federation convention's drafting committee. Barton was, however, wary of their companion in London, the intemperate Charles Kingston, preferring the calmer presence of the current South Australian premier, Frederick Holder.[7]

It was all rather previous, and somewhat clandestine. Barton was keen to contrive opportunities for them to meet, suggesting Deakin accept an invitation to a banquet being given for Barton in Bathurst, 'so no one could suspect us as they now do of arranging Federal Ministries!' Visiting Sydney, Deakin thought it might attract too much attention were he to stay with Barton at his home, Miandetta, in North Sydney.[8]

Less secretively, they were also discussing how to prepare the Liberals for their first federal election. This involved organising across and within each state, and both were daunting tasks. His mission with the Liberals, Deakin wrote to Barton in November was,

> as usual…to unite and bind them together as much as I can…
> The labour party in every colony is organised for the fray and
> unless we take care will anticipate us…We shall have to fight the
> 'ultras'—Tories and Laborites and socialists, but with a progres-
> sive programme and <u>trusted leaders</u> may expect to rally all the
> moderates and thoughtful Liberals under one standard.

Labor's tighter, more cohesive national organisation was to remain a
challenge for Liberals until Robert Menzies formed the Liberal Party of
Australia in 1944–45. In 1900 the challenge was just becoming apparent
and Deakin was keen to prevent the Liberal vote dissipating over rival
candidates. The young men of the ANA were with him, and he would
need to cultivate the protectionist organisations, which 'will mean the
maintenance of existing tariffs with the Victorian as the chief model
subject to Australian interests and considerations'.[9]

Barton was alarmed. 'Don't inscribe on our flag "the maintenance
of existing tariffs with the Victorian as the chief model"…That would
go far to wreck us over here…you must not scare the other colonies
with the idea that this or that colony is to rule the roost.' Barton also
felt that aspects of Deakin's suggested programme were too socialist
for some New South Wales Liberals.[10] Deakin might have been well
placed to construct a Liberal consensus in Victoria, but he still had
much to learn about politics in New South Wales, where free-traders
considered themselves truer Liberals than the protectionists.

In his first letter for the *Morning Post*, written on 29 November 1900,
Deakin worked hard to establish his new identity. Here is how it started:

> Sydney has been simmering rather angrily for the past month,
> despite what may fairly be termed a temperate season, and is
> now fast approaching boiling point. Our preparations for the
> inauguration of the Commonwealth are the immediate cause,
> though the high pressure at which the local Parliament has been
> kept working…has contributed to the general friction. Not that
> the Lyne Ministry is in present peril.

He even adopted a free-trade persona, writing of Barton that 'his Protectionist leanings are not popular with us.' Nevertheless, with Reid out of office, the field is open for him to become the first prime minister: 'in loyalty to the Federal cause, in character, and in political consistency, he stands far above his rivals.'[11]

The Commonwealth of Australia was to be inaugurated on New Year's Day, 1901. The first federal election would follow in March. The imperial government had appointed the first governor-general, Lord Hopetoun, and he had instructions to appoint the first prime minister and ask him to form an interim ministry to start the machinery of government.[12] There was general agreement that the first prime minister should come from the mother colony.

Reid had lost government on a censure motion in September 1899, in part because his twists and turns on federation had created enemies among both federationists and anti-federationists, and in part because he lost the support of Labor. Had he still been premier, he would undoubtedly have been Australia's first prime minister; however, William Lyne was now the premier of New South Wales.

Lyne had been a member of the New South Wales Assembly since 1880, drawn into politics by the agitation to reform the Land Acts. He had begun as a free-trader, but by 1890 was a committed protectionist. At the two referenda he had opposed the constitution as giving too much power to the small states at the expense of New South Wales. As premier from September 1899 to the end of 1900, with the support of Labor, he managed to get a great deal of progressive legislation onto the statute books, including early closing of retail shops and old-age pensions.[13]

These achievements did not soften Deakin's judgement of him: he had opposed federation. Beyond his adherence to protection, Deakin wrote in the *Federal Story*,

> his politics were a chaos and his career contemptible…he appealed at all times to the narrowest Sydney and New South Wales provincialism by the pettiest and meanest acts and proposals. He was an anti-Federalist from the first except upon terms which should

ensure the absolute supremacy of his own colony as a stepping
stone to his own elevation.[14]

Barton and Deakin both expected Hopetoun to send for Barton.
Bolstering Barton's expectations was a private letter from Sir John
Anderson of the Colonial Office discussing arrangements for the
inauguration in a way which suggested that he expected him to be the
first prime minister. Then, a bombshell, a telegram from Barton: 'it is
Lyne have declined to join him.'

This was on Wednesday, 19 December 1900, less than two weeks
before the interim ministry was to be sworn in. The family was at
Point Lonsdale for the summer, and Deakin had come up to town
to wait for the telegram from Barton which would summon him to
Sydney. He had already sent his luggage to the station. Immediately
he rushed off to acquaint George Turner, who was again the premier,
with this extraordinary turn of events and to discuss a course of action.
Both Barton and Deakin would likely refuse to join Lyne, and Deakin
thought he might not even go to Sydney for the inauguration. That
night he wrote Barton a long, agitated letter. 'Your telegram upsets
our house of cards—who could have believed that Hopetoun would
make such a blunder.' That a man with no federal feeling was to be the
Commonwealth's first prime minister—it was beyond comprehension.

Hopetoun's motives were of little interest to Deakin; he had blundered,
and that was that. On 15 December, Hopetoun had arrived from India
weak from typhoid fever to a ticklish political situation. The inauguration
was less than three weeks away. Despite the Colonial Office's expectations
for Barton, after meeting with Reid, Hopetoun had no doubt that from
the perspective of Reid and the free-traders Barton was not a politically
neutral choice. He thus fell back on the man who held the office of the
premier. It seemed a constitutionally safe strategy, but it set off a storm.

The next six days were frantic, as Deakin, Barton and their closest
allies, Turner, Kingston and O'Connor, exchanged telegrams and
letters in a fast-moving series of events and negotiations every bit as
unpredictable and as ruthless as later Australian leadership coups.

When Hopetoun asked Lyne to form a government, he made clear that the ministry must contain 'nothing but first class men from each of the colonies, and that above all Victoria should have her proper share both in quality and quantity'. To ensure this he instructed Lyne to consult with the premiers on the formation of the ministry.[15] There was a chance, then, that if Lyne was unable to form a respectable ministry he could be forced to resign.

On Thursday, 20 December, the day after the bombshell, Deakin was pessimistic in another long, agitated letter to Barton. 'Kingston stands firm but alas no one else does…The whole business makes me sick with disgust.' The *Age* had come out in support of Lyne who was, after all, a protectionist. Lyne summoned the premiers to Sydney to consult with him, offering them each a ministry.[16] Not all were interested and not all could make it. In the event, only Turner and Holder met with Lyne, on Saturday, 22 December. Deakin hoped that Turner would press Lyne to resign his commission in Barton's favour, and that other premiers would join him in this, but the feeling was that Lyne 'will not be deterred by any refusals from forming a scratch team which will do much mischief while in and only serve as a warming pan for Reid'.

Deakin foresaw two possibilities: the first, unlikely, that the premiers would persuade Lyne to resign in Barton's favour, in which case Barton would have to offer Lyne a ministry—this was bad enough. But the second possibility was even worse—that the premiers would fail, and Barton would be asked to serve under Lyne. If so, Deakin agonisingly put it to Barton, it would be his duty to accept. 'It robs the prospect of all its charms, but the situation must be faced somehow.'

On Friday the prospect was even gloomier. The *Age* argued in support of the governor-general's decision, weakening the chance that Turner would be able to convince Lyne to resign. At 7 a.m. Deakin wrote a third agitated letter to Barton, arguing more forcefully than the day before that it was Barton's duty to put aside his personal claims and join Lyne, if, as he expected, Turner's mission failed. 'Australia will suffer if you refuse to crucify yourself.'

The letter is ambiguous as to Deakin's intentions for himself—likely he had not made up his mind. The *Age* had reported that he intended to refuse a portfolio if Lyne offered him one. The same arguments about duty which Deakin was putting to Barton could be applied to him, and Syme was pressing him to accept. 'My action must depend upon yours,' he told Barton. His letter crossed a wire from Barton which made clear that he would not serve under Lyne.

On Saturday morning, 22 December, Deakin wrote to Kingston: 'do you think we should all stand out—if we do Reid comes in and as a party we shall be wrecked at the elections or soon after.' Initially he was 'too ineffably disgusted to think it out' and had decided 'not to join under any circumstances or any conditions—but everyone here condemns this policy and I am fairly puzzled at present as to what to do'.

That afternoon he visited David Syme at his home, Blythswood, in Kew. We don't know exactly what transpired. We know that Syme thought Deakin should accept an offer from Lyne and presumably he argued this. We know that Deakin knew that Barton had said he would not serve under Lyne. We know too that Deakin was intensely loyal to Barton. His diary note reads, 'Lyne's offer. Persuaded DS to wire that Barton was essential.' My surmise is that Syme was far more concerned to secure a place in the cabinet for Deakin, and that Deakin made Barton's inclusion a condition of his own, knowing that Barton would refuse, but not himself refusing directly.

Turner returned from Sydney with an offer for a place in the ministry from Lyne to Deakin, but also with his own mind made up that he himself would not serve under Lyne. Turner told the press that he believed that neither Barton nor Deakin would serve under Lyne, and that he saw 'nothing ahead but strife and trouble if Lyne succeeded in forming a ministry which did not include some of the leading federalists'. He did not want the new nation to start with 'personal bickering'.[17] Deakin's bourgeois shopkeeper had become a statesman.

The South Australian premier, Frederick Holder, also said he would not serve. Other possible cabinet members such as John Forrest and Samuel Griffith had not actually rebuffed Lyne's approaches, but nor had they accepted. Desperate, Lyne told Syme he would accept any two men he liked to nominate, but Syme, after another meeting with Deakin, wired that he would not support a ministry without Turner.

Lyne was defeated, and at 10 p.m. on Christmas Eve he visited Hopetoun at Sydney's gothic-revival Government House to tell him he had failed to form a ministry and to advise that Barton be sent for. On Christmas afternoon Turner sent a one-word telegram to Deakin, now back at Point Lonsdale: 'Come', the agreed signal from Barton for him to go immediately to Sydney. It was not till Deakin read the Boxing Day papers, however, that he was sure they had won.

He hesitated at first, exhausted from the strain of the past few days. Hot north winds were blowing and he had a stomach upset. But he rallied, returned to Melbourne, picked up some luggage from Llanarth and was on the express train to Sydney that night as the cool change arrived, heading for his federal future.

On New Year's Eve, Deakin described the formation of Australia's first ministry for the *Morning Post*. The episode, like 'a well-knit drama', had 'carried men in its sweep from the depths of despair to the heights of triumph…It may now be classed as a comedy, because of its happy ending, though it began like the prologue to a tragedy.' Deakin would be attorney-general in the inaugural ministry, and Charles Kingston the minister for trade and customs. Deakin had persuaded Barton to include Kingston, regarding the three of them as 'federally inseparable' after their battle in London.[18]

Lyne initially hesitated to join, 'because of the political hostility evinced towards him by Mr Deakin'. He told reporters that he would have been able to form a ministry were it not for the Victorians, 'one gentleman refusing to join unless another one would, and the second gentleman declining to come in'.[19] Deakin had effectively vetoed Lyne. In 1909 Deakin recalled, 'Defeated Lyne and placed Barton in power.'[20] In his own mind at least, he was the ringmaster.

There was a short coda to these events for the *Morning Post*'s Australian correspondent. The editor, Nicol Dunn, thought his letter 'a little too straight in its hits on Lyne'.

I know that in the colonies and in America plain speaking about public men is the rule. Here we are more accustomed to diplomatic phrases, our golden rule being that no matter how severely you attack a man you should so express it that you could dine with him immediately afterwards.

It seems that the *Post* took it upon itself to bring Deakin up to their gentlemanly standards of politeness. By mid-1901 Philip Mennell was writing to Deakin in outrage about the *Morning Post*'s garbling of his letters, especially those dealing with the Hopetoun–Reid intrigue: 'I do not believe in your being a curbed force. What people here want to know is Australian opinion not Australian opinion as manufactured and interpreted to suit the M.P.' Mennell advised him to take his talents elsewhere, perhaps to the *Manchester Guardian*, whose editor had approached him only a few weeks after he accepted the offer from the *Post*: 'it must soon happen that the Commonwealth will come into collision with the Colonial Office…then the *MP* will desert you and Federal policy will have no mouthpiece on this side.'[21] Deakin did not take Mennell's advice. He wrote for the *Morning Post* for the next fourteen years, offering an anonymous commentary on political events in which he was a major player.

22

CELEBRATIONS AND BEGINNINGS

THE NEW NATION and the new century began together on 1 January 1901. Deakin shared a carriage with Barton and Richard O'Connor in the grand procession of more than ten thousand dignitaries, floats, mounted imperial troops and contingents representing various trades along an eight-kilometre route from Sydney's Domain to Centennial Park. Crowds lined the streets and filled Centennial Park, including a thousand-voice choir to sing in the new nation, which was to be inaugurated in a white octagonal wedding cake of a pavilion in the middle of the park.

Here the queen's proclamation of the Commonwealth of Australia was to be read, and the governor-general and his ministers were to swear their oaths. The outdoor ceremony accommodated the crowds but it had drawbacks: few could hear the ceremonial words and it was very hot under the midday sun, with humidity high after overnight rain. For the imperial troops in their dress uniforms, it was a test of endurance.[1]

The family had not joined Deakin for the occasion. In the pavilion he seemed 'palpably nervous' and 'clasped the Bible in a very trembling hand', but when he repeated the oath, 'his exquisitely modulated, clear and far-reaching voice was as music to the ears of all within ear shot.'[2] Nervous excitement on the brink of public performance was characteristic for Deakin, but he was also alive to the significance of the occasion, shimmering with the fulfilment of divine purpose for both the new nation and himself as its humble instrument.

The only moving image we have of Deakin is from this day, walking down the steps from the pavilion as the nation's first attorney-general and looking briefly at the camera, his doffed top hat winking in the sun. As premier of the host state, Lyne had asked the Salvation Army's Limelight Studio, then the country's only production unit, to film the procession and the ceremony. With footage taken by five fixed cameras, it is Australia's first documentary: thirty-five minutes of grainy images of gun carriages, troops riding under ceremonial arches, crowds cheering, and the key actors moving jerkily in and out of the pavilion.[3]

The glimpse of Deakin is frustratingly fleeting. He wore ordinary morning dress, as did Barton, though some others were in court dress and Lord Hopetoun was resplendent in the full Windsor uniform. The curling beard of Deakin's younger days was now clipped to a Van Dyke-style point. In the afternoon cabinet met for the first time, and later Deakin met with Frederick Holder, who was angry about being dropped from the ministry in favour of Kingston. Deakin was exhausted, and made only a brief appearance at the evening's celebratory banquet.

Deakin was forty-four when he moved from colonial to federal politics and into the full glare of national history. He was the most widely known of the new ministers after Barton. According to the contemporary historian Henry Gyles Turner, there was no man from whom more was expected:

> The manufacturers looked to him as the great apostle of Protection...The Labor Party hailed him as the author of the first Factories Act, and felt sure that, with Deakin in power, a satisfactory wage would be the law of the land. And in the mother country his

reputation was linked with that of Edmund Barton as representing all that was worth considering in Australian statesmanship.[4]

But Deakin had been here before, as the bearer of others' high expectations, and he had failed to meet them. A 1901 pen portrait of him in the new Sydney-based Liberal quarterly review *United Australia* concludes that his achievements in Victorian politics had not come up to his lofty ideals, or to the expectations of his friends and admirers, and that he had left no enduring legislative monument, not even the Irrigation Act, which had failed: 'the silver tongued orator of Australian federation [is] a more brilliant speaker than a constructive statesman.'[5]

The federal parliament was to open in Melbourne—its first home—in May 1901. Until then Deakin was up and down to Sydney, with the sea or train journey to Queenscliff added on to the Melbourne leg until the family returned to town in early February, and a visit to his mother and sister in Adams Street as he passed through Melbourne. When in Melbourne he worked from the Attorney-General's Department's temporary office in the General Post Office Building, on the corner of Elizabeth and Bourke streets, 'receiving an endless stream of tiresome visitors, and dealing with a great mass of correspondence'.[6] Like other ministers, he was besieged by people eager to work for the Commonwealth government.[7]

Deakin was working on the judiciary, interstate commission and public-service bills, as well as on machinery bills for customs, the post office and defence. It was a punishing regime; and he was missing out on his summer holiday, with only Sundays to rest, stroll and breathe the sea air. He was now also writing his weekly letter for the *Morning Post*, marking every Tuesday in his diary with the initials MP and Roman numerals. In what was becoming a recurring consequence of his hard work, he was frequently unwell, with poor sleep and an upset stomach.

As they began to build the machinery of government, he and Barton also had to organise the Liberal Protectionists for the first federal election, to be held at the end of March. Early in the month Deakin opened his campaign in Ballarat before a large crowd, speaking for one and a half hours without notes. His main message was that voters needed to vote as Australians: 'The great bulk of people were suffering from the habit of looking at every question through parochial spectacles. What they wanted were Federal field glasses…to scan the horizons of the continent.'[8]

This was to be a frequent exhortation during Deakin's federal career. To him the larger, more unified view was always superior, higher and more evolved, less selfish and closer to the divine purpose than the narrow and parochial. Rather hyperbolically, he claimed that the state parliaments could not be considered to have lost power and prestige: 'as they become knotted together in one great national organism, they will attain, even in themselves, a higher and more complex life than belonged to them as separate Parliamentary units.'[9]

At the federation conventions Deakin had argued that the politics of the federation would not be determined by divisions between the smaller and larger states, but between those 'who consider they should march in agreement with the advanced political thought of their time, and their rivals who…desire to go more slowly'.[10] But it was clear that party relations in the federal parliament were to be far more complex than this, with two fractures already apparent which did not fit Deakin's simple model of more and less progressive.

The first was between New South Wales and Victoria, over duties and tariffs on imports. Federation had delivered free trade between the states, but trade policy in relation to other countries, including Britain, was still to be determined. Since they had run out of land to sell, all colonial governments had imposed customs duties to raise revenue, but Victoria had also used tariffs to protect its infant industries. The dividing issue was the purpose and the rate of tariffs, not their existence, although many in New South Wales still regarded free trade as a core Liberal doctrine.

William McMillan, a keen federationist and soon to be the first member for the Sydney seat of Wentworth, objected to Deakin's Liberals appropriating the name Liberal while identifying themselves with a policy that struck a blow against the principles of human liberty. Why, asked McMillan, should free-traders be 'obliged to come before

Mr Deakin's tribunal to prove their Liberal credentials'? Why should they be classed as Conservatives? McMillan was replying to Deakin's account of 'The Liberal Outlook', in the inaugural issue of *United Australia*, which was edited by McMillan's close friend Bruce Smith, another Sydney-based free-trader who was about to enter the federal parliament.

Deakin's piece shows the enduring emotional structure which underlay his construction of the differences between Liberals and Conservatives: 'Upon the Liberal Party there falls, as always, the task of presenting a positive constructive policy to the new constituencies… wherever provincial or personal interests are operative, whenever representatives are returned merely upon past local services or wherever a negative platform is accepted, Conservatism will find its allies.' It was the conflict between the particular and the more universal, between the everlasting Nay and the everlasting Yea, between those who obstructed and those who facilitated the forward movement of the spirit.[11]

The second fracture disturbing Deakin's model of political conflict was the emergence of labour parties capable of winning seats. This was 'the most disturbing element in local politics of late years', he wrote in the *Morning Post*, just before the first federal election in March. Protected by his anonymity, he was frank in his assessment of Labor:

> their platform is selfish and their discipline admirable. They constitute a caste in politics, and refuse to support representatives who have not been selected from among their own numbers. The consequence is that their members are rarely men of sufficient ability to acquire a Parliamentary status. They help to demoralise politics by bartering their tally of votes for concessions to their class and by their indifference to all other issues.[12]

The first federal election returned sixteen Labor candidates to the Representatives. As neither the Conservative free-traders nor the Liberal Protectionists won an absolute majority, Labor would hold the balance of power.[13] Nevertheless, the *Age* described the Victorian result as 'A Great Liberal Triumph', with an overwhelming vote for the protectionists. Deakin won his seat with a majority of three thousand, but there was not yet compulsory voting and the turnout was low. Not even 'the catching phrases from the Deakin word factory' could get the apathetic to the polling booth, and dreadful weather kept many at home.[14] The Federation Drought had settled in, with gale-force north winds blowing topsoil from newly cleared land in the Wimmera and Mallee across Victoria. Deakin was in Ballarat for the declaration of the poll and then straight back to Melbourne, where Pattie was ill again. The doctor ordered her to bed and for the next few weeks, before the arrival of a new housemaid, Deakin started his days with 'Home Duties'.

The protectionists did much better in Victoria than in New South Wales, where the free-traders were far more popular than Deakin had bargained for, winning seats with majorities of thousands rather than hundreds. Commenting on the result in the *Morning Post*, he noted that the 'brains and substance of the first Federal Opposition' will be fifteen hostile representatives from Barton's own state; and that the breach dividing Victoria and New South Wales showed every sign of deepening provincial jealousies. Although Labor would hold the balance of power, it did not have a united position on the tariff: five of its number were for protection, six for free trade and five undeclared. It was fortunate for Barton, he wrote,

> that he had adopted Radical proposals for the exclusion of coloured labour, because it is possible that this may attach to him the votes of the Labor members who are unpledged…It will be a hard task, too, for a man of his somewhat aristocratic tastes to ingratiate himself with the uncourtly members of the working classes who have been elected. Mr Reid is sure to be on friendly terms with them in a very short time.

Nor would the Barton government control the Senate, where free-traders had almost half the seats and there were eight Labor men. Deakin concluded that Barton's 'heart must be inclined to sink when he looks at the material provided out of which he is required to build a new national Parliament and establish a new national policy'.[15]

Deakin's heart sank too, because he knew that he would be doing much of the tactical work needed to steer legislation through two unstable houses. Barton also had to manage a 'cabinet of kings', with five ex-colonial premiers flexing their well-developed muscles in this much larger federal pond. Clashes and arguments among Lyne, Forrest and Kingston were to try Barton's patience sorely over the next few years.[16] Forrest was a big man—literally, at almost twenty stone (127 kilograms)—and used to getting his own way. He had led numerous expeditions of exploration in Western Australia, and after the colony was granted self-government in 1890 he became its first and, until then, only premier.[17]

For the opening of Parliament in May, Australia received its second royal visit. Queen Victoria had died in January, aged eighty-one. She had been queen since 1837, when the grand metropolis of Melbourne was just a few wooden buildings on the Yarra. Her son, Edward, was now king, and he sent his eldest son, the future George V, and his wife to grace the occasion.

As a boy, Deakin had been with his own parents and Catherine in the crowds lining Melbourne's streets in 1867 to glimpse Prince Alfred. Now he was in the official party, welcoming the Duke and Duchess of York when they disembarked at St Kilda, attending the royal levee, dining with Pattie at Government House, the duke and duchess 'very gracious to us both'. Ivy, now almost eighteen, 'came out' into society at a reception at Government House, where she was presented to the duchess and to Lord and Lady Hopetoun.[18] Were it not for the recent death of the queen, it would have been a ball, but gala balls, banquets and race meetings had been replaced with more sedate entertainments, and the dressmakers had been busy with black satin and jet beading for the women's gowns.

The next day Pattie was in the newly decorated Exhibition Building to see her husband sworn in as attorney-general. She wore black voile, a black coat and a handsome steel-sequinned toque. Ivy was 'in a fine grey cloth gown, grey hat trimmed with feathers and a white feather boa'.[19] Catherine was no doubt there too, with her mother, Sarah, whose invitation to this historic event survived in Catherine's papers.[20]

That afternoon the seventy-five new members and thirty-six senators assembled in the Victorian parliamentary chambers, which had been lent to the Commonwealth until such time as it had its own parliament house. In the meantime, the Victorian parliament would meet in the Exhibition Building. Frederick Holder, as a compensation for missing out on a ministry, was elected Speaker. Some few already knew one another from the federation conventions, but most were strangers to each other, and to Melbourne. Over the next few months, Deakin was everywhere, helping the newcomers to feel at home in his city and his Parliament House.

> The tall dark figure of Alfred Deakin flitted about the House...
> like a master of ceremonies, with his bright eyes and smiling face,
> watching every point, prompting here, advising there, one moment
> in the Chamber, another in the lobbies, chatting for a few seconds
> with a member, in consultation with the whip, or cracking a joke
> with his opponents. He appears to be inhabited by the spirit of
> restlessness and to be taking a boyish enjoyment in the situation.

This is from a Sydney reporter. Coming under the spell of Deakin's charm for the first time, he called him 'the dark-eyed gipsy of Australian politics' and marvelled at his protean skills.[21] On that first afternoon, the youngest member of the House of Representatives, the new member for Corio, Richard Crouch, waited nervously to second the address in reply. Deakin, no doubt remembering his own nervous excitement in that same chamber twenty-two years earlier, sent him a note: 'In quietness and confidence be your strength.'[22] Deakin's hostly spirit did not, however, extend to inviting his fellow parliamentarians home. Except for Barton and O'Connor, few ever came to Llanarth for dinner or Sunday tea.

The Commonwealth and its parliament were now launched, but the federated union was still only 'formal and legal rather than vital'. The *Morning Post* correspondent predicted 'much friction, much misunderstanding, and much complaint' in its beginnings.[23] Most of Deakin's

CELEBRATIONS AND BEGINNINGS

letters for 1901 dwell on the difficulties to be overcome to transform the federation from a legal contract into a nation of 'one people': the persistence of parochial loyalties; the difficulties Australia's great distances posed for overcoming them; the state governments' suspicions of the Commonwealth's potential to encroach on their power and status; possible conflict between the House of Representatives and the Senate; the still unresolved question of the tariff; and the instability of the House in which the new ministry's majority depended on the Labor Party, whose success had disrupted the two-party structure Deakin thought indispensable to the proper operations of parliament. The new prime minister would have to cobble together a fresh coalition of support for every major piece of legislation, and Deakin, who was in charge of the House when Barton was away, shared the task.

Deakin was in his prime, alert, full of energy, and doing the work he liked best. Back in 1888, on their sojourn in the Blue Mountains, Deakin had complained to Josiah Royce of the amount of time a minister in the parliamentary system must spend on politics, rather than on administration and legislation. He had never liked the constituency work, with the requests for help with employment, and the lobbying for railways and bridges distracting the legislator from 'matters of a purely public nature', as he had put it when a newly minted member of parliament.[24] Most of this could now be left behind to vex state politicians, while he focussed on the foundational legislation for the new nation.

Much of this legislation was uncontentious machinery legislation to transfer powers and functions from the states to the Commonwealth and to establish the institutions of government. Deakin was not only a great orator, he was a very capable administrator too, methodical, thorough, hard-working, with a quick mind and sharp eye for detail. As attorney-general he was ably assisted by Robert Garran, whom Deakin had requested to be the first secretary of the department.

Garran was a young Sydney lawyer, a passionate federalist like Deakin, and already the author of three books on federation and the constitution, including, with John Quick, *The Annotated Constitution of the Australian Commonwealth*, which quickly became the classic interpretation. Garran found Deakin to have 'the keen analytical mind

of the natural lawyer'. With the draft of a difficult opinion, Deakin
would take the role of counsel for the other side and attack it from
every angle. 'At last he would say, I think you are right but redraft it
and let me see it again.'[25]

In July 1901 Deakin became seriously ill with dysentery and influ-
enza. The press reported the cause as 'overwork' but infection too
played a role, with Pattie and Vera also becoming ill over the next few
weeks.[26] While ill, he wrote another of his out-of-body narratives.
Attending a performance of a Beethoven symphony, as the music soars
he is 'sucked upwards as if out of the body'. Sloughing off his old self,
like a snake shedding its skin, he becomes light, radiant, 'quivering
with energy, sensibility...unfolding as if in rapture', among choruses
of ecstatic soul companions.[27]

To us, the coincidence of this vision with Deakin's illness points to
the effects of fever, and perhaps to a mind under stress, but to Deakin it
was evidence of the existence of the soul and the transience of its bodily
home, a manifestation of the dual nature of reality, with the divine spirit
animating the material world. 'The web & woof of history discloses
the Divine pattern thro' the dim light of understanding. The myriad
unseen influences of individuals living or called dead & the myriads
of unguessed agencies operating upon & among them without which
the secret of life cannot be mastered.'[28]

This is from a prayer written on 4 August 1901, the day after his
forty-fifth birthday. It was his first prayer for eighteen months. For the
next few months he prayed almost weekly, as an escape from the sleepless-
ness which increasingly afflicted him, but also as a form of meditation
with which, amid the rush of daily events, he could centre himself and
scrutinise his motivations. Prayer 'is an effort to put ourselves in rapport
with Him by coming to a better understanding of and with ourselves',
he wrote. 'Virtue is an ordering of the self—continuous, unflagging and
ever wakeful to the best ends one sees.'[29] In a prayer a week later, Deakin
contemplated the idea of progress. 'The most modern of all ideas and the
most fruitful is that of progress, evolution, growth. Swedenborg called it
the doctrine of uses and saw all else subordinate to utilities.'[30]

Linking the ideas of progress, evolution and growth to Swedenborg shows just how far Deakin's thinking was from our own—as well as from his more practically oriented contemporaries. For him, these terms referred to the progress of the spirit in human affairs, the divine pattern dimly disclosed in the 'web and woof' of history. They have nothing to do with material, scientific or technical progress, or with economic growth.

Deakin knew that the idea of progress which dominated western nations had a selfish aspect of insatiable appetite and boundless ambition, yet he believed, nevertheless, that 'progress is towards unselfishness'. If he was to be an instrument in its advance then he had to prepare himself 'by casting out pride, petulance, the aim for superiority of place...and all anxiety to be understood or appreciated, rewarded or enriched even by spiritual growth'. As his energies returned after his illness, he prayed to be sunk in his work and so 'lost to my own recollections or calculation of consequences by being absorbed in Thee'.[31]

23

ATTORNEY-GENERAL AND
ACTING PRIME MINISTER

ON 7 AUGUST 1901 Edmund Barton introduced the Immigration
Restriction Bill to federal parliament. The achievement of a White
Australia had been one of the motivations for federation. It was supported
by all sectional groups, except for the sugar planters of North Queensland,
who wanted to continue to import indentured Pacific Island labourers.
For Labor it was the first item of its platform.

Holding a copy of Charles Pearson's *National Life and Character*,
Barton quoted its warnings: 'We know that coloured and white labour
cannot exist side by side; we are well aware that China can swamp us
with a single year's surplus population.' Restrictive legislation was
thus based on 'the instinct of self-preservation, quickened by experience'.[1] Appealing to the precedent of colonial legislation on the Chinese
question, the aim, Barton said, was uniform legislation to restrict the
immigration of undesirable immigrants. The main target was coloured
immigration, but also to be excluded were the criminal, the insane and
the diseased.

Deakin's eloquent second-reading speech in support of this bill has become the best-known defence of the White Australia policy, quoted repeatedly in history books and school texts. The legislation, he argued, was as much about the projected future nation as the present one, for in a population of around four million people there were only about eighty thousand 'coloured aliens'. (The indigenous population was not included.) Today's Australians, especially the Australian-born, he said, were conscious of their endowment of political freedom and felt an 'obligation to pass on to their children and the generations after them that territory undiminished and uninvaded'. It was the note of nationality, he argued, 'which gives dignity and importance to this debate'.

> The unity of Australia is nothing if it does not imply a united race. A united race means not only that its members can intermix and intermarry and associate without degradation on either side, but implies one inspired by the same ideas, and an aspiration towards the same ideals, of a people possessing a cast of character, tone of thought—the same constitutional training and traditions—a people qualified to live under this Constitution—the broadest and most liberal perhaps the world has yet seen reduced to writing…Unity of race is an absolute essential to the unity of Australia. It is more, actually, in the last resort than any other unity. After all when the period of confused local politics and temporary division was swept aside it was this real unity that made the Commonwealth possible.[2]

Contemporary Australians regard the White Australia policy as a blot on the nation's past, a product of fear and loathing of a racialised other as the new nation turned away from its region to ensure its place in a white man's world. We need to exercise our historical imagination to understand why Australians at the beginning of the twentieth century could regard it as an expression of high ideals. Yes, boundaries keep outsiders out, but they also enable those inside to co-operate to achieve common goals.

In the parliamentary debates and in the press, many different reasons were given for supporting a White Australia: physical repulsion at the prospect of interracial marriage; the protection of Australian workers' wages and conditions from competition with lower-paid workers; avoidance of the interracial violence which had marred the south of the United States and led to the Civil War; the inability of uneducated people who did not speak English to participate as equal citizens in Australian democracy; the creation of vice-ridden ghettoes; fear that the small Australian population just starting its national journey would be swamped by people of a different culture and race; the desire to avoid significant populations of foreign nationals that would give foreign governments an excuse to intervene in Australia's affairs; strategic fears focussed on a modernising, militarising Japan. There is a mix here of nationalism, Social Darwinism, strategic fears, racial loathing, industrial protection and social-liberal aspirations for an active citizenry.[3] As a policy it was massively over-determined, with different sectional groups drawing on different strands that all led to the same conclusion: the immigration of non-white people to Australia should be restricted.

When Deakin said that 'the unity of Australia is nothing if it does not imply a united race' he was making a claim that most westerners at the time regarded as self-evident, that people who shared a culture and history should be united in one self-governing polity. This ideal of the nation-state formed during the nineteenth century in the liberal struggles for constitutional self-government against monarchic, aristocratic and imperial rule. All Australians with an interest in public affairs knew John Stuart Mill's chapter on nationality in his *On Representative Government*, and its arguments informed Deakin's speech:

> A portion of mankind may be said to constitute a Nationality, if they are united among themselves by common sympathies, which do not exist between them and any others—which make them co-operate with each other more willingly than with other people, desire to be under the same government, and desire that it should be government by themselves or a portion of themselves, exclusively…
>
> Free institutions are next to impossible in a country made up of different nationalities. Among people without fellow-feeling,

especially if they read and speak different languages, the united
public opinion, necessary to the working of representative government, cannot exist.[4]

Setting out to build a new nation, which was already almost totally
culturally homogeneous, it was incontrovertible to the Australian
colonists that they would strive to maintain it. Why would they willingly
create the sorts of racial and cultural divisions that, in their experience,
led to violence, conflict and degradation for white and coloured alike?
Over and again the Australians pointed to the racial violence of 'the
Negro problem' in the United States, and of blackbirding in the Pacific.
Indigenous Australians barely figured in these debates. Their welfare
had been left to the states, and they were assumed to be a dying race.
Deakin expressed the pious empty hope that 'in their last hours they
will be able to recognise not simply the justice but the generosity of
the treatment which the white race, who are dispossessing them and
entering into their heritage, are according them'.[5] He told *Morning Post*
readers that 'the aboriginal race has died out in the South and is dying
fast in the North and West even when most gently treated.'[6] Clearly
he gave Australia's native peoples barely a passing thought. They had
no place in his projected future nation, and he had deaf ears and blind
eyes to the violence, exploitation and neglect they had suffered at the
hands of the invaders, and continued to suffer.

Nationalism was a modernising project, building identities and moral
communities which transcended local and parochial identifications. Over
the little more than a hundred years since white settlement began in
Australia, some regional loyalties had developed, but these were weak
compared with the deep-rooted provincial and ethnic identities of the
old world. And the colonists had worked hard to keep sectarian conflict
between Protestants and Catholics in check. For Deakin the nation
manifested humanity's evolution towards higher unities and expressed
both natural law and divine purpose, though this upward progression
had not yet embraced the universal human rights of contemporary
cosmopolitanism.

The only point of contention in the legislation was how the exclusion was to be achieved. Chamberlain had made it clear that any direct reference to race would be painful to Her Majesty, as the head of an empire 'whose traditions make no distinctions in favour or against race or colour'. Her Majesty's Indian subjects would be offended, but so would Britain's new ally, Japan. Japan had no objection to immigration restriction as such, and itself had measures to prevent the immigration of Chinese labourers, but it objected to its civilised subjects being classed with 'Kanakas, Negroes, Pacific Islanders, Indians and other Eastern peoples', and thought the Japanese should be treated in the same way as Europeans.[7]

Faced with a similar dilemma, the small British South African colony of Natal had used an education test, and several Australian colonies had adopted similar solutions. The legislation Barton introduced proposed an English-language test. After objections that this would not exclude the clever Indian, Japanese or Chinese, but would bar many desirable prospective European immigrants, this was amended to a test in any European language. Thus, the notorious dictation test was born, with absolute discretion in the hands of the customs officers administering it to choose the language in which it would be given and so ensure that all non-white applicants would fail.

It was a devious and hypocritical solution. Why couldn't the new nation at its outset adopt a straightforward method of exclusion and say exactly what it meant, asked the acting Opposition leader, Sir William McMillan? Labor agreed, and proposed prohibiting anyone who was an 'aboriginal native of Asia or Africa'.[8] If Australia stood up to Britain, would the monarch really withhold assent to the legislation? Labor and the Opposition argued for the direct approach, the government for respecting Britain's wishes.

Barton and Deakin, proud nationalists though they were, were also loyal imperialists, and were not prepared to push a confrontation with the British government. In the final vote on the method of exclusion the Labor Party voted as one against the dictation test, for the first time pitting its disciplined strength against the government, but the Opposition could not hold all its followers and the government won by a majority of five.

Defeat, wrote Deakin in the *Morning Post*, would almost inevitably have led to the ministry's resignation. 'The flag raised was that of Empire, and a majority against the government would have meant a selfish declaration of local demands made in utter indifference to the interests of Great Britain and to the embarrassment of its international relations.' Not, he reassured his readers, that this vote was an indication of weak imperial feeling.[9] Rather, it was party feeling and party politics, with Reid and the Opposition bidding for Labor's support to bring down the government. Later that year the Commonwealth also passed the Pacific Island Labourers Act to deport the Kanakas from North Queensland who worked in the sugar industry. This was uncontentious, except for the question of timing, to allow Queensland sugar growers to adjust.

On the whole, Deakin's rhetoric on White Australia was more moderate than that of many. He tempered the denigration of other races by arguing that, in the case of many Chinese and Japanese, it was their superior qualities that made them threatening and so warranted their exclusion.[10] Later, when Deakin was prime minister, the secretary of the Department of External Affairs, Atlee Hunt, complained of his inclination to relax the act in individual cases.[11]

Deakin was far more aware of the achievements of Asian civilisations than most of his contemporaries, but he did not hold this line consistently, also talking easily of servile races and subscribing to the fear that the coloured people to Australia's north posed a threat of invasion. In the difficult first parliament beset with provincial suspicions, the still unresolved matter of the tariff and the new Labor Party finding its feet, White Australia was an area of furious political agreement that could be relied on to create a unifying common purpose and so give legitimacy to the new federal institutions.

The commitment to a White Australia was also expressed in the Franchise Act, which was passed in 1902. The constitution provided that no one who already had the vote could lose it when the colonies federated. Women could already vote in South Australia and Western Australia, and the Franchise Act extended this right to all white women for federal elections. It was a great triumph for Australia's suffragists. After New Zealand, Australia was the second nation to grant women the vote. But this did not include indigenous women, nor their menfolk.

Richard O'Connor had introduced legislation for the government which had the broadest possible franchise. Six months' residency was to be the only requirement. After a furious onslaught, replete with dreadful racist attacks on Aborigines, the bill was amended to exclude 'aboriginal natives of Australia, Asia, Africa and the islands of the Pacific, except New Zealand'.[12] Those 'natives' already on the state rolls had to stay there, because of the constitution, but no new applications would be accepted.[13]

During the first year of the federation state governments began to realise just how much power, prestige and possible revenue they had given up, and taxpayers were growing concerned about the cost of another level of government. At the end of 1901 citizens in the Victorian country town of Kyabram formed a league to protest against the extravagant cost of the state and federal parliaments and the growth of government debt. The Kyabram movement quickly became the National Citizens' Reform League, with branches forming across the state, mainly in country districts where drought was exacting a heavy toll, though the league also had strong links with Melbourne business interests.

Robert Menzies' father, James Menzies, attended the league's first conference in Melbourne in April 1902 as the representative of the Dimboola Shire. The league's main target was the Victorian government's salary bill, and it caused a great deal of trouble for Liberal Premier Alexander Peacock, who lost a no-confidence motion in June.[14] Similar sentiments were aired in the other states, creating a mood of cautious parsimony among federal parliamentarians.

In March 1902, when Deakin introduced the Judiciary Bill to create the High Court, general public opinion regarded the creation of yet another federal institution as an extravagance that could be delayed. In the meantime, it was argued, the task of judicial interpretation could be left to judges of the state supreme courts taking turns to act as High Court judges, and to the Privy Council. Deakin spoke in the House for three and a half hours to persuade otherwise: that only a High Court with its own judges, as envisaged by the constitution, could interpret that constitution with the proper federal perspective. 'A new court, strictly Australian and national, created for Australian and national purposes' was essential to lay down the boundary lines between the Commonwealth and the states, he said. The speech was calm, measured and comprehensive, showing Deakin's oratorical skills in another register from the arousal to action, and William McMillan, again acting as leader of the Opposition, congratulated him on its eloquence.[15] But the bill got pushed aside by the interminable debate on the tariff and lapsed when parliament was prorogued at the end of the year. Deakin would have to repeat his arguments in a year's time.

Deakin had begun 1902 in low spirits. The summer break had been marred by Pattie's serious ill health. She was so weak that he had to carry her downstairs to begin their annual journey to the seaside.[16] In February he prayed for inspiration to wash upon 'my fickle feverish irritable spirit' as 'the hour of darkness has continued.'[17] In April he resigned from the ministry, telling Barton that 'my retirement will be a relief from a strain which has been severe at times.'[18] To Herbert Brookes, from whom he sought frequent advice on mining investments, he wrote that he was setting his house in order, as he may find it advisable 'to plough the lonely furrow as of old'.[19] Brookes was now managing a mine at Hollybush, forty kilometres south-west of Ballarat, and a regular weekend visitor to Llanarth.

The precipitating issue for Deakin's resignation was government finances. The government was proposing to raise a loan of six hundred thousand pounds for capital expenditure on post and telephone services, and to increase the allowances of MPs from four to six hundred pounds a year. With most breadwinners lucky to earn one hundred pounds a year, the existing allowance was a windfall for Labor's working-class members, but it would barely sustain a middle-class home and family.[20]

Attending parliament in Melbourne was an expensive business for non-Victorian parliamentarians, who had to maintain an additional residence as well as forgo opportunities to earn other income. George Reid was frequently absent from parliament attending to his Sydney legal practice, which diminished his effectiveness as Opposition leader. Barton saved on accommodation expenses by living in a small improvised bachelor flat in Parliament House. Here he worked after hours, and socialised with his closest cabinet colleagues, Deakin, O'Connor and Forrest, talking till the wee hours and sharing suppers of chops and billy tea cooked on the open fireplace, bush-style.[21] Deakin, always touchy on money issues, resigned rather than support the increased allowance.

Deakin wrote two resignation letters to Barton, one formal, the other more personal, expressing his regret: it is 'a great wrench for me to go. I have never in my life had work that I so much enjoyed doing or which so absorbed all my interest as that of acting as your Attorney General,' but he would stay in parliament, as 'there could not be a worse time to return to the Victorian Bar.' He thought he could do a great deal to help Barton's government as a private member, particularly among the Victorians.[22] Deakin was contemplating returning to the role he had played in the Victorian parliament as chief government adviser without the responsibility and strain of a ministry.

Barton's answer was swift: 'My dear old friend, Don't break my heart…How can I bear the thought of going on without you? Disappointment was hard enough, but I have long been near despair… Your departure now would—though you may not know it—*wreck* the Ministry.'[23] He returned Deakin's formal letter of resignation, but he also dropped the proposal to raise the allowances. Deakin later added this to his list of contemplated resignations: 'Resigned rather than assent payt. of Members increased—Barton reluctantly gave way.'[24] Given the protests about government expenditure, Deakin probably did Barton a favour.

In early May, Barton went to England to attend the coronation of Edward VII and the Imperial Conference. He would be away until early October, leaving Deakin as acting prime minister and minister for external affairs with the assistance of two younger men: Atlee Hunt, the secretary of the Department of External Affairs, and Thomas Bavin, Barton's private secretary.

Hunt, who complained in his diary about Barton's time-wasting socialising and failure to prioritise urgent business, appreciated Deakin's more methodical work habits. Deakin told him that he had never been happier with a permanent head. He also told him that it was his policy never to become intimate with those working under him, neither visiting their houses nor inviting them to his.[25] With Thomas Bavin he was able to relax this stricture after the younger man decided to return to Sydney to work at the bar. They became good friends and frequent correspondents, and Deakin often stayed with the Bavins in Chatswood on his Sydney visits.

Before he left on 6 May, Barton had one messy piece of business to tidy up. Early in 1901 the governor-general, Lord Hopetoun, had requested that his salary of ten thousand pounds be supplemented to take account of his various unavoidable expenses. He would, he calculated, have less money at his disposal for his official duties than the state governors and had already spent fifteen hundred pounds of his own money. Privately Barton had agreed to a supplementary allowance, though he had done nothing about it. On 1 May 1902 he introduced a bill to pay the governor-general an allowance of eight thousand pounds per annum. Labor could barely restrain its indignation, and there was little support elsewhere. The best Barton could get was agreement for a one-off payment of eight thousand pounds. Barton sent Deakin a note: 'Be happy while you may. I am going to hand you over a burden!'[26]

Hopetoun, who believed he was expected to spend lavishly to give the new nation ceremonial weight, was distressed and humiliated by the rejection. Two weeks later, when Chamberlain recalled Hopetoun to England at his own request, it was Deakin as acting prime minister who had to deal with the recriminations in a shocked community. Deakin told the House that, although Hopetoun had been requested to reconsider his position more than once, he had declined 'to discuss any proposition the House might think fit to make with the view of retaining his services'.[27]

Hopetoun wrote frequently to Deakin in the days before his departure. They had known each other since 1889, when he was governor of Victoria, and he found it a comfort 'to open out to such a good old friend as you are'.[28] Deakin travelled to Sydney to farewell him.[29] Hopetoun's resignation gave Deakin 'a remarkably eventful' beginning to his first experience as prime minister: 'the wheels revolve so rapidly that the days fly crowded with incident, variety, responsibility and sometimes anxiety—but surprisingly little of the last on the whole.'[30]

Hopetoun left Australia in July and was replaced by the governor of South Australia, Lord Tennyson, who had inherited his title from his famous poet father. Atlee Hunt recalled that, when he became acting prime minister, Deakin rejected Barton's elaborately formal third-party mode of address to the governor-general. Barton would say, 'Mr Barton presents his humble duty to your Excellency and desires to be allowed to refer your Excellency to Mr Barton's minute of...' According to Hunt, Deakin said, 'That won't do at all. I'm humble enough, Lord knows, but I do not present my humble duty to anyone.'[31]

Almost immediately, Deakin was faced with a delicate constitutional issue involving states' rights in relation to the external-affairs power. In Adelaide some sailors deserted from a Dutch-owned ship, the *Vondel*. When the Dutch consul had requested assistance to apprehend them under the Anglo–Dutch Convention, the South Australian authorities refused. The Dutch government complained to the Colonial Office, which in turn asked Deakin as acting prime minister why assistance had not been given, and he in turn asked the South Australian government. All perfectly straightforward, it would seem, except that the South Australian government objected to receiving communications from the Colonial Office through the Commonwealth government and would only explain itself if the request came from the Colonial Office through the governor of South Australia. It was a belligerent assertion of the states' rights to maintain the direct lines of communication with the Colonial Office they had formerly enjoyed.

Deakin was keen to resolve the incident without confronting the constitutional issue, so he responded diplomatically by claiming only that the Commonwealth was competent to act in the matter, not that it had exclusive competence. The British government might well have directed its enquiry to the South Australian government, he said, but in this case they directed it to the Commonwealth, so could the information please be supplied. But the South Australian government wanted the constitutional issue raised, and ordered its officers not to respond to requests from any other government.

Deakin thus had no choice but to treat it as a constitutional issue and the stand-off became the first test case of the scope of the Commonwealth government's external-affairs power. The conflict continued into 1903, with Chamberlain providing the final clip to the South Australians' wings: 'the people of Australia form one political community, for which the Government of the Commonwealth alone can speak, and for everything affecting external states or communities which takes place within its boundaries that Government is responsible.'[32] This was just one of a number of trials of strength between the Commonwealth and the states as they tried to defend their power and prestige.

The Customs and Tariff Bill was another blow to the power of the states. This was the last of four bills to enable the Commonwealth to start collecting customs revenue, and it included the detailed schedule of the tariffs and duties to be applied to everything from butter and felt hats to the tools and machines needed by farmers and manufacturers. Deakin hated the tedium and self-interest of tariff debates and left their management to Turner and Kingston, turning up only for the divisions.

Members pored over the detail as they tried to balance the interests of the various producer groups among their constituents with those of consumers. Labor members spoke loudest for consumers, arguing for 'a free breakfast table'. When they succeeded in having the House drop duties on the household staples of tea and kerosene, the vertical fiscal imbalance of Australia's federal–state relations became starkly apparent for the first time to 'the astounded politicians of the States' who saw their income suddenly reduced. Deakin spelt out the implications for his *Morning Post* readers: 'The rights of self-government of the States have been fondly supposed to be safeguarded by the Constitution. It left them legally free, but financially bound to the chariot wheels of the federal government. Their need will be its opportunity.'[33]

Finally, the Customs and Tariff Bill passed from the House to the Senate, which was impatient to test its powers. The constitution gave the Senate the power to reject money bills or to request amendment, but not the power to amend the bill itself or to introduce its own money bills. This was a compromise between the Westminster convention of

lower-house control over money bills as essential to responsible government and the smaller colonies' demand that the states' house have real
power. What it would mean in practice, however, was yet to be tested.

At the 1897 Adelaide Convention, Deakin had predicted that, when
considering a money bill, 'Instead of criticising every item and every
figure, and weighing the question of whether a duty should be 10 or
12.5%, I take it that the Senate would look broadly through the tariff.'[34]
How wrong he was. The Senate spent thirty-three days in committee
on the detail and in late July 1902 sent the bill back to the House with
ninety-three requests for amendments. Deakin could no longer avoid
the detail, as cabinet considered the Senate's amendments.

Most proposals were for reductions, such as from threepence to
twopence per pound for raisins, peel and ginger; from 25 per cent to 20
per cent for tilbury carriages, dog-carts, gigs, sulkies and other horse-
drawn vehicles. In some cases the Senate proposed no duty at all, and
for cigars and cigarettes an increase.[35] The House accepted wholly or
in part forty-four of the Senate's proposed amendments, and rejected
forty-nine. The Senate accepted much of the revised legislation, but
now pressed its request for twenty-six.[36] Should the House accept this
request? Wouldn't a repeatedly pressed request, which stalled the bill,
effectively become an amendment?

There were as yet no standing orders to regulate communication
between the two chambers, so acceptance of repeated requests might
establish a constitutional precedent. On the other hand, it was urgent
that the tariff schedule be finalised. Without it, the Commonwealth
could not raise revenue; and the twenty months spent debating tariff
schedules had created uncertainty for business and commerce, as well
as opportunities for anti-federalists to stir up doubts about the wisdom
of the union.

Deakin was disappointed that the tariff was not more protectionist,
but far more concerned about the costs of further delay. On 3 September,
a 'day of intense strain', Deakin persuaded the cabinet and then the
House to receive and consider the request from the Senate, while
postponing the determination of the constitutional issue to a time when
it could be considered separately and on its merits. It was a deft piece

of parliamentary footwork to head off either a constitutional deadlock with the tariff left unresolved, or a resolution determined largely by short-term fiscal considerations but which would have long-lasting constitutional implications. It was, he told his diary, 'a great victory for the wisest course', and it left him exhausted.[37]

Addressing the House he was calm and avoided talk of a crisis; to *Morning Post* readers he revealed just how much he felt had been at stake and how critical was the victory:

> the Union itself can scarcely be exposed again to such a crucial trial as that through which it has so lately passed. The country drew a deep breath of relief simply because, at last, after months of turmoil, a tariff was passed, but the few onlookers, who realised all the consequences of failure, drew a deeper breath still, and felt a more profound relief as they became assured that the Commonwealth itself was out of the toils at last, and fast escaping beyond the reach of its enemies.[38]

The trials of strength with the states and the Senate when he was acting prime minister show Deakin's characteristic preference for compromise, but they also reveal his driving motivation in these early years of the new nation. In the 1890s, at the nadir of his self-belief, Deakin had committed himself to the achievement of federation, and now that it was achieved he was putting his all into protecting it.

Vision is a stale word in political commentary, but it aptly describes Deakin's actions in these early years of the new Commonwealth. Amid conflicts of personalities and sectional interests, Deakin kept his focus steadfastly on the generations to come, striving to avoid actions and decisions which would pre-empt future directions. When persuading the House to consider the Senate's requests, he described the constitution as deliberately general in places, a sketch or outline yet to be filled in, 'a frame into which the people require to breathe the breath of life'.[39]

In this jumble of metaphors, the last is the most telling, endowing the people with life-giving force and imagining the constitution as an evolving, adaptive organism. Its advance was now the focus of his political energies, and its survival the site of his dramatic political sensibility. Deakin had always been prone to see political conflicts in terms of crises and turning points, with the path of progress beset by dangers and obstructions. It was a vision which energised him for the fight and confirmed his sense of purpose. While he soothed and charmed, his friendly smile belied his frequently racing pulse.

The session ended on 10 October 1902. 'Prorogation Thank God,' Deakin underlined in his diary. With Barton's return the following week, the harness loosened and Deakin again collapsed into exhaustion. He had been sleeping badly, and now he became ill. His doctor forbade him to go to Sydney to welcome Barton home. Instead, he and Pattie went to Healesville, in the hills outside Melbourne, for a few days and he started to sleep a little better.

A prayer of 24 August suggests that more than nervous strain had contributed to his poor health. He offers sincere gratitude for the mercy of 'having been saved from sudden death' and ponders the fate of his loved ones 'if I had died this morning'. While he is content to leave his own life to the will of the Father, his faith fails 'in anxiety for my wife and children, mother and sister…At present nothing in life could compensate them for losing me.'[40] I suspect he had experienced a mini-stroke or transient ischaemic attack, a frightening temporary loss of capacity which left no obvious lasting damage and of which he told no one except his God. It was a warning.

As 1902 wound down, so did Deakin, spending November and much of December gardening, writing, and sitting for Arthur Handel Gear, who had been commissioned to paint his portrait by some of his fellow parliamentarians—in recognition, said Sir John Forrest at its presentation, 'of the honour, courtesy and chivalry he showed to all who crossed his path'.[41] On acceptance, Deakin donated it to the Ballarat Art Gallery. It shows him holding a book, eyebrows arched, his hair still dark and his mouth well hidden by his beard.

24

1903

DEAKIN BEGAN THE new year in a pessimistic mood.

> All life is failure, first the inevitable and universal failure to reach
> the Ideal…yet despite the scepticism and disillusion bred of experi-
> ence, ideals one must have, some of them embodied in creeds and
> programmes and these one always seeks to realise…but the actual
> line followed in thought or action too often can only run parallel
> with them, and only rarely do they blend. One such instance was
> in federation—another was irrigation and this failed—another
> was social legislation still trembling in the balance.[1]

The idea of federation had been achieved, but the reality of governing
the new Commonwealth was a difficult business, and he was spending
too much time sorting out Barton's messes.

On his return, Barton had written to Deakin that he was grieved to
hear he was so knocked up, and felt 'quite guilty for having imposed

on your anxieties which must have been too much for you'.[2] But Barton continued to contribute to Deakin's anxieties, nevertheless. In January he became embroiled in a dispute with the new governor-general, Lord Tennyson, over the duties of the secretary to the Executive Council in which the government advises the governor-general, who is bound by convention to follow that advice. Tennyson did not want the secretary to have access to 'secret and confidential information between himself and the Colonial Secretary'. Barton regarded this as revealing Tennyson's intention to withhold information from the Australian government, which was his responsible adviser.

After an acrimonious exchange of letters both turned to Deakin, who was recuperating at Point Lonsdale. He persuaded them to treat the matter as an unfortunate misunderstanding, but he advised them never to deal with matters of this nature '*in writing* until you have first settled the course to be pursued by personal consultation. It pains me deeply to find it possible that evidence of this permanence should be created which remains when the trifling circumstances occasioning the misunderstanding have been utterly forgotten.'[3]

Parliament did not meet again until late May 1903. Deakin could spend more time at home, and began most days by walking the dogs, Kim and Crusoe. He was sitting for Tom Roberts, who was painting his portrait for the 'Big Picture', the painting commissioned to commemorate the opening of federal parliament. They became friends. Deakin invited him and his family for lunch at Point Lonsdale, a very rare privilege, and when Roberts moved to London they corresponded.[4]

For the first time in many years, his diary notes his eclectic reading, including the spiritualist Frederic W. H. Myers' posthumously published two-volume *Human Personality and its Survival of Bodily Death*, which had just come out. His old university friend Richard Hodgson was one of the editors, and an appendix included Hugh Junor Browne's account of his eldest daughter Pattie's extraordinary capacities as a medium.[5]

These had already been revealed in Browne's *The Holy Truth* in 1876, and again in his *The Grand Reality* in 1888, when Browne tells readers that this daughter had become the wife of the chief secretary.[6] Now the revelation of Pattie's gifts was repeated in a major international publication, no doubt causing some consternation to Pattie and Alfred, who generally kept their spiritualist past to themselves. It does not seem to have drawn public comment at the time. When the journalist Zora Cross wrote an extended portrait of Pattie in 1935 it was not mentioned, and only recently has Pattie's childhood experience as a medium been noticed by historians.[7]

Birthdays and anniversaries were important in the Deakin family, and Alfred regularly wrote poems for Pattie on her birthday and their wedding anniversary. This year, their twenty-first, he was 'Stoop shouldered to my load and deeply wailed…but still thy faithful thrall.'[8] He gave Pattie a secretaire. Pattie told Herbert Brookes that they spent the evening at home reminiscing: though we are now really old people, 'our love is young.'[9] Later that year, on 7 July, Deakin wrote in his diary, '22 years ago', marking the anniversary of the day he had asked Hugh Browne for his daughter's hand.

When parliament resumed in May 1903, Deakin again had to take up the cudgels for the establishment of the High Court. He told parliament that it was not simply its choice 'to create or not create, but a direction from the people from whom the Constitution came that the Federal Judiciary be established'.[10] He spoke for three hours, dealing with members' objections and questions and arguing that judicial interpretation was vital for the constitution to adapt to changing circumstances. Again the critics' focus was on cheaper alternatives, such as leaving constitutional interpretation to the state supreme courts and the Privy Council, and again Deakin resisted, urging members to rise above current practicalities and 'lift our eyes forward to the future of the Commonwealth'.[11] But the House was adverse, Deakin recorded in his diary, and the attacks continued with no clear party division on the matter. At the end of July 1903 a compromise bill was passed with three rather than five judges, reduced salaries and no pension entitlements, but not before he had threatened to resign. At the end of the marathon battle he was, again, exhausted.[12]

July was also a month of family troubles, as he mediated the continuing tensions between Pattie and Catherine, and tried to stave off a rupture with Pattie's parents. 'Katie obdurate,' he recorded on 24

July. A week later he sent a lawyer's letter to Hugh Browne after an exchange of letters that had become increasingly frantic on Browne's part, despite Deakin's own strenuous efforts at conciliation, describing one of his letters as a 'final cringe'. Deakin does not record what the dispute was about. Relations between Pattie and her parents had always been difficult, and both she and her father were strong-willed. She felt badly let down by them, for not helping her when she needed their sympathy.[13]

It is not clear when this was: perhaps in her early married life, when she was an inexperienced young mother living at Adams Street; perhaps later, when she was ill and Catherine was taking control of her daughters' education. Browne remained an ardent spiritualist, so perhaps Myers' republication of his account of the child Pattie at the séance table had stirred up past resentments. Deakin himself seemed to have a good relationship with Hugh. But he was loyal to Pattie, telling Brookes that with this final irrevocable and angry rupture 'they are now gone out of our life altogether.'[14]

His birthday dinner with Mama and Catherine at Llanarth was a diminished event without the Brownes. That night he prayed to 'conquer my impatience, intolerance, anger and willingness to give pain', and for special blessings 'to those to whom I have given pain that has not been beneficial to them'. It is an odd prayer, as he also asks for the courage to strike strongly where wrath and punishment may be the truest kindness, showing that the emotions of anger and resentment were not foreign to him, and how responsible he felt for the emotional and moral well-being of his loved ones.[15]

In late July 1903 Deakin had to pick up the Conciliation and Arbitration Bill. This was Charles Kingston's legislation. Shocked by the ferocity of the strikes of the early 1890s, Kingston had become a passionate advocate of the civilising effects of compulsory arbitration and conciliation. With Henry Bournes Higgins he had argued at the federation conventions that the Commonwealth be given the power to establish courts of conciliation and arbitration for disputes that went beyond the boundaries of a single state. There was resistance from Conservatives, who argued for freedom of contract in employment relations, but the clause was eventually accepted by a narrow margin.

Cabinet was generally supportive of Kingston's legislation, but it baulked at its extension to seamen engaged in the coastal trade. Barton thought that a domestic bill could not properly regulate foreign vessels, and that this should be left to a later navigation act. Forrest, who clashed frequently with Kingston, objected that it would raise the costs of Western Australia's communications with the rest of the country. Kingston argued that 'cheap crews—not Australian—which invade our coastal trade' would make the bill a mockery.[16] Unable to persuade the cabinet, and lacking Deakin's ability to compromise, Kingston resigned. So it was Deakin who made the second-reading speech on 30 July 1903.

Deakin argued for the bill as an extension of the civilising power of the law, the laying aside of weapons of strife for the weapons of argument, preventing 'the strikes and lockouts...which breach the social peace and bring disorder, destruction and loss'. He also argued that 'Under the influence of a sense of injustice, unfairness and helplessness the working population of the world cannot be expected to submit to their lot. There must be held out to them the prospect of betterment and advancement.' The pronouns here tell the story. For Deakin the workers would always be 'them', separated from him by an experiential gulf of which he was only partially aware. He wanted 'a gradual, slow, but sure achievement of fair hours, fair wages, fair conditions of labour', 'to bring both employer and employee before the bar of a tribunal which would mete out even-handed justice'.[17]

Deakin was a middle-class liberal lawyer who never squarely faced the imbalance of power between employers and employees, or understood the urgent emotions driving labour politics. Conservative Premier William 'Iceberg' Irvine's ruthless defeat of a strike of Victorian railway workers in May 1903 had made federal Labor determined to bring state employees under federal legislation. An amendment to extend the bill to state employees was narrowly defeated, but one to cover railway workers succeeded, with the mischievous support of members of the Opposition. Deakin regarded this as an unconstitutional extension of the Commonwealth's powers into the state's jurisdiction and the entire bill was dropped.

Labor was stunned. The government had given no warning that the amendment would be a deal-breaker. Dropping the bill which it had long promised on such inadequate grounds was evidence of its 'absolute insincerity', said the Labor leader, Chris Watson. Mocking the high-flown rhetoric of Deakin's second-reading speech, the Labor member for West Sydney, Billy Hughes, asked how the crowning effort of civilisation, which promised to bring about industrial peace, could be dropped on such a small amendment.[18] Labor had overplayed its hand, but this was not to be the last of the issue. Compulsory arbitration was the second item on the federal Labor Party's fighting platform after a White Australia, and the bill to bring it about was to be the catalyst for the fall of two governments, as well as a rallying cause for the Labor Party's growing political power and electoral strength.[19]

By the time the bill was dropped in early September, Barton and Deakin were both preoccupied with their futures. With the High Court now legislated, the three judges needed to be appointed. Deakin had long wanted the Queenslander Sir Samuel Griffith for Chief Justice. Griffith had been the major drafter of the 1891 constitution, and Deakin had admired his patience and courtesy as he turned the fragile consensus of those meetings into terse, clear clauses.[20]

Barton had promised a judicial seat to Richard O'Connor, who had led a difficult Senate with great skill and no remuneration beyond a member's allowance; and Barton was considering himself for the third. Tired of politics, in debt and missing his family, he would be happy to retire to the well-paid serenity of the bench. His doctor had provided him with written advice, which he showed to Deakin, that the excessive strain of politics was affecting his life expectancy.

Appointment to the High Court was a matter for cabinet and, as there are no papers for this period, we don't know how discussion proceeded. It was clearly difficult, however, for on 28 August 1903 Deakin wrote in his diary, 'Determined to resign re High Court.'[21] Deakin was entering yet another period of crisis about his future. He had just turned forty-seven. In his prayer diary he wrote, 'I have this year for the first time realised age—the beginning of old age, of enfeeblement, of withdrawal, of a spent force.'[22]

If Barton were to go to the High Court, who would become prime minister? Deakin was the obvious candidate, but did he want it? And would it be for the best, for the party and for the country? On the first Saturday in September, he took the train to the outer Melbourne suburb of Eltham and walked 'solus' along the Yarra the eight kilometres or so back to Heidelberg, where he caught the train home. Walking through the bush beside the tranquil river on a fine day, he could let his mind drift over his choices. On Sunday he read Gottfried Ephraim Lessing's essay *Laocoon*, his book about the limits of art and literature. In the afternoon, as he always did when in Melbourne, he visited his mother and sister at Adams Street. That night he dreamt that a gigantic and heroic figure fell near Adams Street and the head broke off.[23]

Did the fallen statue recall Barton, whom he often associated with classical imagery: did he wish for or fear his imminent departure? Or did the fallen hero signify his disappointment that Barton was not made of sterner stuff? Deakin's portrait of Barton in *The Federal Story* shows him aware from the first of Barton's limitations, 'his Apollo-like brow and brilliant capacities...chained to the earth by his love of good living.'[24] But he admired the skill and dedication Barton had brought to chairing the constitutional drafting committee at the 1898 convention and his energetic championing of federation in the hostile territory of New South Wales. He also valued his loyal and affectionate friendship. Nevertheless, Deakin must have been irritated when he had to sort out the various problems caused by Barton's carelessness and procrastination; and now Barton planned to leave his 'dear old friend' with responsibility for both the government and the protectionist cause.

After Barton made clear his intention to go, Deakin concluded that it might be best if he, Deakin, stood aside to give Lyne a chance at the prime ministership. He, Pattie and Vera went to Woodend in the hills north of Melbourne for five days, from Tuesday, 15 to Saturday, 19 September. While there he wrote a long letter to Barton which shows how precarious he judged the political situation to be. The government would not survive the election due at the end of the year; his and O'Connor's seats might well be lost; and there would be some popular reaction against Barton's move to the High Court.

The letter canvasses various scenarios, including the familiar one of Deakin retiring to the backbench, with Lyne as prime minister. Deakin thought Lyne might be the best chance of a good protectionist government, but was not sure he wanted it, especially as Lyne thought Barton's move to the High Court was highly improper. In his 1909 list of contemplated resignations, Deakin records, 'Offered Lyne P. Ministership and only reformed government on his failure.'[25]

It is hard to judge how eager Deakin was for the prime ministership. His letter to Barton obliquely refers to his personal ambition as being served by Barton's decision, and the suggestion that he might go to the backbench seems hardly serious, given that he had no plans as to how he would maintain his income. He would not have been disappointed, I think, had Barton changed his mind, but Barton was determined.

Events moved quickly once Deakin returned to Melbourne. On Sunday, 20 September he prayed for insight into 'the public consequences of my choice sufficient to enable me to decide by them and without the shadow of personal motive'. On Monday he consulted his old mentor David Syme who said, 'take PM', and discussed the ministry with Lyne. On Wednesday he gave an interview to a Melbourne *Punch* journalist. On Thursday, Barton resigned, the governor-general sent for Deakin to come to his official residence at Melbourne's Government House and the new ministry was announced and sworn in. Lyne became minister for trade and customs, and second in cabinet precedence.

His prayer that night was for guidance and support 'to discern those things which are necessary for the welfare of the people at large and in which something practical may be accomplished'.[26] For the next few days he received 'Torrents of congratulations', including from his old schoolteacher John Henning Thompson, and this observation from a Ballarat constituent: 'I trust the strain will not prove too great for you. The coarse fibred man seems to stand the tension best and from your temperament I should judge you to be extremely sensitive and highly strung.'[27]

Punch had scored a coup, able to publish its interview the following week with the prime minister. The seventh in a series on 'Victoria's Representative Men at Home', it has photos of Deakin in his garden with the dogs, on his balcony looking out across the bay, and in his library among his books and the busts of great men. He shows the reporter his copy of *Sartor Resartus*, the first work that 'turned my thoughts to more serious channels', and tells him that the past three years were only the first stage of federation, providing the means for 'the localisms and sectionalisms still rampant among us, with their long train of jealousies and misunderstandings' to be 'absorbed by an all-embracing national feeling'.[28]

25

PRIME MINISTER I

DEAKIN BECAME PRIME minister of Australia for the first time at the end of September 1903. He believed that the future dynamic of federal politics would be the continuing trials of strength between the parochial states and a Commonwealth government representing a unified national destiny, and that sectional divisions would gradually dissolve in a higher unity that he would serve. This was the deep narrative that had shaped his political life, informed by a profound conviction in the divinely sanctioned unity of the universe.

Labor's class-based challenge and the equally class-based political response of employers were not part of this story, and Deakin was poorly equipped to understand them. He was a nineteenth-century man, shaped by its religious debates and solutions and by its political practices; and he remained a nineteenth-century man as the class politics of twentieth-century Australia took shape around him.

The catalyst for change was the Labor Party, which upset established parliamentary practices. Labour parties had first formed in Australia in the early 1890s, after the failed strikes. The trade-union movement decided to stand working men for parliament on a labour platform. The strategy was immediately successful, especially in New South Wales, where Labor captured 21.8 per cent of the vote at the 1891 election. With thirty-five members in a chamber of 141 it held the balance of power.[1] But, as all new parties soon discover, a parliamentary as well as an electoral strategy was needed to make effective use of parliamentary numbers, and the thirty-five was soon reduced to seventeen as newly elected members defected.

Labor's solution was to impose rigid party discipline on its members, requiring them to pledge themselves to support the party platform and to vote in the House as the majority of the party sitting in caucus would determine. At the 1894 New South Wales election there were two groups of Labor candidates: 'solidarities', who had signed the pledge; and independent Labor candidates, who would not. Some independents were concerned that, as either a protectionist or a free-trader, they might be forced to support the other side. Others had more fundamental worries about the effect a pledge to an organisation outside the parliament would have on their parliamentary duties. Joseph Cook, an ex-coalminer and a devout Primitive Methodist who was for a short time leader of the New South Wales parliamentary Labor Party, refused to sign because 'the pledge destroyed the representative character of a member and abrogated the electoral privileges of a constituency.'[2]

The deviation from current notions of representative parliamentary government which disturbed Cook was threefold. First, it positioned parliamentarians as delegates of the labour movement, rather than as representatives of their electorate. Second, it rejected the idea of the parliamentarian as a trustee who brought his independent judgement and conscience to the affairs of state. Third, as labour policy was made in labour's own deliberative bodies, it challenged the primacy of parliament itself. What was the point of parliamentary debates if parliamentarians were already locked into policies formed outside parliament?[3] These arguments were repeated again and again to mark the line in the sand between progressive Liberals and their working-class challengers, whose policies on most issues were indistinguishable.

The first federal parliament ended on 22 October 1903, with an election
to be held on 16 December. Deakin's opening policy speech in Ballarat
was something of a grab bag: a survey of the federation's short history, a
defence of the ministry's record; a list of promises still to be implemented,
including the Conciliation and Arbitration Bill; a plea for a truce in
the fiscal contest between free trade and protection; and the passionate
advocacy of his new cause of imperial preference, which would turn
the empire into a free-trade zone.

The crux of the election, he told his supporters, was to protect the
tariff. 'Social, sectoral, class and personal appeals are being made to
everyone…to tempt electors to vote on every issue except the real one
now at stake.' It was a case of the general fighting the last war with the
last war's weapons and the last war's troops. Not until the end of the
speech did he acknowledge that women were now part of the federal
electorate when he added to 'the men of Australia' 'the women of
Australia who at this election are going to cast their virgin vote'.[4] This
was his only comment on the historic moment when Australia led the
world in progressive democratic reform; and it was only half right, as
women in both Western Australia and South Australia had been able
to vote in the 1901 election.

The speech's final, rallying banner was 'Fiscal peace and preferential trade for a White Australia', and to his *Morning Post* readers he
presented imperial preference as giving the prime minister's policy its
'harmonious' structure and design. If Britain were to give Australian
primary produce preference, then more people could be settled on
the land and the nation could grow; in return, Australia would give
preference to British imports. Deakin's *Morning Post* Sydney persona
even claimed that though the city was no friend of high duties, it would
be a different matter if these were to be applied 'out of attachment to
the Mother Country and in order to unite us as an Empire'.[5]

Deakin had been courted by enthusiasts for imperial federation
on his first visit to England in 1887. At that time he had argued that
Australia must federate first. Now that federation was achieved, a
closer form of imperial union seemed the next step to a higher unity.

In September 1903, when Joseph Chamberlain resigned from the British cabinet because of the lack of support for his campaign for imperial trade preferences, the moment seemed right. From London, Philip Mennell kept Deakin abreast of Chamberlain's Tariff Reform campaign, and let Chamberlain know of Deakin's support. Together, Chamberlain wrote to Mennell, the colonies and the mother country can hold their own against all comers.[6]

Deakin used his *Morning Post* letters to signal Australia's support for Chamberlain to the British elite. Next to royalty, Chamberlain would be the most popular visitor the mother country could send us, he wrote. 'The whole strength of the Imperial sentiment among our people…would blaze into force and flame at his approach.'[7] Did he really think the cause of imperial preference had such power to ignite the people's passions?

Imperial politics offered Deakin the chance to serve the Ideal on both a higher plane and a larger stage with a much larger audience, to be an imperial not just a colonial or national statesman. Deakin always disavowed the lure of the world's rewards, but he was no doubt gratified when Hammond Hall, the editor of the illustrated London newspaper the *Daily Graphic*, requested a portrait of him for a series on leading imperialists which included Chamberlain and Balfour.[8]

George Reid was having none of either imperial preference or the plea for fiscal peace and fought the election as he had the last, as a champion of free trade. He did not propose tearing up the tariff legislation altogether, as the Commonwealth's reliance on customs revenue would not allow it. But he wanted a reduction of duties on 'the common necessities of life' and on items required for the development of primary industry. Unlike Deakin, Reid was quick to adjust his policies to the interests of the newly enfranchised women struggling to stretch their housekeeping money. He was also sceptical about Chamberlain's motives for pursuing imperial preference, querying just how much benefit the policy would bring to Australia.[9] In fact, there was little popular demand for imperial preference; and it was hard to see how it squared with Deakin's passionate commitment to the protective tariff, given that it would reduce the price of British imports.

At the December election Deakin was returned unopposed, but his Liberal Protectionists lost seven seats. Labor, which had campaigned hard on the Conciliation and Arbitration Bill, gained nine and also did extremely well in the Senate, winning ten of the nineteen seats it contested. Although the free-traders' numbers were reduced by Labor, they won three seats from the protectionists in New South Wales. The final line-up was Liberal Protectionist twenty-five, Labor twenty-five, Free Trade twenty-four, and one independent.[10] Parliament would not meet until early March. Until then, the government stayed in place and Deakin was still the prime minister, but what would happen when parliament met was uncertain.

In January 1904 the governor-general, Lord Tennyson, returned to England. Deakin travelled to Adelaide to farewell him. The third Ashes Test was in full swing, with Australia's Victor Trumper putting on virtuosic displays of batting. Never a cricket enthusiast, Deakin did not attend, but he turned to the sport two weeks later for a 'homely illustration of the difficulty the Federal Parliament had to solve'. Addressing the annual luncheon of the ANA at the Exhibition Building in Melbourne, he asked,

> What kind of a game of cricket…could they play if they had three elevens instead of two—one team playing sometimes with one side, sometimes with the other and sometimes for itself…It was absolutely essential that as soon as possible the three parties somehow or other should be resolved into two—either as parties or parts of parties—in order that constitutional government might be carried on. He had not the slightest idea as yet which two parties were going to endeavour to unite, but unite they must…Someone must give way for the benefit of the State, and which was to give way was the delicate issue.

There should, he stressed, be no secret compacts, with the terms of any treaty of alliance made known to the world. Until such time as this happened, the duty of the ministry of the day was 'to go straight on with the programme they submitted and the business of the country'. He told the *Morning Post* readers that Deakin's candid account of the federal political situation had 'sent the echoes flying'. Mr Deakin, said the *Age*, was only saying what everyone had been whispering since the election, but he was saying it aloud and as prime minister. Disingenuously, he asked his *Morning Post* readers, 'What does this frankness mean?'[11]

The challenge was clear enough. When parliament resumed, the government would stay put until parliament put it out. Deakin was used to coalition ministries being put together after elections, and he was used to ministries being unable to pass all their legislation. But this parliament, with three equal and opposed blocks, was different. Over the summer he had tested the possibility of an 'understanding' with Labor, but nothing eventuated.[12]

During the first parliament Labor's strategy had been support in return for concessions but, although its support had been crucial to Barton's government, the concessions won were not obvious. It did achieve the strong legislative foundation for a White Australia, but this was hardly a concession, as the Barton government was already committed to it and rejected Labor's preferred direct method of exclusion. The Conciliation and Arbitration Bill loomed as the first real test of Labor's strategy in relation to a core policy, and Deakin was resigned to the likely outcome.

Labor's federal parliamentary leader was Chris Watson, a trade unionist and a foundation member of the New South Wales Labor Party. He won a seat in the colony's parliament in 1894 as one of fifteen 'solidarity' Labor members who signed the pledge. In 1901 he contested and won a federal seat, and was elected the parliamentary Labor Party's first leader. Watson was an ardent protectionist. He did not much like Barton, but he got on well with Deakin and shared his capacity for compromise.[13] But there was to be no compromise from either man on the Conciliation and Arbitration Bill.

On 22 March 1904, when parliament met, Deakin reintroduced a modified bill, but its provisions still did not extend to state public servants. Deakin told the House that his objection to such extension was 'unswerving'. As a lawyer he did not think the federal government was competent to include them; it would breach the federal nature of the constitution and be antagonistic to states' rights.[14] Labor, though, was not convinced. Both Isaac Isaacs and Henry Bournes Higgins thought the extension was constitutional. Given that opinions differed, Labor argued that it was for the High Court to decide and that parliament should not pre-empt the matter.

There the matter rested while Deakin and other federal politicians went on a tour to East Gippsland and the Snowy Mountains to inspect potential sites for the capital. He returned greatly refreshed. Pattie wrote to Herbert Brookes, 'My dear man came home Monday looking splendidly fresh and free of the worried look he went away with.'[15] Atlee Hunt observed that, although Deakin had told him that he did not expect his government to last the week, he went about his work 'just as usual keen and careful for the future as if he was to be in office always. For a nervous excitable man he betrays few signs of being much troubled.' In fact he seemed in excellent spirits, as he looked forward to 'a relief from the burden of his responsibilities'.[16] Deakin wrote to Tom Bavin in Sydney that he soon expected to be 'kicking up his heels in his library like an old horse turned out to grass'.[17]

On 22 April 1904 Andrew Fisher moved the expected amendment.[18] By having Fisher move the amendment rather than Watson, Labor hoped to avoid Deakin regarding the matter as one of confidence, but Deakin's mind was made up. If the House voted to include state public servants, he would resign. Pattie, Catherine, Ivy and Stella were there to witness what might well have been his final evening in the House as prime minister.

As Deakin expected, the government lost the division, twenty-nine to thirty-eight, and he informed the House that as a consequence he would be 'ceasing to discharge the duties of Prime Minister'.[19] On 22 April he tendered his resignation to the new governor-general, Lord Northcote, and advised that Watson be sent for. Next day, a Saturday, Watson told a special meeting of caucus that he had been asked to form a ministry. It would be the first Labor government in the world. Deakin was, he prayed, 'grateful for the gift of political power, for

what it has enabled me to do and for the manner in which I am able
to relinquish it with joy'.[20]

Why did Deakin dig his heels in at the bill's inclusion of state public
servants? Why was he so uncharacteristically stubborn, particularly
given the parliamentary mayhem caused by his refusal to compromise?
To Bavin he wrote that he had the 'satisfaction of going down for a
great cause',[21] but was it really so great? He could have allowed the
legislation to pass and then be tested in the High Court. After all,
he himself had argued strenuously that a High Court was needed to
interpret the constitution and adjust it to a changing community. Why
not let it do its job?

Labor would have done anything it could to have avoided taking
office, and regarded Deakin's making the amendment a matter of
confidence as unprecedented.[22] There was something reckless in Deakin's
actions, as if, by forcing a crisis, he was creating the space for Providence
to show its hand. He was at least taking the opportunity to teach Labor
the limits of its political power, as it was forced into a minority government for which it was unprepared.

At a personal level, perhaps he was simply courting defeat to relieve
himself of the burden of office. Deakin was going through another
periodic crisis of his political vocation. On 21 February 1904, after only
six months as prime minister, he had prayed:

> Gracious God lift the sense of my burden from me...the duties cast
> upon me are beyond me, not beyond my desire and aspiration but
> beyond my capacity. Knowing this I pray that...by self-sacrifice,
> meekness, patience, unceasing effort and sincere prayer I may
> subdue all that is in me so that it is available for doing the best
> that is possible to me.

A few days later he described his prayer's answer:

> I woke in utter darkness and the world's weight crushing me.
> Life seemed leaden without a vista that was not failure, shame,
> collapse. Suddenly in the midst of a universe of blackness and

despair appeared less than a pin's point of light almost infinitesimal that I felt was Divine light and was near me. The weight vanished and the darkness was forgotten.[23]

Deakin's basic prayer of 'O God, show me the way' had been joined by 'O God, give me the strength.'

26

LABOR IN, LABOR OUT

WHEN PARLIAMENT MET a week later, on 27 April 1904, Deakin promised to extend 'the utmost fair play' to the new government, but he also pointed out the obvious: as Labor did not have a majority in the House, its position was untenable. It must therefore acquire a majority; and so long as the government was 'moderate enough to afford us the opportunity of joining with them' we owed it to the electors to lend them every assistance. He was confident that 'the tact and consideration' with which Watson had led Labor would continue, that Watson would 'lay before the Chamber no chimerical or impossible schemes', and that 'the sobering responsibilities of office' would enable him to quell his party's less restrained elements.[1]

Deakin's metaphor of three elevens was misleading, because it presented the parliamentary situation as triangular, as if alliances were possible among any of the teams. They were not. Reid had experienced Labor in parliament when he was premier of New South Wales, both enjoying its support and suffering when, on the brink of federation, it supported Lyne, brought down his government and robbed him of Australia's first prime ministership.

Like Deakin, Reid had a great deal of sympathy for working people, and with Labor support he had introduced much progressive legislation, including factories and shops legislation, but he had come to abhor Labor's restrictions on the freedom of its parliamentarians and would never consider an alliance.[2] There were thus only two possibilities: Deakin's Liberal Protectionists in alliance with either Labor or the free-traders. When he resigned, Deakin later told parliament, 'we had two doors, one on each side and we left them both open,' inviting overtures; if the overture had come from the Conservative free-traders the issue would be of policy, if from Labor of organisation.[3] He implied that either of these would resolve the situation, but Deakin's judgement was wrong, because the Liberal Protectionists themselves were split, with a clear majority favouring an alliance with Reid.

John Forrest advised Deakin not to give Watson more than a fortnight, and to pursue a coalition with Reid. Forrest told Deakin that he would not countenance an alliance with the Labor extremists, and that he could never subordinate his independence to caucus. Doing the numbers, Forrest believed that the majority of the Liberal Protectionists felt similarly and that only six 'malcontents' would hold out for Labor.[4] Even if Watson had approached Deakin through the door to his left, and Deakin had been able to strike satisfactory terms, the majority of his party would have deserted him to the right, and Reid would have become prime minister anyway.

Deakin was also receiving advice to go left. Bernhard Wise, who was attorney-general in the Liberal Protectionist New South Wales government, advised Deakin to give Watson time to find his feet, and warned that defeating Watson would only increase the influence of the extremists. 'You seem to me to judge too much from the Victorian experience. The Labor Party there is wild and unrestrained largely because of the alliance formed against it.' Did he want the Victorian experience in every colony?[5] Wise was optimistic that, given time, the moderates in the Labor Party would prevail and the caucus system be modified to accommodate the Liberals' views on representation and parliamentary government. In a later letter, he wrote, 'There is a dementia of high-mindedness more subtle than a dementia of self-seeking.'[6]

The Labor caucus left the choosing of the world's first labour ministry to Watson. There was a difficulty filling the position of attorney-general, as the only Labor man with a law degree was Billy Hughes and even he thought he had insufficient experience. With Deakin's approval, Henry Bournes Higgins was invited to fill the position. But caucus did not authorise Watson to seek any alliances.[7] By the time caucus did authorise Watson to open formal discussions with Deakin, it was too late; Deakin had already negotiated an agreement with Reid.

By mid-May, Deakin and Reid had a draft agreement to take to their respective parties. Its preamble summed up the challenge Labor posed to parliament's traditional modes of operating:

> Unfortunately the party now in office quite apart from any question relating to its programme, maintains a control of its minority by its majority and an antagonism to all who do not submit themselves to its organization and decisions, which makes it hopeless to approach its members on any terms of equality, even under the present exceptional circumstances.

Deakin and Reid agreed that the tariff would not be revisited during this parliamentary term, except by mutual agreement; that imperial preference would not be pursued; that the old-age pension, immigration and rural development were matters of priority; and that determination of the site of the national capital and the resolution of the troublesome Arbitration Bill were urgent. In a future coalition government, there would be equal numbers of ministers from the Liberal Protectionists and the Free Trade Party. Reid would be prime minister and Deakin, again planning to advise from the backbench, would not take a ministry.[8]

The Liberal Protectionists were appalled by the prospect of Deakin abandoning them and rejected the agreement. Forrest judged that, with Deakin as leader, the majority of the party would follow him into a coalition with Reid, but 'without you all is chaos.'[9] The day after the Liberal Protectionists rejected the agreement, Deakin decided on impulse to explain himself to parliament. The party caucus, which had met in the morning, was insisting on his leadership. He went home for tea, talked with Herbert Brookes, who was staying at Llanarth, and returned to parliament to make public some of the moral and tactical reasoning behind his actions. He had conceived it to be his duty, he said in this 'Apologia', to expedite the restoration of normal conditions of government, and believed he would be able to bring about a working coalition. It was now clear to him that he could not do this without his Liberal Protectionist party splitting.

He had therefore decided that his duties would be fulfilled if he brought about the restoration of responsible government, that he would sit behind whichever government resulted, but that 'he was not called upon to undergo the trial of separation from old colleagues and supporters.' Nor, as his party would be the weaker in any coalition ministry, did he want to be bound by cabinet solidarity but to remain free to defend his Liberal Protectionist principles. He had gone to the backbench before in the Victorian parliament, he said, and believed this had been beneficial to his ministerial colleagues. He had once been persuaded to withdraw his tendered resignation and sacrifice his own views to those of others, and he now regarded this as a 'fatal mistake'.[10] Given how frequently Deakin contemplated resigning, it is not certain which occasion he had in mind. Was it 1902, when Barton appealed to his dear old friend not to break his heart? Or earlier, in 1889, when he did not resign from the Victorian ministry and later recorded his regret?[11]

Deakin was keen to convince himself and others that he was not shirking his responsibility, but he also did not really know what to do. Privately, to Reid, he pleaded 'his state of health', and his diary reveals that Pattie was again ill.[12] Since Barton had left parliament, he had no one really simpatico to talk with who understood the complexity of the situation. Perhaps he talked a little to Brookes, who would have given him emotional support; and he prayed to the God of Mercy to 'grant my soul light that it may hew its way through the forest of perplexities through which I am moving'.[13]

Late in May, Watson finally received caucus authorisation to approach Deakin. Deakin told him that since they had discussed the situation three months earlier, much had happened and the obstacles had multiplied. Deakin now knew he could not bring his whole party with him into any agreement with Labor, so in any alliance Liberal Protectionists would always be in a minority; and with Labor members already locked into their positions, how could they have any influence?[14]

In his 'Apologia', Deakin had spoken bitterly of another stumbling block: three-cornered electoral contests, in which Labor men opposed radical Liberal Protectionists holding almost indistinguishable policies. By early June it was clear that Deakin and the Liberal Protectionists would enter an alliance with neither Labor nor the Free Trade Party and that the Labor ministry would survive only until Reid moved a no-confidence motion, when Deakin's supporters would split, some voting with the Labor government and some with Reid and the Opposition.

Deakin's sense of personal isolation increased when he had a major falling-out with David Syme over a speech Deakin delivered in Ballarat on 1 August 1904 to launch the National Political League. The league was a local initiative. The shock of a Labor government had turned the minds of Ballarat's professional, business and mining men to the need for a new anti-socialist organisation able to match Labor's organisation and unity.[15] Deakin's speech passed lightly over the Labor programme, to attack its organisation. Political machinery was necessary, but it should not dominate, said Deakin. Of course men needed to be able to trust and rely on each other, but it was demeaning to bind them with a pledge. Local committees to select candidates were a good thing, but not when they were made up of 'wire pullers, swayed by personal considerations'. Labor was pushing organisation to extreme, 'to turn voters into dummies, representatives into pawns, and Ministers into figure heads'.[16]

Deakin was facing a dilemma. His preferred opposition, between liberals and conservatives as more or less advanced in their acceptance of the inevitable, evolutionary advance of human progress, between facilitators and obstructionists, was being disturbed by another quite different dichotomy: between Carlyle's living world of the spirit and the mechanical material world of class-based self-interest, of which Labor was the harbinger. Reid's free-traders were conservatives and obstructionist, but the Labor machine was death to the spirit. What should the progressive liberal do?

John Forrest was delighted with Deakin's speech, and told him so when they met by chance in Collins Street next day. Labor and the radical Liberals were perplexed. Two days later the *Age* launched a full-scale attack on Deakin's 'transcendental musings concerning the precise line where party organisation is too little or too much'. For the *Age* the main game was still the fight for protection, and it called for an immediate revision of the tariff which, it claimed, was too low and causing suffering to tens of thousands of working people as imported manufactured goods put them out of work. It argued that a majority of the parliamentarians were protectionists and that all that was wanting was 'a capable Protectionist leader', and that Deakin had 'lost himself in the clouds amongst politico-philosophical questions', making 'a series of windy speeches' instead of giving practical leadership.[17]

The attack cut Deakin to the quick and he wrote to Syme. The two men had discussed the speech before Deakin gave it and he believed that Syme had endorsed every point of it, 'yet when it was made you treated it with derision. I must insist that such conduct is indefensible.' Syme responded that nothing he had approved of in private was contradicted; the *Age* editorial leader had discussed another subject altogether.

'I have been more deeply upset by this incident than by any during my political life,' Deakin wrote in a second letter to Syme. The *Age* had attacked him before, but 'this is the first and only time in which you and I have come directly into conflict. I feel this acutely.' Syme thought Deakin should apologise to him for making the charges he did, and requested that his letters be returned.

Deakin was hurt not just by Syme's betrayal of trust, but by the accusation of 'transcendental musings'. His hostility to Labor's organisation was far more than a matter of differing theories of political representation; in today's terms it was an identity issue, a matter of who he was and what he could tolerate emotionally and psychologically. 'I have no ambition to retain even a place in Parliament except as a free man and an independent representative,' he told Syme. 'I would rather lose my seat a hundred times than sully it by subservience to any "machine".'[18]

This granitey old man was Deakin's last link with the mentors of his early political life: Graham Berry had died early in 1904, Charles Pearson in 1894 and James Service in 1899. His coalition partner, Duncan Gillies, had died in 1903, and since the financial disasters of the early 1890s his friendships with Theodore Fink and Fred Derham had cooled. Though he later re-established relations with Syme, they were never again as close.

After 1901 Deakin's diary records little that is not either political business or family events. The *Age* attack had been published on the morning of his forty-eighth birthday and, as was his habit on his birthday, he marked it with a prayer reflecting on his life's direction.

> The providence of God in my life makes for self-reliance. Few people so far as I can judge are more receptive of influence. Yet there has been no one on whom I can lean or have leant for years in public affairs or even in private. All have failed me or I have had to withdraw from them...none of them reach me now except momentarily and by sympathy—all touch me there and draw me—but I act alone, live alone and think alone.[19]

He would, 'By the grace of God...stand firmly on my own feet leaning on no one and looking nowhere for support.'[20]

Deakin's warm affectionate nature, his quick responsiveness to others, was not a pretence but he hated overt personal conflict and, as he grew older and its sources multiplied in his private and public lives, he retreated into himself. With a wife who shared his intellectual interests, with a sister preoccupied with her own family, in a career that took less from him, in more stable political circumstances, he might not have been so lonely.

Syme was angry because he took the Ballarat speech to indicate that Deakin thought his objections to Labor's organisation were more important than advancing protection, that Labor not the Free Trade

Party was the main enemy, and that he was ready to cut a deal with Reid. Others, including Reid, drew the same conclusion, and within a week the whips knew which Liberal Protectionists would follow Deakin through the door to the right.[21]

Believing that an alliance with Deakin was possible, Reid moved to force Labor out, using the Conciliation and Arbitration Bill as the trigger.[22] The extension of the bill to state public servants had been passed, after opponents decided to let the issue go to the High Court, confident that it would be rejected. But a new point of contention had emerged: the inclusion of a clause to give the Arbitration Court the power to award preference to unionists. The Opposition successfully moved an amendment that this required the approval of a majority of workers in the industry. The Labor government regarded this as making the preference provision unworkable, and on 12 August 1904 Watson moved to recommit the bill with a view to removing the amendment. When the recommittal motion was lost by two votes, Watson chose to regard it as a matter of confidence, and when Northcote refused his request for a new election he resigned.[23]

Normal parliamentary procedure was to support a recommittal motion to allow debate, so this was a tricky political manoeuvre on Reid's part. Deakin had voted with the government on preference for unionists but had opposed the recommittal. In the acrimonious debates that followed Watson's resignation he maintained that he did not know Watson would make it a matter of confidence. As with Deakin's own resignation over an amendment to this same bill, the issue of union preference did not in itself justify the government's resignation, but it did reveal its tenuous control of the House and the near impossibility of legislating its programme. Watson had concluded, as he wrote to Higgins, 'It is distinctly better that Reid should be guilty of inaction than ourselves.'[24]

The world's first Labor government had held office for only four months, but it had much to be proud of. Labor had not sought office, but had had it thrust upon it by Deakin's resignation. Taking up the challenge, it had shown that Labor could provide competent administration, and so taken it a step nearer to becoming a party of government.

.

Not all Labor men took defeat as calmly as Watson. On 12 August, the day of the fateful vote, Labor's master of invective, Billy Hughes, singled out for blame 'the chivalrous member for Ballaarat' who 'retains the mask of fair play towards us, though he…remains ominously silent' during the debate on the bill he himself claimed would take Australia into the promised land of industrial peace: 'not one word have we heard from him to justify this most amazing, this unexampled, this treacherous change of front.'[25]

Hughes told Atlee Hunt that his purpose was to draw Deakin and he was delighted that he had made him 'real angry'.[26] *Punch* described just how angry: 'with pallid face, blazing eyes and bristling hair…the habitual courtesy, kid-gloved chivalrous methods' fell away and 'roused to a frenzy of indignation' he delivered a 'whirling, biting, prophetic denunciation of the Labor machine'. 'For nearly a decade Mr Deakin has not been heard to such effect.'[27] Deakin began with a contemptuous dismissal of Hughes:

> It happens sometimes to all of us, that as we pass along the streets of the city, we meet men engaged in filling drays with dirt and garbage, and unless one is discreet some of that dirt and refuse may drift upon him. When it does happen that the dust reaches us, we brush it off and pass on; that is the proper treatment for a speech of the character to which we have just listened.[28]

This was subtly pointed. Hughes was president of the New South Wales Trolley, Draymen's and Carter's Union, and had recently appeared for it in the Arbitration Court. It was a personal landmark for Hughes, his first important case after his admission to the bar at the end of 1903. He had not slipped into legal life from a comfortable home, but had qualified when he was over forty and already in federal parliament by dint of his native intelligence and hard work.

Hughes was a complicated, clever, proud, ambitious man who had migrated to Australia as a twenty-two-year-old in 1884 after a difficult childhood. During the 1890s he joined the nascent Labor Party and

became a union organiser, and in 1894 he was one of the 'solidarities'
to win a seat in the New South Wales parliament. At the 1901 election
he won the federal seat of West Sydney.[29]

Hughes was always quick to call out class condescension. The next
Monday, 15 August, in a speech to the Ballarat branch of the Political
Labour Council, he repeated his attack on Deakin, the professed radical,
for voting against the Watson ministry, and added an astute observation
on the ambivalence of middle-class men like Deakin towards working-
class political agency: 'while the Labor party hewed political wood and
drew political water for its detractors it was all right, but as soon as it
commenced to hew wood and draw water for itself affairs took on a
very different complexion.'[30]

In a speech to the East Ballarat ANA the following Monday, Deakin
again let his courtesy slip: he would not answer Hughes, 'excepting to
say that the gentleman reminded him of the ill-bred urchin one saw
dragged from a tart shop kicking, screeching and scratching'.[31] The voice
was mild, delivered to raise a laugh, but the image was cruel, drawing
attention to Hughes's small stature—he was slight and 167 centimetres
tall—as well as to his lower-class origins. Anger had gripped Deakin's
tongue twice in replying to Hughes, and the break in his detachment
unsettled him; this was not the calm goodness he so often prayed for.

Months later, on 12 October, Deakin apologised in the House for
having allowed himself a rather flippant remark in his 'tart' reply
to Hughes, even though it was under the provocation of Hughes's
caricature of his own speech to the Ballarat National Political League.

> It was merely a political retort. I recognise the honourable and
> learned member's achievements and honour him for them. He
> started where I did, as a teacher. He earned his living as I did by
> that means. He has now joined the profession to which I am proud
> to belong; and any man who could achieve his position under the
> difficulties which he had to surmount is entitled to the respect of
> every honourable member of the House.[32]

Although a courteous gesture, the comparison between his own and

Hughes's youth showed how little Deakin understood the injuries of class.

After Northcote refused Watson an election, he commissioned Reid, so giving the third of the three elevens a chance to govern and Australia its fourth prime minister in under four years. Reid consulted with Deakin and offered him a ministry, which he refused, although he used his influence to persuade Turner to accept the position of treasurer in the new government.[33] Turner would rather have 'stood out' with Deakin. Pleading ill health, he refused to take on the responsibilities of the leader of the Liberal Protectionists. This instead went to Allan McLean and the government became known as the Reid–McLean government.

That Deakin would allow the party's leadership to pass to this man shows just how detached from politics he was feeling and how thin were his ranks. McLean was from one of the Scottish Highland families who had driven the Kurnai out of Gippsland.[34] This is not likely to have troubled Deakin, who never thought hard about the fate of the Aborigines, but as the Victorian premier from 1899 to 1900 McLean had opposed federation and saw himself primarily as a representative of rural rather than national interests. Protectionist he may have been, but he was also parochial, far more parochial in fact than Reid and most of the free-traders.[35]

Not all the Liberal Protectionists were prepared to support Reid, with a radical group including Isaacs, Higgins and Lyne sitting on the crossbenches. Reid was finally prime minister, but with a reliable majority of only two, no formal agreement between his party and its Liberal Protectionist supporters, and the number of party groupings increased to four. Nor did he control the Senate.

Like the previous two ministries, Reid's capacity to pass legislation was limited and much of the remainder of 1904 was filled with acrimonious exchanges across the House to the exclusion of real business. In October, Deakin made a four-and-a-half-hour speech in which he went in great detail over the events of the previous few months. Pattie, Ivy, Stella and Herbert Brookes were all in the parliament to hear him speak 'from no merely partisan view point, avoiding every personal consideration and every party consideration'. From this lofty

stance, admitting of no bitter or angry feelings, he justified every one
of his actions, went back over his statements to the House and in the
press, what he did and did not know, what he did and did not intend.[36]
Always he was in the right.

Reid did finally manage to pass the troublesome Conciliation and
Arbitration Bill, as well as some other uncontentious measures, but when
the House rose in December for the summer recess it ended a year which
had achieved little, and with the parliamentary situation still unresolved.

In July of this difficult year, Deakin's 'darling Ivy' turned twenty-one.
There was a surprise party and the dancing went late. Deakin's prayer
that night was thankful for her 'goodness and trueness' and craved
'thy perpetual presence, light and grace...through all the days of her
life'.[37] Ivy still appeared more frequently than her sisters in Deakin's
diary, though he did record Stella's academic achievements: the school
prizes, and exhibitions and first-class honours at university, where she
was studying science. Catherine had taught her three nieces music, and
Ivy and Vera both pursued its study, Ivy singing and the violin, and
Vera the cello. Deakin attended their concerts when he could, adding
an appreciation of music to his cultural repertoire.

In 1901 Ivy had enrolled as a pupil at George Marshall-Hall's
Conservatorium in East Melbourne. Marshall-Hall had come to
Melbourne in 1891 as the foundation chair of music at the University
of Melbourne. Friends with the Heidelberg School painters and with
Lionel and Norman Lindsay, Marshall-Hall was a flamboyant bohemian
dedicated to the service of art, in his case music. In 1900 he was forced
from his chair after he published a book of rather indifferent erotic
poetry. Accused of lewdness, lasciviousness and anti-clericalism, he was
deemed unsuitable to be a teacher of young women.

The orchestra he established while at the university brought new
music to Melbourne audiences. After he left, the orchestra continued,
as did his teaching, with a loyal band of staff at the now independent
Conservatorium of Music, later the Melba Conservatorium.[38] Allowing
Ivy to attend Marshall-Hall's Conservatorium, the Deakins were clearly
siding with him against Melbourne's puritanical bigots. The anxieties

behind Deakin's earlier moral panic at the thought of servant girls reading Zola seem to have receded.

Ivy was tall, six foot and not a hint of a stoop, thin and with a long face. She was not a beauty, but she was warm and natural and everyone liked her. She was also serious-minded, seemingly content with the ideal of womanhood her father had set for his daughters in the Testament of 1890, 'quiet cheerfulness, intellectual in cast and unselfish in end'. In 1903 she began attending the university conservatorium, where she studied singing, though she continued to play in Marshall-Hall's orchestra.

Ivy was not an outstanding pupil, and at the end of 1904 when Stella received first-class honours and the exhibition in her science degree, she was 'shamefully plucked' (a now outdated way of saying she failed). By this time, however, Ivy no longer needed to worry about her future. In October 1904 Herbert Brookes had formally asked her father for her hand and he had gladly given it, marking their engagement with a prayer that they may elevate each other and those around them 'in purity, simplicity, brightness and usefulness'.[39] Brookes was thirty-six, fifteen and a half years older than Ivy.

Since he had travelled with the Deakins to Europe in 1900 for the passing of the Commonwealth Act, Brookes had become like one of the family. Still working out of town as a mine manager, he was a regular visitor to Llanarth, often staying overnight or for the weekend, rather than with his own family at Brookwood in Queens Road, or with his former in-laws, the Strongs, where a room was kept ready for him.[40] He corresponded with each of the sisters, as well as with Pattie, who kept him up to date on the health and overwork of her 'dear old man'.

Ivy's letters to the man who would become her husband are artless and matter-of-fact, as she reports on the household's comings and goings, her music practice, reading, social engagements, chores and good works, and enquires after his health and the well-being of his pet dogs. Not a hint of passion disturbs her cheerful schoolgirl demeanour, so it is hard to discern the point at which his brotherly interest turned to courtship, though he did send her a bouquet of flowers for the end-of-year concert in 1903.[41] The only discernible change is her becoming more solicitous of his good opinion, and the letters including more earnest discussions of books.

By early in 1904 an understanding had developed between Herbert and Ivy that they were courting. In a girlish game that autumn the three sisters 'confessed' to each other their ideal man. Here is Ivy's:

> My ideal man is a man of moral courage, sincerity, truthfulness and manliness, accompanied with the greatest love of myself...He must be fond of helping others in their troubles, unselfish, patient and generous, not a lover of wealth...This character sketch is not only an ideal but an ideal of life, one whom I have met and loved and still love. He is fair with deep blue eyes, tall and sad and to be worthy of him I must ever look upward.[42]

Apart from the sadness and the blue eyes, it could be a description of her father.

The mine Herbert was managing at Hollybush near Ballarat was running out, destined like so many of Victoria's mining settlements to become just another name on a map. Herbert decided to leave mine management for a city job, and accepted an appointment as secretary of the Austral Otis Elevator and Engineering Company. He rented Winwick, the house next door to Llanarth, for himself and his bride. They later bought it. He hoped, he wrote to Deakin, 'that the little house next door may become a home shadow of the home haven next door. Both your own dear Ivy and myself are looking calmly, hopefully and joyfully to our union which seems the most natural thing in the world.'[43]

He did not tell his own parents of their engagement until two months after the event; and he had let the Strongs, to whom he was once so close, go out of his life.[44] The Deakins were now his family. Pattie was soon addressing him as 'dear Son' and Vera called him 'my dearest Brother'.[45] He did not forget his first wife, Jenny, however, and dutiful Ivy supported his remembering. They called their only daughter after her, and he visited her grave at least twice a year, on the anniversaries of their wedding and of her death. He also wrote occasional memorial poems to the 'wondrous bloom' of his passionate first-love.[46] Photos

of Ivy in the early years of her marriage show a sad young woman.
Perhaps she had taken on some of the burden of his grief, or perhaps
she knew she could never fully assuage it.

The other momentous event for the family in the second half of 1904
was the purchase of seven acres of land at Point Lonsdale. A wooden
house was moved onto it, just as William had moved the Adams Street
house from Fitzroy to South Yarra all those years ago. They called the
house Ballara, after Deakin's electorate of Ballarat. Herbert helped
Deakin as he moved the family into the unfinished house, built fences
and cleared scrub. The purchase was made possible by a bequest from
the will of Alexander Strachan, who had died in 1891, leaving his estate
to Deakin and Pattie after the death of his wife, Kate, which occurred
in 1904. The Strachans were spiritualists and friends of Hugh Browne,
and Kate was a sister-in-law of Sydney Watson, the spiritualist grazier
Deakin had accompanied to Fiji in 1879 and who was also a close friend
of Browne. By 1904 Deakin and Pattie has pushed their spiritualist
experiences well into the past, but it had brought them together, and
it now gave them a house by the sea where they could retreat from the
world.[47]

27

ANOTHER PATH?

ON 10 APRIL 1904, as he returned from the Snowy Mountains to lead his government to inevitable defeat over the Conciliation and Arbitration Bill, Deakin began another of his rambling narratives about a solitary wanderer in his familiar dreamscape of plains, misty chasms and steep ridges. As with his sojourns in the Blue Mountains, the Snowy Mountains scenery stirred his yearning for the Unseen and a simpler, more solitary life. The 'story', titled simply 'M.S.', reveals just how relentlessly events were pressing in on Deakin, threatening to extinguish the core of his self. Beginning in the first person, then shifting to the third, he writes of the strife and strain of a world like a whirlpool which absorbs life and mind into it, until 'dead dreams beset the soul like clouds of insects... he struggled to be free, prayed for release...the strain became unendurable...Cheerful friends are setting out contented with life...haunted by no dreams—by no sense of vanishing opportunities—or a lost path.'

The silent landscape slowly revives the nameless hero and the faculties forced out of action by the exigencies of daily life reassert themselves and demand expression: 'the mind sloughing off its impressions of the world…a new birth seemed at hand…until his sphere of life and occupation, his relations, friends, were all expunged from his consciousness…He felt his self emerge. He had arrived.'[1] As Deakin was driven through the clear blue and soft grey-greens of an Australian alpine autumn, his inner self revived and he confronted again the psychological costs of political office.

The first few pages of this prolix religious narrative describe a self which is overwhelmed by the flux of events. Deakin was remarkably receptive to others, to moods and to the ideas in the air, as if he absorbed the world into himself by osmosis, but he needed long periods of solitude, walking and cycling, reading and writing, communing with the sea and sky, and praying to his God. He interpreted this as a spiritual rather than a psychological need, as he searched for meanings in fleeting sensations and events. When his reflective spaces were crowded out by events, he felt himself going off balance.

Since he had first placed his youthful feet on the political path, more than twenty years ago, Deakin had never entirely given up the possibility of a less worldly vocation. Following Carlyle's prescription he had taken up the duty which lay nearest to him, and this had been given spiritual heft by Swedenborg's doctrine of uses, but just where the Ideal lay and how to serve it was proving hard to discover in the unstable parliament of the early Commonwealth. In the fifteen months between April 1904, when he resigned as prime minister, and July 1905, Deakin produced more than four hundred pages of religious writing: prayers, meditations, journals and devotional poetry, including an exegesis of both the Koran and the Bhagavad-gita.[2] Briefly, early in 1905, he entertained the idea of becoming a preacher: 'If I had followed my heart I should have taken this step many years ago.'[3] In June 1904, as Labor struggled to govern without a majority, he had written, 'Merciful Father, what I crave is a new life'; and a prayer early in 1905 referred to 'glimpses of the new path, the new duty, the new message—Search me & try me that I may search & try myself & my fitness for so great a change.'[4]

Herbert Brookes was urging such a change. In February 1905 he wrote to him: 'I have often said I would like to see you in the pulpit…I am deeply delighted to think you are beginning to think of crowning your life career with such an Act…Federal politics is not your element, religion is.' Brookes had even made contact among his fellow Methodists with a group of 'liberal minded thoughtful men and women' who were looking for a preacher for a new Free Thought-style church.[5] Deakin noted in his diary that he and Brookes discussed this in February, and he met with him every few days over the next month or so.

It is difficult to know how seriously Deakin considered this career change. Whatever its allures, Deakin still had to earn a comfortable middle-class income, as Pattie is unlikely to have welcomed living on a preacher's stipend. Even if he was seriously discussing the possibility with Brookes, he was also keeping his political options alive in meetings with Watson, Reid, Syme and others. And he sought another anonymous writing commitment which depended on his staying in public life, with the *National Review*, a British monthly aligned with the Conservative Party and focussed on imperial and foreign policy. Like the *Morning Post*, it strongly supported Chamberlain's campaign for imperial preference.[6]

When he was considering resigning as attorney-general in mid-1903, Deakin had drafted a letter to the editor of the *National Review*, Leo Maxse, suggesting he write a monthly article on Australia and spruiking his qualifications. The letter seems not to have been sent, and Deakin was soon embarked on the prime ministership. He wrote to Maxse again on 25 April 1904, a few days after he had resigned as prime minister. He was, he said, too involved in politics to contemplate a return to the bar, and so desired to supplement his income with his pen, 'and the first idea that suggests itself—would the *National Review* engage me as a regular contributor?'[7]

After some toing and froing Deakin was engaged to write monthly articles on Australia and her place in the empire at twenty pounds each. Deakin did not tell Maxse of his similar arrangement with the *Morning Post*, and as these contributions too were to be anonymous he presumably thought he could get away with it. This time he wrote as if from South Australia and used the initials CR, for Commonwealth Representative.[8] Over the next year he wrote ten long articles for the

National Review, and so for a short time Deakin was the anonymous Australian correspondent for two London publications.

On 5 April 1905 Deakin wrote to Forrest with a gloomy forecast that the three parties would continue to confront each other, the bargaining for power and the instability would continue, and the Labor Party would become ascendant.

> It is quite probable that if this forecast is correct I shall retire soon from any leadership position and scarcely less probable that I shall retire soon from politics altogether—State and federal—because I see no opportunity for real work such as I care for done as I think it ought to be done.[9]

On the day he wrote to Forrest, Deakin began a new notebook in which he weighed the religious against the political life, the preacher against the legislator, and both against the ultimate purpose of existence. He was dissatisfied with politics because of its dependence on causes, forces and motives that politicians hardly touch. Legislation, such as to repress criminality or breaches of social justice, was not useless, he wrote, but it was exterior effort. 'The root of social injustice is interior' and only to be reached through religion in its widest sense—'recognition of a Divine Order in the Universe' which could only be achieved by individuals: 'Not until every man is his own policeman, his own legislator, his own shepherd and his own pastor…can he reap the full benefits of the efforts of those who try to help him as legislators and pastors.'[10]

This argument pointed to the work of the preacher, but Deakin's religious beliefs were so austere and uncompromisingly individualistic that it was hard for him to imagine a church that could accommodate him. It must have no binding rites, no claims to infallibility, no dogma, and he even wondered if it should have a building. Its only faith was to be in human growth towards the Truth: 'doubts, questioning, hesitations, and particularly suspensions of judgement are to be welcomed with confidence as necessary stages in mental unfoldment…without even a creed to which I myself am bound…Free to unsay as well as to say.'[11]

His claim to leadership was his fifty years of life, and his effort to articulate thoughts and feelings long accumulated. Asking himself what success would be, he concluded that it would be when his listeners knew what he knew, saw and felt what he saw and felt, and could dispense with him and go their own ways. 'I may or may not join,' he added. This comment shows the psychological impossibility for Deakin of his other path, no matter how profound he believed his religious insights to be. In politics he could always hold something of himself back, could choose to join or not join, but as a preacher of the Truth he would have to be fully present, revealing his own heart and life and abandoning his characteristic detachment.

A week into this conversation with himself, on 12 April 1905, Deakin had an 'Interesting and Important' interview with General William Booth, the elderly founder of the Salvation Army, who was on one of his regular visits to Australia. Talking with Booth 'providentially made a great deal plain to me'. The simple sincerity of the committed evangelist opened Deakin's eyes to the folly of religion not finding constant expression in works. Truth is not academic: 'the Truth that saves must be valuable for life…Unless it sways the life & thought of the man who receives it, it is nothing.'[12]

Deakin concluded that 'Light, heat and leading' were absent from his open-ended approach to religious faith. Without them the preacher could not hope to arouse the passion to effect the transformation of the self that was the goal of evangelical preaching.[13] Deakin admired the Salvation Army and met with Booth a number of times during his visit, chairing his meeting at the Exhibition Building and welcoming him to a vegetarian breakfast with the family at Llanarth, where his home-centred piety was on full display. One of the daughters, probably Ivy, sang the hymn 'Just as I Am Without One Plea', and Booth led the family in prayer.[14]

The notebook contains some pieces that look like partial drafts of sermons, and these too show how unsuitable Deakin was to be a preacher. Starting with a conventional evocation of the shortness and uncertainty of life, instead of leading the listener to visions of salvation or redemption Deakin dissolves all certainty in a cascade of rhetorical questions:

> What play is it that is being produced on this magnificent stage
> of the Cosmos? Who prepared the pieces, teaches the actors,
> manages the production? Where shall we be when the curtain
> falls?…What is life? What is destiny?…Churches, schools of
> thought, philosophies offer conflicting explanations. Where
> shall the perplexed find an interpretation?…Stretching to the
> stars—taking soundings in the grave…probing the wounds of
> life—Measuring its drops of blood—Haunting the birth chamber
> & peering under the shroud.[15]

When Deakin's conversation with himself turned to politics, its focus
was the new era emerging from the present. He foresaw both a turn to
socialism and growing world interdependence: 'Despite wars, nationali-
ties, languages, we are part of a world State…We need individual men
and women who think out our condition and future as citizens of the
world. In that capacity we rise above realms and races to the standard
of common humanity.' But Deakin had no idea how humanity would
reach this standard, except, in his millennial imagination, through a
great world crisis, 'a storm threatening all peoples, their governments,
their creeds and political economies'. It is no easy task, he concluded,
to penetrate the true causes of the earth tremors, to understand 'the
hopeless tangle of an age'.[16] His long conversation with himself about
both politics and religion had led only to uncertainty and puzzlement.

Through all this private questing, Deakin maintained an enigmatic
public silence on the fortunes of the Reid–McLean government. Having
kept his government in office till the end of 1904, Reid was in no hurry
to test its majority, and parliament remained in recess till late June 1905.
The new prime minister believed that a fusion of the non-Labor parties
was inevitable, but for this to happen the issue of free trade versus
protection had to be buried. A fiscal truce was needed. At the 1904
New South Wales election Joseph Carruthers had become premier by
marginalising protectionists and campaigning against Labor's socialism.
Reid hoped to repeat this at the federal level, launching anti-socialist
electoral leagues and undertaking a national speaking tour on the

dangers of the Labor Party.

Reid and Deakin had agreed on a fiscal truce on the issue of tariffs until the election due in 1906, creating, Reid hoped, the opportunity for socialism to become the dividing electoral issue if parliament were dissolved before then.[17] He met several times with Deakin in the first half of 1905 to endeavour to persuade him to support the creation of anti-socialist leagues across the country to counter 'the destruction of the rights of private enterprise, private property and personal freedom'.[18]

In July, Labor's federal conference adopted as an objective the 'collective ownership of monopolies and the extension of the industrial and economic functions of the State and the Municipality'. This was weaker than the Victorian and Queensland Labor parties' corresponding objectives, which sought 'the gradual nationalisation of the means of production, distribution and exchange', but it was enough to give momentum to Reid's campaign.[19]

Deakin was not drawn, however, and anti-socialist leagues did not do well in Victoria. Reid tried and failed to win the support of David Syme, who wrote to Deakin that he had 'seen our friend but I can do nothing with him…I have come to the conclusion that he is no friend to us or our party and that we should do well to avoid him.'[20] The exception was the conservative Australian Women's National League, which had been formed in Melbourne in March 1904 by the leader of Melbourne society Lady Janet Clarke and her sister Eva Hughes, who was to prove a formidable political organiser.[21] Reid was quick to see that anti-socialism could appeal to home-centred women and the AWNL soon established itself as the strongest anti-labour organisation in Victoria.

At the end of 1904 Reid had agreed to establish a commission on the tariff in response to pressure from Syme and the radical protectionists, who claimed that businesses were being destroyed and men thrown from work because many tariffs were too low.[22] This was a fatal mistake on Reid's part, for it is hard to see how the commission's report would not reopen the fiscal debate and so end the fiscal truce on which his government's survival depended.

Deakin said very little publicly during the long recess in the first half of 1905. He was not well for much of it and, preoccupied with his religious writing, he was also not at all sure where his future lay. In May he accepted an invitation from John Forrest to visit Western Australia: 'It would do you and your party a lot of good, and I can promise you a good time.' Deakin had only ever visited briefly on a boat stopover and had never ventured beyond Perth and Fremantle.

He was hosted during his visit by Forrest's political ally Winthrop Hackett, who was the editor and part-owner of the *West Australian* and an influential member of the Legislative Council. Deakin also met the Anglican Bishop, Charles Riley. Forrest, Hackett and Riley formed a triumvirate with a shared commitment to the state's development. Together they had backed the vision of the chief engineer, Charles Yelverton O'Connor, to build a pipeline bringing bring fresh water to the Coolgardie goldfields.[23]

When Forrest turned on the tap in 1903, Deakin described the pipeline in detail to his *Morning Post* readers as 'one of the most daring engineering schemes undertaken in any part of the world'.[24] Now Deakin visited the settlements of Coolgardie and Kalgoorlie and inspected the new reservoir. This was the sort of inspired development which he believed held the promise for Australia's future. He made one major speech in Perth, but it gave no indication of his stance towards the government. Thanking him, the chairman congratulated him on 'his skill in avoiding definite expressions of opinion'.[25]

Deakin's trip reinvigorated his political energies and seems to have marked the end of his ambitions to be a preacher. On the journey there and back, he read Phillips Brooks' *Lectures on Preaching* and recoiled from the audacity of the preacher's claim to be a messenger from God; this seemed to him near to blasphemy.[26] He felt better able to live with uncertainty. 'The Sphinx of Life is not so much incomprehensible because no reading of its riddle is possible as because there are many readings that are irreconcilable. Each falls short. Each implies its antithesis.'[27]

While in Western Australia, Deakin had plenty of opportunities to discuss the political situation with Forrest, and also with Austin Chapman, a protectionist from New South Wales who had been minister for defence under Deakin, and was, coincidentally, also visiting the west. Once back in Melbourne he met with Reid and, according to his diary, issued 'Warnings'.[28] Deakin was worried that an early report from the tariff commission would reopen the fiscal debate, but a deeper fear was that Reid would be granted a dissolution, and that the Liberal Protectionists would do poorly in the ensuing election.

Chapman urged Deakin to take up the fight, telling him that Reid was unpopular in Queensland because of his undecided views on protection for the sugar industry, and that several Labor men were saying they wanted Deakin to take the lead.[29] Others were doing the same. Octavius Beale, a piano and sewing-machine manufacturer and influential New South Wales protectionist, told him on 4 June that the New South Wales manufacturers would not join the anti-socialist leagues and preferred to take their chance with Labor. Beale added a new argument to the protectionists' armoury. Referring to Japan's annihilation of the Russian naval fleet a week before, on 27 and 28 May, he urged Deakin to recognise that the world's centre had shifted. 'Must we always depend on foreign firms for our rifles and cartridges?'[30]

Deakin was due to give a speech to his Ballarat constituents on Saturday, 24 June. Everyone was wondering what he would say. Joseph Carruthers urged him, at this turning point in the party's history, to co-operate with Reid against the 'dirty hands' of Labor.[31] Beale wrote to him, 'You are the one leader to whom our minds turn,' and said that Hughes had told him privately that 'they all want you, yourself.'[32] Finally, just before the Ballarat speech, Watson wrote to him that he believed Deakin may be willing again 'to take up the head of government and if so, you will have our active support. We and especially myself don't want office, but I have the utmost anxiety to stop the retrogressive movement which Reid is heading.'[33]

Ballarat was wet and windy, and Deakin had a severe cold. Despite this affliction, he spoke for nearly two hours, explaining that his six months of virtual silence on the political situation was the result of ill health, but also of his indecision about whether to stay in public life when the sacrifices it demanded proved fruitless. If Reid was to be successful in getting parliament dissolved and there was an election, then the tariff, not anti-socialism, should be the central issue, he said, and he attacked Reid's anti-socialist crusade as so vague and indefinite, so lacking in practical proposals, that to vote for him would be to give him a 'blank cheque'.

He also attacked Labor's socialist objectives as vague and insubstantial. He rejected socialism if it meant 'that all activities of life should be subsumed by the State and worked by state machinery'; but he defended state socialism if it meant using the machinery of the state to remedy evils and injustices. The choice, he said, was not between nationalisation on one side and unrestrained capitalism on the other. Between these two points was all the range of regulation, and what was needed were practical proposals to solve particular problems.

Deakin was here sketching out the middle ground for Australia's mixed economy and arguing for a pragmatic rather than a 'philosophical' approach—we would use the term ideological—to questions of public policy. It was the same centrist stance that Robert Menzies took after World War Two, when he had to readjust Liberal Party philosophy to accommodate the post-war consensus for an expanded welfare state and counter Labor's programme of extensive post-war planning. Deakin criticised both Reid's anti-socialism and Labor's socialism, but he said nothing about the Labor Party machine. Instead, in a convoluted piece of reasoning, Deakin argued that, by establishing the Tariff Commission, Reid had already broken the fiscal truce (even though he, Deakin, had agreed to the commission's establishment).

The speech caused a sensation, not only because of its content but because the *Age* upped the ante by claiming on Monday, 26 June that 'Mr Deakin's Ballarat speech, read in any light, is a notice to Mr Reid to quit.'[34] Thus it was read by everyone except the man himself, who claimed it was merely a warning. But the speech gave Syme his chance to force Deakin to step up to Reid and he took it.

The thunderstruck government concluded that Deakin had withdrawn his support. 'A frank and loyal supporter of his Government', Reid said, could never have made such a speech; 'the spirit and soul' of the coalition agreement had gone.[35] Under these circumstances his ministry decided it could not go on, and when parliament resumed

on Wednesday, 28 June, instead of the governor-general setting out a
full programme for the future session, only an electoral redistribution
was foreshadowed. The implication was that, if the House accepted this
truncated programme, a dissolution would be sought after the Electoral
Redistribution Bill was passed. But Reid was in little doubt that the
House would reject the minimal programme. Like Deakin and Watson
before him, Reid had tired of governing with an insecure majority.

On Wednesday, before parliament met, Deakin replied to Watson's
offer of parliamentary support and invited him home to tea for a chat
on the following weekend. He still believed that leaders of goodwill
meeting face to face could manage the parliament, and that principle
could trump party. 'Even our parties are less than the Commonwealth
and are only to be valued for their service to the public as a whole.
Cannot we agree to sit down together soberly and without haste in
order to thrash out all the contingencies?'[36] But events overtook them
and they in fact met that very evening to 'confer re situation'.[37]

Thursday, 29 June was the day of reckoning. Watson opened
proceedings with an attack on the government, concluding that 'we
should all welcome the disappearance of a ministry which has neither
achievement in the past, policy in the present, nor prospects in the
future, to justify its existence,' but he did not move a censure motion.
Reid replied, explaining his reaction to Deakin's speech, wondering
why he had not been warned as one would expect from a friend. He
puzzled over why Deakin had now apparently withdrawn his support
and what he intended to do. Throughout, he was unfailingly polite: 'I
have never, in the bitterest hours of our controversy...used an unkind
word of my honourable and learned friend,' for whom he had 'unstinting admiration'.[38]

Deakin did not reply in kind. He acknowledged that Reid spoke
without personal bitterness, but said that his speech bristled with
implications that 'I have been a traitor and a plotter and have betrayed
my old friends in the Ministry.' Deakin's reply was defensive and not
especially convincing. There was no reason why the government should
not lead us through a productive and useful session, he said, but they
have chosen to do otherwise; just because the newspapers interpreted

his speech in a certain way does not mean it was intended that way. After his lengthy disavowal of any prior intention to put the government out, Deakin produced from his pocket a motion of amendment that added to the Address in Reply the words, 'But are of the opinion that practical matters should be proceeded with.' 'Here is the dagger,' said Reid. 'He had it in his pocket all the time.'[39] By convention, amendments to the Address in Reply are equivalent to a motion of no-confidence. When the vote was taken the following afternoon, the majority for the amendment was seventeen, and Reid went to the governor-general to request a dissolution.

As Liberal Protectionists in the ministry, George Turner and Allan McLean felt badly let down by Deakin—Turner in particular, who only joined the ministry, he said, because of pressure from Deakin and with his approval. Deakin denied this. He had not objected to their joining the ministry, he told parliament, but 'they must take upon themselves the burden of responsibility of a choice of that kind.'[40] This is certainly not how they saw it. Deakin was their chief. Said Turner, 'Many time he has sat in the Ministerial corner and has by means of one magnetic look persuaded me to give way.'[41]

Deakin would never admit that his dealings with others were anything but frank and upright. In a draft letter to Turner he defended himself against what he regarded as a grave and unwarranted accusation of injustice. The draft shows him poring over Hansard for the detail of what he and Turner said, quibbling about dates and exact wording, and it reads like a lawyer's defence.[42] It is not clear if the letter was ever sent, but had it been it is unlikely to have mollified Turner, whose account of events comes through the historical record as far more convincing than Deakin's.

On one other crucial matter Deakin seems to have lied. In August he told parliament that he did not meet with Watson on the day of the opening of parliament, 'nor I think the night. I had no communication with Mr. Watson, nor had he any communication with me upon the amendment.' This last may have been true, but his diary for Wednesday clearly records, 'Watson for tea and confer re situation.'[43] Did he imagine

'I think' would be sufficient cover should his claim be probed? Or was it a record of his intention to invite Watson for tea the following weekend, which seems unlikely?

Deakin rejected any suggestion that he had engaged in anything other than the most transparent and honourable behaviour. He wrote to Tom Bavin that he had 'no alternative' when Reid turned his Ballarat speech into a *casus belli*, and he told his *Morning Post* readers that Mr Reid himself was responsible for the prominence of the speech by failing to put forward a programme.[44]

But it was Syme who gave the speech its prominence, and forced Reid to test his support. And in the two days between the *Age* 'Notice to Quit' leader on Monday, 26 June and the opening of parliament on Wednesday, Deakin kept silent, speaking neither to the Protectionists in cabinet nor to Reid to reassure them that the *Age* was mistaken and his support was not withdrawn. Writing his *Reminiscences*, over a decade later, Reid still thought Deakin was culpable for this: if he wished us to carry on, he should not have said anything to weaken us; and if he had determined to forsake us, he might have warned us, or at least Sir George Turner. 'However it is an old story now.'[45]

In February 1909, Deakin wrote of these events, 'When I passed through the flaming furnace of 1905 owing to Reid's betrayal of his trust and of my confidence...'[46] This is projection, with Deakin in the role of victim, for if anyone betrayed trust and confidence it was Deakin himself. It is a clue to the role Reid played in Deakin's political imagination, as the bearer of all the grubby aspects of political life—the personal ambition, the self-interest, the plotting, the disloyalty and the betrayals—while he, Deakin, stayed above it all, focussed on the service of the Ideal.

Reid had gone out of his way to accommodate Deakin. On New Year's Day, 1905 he had sent him cordial good wishes, and had praised him for his self-sacrifice and forgetfulness of self in his conduct towards him.[47] He had allowed Deakin to move a vague motion in support of imperial preference, a cause for which Reid had no sympathy.[48] He acted as if there was no personal animus between them. Of course he could not know the identity of the *Morning Post* correspondent who commented so frequently on his negative attitudes, lack of policies and penchant for political expediency, nor of the cruel caricature lying in wait on his posthumous reputation in Deakin's bottom drawer.

The day after the government's defeat, a Saturday, Watson came to tea at Llanarth for another of their quiet chats about policy and procedure. The house was busy with preparations for Ivy's marriage to Herbert Brookes on the coming Monday. Watson assured Deakin that 'he is authorised to promise me a cordial and genuine support for this Parliament...There is a general agreement between us as to policy and a pledge to co-operate in both Houses.'[49] Labor's short period of minority government had left its parliamentarians shell-shocked, and they were not keen to repeat the experience of responsibility without power. So Labor offered general support until the next election, but it would not enter a coalition. It was a transitional arrangement, bridging the coalition ministries of the colonial parliaments and the single-party ministries that were to come. As with Watson before him, Northcote would not grant Reid a dissolution and instead, on Monday, 3 July, a week after the *Age* had issued Reid's 'Notice to Quit', he sent for Deakin to discuss the situation. Northcote required assurances from Deakin that he could form a more enduring ministry than his first, in 1903. The following day he asked him to form a ministry.

Monday was Ivy's wedding day. There was a morning service, then the wedding breakfast at Llanarth, so Deakin did not see Northcote till four in the afternoon. This was not the simple civil ceremony of Alfred and Pattie. Wearing an elaborate Edwardian wedding dress of ivory duchesse satin and her mother's bridal veil, with Stella and Vera as bridesmaids in pale-blue satin and enormous hats, she and Herbert were married by the Reverend Edward Sugden at Punt Road Methodist Church. Sugden was a liberal Methodist who was master of Queen's College and the only one of the university college heads to defend George Marshall-Hall. Although the invited guests were mostly relatives, Ivy was popular and her girlfriends filled the church to see her married.[50]

How are we to interpret Deakin's actions over the fifteen months since his resignation in April 1904? If we only consider the outcome, it can seem as if Deakin were the master tactician, as he put Labor in, then out; Reid and the Free Trade Party in, then out; until he emerged triumphant to pick up the crown. But this interpretation over-emphasises Deakin's intention and control of events. Deakin did not actively seek to return as prime minister in 1905. For much of 1904 and the first months of 1905 he was preoccupied with deciding whether to forsake politics altogether. He only returned his attention to politics when he realised he was not suited for preaching. Even then, it was Syme who forced his hand.

He did know, though, how it looked to others. On the night of Monday, 3 July, with Ivy married in the morning and the prime minister-ship offered him in the afternoon, he wrote his letter for the *Morning Post* on his Ballarat speech, canvassing Mr Deakin's likely motivations and concluding:

> It is, indeed, hard to understand how as experienced a leader as Mr Deakin could have been as guileless as Sir John Forrest and his friends protest. No one knew better than he the inflammable condition of Federal politics or the great risk, whatever the pretext, of carrying a torch through the magazine.[51]

Reid did not see Deakin as the crucial agent. It was, he wrote, 'the Labor Party who put us out and brought Mr Deakin and his friends back, a sensible move from their point of view because we were not likely to pass their class legislation.'[52] Reid was much quicker to see Labor's fast-growing political agency than most but, despite this, until either Labor or the Free Trade Party achieved an absolute majority, it was always up to Deakin as the leader of the centre party. As his friends and allies kept telling him: take the lead and we will follow.

His approach through these fifteen months is perhaps best described as wait-and-see, as he let possibilities play themselves out and events unfold. He did not, as he had on previous occasions of indecision, seek occult help; there were no séances, nor divinations.[53] But his providential imagination did accept the way events unfolded as evidence of divine intent. So he kept talking to his political allies, to Syme and to Watson, whom Deakin liked and trusted, and who admired and trusted him. The task now was to salvage something from the remaining fifteen months of what had so far been an almost fruitless parliamentary session.

28

PRIME MINISTER II

WHEN HE BECAME prime minister for the second time, Deakin was just about to turn forty-nine. To all outward appearances he was in good health, hair and beard still dark and his step vigorous. But to the always vigilant inner monitor of his flows of psychic and physical energies, there were worrying signs. A year earlier, in October 1904, he had written 'that the first jet of life has passed': 'There is a cloud between me and everything I see & feel—a cloud of memories, suggestions unfledged half-formed thoughts sentiments...so that I recede inwards—a thicker veil forms between me and the spring, between me and all beauty, music, even love.'[1] He had been ill during the first months of 1905, and his insomnia was now chronic.

Over the next few months he and Pattie consulted Dr Thomas Beckett, 'a medical electrician and skin graphist', who was in charge of the Alfred Hospital's new X-ray machine.[2] Electrical currents were used to treat a range of ailments in the early twentieth century, and Pattie's continuing gynaecological complaint may have been the initial reason for the visits. But Deakin also went alone, and an entry in his diary, 'Dr Beckett and sex', suggests that he too may have had reason to seek electrical stimulation.

Pattie and Alfred's sexual relationship was important to them both. For Pattie it was the basis of her confidence in Alfred's love for her; for Alfred, who nurtured the memory of their young passion in his annual anniversary poems, it held his love, but was also a manifestation of his vitality. Together with the likely mini-stroke of 1902, and his chronic insomnia, Deakin's mental and physical health may have already passed their peak.

Does this matter? There is no evidence that Deakin's judgement or cognitive capacities were seriously impaired, but he was finding life and work a harder struggle, and was driven deeper into himself to protect his energies. Still, with the return to power the other path had lost its allure. On Sunday, 10 September 1905 he concluded the religious notebook he had begun in April 1904 with 'another mistake avoided—"Sermons never convince" but are useful in an explanatory way—talking at people from a pulpit saves only a very few.' So he returned to the path of the legislator, as his best means of serving the Ideal. That same Sunday he began a new series of prayers, and a month later he prayed, 'Thou God of ideals & source of all ideals grant that I may master the real, bow to it or ignore it, so that I help to body forth the ideal in and around me.'[3]

For the rest of July and into August, Deakin was subjected, in his words, to 'Floods of Slander'.[4] The Sydney papers were furious with him for deserting Reid. In parliament Reid kept up the attack: Deakin 'after denouncing the Labour Party as the enemy of true party government has become their instrument', he said. Reid's accusations and Deakin's defence went back and forth for days in the parliament, until Reid quipped, 'I wronged the honourable and learned member into the position of PM again, so that he need not be too bitter.' To which Deakin replied, 'I would much rather that the right honourable gentleman had retained the position...I do dread the arduous burden which it imposes upon us.'[5] In a draft letter for the *Morning Post*, he interviewed himself on the charge of 'treachery'. His defence was that he put policy first and parties second, so 'if any person accepted the Deakin policy he became a member of the Deakin party.'[6]

Deakin did not expect his ministry to survive the election due at the end of 1906:

> the position of my Ministry [was] so perilous, and the annihilation of my party at the next election so apparently inevitable, that I learned to fight a hopeless campaign happily though never able to see with certainty a day ahead and subject to unnumbered dangers...I came first and last to feel my own or my party's future irrelevant, so clear was it my duty to go on until relieved of responsibility, and steeled myself to do what I thought right for Australia without hope and without fear.[7]

His task was to pick up where he had left off in April 1904, adhering 'to the practical policy sanctioned by the country at the last general election'—the same party, with the same policy and almost the same cabinet. None of the legislation initiated by Deakin's first government had yet made it onto the statute book, and Deakin presented the parliament with a long list of planned legislation, much of it minor bills to enhance the ordinary machinery of administration: bills concerned with lighthouses, quarantine, copyright, wireless telegraphy and the census. There would also be major bills 'embodying a progressive policy of development of the resources of the Commonwealth, to be carried out by systematic effort here and in the Mother Country': the encouragement of British migrants, preferential trade with Britain, and bounties for new primary products with which Deakin hoped to resurrect the optimistic agenda of the 1880s that had been so badly disrupted by the bank crashes and the Federation Drought.[8]

This second prime ministership became Deakin's apogee. His government committed to the New Protection, which linked tariff protection to a fair and reasonable wage for workers, and laid down the contours of Australia's defence and foreign policy. These achievements make him Australia's most constructive prime minister before the emergency of World War Two forced Labor into a radical rethinking

of the Commonwealth's capacities. But the origins of Deakin's achievements go back well beyond the agenda of April 1904, beyond the first
Barton government and its unfinished business, to the covenant he
believed had been made between the politicians who had argued for
federation and the Australian people who had voted for it; and further
again, to the convictions he formed in the Victorian parliament under
the influence of David Syme and James Service.

For his thinking about defence and foreign policy, the key event
was much more recent: Japan's destruction of Russia's Baltic Fleet in
the Tsushima Strait at the end of May 1905. Russia and Japan had
been at war since February 1904, when a surprise attack by Japan
destroyed the Russian fleet at Port Arthur on Manchuria's Liaodong
Peninsula. Now the Baltic Fleet Russia sent to relieve it was gone too.
Russia would soon sue for peace and Korea would become a Japanese
protectorate. It was a seismic shock to the balance of world power. A
European empire had been defeated by a rising Asian empire. Japan
was now the dominant naval power in the Pacific and expanding its
reach on the Asian mainland.

Two weeks later, Deakin was interviewed by the Melbourne *Herald*
about these developments. Not since the Napoleonic Wars had Britain's
sea power been challenged, he said, but in the last few years three new
naval powers had arisen: Germany, Japan and the United States. This
was a new situation, and the public needed to be alerted to its risks and
the responsibility of Australia to develop effective defences. Australia
could no longer 'depend largely on its isolation for security'. Japan was
now the nearest of all the great naval powers to Australia. When Deakin
gave this interview, he did not know that in a few weeks he would be
back at the helm, but he was already thinking hard about Australia's
security in this more threatening world. In August the interview was
tabled in the Senate, and it began a new conversation among Australia's
political leaders about the country's place in the world.[9]

Deakin was still writing weekly for the *Morning Post* and monthly for
the *National Review*, but in the whirl of events he neglected to write
his August letter for the *Post*. A few weeks later he resigned from the

National Review and his last article was published in October,[10] though he continued his anonymous letters for the *Morning Post*.

When he was a member of the Victorian parliament, Deakin had unsuccessfully supported some government provision for the impoverished widow of Marcus Clarke. In June 1906 Higgins requested that the federal parliament make a grant to the impoverished family of another writer, the poet Victor Daley, who had died the previous year. Deakin was sympathetic and five hundred pounds was included in the 1906 estimates for a fund for Australian Men of Letters. Deakin argued for it vigorously against the sceptics who thought poets and literary men were generally irresponsible sorts of people. A committee was appointed to draw up a scheme, which recommended the establishment of the Commonwealth Literary Fund to provide modest pensions for needy authors or their distressed families. Parliament agreed and an independent committee of 'three gentlemen' was established to consider applications and make recommendations to the government.[11]

In early December 1905, Hugh Browne died suddenly and Pattie, who was already at Ballara in Point Lonsdale for the summer, came up for the small family funeral. Pattie had not reconciled with her father before he died and when Ventnor, the Brownes' home in Walsh Street, was sold some years on she wanted nothing from it, not even her own paintings.[12] She did, however, nurse her mother in her last illness. A few weeks later, 'thoroughly exhausted' as he now was at the end of every year, Deakin took the boat to Queenscliff and his refuge by the sea. On New Year's Day, Pattie's forty-third birthday, he wrote:

> Life's shadow play is over for the year
> Set free afoot upon this sandy rise
> In ocean breath, wild verdure wilder skies
> To home, heaven and Thy heart I draw more near.[13]

Ballara had become his and Pattie's haven from his public self. In a letter to Ivy and Herbert, Pattie described their time together in the early weeks of 1906. 'We were lovers resting as of old and…talked of our love and happiness past and present. We sauntered home gathering

blackberries and some young Groundsell plants...Father read us some
Byron and...we all sat after tea for over two hours watching the glories
of the sunset.'[14]

As was now his habit, Deakin took his bicycle to Point Lonsdale, a new
one bought in September 1905.[15] The increasing number of bicycles on
Melbourne's streets was drawing greater police attention, and twice
during 1906 Deakin and his bicycle brushed with the law. In January
he was stopped for riding on the wrong side of the road in the middle
of Melbourne, at the corner of Flinders and Swanston streets. The
incident would have disappeared from view, except that a cab driver
also driving down the wrong side of the same road was charged, while
Deakin was not, and the Cabmen's Union complained. Was it only
prime ministers who were allowed to break the regulations?[16] Playing
on Deakin's recent political manoeuvres, Melbourne's *Punch* asked if
he was unable to tell his left from his right:

> To me, they never seem the same for long.
> I am a bubble blown that way and this
> To some ideal that I always miss...
> A compass is not easy to obey
> Which every morning points a different way.[17]

In June he was among a dozen people charged in the District Court
with riding on the footpath on his usual route between Llanarth and
parliament.[18] Deakin did not see himself as a man of the people, he
was too private and intellectual for that, but he wore his office lightly
and saw nothing odd in the prime minister cycling to work with other
Melburnians. Andrew Fisher, who was to succeed him as prime minister
in 1908, thought he had insufficient sense of the dignity of the office
and ordered the first prime-ministerial car.[19]

Deakin's private secretary, Malcolm Shepherd, complained that
even when Deakin was at his busiest he resisted Shepherd's help to
deal with his correspondence, which would have meant typewritten
replies, because, he told Shepherd, 'as they had written to him in their

own handwriting, he felt he should answer them.'[20] It was appreciated. Vida Goldstein, the advocate of women's rights, who had written to him about the federal marriage and divorce bill, thanked him for a letter that was 'personal not dictated'.[21]

In July 1906 the *Argus* reported a rumour that Deakin was planning to retire at the end of the year, which he denied. This had been his intention two years ago, he said, but now 'the unexpected obligations cast upon him had entirely altered that purpose.'[22] Still, as the election at the end of the year approached, with no likelihood of producing a government with a workable majority, some of Deakin's colleagues were urging him to leave parliament for easier berths. Just as Deakin had predicted, there was too much High Court work for three judges to handle and in August parliament authorised the appointment of two extra, bringing the bench to the five Deakin had fought so hard for in 1903. His cabinet thought he should take one of the appointments himself.[23] From London, Bernhard Wise and Walter James, then the Western Australian agent-general, wanted him to become high commissioner.[24]

Deakin seems never to have seriously considered himself a candidate for the High Court, regarding his legal experience as inadequate to the task.[25] And London held few attractions. He disliked what passed for society in the imperial capital, and with Ivy and Herbert's first child born in April 1906, he and Pattie now had a grandson, Wilfred, next door at Winwick. Traffic between the two houses was constant, and Deakin still made his regular Sunday visits to his sister and elderly mother in Adams Street.

Deakin's prayer diary shows that his commitment to staying the course drew as well on deeper sources. In August, two days after his fiftieth birthday, he wrote that 'after fifty years of halting and unprofit-able apprenticeship...I seem near & am perhaps near to the springs of some influence & authority.' In October he prayed, 'Let me not release my grip upon reality, my appreciation of opportunities and power of using them while & where I can be of use in furthering the true welfare of my time and country. Make me strong to bear, to strive, to persist.'[26] Swedenborg's theory of uses was still guiding his decisions, and while there was a chance he could influence political outcomes he would stay.

Deakin was also the minister for external affairs, where much could be done by executive action. He immediately returned to the issue of Britain's annexation of the New Hebrides. Ten days after taking office he cabled the British government for information about the state of negotiations between France and Britain over the islands. Was a joint protectorate being considered? In August 1905 Britain and France had announced their intention to discuss arrangements to settle jurisdiction and land claims, but nothing had yet happened. Britain, it seemed, was continuing to ignore Australia's claims. Deakin's return to external affairs was a signal to supporters of annexation to renew the pressure, and parliament supported a call for British annexation.[27]

As a young minister in the Victorian parliament Deakin had taken on James Service's paired dreams of federation and an Australian Pacific empire. With the first realised, Deakin could now pursue the second. In a February letter for the *Morning Post* he railed against the cold indifference of the Colonial Office to the spirited ambitions of the colonials towards nearby Pacific islands, and claimed that 'The New Hebrides were ours by every right.'[28] That other progressive new-world nation the United States had entered the colonial club in 1898 with the acquisition from Spain of the Philippines, Guam, Cuba and Puerto Rico. Why not Australia too? Extending Australian sovereignty into the South Pacific would be a fitting expression of its new national status.

The ANA was a vociferous supporter, and the Presbyterians never gave up lobbying on behalf of their missionaries. The loss of the northern part of New Guinea to Germany in 1884 still rankled, as did French control of New Caledonia. Deakin spoke for many when he insisted there be no more foreign incursions into Australia's part of the world.

Britain, however, had no intention of antagonising France over a few Pacific islands as she negotiated the Entente Cordiale with her to combat Germany's growing power. Settling differences over the New Hebrides was far down the list, behind Morocco, Egypt, the borders of Nigeria and French fishing rights off Newfoundland. But insignificant as the issue of the New Hebrides was, it proved intractable. When an agreement was concluded in April 1904, the solution to competing claims over the New Hebrides had been postponed, pending further discussions. In fact, were it not for the damage it would do to its relations with Australia and New Zealand, Britain would have been quite happy for France to have the islands. Deakin learned about the postponement from press reports, and he was furious. Here was yet another example of the faraway British government acting without the courtesy of consultation on a matter of direct concern to Australia and New Zealand.[29]

Late in 1905, again without the knowledge of either the Australian or New Zealand governments, the French and British established a New Hebrides commission with terms of reference including discussion of a joint protectorate. Again, Deakin only learned of this from a newspaper report. While the commission was meeting, Britain's Conservative government lost office to the Liberals, and the excuse was later made that, in the confusion of the changeover, the need to inform Australia and New Zealand of the new commission was overlooked. More likely, the Foreign Office which was responsible for the negotiations did not want any interference from the 'colonials'.[30] This was certainly Deakin's conclusion.

The agreement, concluded in March 1906, was for a joint protectorate. It was submitted to the Australian and New Zealand governments for their approval, but this was a formality, as there was no prospect of Britain achieving a more acceptable agreement with the French government: 'The draft convention must therefore be confirmed or rejected practically as it stands,' they were told.[31] Both Australia and New Zealand declined to support the joint protectorate. Deakin's anger seeps through the formal language of his communications with the new secretary of state for the colonies, Lord Elgin, as he records his government's 'respectful but earnest protest' at the Colonial Office's handling of the matter, notes that the withholding of information had left his ministry dependent on press reports, and complains that he has received no reply to his letter of enquiry of last August.[32]

Deakin made detailed suggestions for amendment. He was especially

troubled by the operation of two systems of law and by the arrangements for the oversight of native labour. When news broke that a
German company was negotiating to buy a large property in the New
Hebrides, the Australians felt they had no choice but to abandon their
opposition. Deakin cabled that, not having been consulted during the
negotiations and the suggested amendments not having the support of
His Majesty's Government, and being unable at this distance to judge
either the possibility of obtaining amendments or the risk of further
delay, 'the Commonwealth Government has no option except to leave
the whole responsibility to His Majesty's Government.'[33] Deakin would
take his anger and frustration with the Colonial Office and the British
government with him to the 1907 Imperial Conference.

Australia did still have one colonial responsibility: British New Guinea,
or Papua. Britain had administered the south-eastern half of New Guinea
since November 1884, when it established a protectorate. In 1888 this
became the colony of British New Guinea, with the colonies contributing fifteen thousand pounds per annum to the costs of administration.
Britain was only ever in New Guinea because of Australian pressure,
and once Australia was federated it made clear to Australia that it must
assume control and bear all the costs. The new Commonwealth was
now obliged to accept responsibility for the territory. An act to regulate
the Commonwealth's control of its affairs and to establish its internal
government was yet another major item of unfinished business for
Deakin's second government.[34]

The Possession, as it was called, was costing the Commonwealth
twenty thousand pounds a year. Its administration was in turmoil after
the acting administrator, Christopher Robinson, had shot himself beneath
the government flagpole following a badly mishandled confrontation
on the notorious cannibal island of Goaribari in which eight natives
were killed.[35] The tiny European population of around six hundred
had fallen into two warring camps: the official administration, mostly
appointed by the Colonial Office, who saw their task as the protection
of the natives' welfare; and the mostly Australian miners and planters,
who wanted development and access to land.

Since 1901 the public servant Atlee Hunt, who was the secretary of external affairs, had provided administrative continuity. In 1904 Reid sent him to Papua to report on ways to promote settlement while preserving the best interests of the natives, but when he returned Reid had lost power and Hunt made his rather optimistic report about the possibilities of European agriculture to Deakin.

Deakin found it all very vexing. No other of his duties occupied more of his time or attention or gave him more anxiety than the affairs of Papua, he told the House, 'a Territory 2000 miles away which I have never seen'.

> The whole history of this Possession has been marred by ill-fortune. In the first place, it includes only half of the area we ought to have obtained; in the next, when, in consequence of pressure from Australia, control was accepted by the Imperial Government, it was used unwillingly, and in the most grudging fashion...Then in my opinion it was prematurely forced upon the Commonwealth... when because of pressure of other responsibilities Parliament could not give the matter the attention it needed.

Like the refusal to annexe the New Hebrides, for Deakin, Britain's half-hearted acquisition of British New Guinea was a symbol of its reluctance to recognise Australia's independent nationhood and to take seriously Australia's fears of the incursion of European powers into its backyard. Now that he was responsible for Papua as minister for external affairs, he wanted to act 'justly and wisely' towards the place and its people. 'Our policy is Papua for the Papuans and then for the Australians,' Deakin told the parliament, and if their interests clashed the Papuans' well-being should come first.[36]

At the end of October 1905, after a very long debate about whether alcohol should be banned totally from the territory or only for the natives, the Papua Bill was finally passed, providing for the territory's administration by a lieutenant-governor. However, it took until 1908 for a permanent appointment to be made, as rival groups among the administrators and settlers pushed their men and interests. Deakin received conflicting reports and much gossip. It was the sort of personal conflict he hated and, after receiving a confidential report from the chief judicial officer, John Hubert Murray, his solution was the arms-length adjudication of a royal commission, which optimistically saw the territory's future in large-scale agricultural development. The situation did not stabilise until the end of 1908, when cabinet recommended the appointment of Murray as the lieutenant-governor. He remained in office until his death in 1940.

Then there was the problem of Japan. Japan had been an ally of Britain since 1902 and in 1905 the alliance was extended. Yet Japan was a troubling presence for Australia. Since 1901 the Japanese empire had been objecting to the Immigration Restriction Act. Japan had no objection to the Australian government excluding its people; it claimed the same right for itself. What it objected to was the means, and to Japanese being classed as aliens along with 'Kanakas, Negroes, Pacific Islanders, Indians or other Eastern peoples', because 'its standard of civilisation is so much higher'.[37] Britain agreed that the Japanese should not be treated as belonging to an inferior race.

Both Reid's government and Deakin's second government sought to appease the Japanese by modifying the Immigration Act and the way it was administered, excusing them from the dictation test and relying instead on a visa issued by the Japanese government to prevent permanent settlement. As prime minister, Deakin negotiated this himself through the Japanese consul-general, bypassing the Colonial Office, which expected that all Australia's diplomatic communications would go through it. This was audacious of Deakin, but he preferred the displeasure of the Colonial Office to its interference.

The Colonial Office was indeed displeased, but contented itself with reminding Deakin that it expected Australia to conduct any dealings with a foreign power through London. Deakin replied that, though he agreed with this in principle, he reserved the right to conduct preliminary and unofficial discussions.[38] The difference between Australia's national interests in the Pacific and Britain's global imperial interests was sharpening.

29

IMPERIALIST

THE ELECTION WAS not due until December 1906, so Deakin had a year
to prepare the Liberal Protectionists. On 24 March 1906 he addressed a
meeting of his constituents. The hall was cold and the meeting poorly
attended, with most of Ballarat having spent the day at the picnic races.
Deakin seemed ill at ease, and there was little applause to stimulate
his oratory.[1] Two-thirds of the speech was about Reid, as he went yet
again over the reasons for breaking the coalition, and attacked Reid's
anti-socialism as 'a necklace of negatives—no tariff reform, no relief for
injured industries, no assistance to rural producers, no more protection
in any circumstances.'[2]

Deakin's obsession with Reid was clouding his political judgement.
From Western Australia, Winthrop Hackett gently advised him to
leave the battle with Reid over the past alone, and even to consider
working with him again: 'I do not think an understanding between your
party and his quite impossible.'[3] But protection was not the defining
political issue for West Australians that it was for Victorians. Syme

was furious at what he saw as Deakin's weak support for protection: 'Between Watson's socialism and Reid's anti-socialism, where are we? What have we to offer that will carry the election? Your friends are in despair and your enemies delighted'; 'There will be no Protectionist party left if you maintain your present attitude.'[4]

Deakin's speech in Adelaide the following week was much better, more about the future than the past, but Reid was still his main target. In 1905 Reid had hoped to convince Deakin's Liberal Protectionists to join him in a united anti-socialist party, but Deakin told Hackett that nothing would induce him to work with Reid or accept his alliance.[5] Reid's goal now was to win a majority in his own right on an anti-socialist platform, and for the Liberal Protectionists to shatter into irrelevance, with whoever survived the election forced to choose between Labor and his anti-socialists. After parliament opened in June 1906, Reid was scarcely in Melbourne. Either in Sydney at the bar earning an income or on anti-socialist speaking tours, he left Joseph Cook to lead the Opposition.[6]

Cook had begun his political life as a labour man. He was a miner in Britain before emigrating to Lithgow, and had early experience with British trade unions. He was elected as a Labor representative to the New South Wales parliament in 1891, but after refusing to sign the pledge he stood successfully as an independent labour candidate. Keen to show his sympathies with working men's aspirations, Reid rewarded him with the position of postmaster-general, which had a salary of fifteen hundred pounds, and he had been steadfastly loyal to Reid ever since. As a Primitive Methodist, Cook was an exemplar of the benefits of its advocacy of hard work, self-improvement and total abstinence. He was humourless and a dogged parliamentary combatant for his chief.[7]

The agreement between Deakin's Liberal Protectionists and Labor lasted only until the end of the year, when they would face the electors as separate and independent parties. Deakin had to differentiate his party from Labor while at the same time depending on its votes to pass his legislation. It was tricky. Compared with his assaults on Reid, his criticisms of Labor were muted and conditional. They took two main lines. The first was to criticise Labor for impractical proposals which were impossible to achieve within the present federal constitution.[8] The second was to divide Labor between its parliamentarians, 'men of experience, training and knowledge' with whom we have been able to work, and 'the machine outside which dictates to them'.[9] For Chris Watson he had nothing but praise.

Deakin's hope was that Watson could moderate Labor's extremists. For his part, Watson wanted the Labor caucus to be able to judge the wisdom of alliances for itself, and to be able to offer electoral immunity to sitting Liberals, promising that Labor would not run candidates against them. But the 1905 Federal Labor Conference, which had supported the alliance with Deakin for the current parliament, would not give electoral immunity to Liberal Protectionists, many of whom held the inner urban seats Labor planned to win as it built its numbers towards governing in its own right.[10]

Labor had broken Deakin's simple model of the political world as divided between progressive Liberals and reactionary obstructionists. Now there were three, and he was in the centre. But the centre is only a point on a spectrum. How could he give it progressive content? His solution was to stand on the solid territory of the nation continent, reminding his audience that they were no longer just Victorians or South Australians, but were now Australians who must develop a wide view and a federal outlook. The Liberal programme, he said, was itself the fruit of this wide Australian experience: completing the institutional foundations; developing the industries; building the population; filling the empty land with people of British blood; 'turning it into a white man's country from north to south'. These were goals of Australian origin and character, and Liberals put forward practical proposals to achieve them.[11] Deakin was claiming the nation as progressive liberalism's consensual centre, and what was crucial for the long-term historical significance of his claim was not only the whiteness but the space of the nation, the imaginative projection of a national community of interest and shared destiny across a vast territory and into an unknowable future.

During 1906 Deakin received a steady stream of advice on how to resolve his political dilemma. John Forrest feared the Liberal Protectionists

would become the tail of the Labor Party, and that an anti-caucus party
with a protectionist leader was their only chance to avoid destruction.[12]
Watson urged him to commit to a land tax and old-age pensions; perhaps
then Labor would hesitate to run candidates against him, but 'if the
only idea of progress put forward by the Ministry is Protection, then I
say flatly it won't fill the bill.'[13] In the *Bulletin* the journalist Frank Fox
urged him to 'come forward as the Man of Today', 'a fighting leader
with a fighting platform'. Fox was almost twenty years younger than
Deakin, and they were friends, but he was much more jingoistic. With
Australia threatened from the north by Asiatics, and Britain unable to
defend her, with tariff protection needed to protect our market against
'foreign invaders', he asked of Deakin: would the urgency of the situation
'shake him out of dreams and doubts and give him a zealot's passion'?[14]

Deakin delivered his opening speech of the election campaign in Ballarat
on Wednesday, 17 October. The *Herald* sent Ernest Scott to report, with
instructions to describe his delivery. In the absence of visual or sound
recordings, it is the most detailed account we have of Deakin in full
oratorical flight, 'a leader of men…using the ear of Ballarat' to address
a continent. Parliament, wrote Scott, had never heard Mr Deakin 'when
he is letting himself go…a man does not address Parliament as he does a
public meeting…But on the Albert Hall platform…body spoke as well
as tongue, and every sentence was animated by the appropriate gesture.'

> For two hours every variety of gesture, from a simply lifted forefin-
> ger to a windmill whirl of arms, gave emphasis to an unfaltering
> flow of language…passages shot out of the mouth like lightning
> flashes, swift and fiery; passages accented by the emphatic beat
> of fist upon open palm; passages spoken in an eager stride across
> the platform; passages delivered in the attitude of a boxer facing
> an assailant; passages rhythmic with movement and glowing
> with fervour.

Usual oratorical practice was to start quietly and build to a rousing
climax, but on this occasion as he approached the end Deakin 'slowed

down his speed, folded his arms across his chest, stood quietly by the table, and drew to a quiet and earnest conclusion'.[15]

At the election in December 1906 Labor did not contest every Liberal Protectionist seat, but it did stand a man against Deakin in Ballarat: a young Catholic grocer, Jim Scullin. Watson thought this a great mistake, but electoral nominations were in the hands of the party organisation and Labor's Ballarat branches were against electoral immunity.[16] Scullin was a good campaigner. A local wrote to Deakin that, after attending his and Reid's meetings, Scullin's was an eye-opener: 'Never since meetings at the Town Hall during the South African trouble have I witnessed such a one man sentiment…hundreds more present than when you addressed your constituents.' He predicted that Deakin would have a bad beating. Deakin expected it too.[17]

Both were wrong, and Deakin easily defeated Scullin, with almost twice his vote.[18] Nationally, however, the Liberal Protectionists did not fare well and came in at third place, with 21.3 per cent of the vote, well behind the free-trade anti-socialists, with 36 per cent, and Labor, with 34.7 per cent. They lost nine seats, including four to the Independent Protectionists, who were hostile to Deakin's alliance with Labor. The final seat tally was Anti-Socialists thirty-two, Labor twenty-six, Deakin Protectionists seventeen, Independent Protectionists four, Western Australia Party two.[19] The majority of the Labor men were protectionists, so protection seemed safe; but, as in 1903, no one party could govern alone.

With no clear winner, Deakin would remain prime minister until he either resigned or lost a no-confidence motion. From Sydney, Watson wrote to him that Labor was not anxious for office as a minority government, and he urged Deakin to stay on at least until he had seen the legislation on the tariff through. Parliament would not meet till February, so they both had the summer holiday to ponder the situation. Watson was going camping in the Blue Mountains, and Deakin to Ballara.

Deakin quailed at the prospect of repeating history. He could not, he told Watson, accept even a check in parliament without taking it as a challenge, so soon either he, Watson or Reid would be sent for to form a government. From his camp on the Duckmaloi River near Oberon, Watson urged Deakin to stay on, arguing that without him protection was still at risk and that he magnified the chance of friction with Labor.[20] Deakin's reply shows that by early January he had settled into his familiar stance of letting events unfold. He predicted that his party would soon split and that he could do nothing to prevent it, though good luck might postpone the day.

> Personally I am not troubled by the outlook. I would much rather be out of office under the present conditions and the sooner the better, but of course I have responsibilities that I must discharge—to the country, to the party, to my colleagues—of these I cannot relieve myself at my own pleasure. A solution to this situation which would relieve me would be welcome but until it arrives naturally I am bound to do my best to keep the flag flying.[21]

A great deal is carried for Deakin in that small word 'naturally'. On Christmas Day, 1906 he had written a long prayer, in which he contemplated what life would be like, if there were 'no God…and no future for me beyond this life'. He would still aspire 'to make the best use of life & thought for the best service of all living things', but his

> standards would sink…& ideas dwindle so that the present would outweigh the future and immediate ease, relief and hope be the safest gifts to distribute hastily before the endless night came to us all. Happiness in itself might not be much but it would be all that there was to gain.

Contemplating how he might have resolved his perplexity of choice were he without religious faith, Deakin reveals the religious centre that disciplined his worldly aspirations and sustained the uncertainties and sacrifices of his political life. The prayer concluded,

> I can but act as usher to Thy doors. In public & private life, in thought & dreams as well as a patient dutifulness, absorbed energy,

meek self-suppression, glad acceptance of any office no matter how mean...I will rejoice in it though it bow me to the dust.[22]

There was another urgent matter pressing on Deakin's decision. Whoever was prime minister would attend the next Imperial Conference, which began on 15 April 1907. There would scarcely be time for parliament to meet, show its lack of confidence in Deakin's ministry, and the governor-general to send for another man before the new prime minister would need to board the boat to London. Neither Reid nor Watson could represent Australia in the imperial centre with the grace and conviction of Deakin, so for Australia's sake Deakin had little choice but to stay on.

On 20 February parliament met briefly to attend to post-election formalities. No one challenged the government, and Deakin presented the resolutions he would take to London. Parliament would not meet again until he returned. Atlee Hunt would accompany him as his secretary. He had organised for William Lyne to be in London to attend a conference on navigation as minister for customs—a wise move, Hunt thought, as Lyne would make mischief if left at home.[23] John Forrest would be acting prime minister.

Before he left, Deakin made a quick trip to Sydney to ask Tom Bavin to take over his *Morning Post* letters while he was away. Bavin agreed, and was rewarded with a great deal of advice from Deakin, which shows how methodical Deakin was with his journalism and how attentive to detail. Bavin was to send the letters to Deakin, who would edit them to better match his own style: topping and tailing to link to those that have gone before, removing tautologies, softening adjectives to give a more detached view, and removing the pronoun 'I', which he hardly ever used. Remember, he told Bavin, you are writing for a Tory paper which allows you to say anything but wishes it said 'politely, deprecatingly or by implication to spare its readers' sensibilities'.[24]

Deakin left Melbourne in early March 1907 accompanied by Pattie, who was initially reluctant. There had been some thought that Catherine, Vera and Stella would go too, repeating the family excursion of 1900, but in the end Pattie and Alfred went alone. Vera and Stella would stay at

Adams Street. All the family gathered for a farewell dinner, including Sarah Deakin, who was now a frail eighty-four, and baby Wilfred.

In early February, Deakin's prayer diary had mentioned more conflict in the family, which may explain his extraordinary parting homily.[25] He read to them a short sermon by Phillips Brooks on the unifying spirit of Christ, and then, according to Catherine, he told them that 'We must apply it and fulfil Alfred's spirit in the same way all the more fully in his absence—love one another and keep united.'[26] It was as if he felt that without him things might fall apart.

The voyage over was uneventful. Deakin skipped vigorously most days, before settling down in a secluded part of the deck with his papers to prepare for the conference. Pattie was bored and lonely, and wondered why she'd come.[27] They arrived in London on 8 April 1907 and settled into their sumptuous suite in the Hotel Cecil with the other visiting dignitaries. The hotel, the biggest in Europe when it was opened ten years earlier, filled a block from the Strand to the Thames Embankment. Their luxurious sitting room, with its salmon-pink Axminster and rosewood furniture, overlooked the river and the Houses of Parliament.[28] Deakin was immediately in the whirl of events, responding to an avalanche of letters and callers, his days and nights crammed with engagements.

Deakin had come to the conference with large aims for the reorganisation of the empire, and he expected opposition. 'Battle with Elgin and C.O. begins,' he wrote on the day the conference opened. The Colonial Office would jealously guard its powers, which he was determined to challenge, especially as the new Liberal government was far less imperially minded than the defeated Unionists.

Deakin's vision was one in which the self-governing colonial nations would have more autonomy, but this autonomy would be balanced by a system of reciprocal preferential trade to strengthen the empire's unity, supplementing sentimental ties of culture and kinship with economic interdependence and mutual self-interest. He proposed that the Imperial Council should become a permanent body, made up of representatives of the British government and the self-governing colonies, and with a permanent secretariat independent of the Colonial Office. Governments would deal directly with each other and with the British government, without the Colonial Office as an intermediary.

When Deakin first took up the cause of imperial trade preferences it had some prospect of becoming British policy. But during 1906 it suffered two fatal blows. At the election in February the Conservative Unionist government lost in a landslide to the Liberals, who had campaigned hard against trade preferences, arguing they would lead to increased food prices. They were supported in this by the small Labour Party. And in July, Joseph Chamberlain suffered a major stroke, depriving the Tariff Reformers of his leadership. Just prior to this, Chamberlain had written to Deakin, expressing his support for colonial proposals for reciprocal preferential trade, and foreshadowing the importance of the conference, but he was now out of the game.[29]

Deakin was extremely frustrated that the opening of the conference was not to be public, and wrote to the new prime minister, Henry Campbell-Bannerman, to complain:

> We have come long distances on what we believe to be a great mission for which we have postponed public business of an urgent character, adjourned our legislatures and divided our executives. It appears to us to be an extremely inappropriate commencement of its labours...that the occasion should be treated as if it were merely a departmental gathering of the Colonial Office.[30]

The government was not persuaded, and so the delegates turned to public gatherings to press their causes. Deakin's strategy was the same one he had used in 1900 to rouse public sympathy over the role of the Privy Council in the constitution. He would address every banquet, luncheon and public meeting he could, so that his vision of empire could be reported in the press and read by the British public.

The other leaders did not share his desire for stronger institutions of imperial governance. Wilfrid Laurier, the Canadian prime minister, and Louis Botha from South Africa both had major domestic constituencies wary of Britain, and Laurier did not want to disrupt Canada's crucial relationship with the United States. Canada submitted no resolutions to the conference and Botha barely spoke.

Australia, on the other hand, submitted twenty-one and Deakin spoke more often and at greater length than any of the other premiers.[31] But he made only a little headway. It was agreed that the Imperial Conference should meet every four years, and that the self-governing colonies would adopt the Canadian name of dominion; however, their relations with the British government would continue to be controlled by the Colonial Office.

Deakin's plans for new institutions of imperial governance included neither India nor the crown colonies. Only the self-governing white dominions were to be represented on his Imperial Council and to have direct relations with the British government. This might have been acceptable with regard to the crown colonies; India was another matter. Deakin had objected to India being included in the conference as it was not self-governing. But India was the jewel in the imperial crown, the source of much of Britain's wealth and its status as a world power. John Morley, the current secretary for India, wrote, 'I laugh when I think of a man who blows the imperial trumpet louder than other people and yet would banish India.'[32] Any effective imperial trade policy would have to take account of Britain's trade with the subcontinent. Deakin's failure to think hard about how India would fit into his more unified empire reveals his race patriotism, but also his anxious need to magnify the significance to Britain of her white dominions.

At the banquets and speeches Deakin gave his usual virtuosic oratorical performances, bringing passionate appeals to the bonds of empire from the 'land of hope and sunshine' and rousing the cheers. He records the stampedes of congratulations in his diary. According to Hunt he so outshone Laurier that after two or three nights Laurier failed to appear.[33] Some of the enthusiasm may have been for his performances rather than his opinions, and his outspokenness annoyed the government. Tennyson, Australia's one-time governor-general, wrote to him after one speech that some of those present were 'highly irritated…you have said your say boldly against the CO for their New Hebrides muddle. Now let it stop.'[34]

In his strenuous campaign for imperial trade preferences, Deakin was effectively taking sides in a contentious domestic issue against a government which had just won a resounding electoral victory for free trade. Courteously, H. H. Asquith, who was Chancellor of the Exchequer, pointed out that, just as Britain respected the fiscal autonomy of the protectionist colonies, she retained the same autonomy for herself and was committed to free trade.[35] No matter how uplifting were Deakin's evocations of the stronger and more united empire that trade preferences would create, the British public, which elected the British government, did not support them.

Deakin's eloquent championing of empire was a tonic to the Unionists sidelined by the Liberal government and looking for ways to keep their imperial project alive. The Unionist-sympathising press reprinted his speeches to give them wider circulation. Deakin met often with Leo Maxse of the *National Review* and Fabian Ware of the *Morning Post*, as well as with Leo Amery, who was writing on imperial affairs for *The Times*, and with Richard Jebb, whose recently published book, *Studies in Colonial Nationalism*, argued that the nationalism of the settler colonies did not presage a weakening of their imperial sentiment and could indeed be a source of strength for the empire.[36]

In mid-May, Deakin was approached by Maxse, Amery and another journalist, Howell Arthur Gwynne, to consider bringing his energies to British politics. Maxse even thought he could straightaway become the Unionist leader, over the heads of all the 'Mandarins', or at least leader of the tariff-reform movement.[37] In 1909 Deakin included in the list of his political choices, 'Offers in London enter British politics seat etc provided in many forms all declined.'[38]

It is unlikely he seriously considered the offer. Pattie, for one, would never have agreed; and Maxse and Amery were not party powerbrokers. But in a letter to Amery after he left London, Deakin adopted his characteristically passive stance towards the course of his political life, which here seems almost fey. He will do nothing to make it happen—but he cannot vouchsafe for Providence.

Life is so unexpected and my own has been so adventurous and

full of surprises that nothing is absolutely impossible—At present
the whole project appears Quixotic in the extreme and may be
dismissed without hesitation. My duties so far as they are public
lie in Australia and nowhere else—But it is just within the bounds
of possibility that something akin to what you proposed may be
required of me in the discharge of these very duties...I would
wager all I am worth that this contingency will not occur—but
for all that it might...[39]

Empire defence was also on the agenda. One of the propositions
Deakin brought to the conference was that the colonies should be
represented on the Imperial Council of Defence. It was never likely
that the lords of the empire would accept this, but it was agreed that
a dominion representative might attend discussions of relevant local
issues. Deakin also wanted reconsideration of the 1902 Naval Defence
Agreement: 'the people of Australia regard the present contribution
of £200,000 to the cost of the Imperial Navy as being somewhat in the
nature of a tribute,' he told representatives of the Admiralty. Australia
wanted to co-operate with the Admiralty in the defence of the empire,
and he proposed a local defence force under the political control of the
Commonwealth.[40]

The Admiralty indicated it was sympathetic, and would wait for
the Commonwealth to bring forward detailed proposals for a revised
agreement. But the Admiralty was stonewalling. Britain refused to
see its ally Japan as a threat and so saw no urgent need for Australia
to develop an independent naval capacity.[41] As Deakin had written to
Jebb about an earlier incident of Admiralty stonewalling, 'What can
you do with such people?'[42]

Deakin made one substantial blunder in London in relation to
Australia's politics. At a meeting of investors, where he believed he
was speaking privately, he dismissed Labor's electoral chances. The
Australian press reported the meeting, and Labor was not impressed.
'The Labor Party has come to stay,' responded the West Australian
Labor senator George Pearce, 'and will become a dominant political
power in Australia.'[43]

•

On this visit Deakin saw nothing of the theatre and galleries, but he did enjoy a few purely social engagements. He met with his Australian friends Tom Roberts and Bernhard Wise, visited the elderly novelist George Meredith, and lunched with Frank Harris from *Vanity Fair*, who remembered that when they had dined together twenty years ago, 'we talked the stars down from the skies.'[44] Just before he left London he met with Rudyard Kipling. Hunt, who went with him, had never heard such wonderful talk: 'it was one of the events of my life.'[45] Deakin and Pattie were welcomed warmly by ex-governors and governor-generals now back Home. Hopetoun met them at Dover and they spent a weekend with the Tennysons on the Isle of Wight.

For much of the time, however, Pattie was left to her own devices. She was lonely and exhausted by the never-ending social demands in 'a life of rush and scurry'. 'My nerves are quite gone—I can sit and weep at any moment…As for father he scarcely ever says one word to me—writing or seeing men all the time we are together'; 'It is one long whirl of dressing, motoring, dining and talking, and I am weary and homesick.'

She was proud though of the impression Alfred was making, telling Ivy, 'They receive him everywhere as they receive no one else.' After he had received the Freedom of the City of London she drove with him through the cheering crowds, both bowing and waving as if they were royalty. And she enjoyed meeting royalty, though on one occasion was rapped across the knuckles by the elderly society hostess Lady Dorothy Neville for failing to bob to a minor German aristocrat. Pattie had not known he was a prince. The wealth and power of the leading families shocked her, as did the squalor, cold and hunger endured by the poor. 'Oh for Australia, sunshine and freedom.'[46]

For Pattie the trip was a turning point. In Melbourne she only occasionally accompanied Alfred to official events; and when they were in London in 1900 her poor health had mostly confined her to quarters. This trip her days were filled with official engagements, and she was a success. Significantly, she spoke in public for the first time. Lady Jersey, wife of a former governor of New South Wales, asked her at short notice to address a luncheon of the Victoria League for the wives and daughters of the visiting premiers. She quaked and her thoughts all fled, but she managed to get through and 'everyone said my voice was modulated nicely.' Alfred was shocked when he saw a sandwich man with a placard, 'Mrs Deakin addresses the women of England.' 'Good God Pattie, what have you been doing?'[47]

Once back home, Pattie began to participate in public life. This was not only a matter of confidence, as she also seems to have become stronger, with fewer bouts of illness. Pattie was now forty-four, and the most likely explanation is that menopause was bringing relief from her monthly ordeals, and a new sense of physical well-being. She joined the organisation of the massive Exhibition of Women's Work, which was the brainchild of the governor-general's wife, Lady Northcote, and a prime example of first-wave Australian feminism's champion-ing of women's contribution to the new nation. Held in Melbourne's Exhibition Building, it demonstrated that women's work had relevance beyond their homes.[48] It emphasised motherhood and the domestic arts, making it the perfect launching pad for Pattie into her new public life. She chaired the committee which organised a crèche, and was soon also active in the Kindergarten Union and the Victorian Neglected Children's Society.[49]

Pattie and Alfred left London on 20 May 1907, spending a few days in Paris, where he met with a friend of his youth, A. van Rijn van Alkemade, a Dutch adventurer. Deakin's correspondence files include many long letters from Alkemade telling of his bohemian adventures and various failed attempts to make his fortune, in Australia, New Guinea, the United States and the Dutch East Indies. Light-hearted, frank and self-deprecating, they are addressed to the brilliant Australian friend he first knew in the late 1870s, when they were both full of ambition and youthful enthusiasm, and Deakin's great strength of will, unbounded energy and powers of mind marked him out for success.

The friends of youth can know one as later friends never do, when one is still playing with possible selves and futures, before the adult persona and its defences are in place. Deakin made more use of these defences than most, and in Melbourne he had let his early friends drop

away. But he retained his friendship with Alkemade to the end. After
the gruelling six weeks in London, in Paris he could relax with an old
friend who was just happy to be in his company.[50]

Once on board the boat home, Deakin collapsed with exhaustion.
Pattie remembered that she was up all night with him on several
occasions, and that he was never the same man again.[51] In family memory,
Deakin's overwork on the London trip was the cause of his later cognitive
decline, though this is hard to establish from the available evidence.

He was returning with slim pickings. As he told a crowded meeting
when the ship was in Perth, the propositions he took to London dealt
with questions of policy which affected the British public. It would
have been easier simply to have enjoyed the glamour of the imperial
surroundings and to have carved 'out of civic generalities some paltry
political bric-a-brac of the customary kind', but this would have been
to evade responsibility. 'We might have sown dead seed, but it was
impossible...to sacrifice duty to complaisance.'[52]

This was not the triumphant homecoming of 1887, or even 1900,
when Australia finally achieved a federal constitution. There were
the same welcome dinners and receptions, but without the same inner
elation. He had mobilised his performative self for a manic six weeks in
the service of a largely doomed enterprise, and in retrospect it was all
a blur, 'an inexpressible experience of which I can determine nothing
except that moving in a conspicuous way among my kinsmen and
kinswomen, my wife & myself have floated an instant high on the crest
of a wave of publicity, prominence, in feverish activity'. It had been a
high-risk enterprise, 'a place of trial in which I might have been stripped
to the skin & disclosed in all my native poverty, meanness, weakness
& crudity, to the full blaze of piercing contempt and life-long shame
of obvious failure'. God be thanked that he had come safely home, 'to
my familiar place'.[53]

30

DEFENCE AND THE
NEW PROTECTION

ON HIS RETURN from London, Deakin was immediately back in the thick of events. Parliament opened on 3 July 1907, and the governor-general set out an ambitious programme for the rest of the session. But Deakin was 'fagged', and walking into the House one day he was overcome with dizziness. The dizziness persisted, and at the end of the week his doctor, Dr Marcel Crivelli, recommended a complete rest, diagnosing problems with his heart and eyes. Deakin took leave from parliament, and he and Pattie went to Ballara. He hoped he would be better in a week, but he did not fully return to parliament until the end of October.

For the next few months he worked assiduously to regain his health. At Ballara he followed a regimen of vigorous physical exercise—skipping, chopping wood, burning off grass trees and bathing in the sea most days, despite the winter cold. When he came up to town, Dr Crivelli administered injections, and he had a series of electrotherapy treatments from Dr Beckett, as well as regular massages. He also met with political colleagues, and when at Ballara kept in touch with events by the newly installed telephone.

To add to Deakin's worries, Forrest was retiring from the government. He had fought the 1906 election as an opponent of the Labor Party and felt it was dishonourable and a breach of confidence with his electors now to be effectively in alliance with them, he told Deakin. Forrest sent an official letter of resignation for Deakin to read to the parliament, and a personal one, to be torn up after reading, though Deakin kept the letter.

> I am truly sorry to leave you with one who does not care for you [William Lyne] and in the hands of Philistines who will leave you not a shred of consistency before they are done with you...You are not fit to bear the worry and strain just now—get out of it quickly is my advice. It will save your life and save your reputation too.[1]

Deakin and Pattie stayed at Ballara till his birthday at the start of August, which he marked with the resolve to seek deeper intimacy with his family, and to live a life of quiet, calm, confident peacefulness.[2] He was now fifty-one. A few days later he met with Lyne and offered to retire from the leadership in his favour, but Lyne repelled the proposal.[3] Later in the month, still unwell, he decided he must get away and embarked on a long train trip to Far North Queensland. This seems an odd decision and anything but restful, sleeping on trains and meeting with political colleagues in the towns. But it gave him the space to read, and perhaps he hoped that new sights would lift his spirits and the rhythm of the wheels soothe his restlessness, even that he might recapture something of the excitement of his first long train trips through America.

But Deakin could not leave politics behind, and getting away turned into something of a research trip. Queensland sugar growers had fought hard against the Pacific Island Labourers Act, which mandated the deportation of thousands of Pacific Islanders who had been working in the sugar industry. The sugar growers claimed they depended on their cheap labour. As compensation, the growers were given a rebate on the sugar excise if they employed only white labour, and in 1905 this was amended to require claimants to prove that they were paying the wages 'standard in the district'; otherwise, no rebate. The 1905 Sugar Bounty Act was the first Commonwealth legislation to embody the principles of the New Protection: that producers who received the benefits of protection must share them with their white workers in the form of higher wages.[4] The repatriation of Pacific Islanders had begun in late 1906, though not all were repatriated. Travelling through the sugar districts, Deakin noted the race of the cane cutters he saw from the train window and made enquiries about wages.

Back in Melbourne in September, Deakin was still nervy. He added missing breakfast and sleeping out on the balcony to his regime of self-medication. Billy Hughes wrote to the English journalist Richard Jebb that Deakin 'ought to go away for a trip where the wire stretches not nor does the phone tintinnabulate. But he dodges about like a fly near paper which to him spells death but smells like life.'[5]

Deakin's prayer diary shows that he thought constantly about retiring, but was paralysed by uncertainty. 'It cannot be that the choice of any one man can be final in anything,' he wrote.[6] Yet he must have known that, were he to retire, what was left of the Liberal Protectionist Party would collapse. Forrest was gone, and Lyne, now acting prime minister and treasurer, was not the man to defend the Liberal Protectionists in a difficult parliament in which the ministry depended on Labor's support. Lyne was much closer to Labor than Deakin was and did not even try to disguise the ministry's dependence on it. He was also irritable and short-tempered—a contrast, wrote the contemporary observer Henry Gyles Turner, with Mr Deakin, who

> had an exceptional faculty, not only for looking on the bright side of things himself, but for leading others to do the same. If the Labor Party regulated his proceedings, he invariably assumed they were following his directions…and so deftly did he handle the situation that he often saved it from anarchic confusion by a few well-timed sentences, committing him to nothing, but sufficing to divert attack.[7]

There was really no one to take the leadership, so at the end of September
he returned to parliament and his prime-ministerial duties.

In early August 1907 Lyne had introduced the new tariff schedules,
which included preference for British manufactures. Deakin contemplated resigning if parliament rejected the measure. David Syme,
for whom British preference was an annoying distraction from the
protectionists' main game, was alarmed: 'You do not seriously consider
resigning for such a cause? You are only incidentally committed to
Preference—which is comparatively unimportant—but pledged to the
Tariff.' Syme suggested that Deakin take six months' leave and offered
to organise a private testimonial to make it possible, but Deakin assured
him he was fit to carry on.[8]

On 23 October, Deakin recorded his relief: 'Preference carried
without a division!' Many Labor members were not keen on imperial
preference, but they were biding their time till the New Protection
was in place and so they voted for the bill. Next day, Deakin learned
that Chris Watson had resigned as Labor's leader. Watson had been
talking of resigning for some time, citing nerves frayed by the strain of
office as well as his long absences from home. Party members pleaded
with him to reconsider, but to no avail. A delegation of Labor women
even visited his wife to elicit her support, but she replied, 'I only want
what all women want, my husband home with me.'[9]

Watson's resignation was a blow to Deakin. He liked him, and
they had established a congenial working relationship. Behind the
anonymity of the *Morning Post*, he praised Watson, 'an honorable,
capable, open-minded and amiable public man', for his soundness
of judgement, his dignity and his lack of malice. His 'clear-sighted
moderation has safeguarded his often unruly associates against many...
serious blunders.'[10]

With Watson gone, Deakin knew the 'ultras' would soon be flexing
their muscles. The Labor caucus elected the forty-five-year-old Scotsman
Andrew Fisher as its new leader. Fisher was an ex-miner who had
been in the parliament since 1901 as the member for Gympie and had
long experience in union politics, both in Ayrshire and in Queensland.
Like Deakin, his physical presence was one of his many political assets.

He was tall and muscular, with thick hair and moustache, and well-chiselled features. He was committed to improving the workers' standard of living and working conditions, and to reining in the speculators and monopolists. Significantly, he took a harder line than Watson on parliamentary alliances and electoral immunity.[11]

Late in 1907, on the last sitting day before parliament rose for Christmas, Deakin made a major speech on defence; and he tabled an explanatory memorandum on the New Protection. For Deakin both were unfinished business of the federation. In May two hundred and fifty thousand pounds had been set aside for Commonwealth defence, but spending it required legislation. The speech set out a comprehensive plan for the development of Australia's naval capacity. Australia would continue to rely on Britain for defence of the high seas, but would take responsibility for its own coastal defence, building, manning and maintaining at its own expense a flotilla of submarines and destroyers. Deakin was adamant that if the Commonwealth paid for local naval vessels with the taxes of a self-governing community, then on constitutional grounds its government should control them, but Admiralty was not happy with the prospect of divided command. Deakin suggested a compromise in which the Commonwealth controlled the vessels in times of peace, but the parliament could vote to place the vessels under the British commander-in-chief of the Eastern Squadron if required, thus satisfying his scruples about self-government. Admiralty accepted the compromise.

For military defence, he proposed a citizen army, with a system of universal military training for young men. The training would not be arduous: sixteen days a year for three years between the ages of nineteen and twenty-one, after which the trainees would become members of a reserve force. He hoped it would never be needed in warfare, but would instead foster the national spirit: 'Those of us who have worn the military uniform, as many of us have, those who have stood shoulder to shoulder in the ranks answering to the volunteer bugle call know how powerfully such an outward summons appeals.'[12]

Deakin was greatly amplifying his brief experience with the volunteers, which ended when he was eighteen and became 'an advocate for

peace'.[13] But times had changed. The sentimental models of manhood
still powerful in Deakin's youth had been swept away by the martial
masculinity of imperial expansion and defence. The nations of the
world were arming in 'feverish haste' and Australia was 'not outside
the area of world conflict', so he did his best to channel a military spirit
through the language of duty and citizenship with which he was more
comfortable: 'when men rally round their hearth and homes to safeguard
those they love, they discharge a duty.' We aim for 'the maximum of
good citizenship, with the spirit of patriotism as the chief motive of a
civil defence force...for a military not a martial spirit.'[14]

New Protection was closer to his humanitarian heart. Deakin himself
wrote the memorandum he tabled. He had fought for the regulation
of workers' wages and conditions in the Factory Act when he was
Victoria's chief secretary, and he had been active in the Anti-Sweating
League. But the results had been disappointing. New Protection was
another chance, using the Commonwealth's power over taxation to
influence wages and conditions, which were prima facie state issues.

The mechanism was simple: an excise would be imposed on a
category of manufactured goods which enjoyed a protective tariff, and
then waived if the manufacturer paid fair and reasonable wages. 'The
"old" Protection contented itself with making good wages possible.
The "new" Protection seeks to make them actual,' he wrote. Deakin
was well aware of New Protection's constitutional daring, but argued
in the memorandum that to restrict the powers of the Commonwealth
to the imposition of duties while the conditions for the manufacture of
protected items differed so much between states 'would be to permit
inequality, discrimination and discord. The ideal of the Constitution
is equality and uniformity in all national matters.'[15]

By the end of 1907 New Protection had gained a good deal of
momentum. It had been used in 1905 and 1906 to protect Australian
manufacturers of agricultural implements, harvesters in particular, from
the threat of hostile dumping by American and Canadian manufacturers.
The industry was a big employer, and Labor and Liberal Protectionists,
as well as the public, demanded it be safeguarded. Labor's free-traders
were more cautious, but they could not stand by while fellow workers

lost their jobs, and they agreed to a special tariff so long as its benefits were shared with the workers in the form of 'fair and reasonable wages'. Labor's suggestion was embodied in the *Excise Tariff (Agricultural Machinery) Act 1906*, but it failed to define a fair and reasonable wage. This was determined on 8 November by Justice Higgins in his first case as president of the Arbitration Court, when he handed down his famous Harvester Judgment.

Higgins based his determination of a fair and reasonable wage on 'the normal needs of the average employee, regarded as a human being living in a civilized community', food, shelter, clothing and 'a condition of frugal comfort estimated by current human standards'. He questioned the housewives of Sunshine, where H. V. McKay's harvester factory was situated, on their household budgets and set the monetary value of a fair and reasonable wage at seven shillings a day for an unskilled labourer. This was more than the minimum wage McKay paid his workers, and Higgins' judgment was immediately appealed to the High Court. It ruled, three to two, that the relevant sections of the act were invalid as they were an attempt to regulate conditions of employment which did not come under any existing Commonwealth power.

The High Court's ruling did not stop the Harvester Judgment's transformative power. Higgins continued to use its criteria to determine wages in cases that came before him, and within five years his lucid reasoning had been adopted by three Labor state governments to determine the basic wage. By the 1920s a minimum wage based on the cost of living was entrenched in industrial law and joined the eight-hour day as the bedrock of Labor's demands for a civilised capitalism.[16] But all this was yet to come. At the end of 1907 Deakin was confident that the constitutional basis of the New Protection would hold, and his commitment to it gave Labor a reason to continue to support his government.

Deakin attended to one other matter on the last sitting day of 1907. Early in December he had lunched with the Anglo-Irish explorer Ernest Shackleton, who asked for government financial assistance for his second Antarctic expedition. It was an appeal to excite Deakin's romantic imagination. In a motion without notice, Deakin proposed to grant the expedition five thousand pounds. His justifications were prosaic:

meteorological knowledge, scientific specimens of flora and fauna for Australia's museums, and the benefit of 'any economic possibilities in these Antarctic lands'. Joseph Cook, who was leading the Opposition, and Andrew Fisher were both supportive. In gratitude, Shackleton named the mountains to the east of the just discovered Beardmore Glacier Commonwealth Range and one of its peaks Mount Deakin.[17]

The past year, as Deakin led his minority government, had been trying. In a cluster of prayers written over Christmas and early January he searched for the 'ideals that are the map of life' in 'our obscure lilliputian mode of being'. From the peace of Ballara he thanked God for reprieve from the metropolis, and in early February 1908 he was ready to return to 'whatever tasks may fall to me'. 'Valuing little what most value much,' he wrote, 'let me not be led into indifference or egotistical self-confidence.'[18]

These prayers are a window into a paradox in Deakin's selfless ambition. The young man's triumphant records of personal success have long gone. He has achieved more than he could ever have dreamed and is grateful. Yet God may still have more for him to do, more service towards the Ideal. Eschewing worldly motives and rewards, he sets himself apart as the instrument of a higher purpose pursued in a political life where others value more worldly ends. No wonder he felt compelled to stay on. By this reasoning he was indispensable to God's purpose.

On 14 February 1908 David Syme died from oesophageal cancer. Deakin had visited him for the last time at his home in Kew just before Christmas and the *Age* featured a tribute from him on the day of Syme's funeral. A biography by Ambrose Pratt was already underway, commissioned by Syme himself, who provided much of the material and who had asked Deakin to write the introduction. After some hesitation, he granted the old man's request and wrote it in the few weeks following his death. 'Without leisure to refer to diaries or documents…for the refreshment of a jaded memory,' he managed only 'a few cursory and hasty glimpses…slight and fragmentary'.[19]

For once Deakin's habitual self-deprecation was warranted. His introduction was a rather shapeless piece of writing, with little verve and none of the acute psychological insight of the federation portraits.

Syme was a complicated, driven and immensely able man, shaped by
the collapse of conventional religious belief as Deakin was, and who
invested politics with the moral and spiritual urgency his father had
found in the kirk.

Parliament resumed sitting in March 1908, and Deakin was soon
confronted with the reality of his tenuous control. There were problems
with the administration of the post office, and some members were
pressing for a royal commission. Deakin offered a committee of the
cabinet to investigate, but on Friday, 10 April a Labor member moved
a motion to appoint a royal commission. Several Labor members voted
in support, as did the Opposition, which took the chance to humiliate
Deakin. The ministry was defeated and Deakin moved an adjournment
to consider the situation.[20]

The issue of the post office was relatively trivial, but the motion
had displaced Deakin's planned order of business for the day, which
was finally to settle the site for the national capital. He was the tail
being publicly wagged by the Labor dog and yet again he contemplated
resignation. 'So scant & intermittent are the gleams of the ideal upon
the surface of events and persons that one falters before the chaos of life
almost paralysed by its apparent purposelessness showing but vague
inconsecutive advances.'[21]

That Friday he told Lyne, Fisher and Watson that he would resign
and offered to support a Lyne–Fisher coalition, and on Saturday the
papers reported that a new government was imminent.[22] From all sides
Deakin was pressed to stay on. The revised Tariff Bill, introduced to the
House in October 1907, was now before the Senate. With the promise
of New Protection before it, when parliament met on Wednesday,
15 April, Labor withdrew its support for a royal commission.[23] The
crisis had passed, for now. Behind the scenes, though, Deakin was
still talking of resigning and talks with Fisher made it clear to him
that Labor was keen for office. 'End in sight,' he wrote on 30 April
1908.[24] But when parliament rose for the recess on 11 June, Fisher had
made no move. As parliament did not meet again until 16 September,
Deakin would be prime minister at least till then. In the *Morning Post*

he predicted that the prime minister would resign 'as soon as the Tariff is settled'.[25]

In the early hours of Wednesday, 3 June, his mother, Sarah, died. She was eighty-five and had succumbed to a cold. When Alfred had visited Adams Street the previous Sunday she was well. 'She kissed him when he said, as usual, take care of yourself. She replied, as usual, Oh! It does not matter about me—it is you!' wrote lonely, grieving Catherine as she recorded her mother's last few days in loving detail. Sister and brother knelt beside the body that had given them life and prayed for her soul, which they believed would now be joining William in a new birth.

'Should she need consolation,' Deakin prayed that night,

> let her realisation of our debt and gratitude stream up to her & surround with the joy of duty done & of repose well-earned. Bless and enrich her & her husband in themselves & in each other with the knowledge of all the good they have done for us and for others.

Next day, under a leaden sky, Dr Strong officiated at the graveside as Sarah was laid to rest by William's side.[26]

31

THE GREAT WHITE FLEET

OVER THE COURSE of 1907 discussions with the British government about an Australian navy had made no progress. Deakin was impatient to begin legislating his defence scheme, but he needed Britain's approval, as well as support from the public and the parliament. So he decided to hurry things along. Deakin knew that the American president, Theodore Roosevelt, had decided to send sixteen battleships and attendant vessels from the Atlantic fleet on a world tour to display the naval power of the United States. On Christmas Eve, 1907 Deakin wrote to the American consul in Sydney, John Bray, about the possibility of the fleet visiting Australia. He sent a similar letter in early January 1908 to the American ambassador in Britain, Whitelaw Reid. As with his 'unofficial' communications with Japanese diplomats in 1905 on the matter of the Immigration Restriction Act, Deakin was bypassing the expected lines of imperial communication through London. Deakin's letters to the American diplomats stressed how much Australia and the United States had in common:

I doubt whether any two people could be found who are in nearer touch with each other and are likely to benefit more by anything that tends to knit their relations more closely…[We are anxious] to have some opportunity of expressing our sympathy with our kinsmen in their timely demonstration of naval power in what may loosely be termed our Oceanic neighbourhood.[1]

The warships were painted white to display their peaceful purposes, and the armada of steel and steam became known as the Great White Fleet.

The United States now had significant territory in the Pacific as a result of its annexation of Hawaii and its victory over Spain in 1898, and Roosevelt wanted to show that the Pacific was as much its home waters as the Atlantic—to Britain, Germany and France, but most especially to Japan. During 1907 relations with Japan had been tense. Japan, which admired the United States and viewed it as a friend, was shocked and humiliated by riots of white settlers on the Pacific coast against Japanese immigration.

Japan regarded itself as a modern civilised industrial power, but its people could not change the colour of their skin. The situation was resolved through 'gentlemen's agreements', like the one Deakin had negotiated, in which the Japanese government agreed to restrict the emigration of labourers. The fleet would visit Japan in a display of goodwill, but the United States was staking a claim to sea power in the Pacific: speaking softly but carrying a big stick, as Roosevelt liked to describe his preferred diplomatic strategy.[2]

Deakin waited until 28 January 1908 before requesting the Colonial Office, through a dispatch from the governor-general by sea mail, to issue an invitation to the United States on Australia's behalf. This would give time enough for his 'unofficial' letters to get to the American government without risk of interference from the Colonial Office. By early February there was such public speculation about the possibility of a visit from the fleet that Deakin had to cable the request to London. This was the first the Colonial Office had heard of the plan.

The Americans were 'gratified' by the invitation and, in late February, Deakin was able to announce, in advance of an official acceptance, the possibility that the fleet might visit Australian waters.[3] The British government had no choice but to support the visit, but it was furious at Deakin's temerity. Foreign Secretary Edward Grey wrote to Colonial Secretary Lord Elgin that Deakin should be admonished, as 'invitations to foreign governments should not be given except through us as circumstances are conceivable in which grave inconveniences might result.'[4] Deakin claimed that his letters were 'preliminary' and 'unofficial'. But, complained Charles Lucas, the head of the Dominion Secretariat, 'A prime minister cannot write as he wrote to an American consul-general & treat it as unofficial.'[5]

Deakin learned by cable that his invitation had been accepted on 13 March, just before he was to make a major speech on defence in Sydney's Centennial Hall. At the conclusion, he announced that the American fleet would visit Melbourne and Sydney. 'I have waited for this for a long time. I have hoped for it more than I can say,' he said, and led the crowd in three rousing cheers for the United States.[6]

Deakin's challenge to a paternalistic Whitehall drew on his pride and colonial self-assertion, but these were not the prime motives for his audacity. The rise of Japan was creating a fault line between Australian and imperial interests. For Britain, the alliance with Japan was designed to check the expansion of Russia and Germany. For Australia, Japan had become a major power in the Pacific, close enough to invade and potentially hostile, given Australia's immigration policy. Britain had already moved battleships from the Pacific to the North Sea in response to the build-up of the German navy and many doubted it could defend Australia should Japan invade. In accepting the invitation, the United States was also thinking strategically, and included a visit to New Zealand. Should the tensions with Japan over immigration erupt into war, dominion allies in the Pacific would be welcome.[7]

Although Deakin never spoke of the possibility of a Japanese invasion, plenty of other people did, in the press and in popular literature, expressing Australia's sense of cultural isolation and fear of the Yellow Peril. In October 1908 Deakin's jingoistic young friend Frank Fox began a serialised invasion story set in the future, 'The Commonwealth Crisis', in the *Lone Hand*, a literary offshoot of the *Bulletin*.[8] The story began in 1912 and 1913, when Japanese soldier-settlers landed in the unpopulated Northern Territory and Britain's Royal Navy was fully occupied defending the heart of empire against European rivals.

Fox intended the story as a warning of the dangers facing the Commonwealth in the context of a global race war in which 'Australia is the precious front buckle in the white girdle of power and progress encircling the globe.'[9] Fox had written to Deakin after his defence speech to the parliament, urging him on. Deakin replied that although Fox's 'alarmism' was useful in rousing public support for defence spending, he did not himself think China or Japan were immediate threats.[10] Fox's tale was not published until after the fleet's departure from Perth on 18 September, but it captures much of the popular response to the American visit—as does a play by another of Deakin's younger friends, the journalist and mining speculator Randolph Bedford, who sometimes gave Deakin investment advice. *White Australia, or, The Empty North* dramatises the defeat of a Japanese naval invasion.[11] Race was in the air and on the waters of the Pacific. Deakin wrote to Richard Jebb that the fleet was welcomed 'not so much because of our blood affection for the Americans though that is sincere but because of our distrust of the yellow races in the Pacific and our recognition of the "entente cordiale" spreading amongst all white races who realise the Yellow Peril to Caucasian civilisation creeds and politics.'[12]

The fault line in Australia's relations with Great Britain did not fracture till World War Two, when John Curtin confronted Churchill over the diversion of the 7th AIF Division to Burma and demanded it be sent home to defend Australia against the Japanese. Churchill's imperviousness to Australia's defence needs was already apparent in 1908. The young undersecretary for the colonies advised that the visit of the fleet to Australia 'ought certainly to be discouraged' and he was dismissive of what he saw as Australia's naval pretensions: 'they will never provide any ships of any serious value…But a few ineffective vessels under an Australian flag may easily cause a nasty diplomatic situation.'[13]

•

The Great White Fleet steamed into a sparkling Port Jackson on Thursday, 20 August 1908, watched by hundreds of thousands of spectators, most of whom had never before seen a battleship. Messages of welcome were couriered to the fleet's commanding officer, Admiral Sperry. Deakin evoked Sir Henry Parkes' 'crimson thread of kinship' as he welcomed the sailors of the great republic as 'native to our race and to our ancestors…invisible ties drawing us together as states united in affection, in our heritage of freedom, and in our ideals'.[14]

The fleet was welcomed like royalty, with decorated streets, illuminations, ceremonial arches, processions, military reviews, fireworks, receptions and dinners. Sydney enjoyed a two-day public holiday, as did many country towns, so that people could journey to the city for the festivities. Every evening, the ships were 'starred from stem to stern, up masts, and around their funnels with hundreds of electric lights'.[15]

A week later the fleet visited Melbourne, where the Deakin family watched its arrival from the paddle steamer *Hygeia*. As the fleet entered the heads, Catherine wrote in her diary, 'the sun burst forth its rays picking out each white and yellow monster from a background of smoke and cloud. A weird and grand effect.' Two days later she watched her brother, looking 'handsome and modest and dignified as usual', make a presentation to the admiral; tears of pride and sympathy welled as she thought 'how proud our dear Mother and Father would have been'.[16]

Deakin was well satisfied with the visit. Although it was popularly associated with recent racial disputes and with ties of kinship, he wrote in the *Morning Post*, for the prime minister the key issue was to get public support for his defence scheme. The Australian correspondent felt that the mere appearance of the men-of-war in Australian waters would serve the prime minister's cause by provoking 'a closer consideration of the many problems of national defence'.[17]

Deakin hoped the American visit might encourage Britain to take Australia's security more seriously, and suggested to the Colonial Office that the British fleet might also visit Australia. But an angry Colonial Office did not want to appear to be competing with America for Australia's support, and anyway it did not have the capacity to match the United States' display of naval power. When Deakin followed this suggestion with an invitation in 1909 to President Roosevelt to visit Australia after his retirement, British officials concluded that Deakin was playing Britain off against the United States in order to undermine Britain's alliance with Japan. According to the historian of Australia's search for security in the Pacific, Neville Meaney, this was a frequent British misunderstanding of Deakin's intentions. He never wanted the British to renounce the alliance with Japan, only to recognise that it was insufficient to protect imperial interests in the Pacific.[18]

Immediately after the farewell banquet Deakin and Pattie headed for Point Lonsdale. Pattie had not gone with him to Sydney, and she was feeling neglected while he attended the many formal celebrations. They were building a spacious new holiday house in the fashionable federation-bungalow style, with dormer windows and a wide verandah, and whenever they could during the year had spent the weekend at Point Lonsdale inspecting the progress and laying out the garden. The stucco and half-timbered house is still in the family, with some rooms little altered since Alfred and Pattie's time, though the view to the sea is now obscured. Herbert and Ivy had bought adjoining land early in 1907, and later built a very similar house, which they called Arilpa, an Aboriginal word meaning moon.[19] Despite Alfred's vigorous clearing of scrub and grass trees, the combined properties are now one of the few blocks of remnant vegetation on the Bellarine Peninsula.

Before the distraction of the visit of the Great White Fleet, Deakin had suffered 'a period of depression, weakness & perhaps consequent discontent & faithlessness, a jaundiced view of the pains and failures of history...physically out of key with loss of self-command'. He now faced the new parliamentary session, which opened on 16 September, with some trepidation, 'asking neither to remain nor be released'.[20] It was clear that he would not have Labor's support for much longer.

In late May the Tariff Act had finally passed all stages, removing Labor's reason for staying its hand, but a few weeks later the High Court ruled that the Commonwealth could not use its taxation power to regulate wages and conditions. At its interstate conference in July, an indignant federal Labor Party added to its platform 'Amendment of the Constitution to ensure effective Federal legislation for New Protection and Arbitration'. It also moved a motion opposing alliances and electoral immunity. No matter what parliamentarians like Watson felt, they were now bound by the external party. The Victorian Political Labor Council was the most adamant that the 'good-as-Labor men' should be opposed.[21] In the final weeks of the last session the Invalid and Old Age Pension Act was finally passed, removing another reason for Labor to continue to support Deakin.

Through the rest of September and October a demoralised House went through the motions as they waited for the inevitable. Most mornings Deakin had his early breakfast with his grandson, Wilfred, starting the day in the company of a sturdy, uncomplicated two-year-old before he faced the grind of parliamentary business. A no-confidence motion moved by Reid failed to dislodge Labor's support but, from discussions with Fisher, Deakin knew the end was near. He and Pattie got the keys to the new Ballara on Saturday, 31 October, and the following Tuesday they went to the Melbourne Cup.

On Wednesday, 4 November the Labor caucus supported a motion to withdraw its support and the next day Fisher warned Deakin what to expect. On Friday, Fisher addressed the House, telling members what he had already told the prime minister: that the Labor Party could no longer support the government. This withdrawal of support was not happening in a situation of crisis but was following 'a course of decency and order', said Fisher. But he moved no motion; for now, he said, he proposed to take no further steps.[22] Cabinet met on the morning of Saturday, 7 November to consider the situation, and after this last meeting of his ministry Deakin went to Ballara to spend a restless first night with Pattie in the new house.[23]

Deakin's second government fell without rancour and recrimination, in a graceful departure which he orchestrated. His ministerial statement to the House when it met the following Tuesday afternoon shows Deakin thinking through his political position in ways quite different from today's partisan parliamentary politics. He pointed out that the Labor government would still depend on the consent of the Liberals, who would support Labor 'while their conduct does not conflict with the principles on which we were returned or the interests of the Commonwealth…we have consistently put our policy in first place. It is for that policy we have politically lived.'

Deakin did not see this policy as belonging to the Liberal Party but to the nation. 'It will remain after us, widening in its popularity…the policy has made us and not we the policy…we remain the party of the centre…which allows the unfoldment of a democratic community.' For Deakin the centre was the place where politics connected with Australian experience and with the nation's needs—for defence, for development, for workable institutions of governance, for civilised wages and working conditions.

To make it easy for everyone, Deakin moved a trivial motion, 'That the House at its rising adjourn until tomorrow at 3 o'clock,' and he invited alteration, no matter how slight, to dispatch his government. Fisher moved that all the words after 'that' be left out, and the house divided thirteen votes to forty-nine.[24] The next day Deakin visited the new governor-general, Lord Dudley, and resigned. Dudley sent for Fisher and a week later Labor was back on the Treasury benches for a second turn at minority government. Deakin was less gracious in the *Morning Post* than he was in the House: 'Mr Fisher will be Prime Minister as long as Mr Deakin thinks fit to leave him there.'[25]

A week after Deakin's second government fell George Reid resigned as leader of the Opposition. The fight over trade policy which had shaped parliamentary alignments since federation was over and protection was safe, freeing Deakin to focus on his differences with Labor. Reid believed that a fusion of non-labour groupings was inevitable but he also knew that he was an insurmountable obstacle to Deakin. So he removed his bulky self from the picture and Joseph Cook was elected leader.[26] The term 'fusion' was already in use in American politics to refer to previously separate parties agreeing to put up only one candidate for election to improve the chance of defeating a common enemy. Although the Australian situation was focussed on parliamentary co-operation, the term was borrowed to describe the impending combined anti-labour party.

Deakin's Liberals supported Labor till parliament rose for Christmas in the middle of December, but had Fisher known the identity of the Australian correspondent in the *Morning Post*, he would have found ominous signs for the new year.

> The roads must soon divide…Mr Deakin framing the policy and Mr Fisher finding the votes which give it a majority is not the same as Mr Fisher finding the policy and Mr Deakin holding the balance of power as between him and the Opposition. While the Labour Party, or most of it, agrees with nearly all Mr Deakin's policy, neither he nor his followers will or can accept the lengths to which the Labour platform goes.[27]

Deakin was clear: Labor might hold office, but it did not have the power to implement any part of its programme which he did not support. He had much thinking to do over the summer and headed to Ballara as soon as he could, into a family storm that had been brewing for years.

32

FUSION

STELLA, NOW TWENTY-TWO, was going overseas to study, taking her Aunt Catherine as a chaperone; and Pattie was not at all happy about it. Stella, who did not share her sisters' musical interests, had studied science at Melbourne University. One of only two girls studying senior chemistry, she was ambitious and strong-willed, heading to Berlin to further her studies and to be closer to her future husband, the brilliant young chemist David Rivett, who was a Rhodes Scholar at Oxford. They had met in the chemistry lab and already had 'an understanding'. Stella had started planning the trip in June 1908, a week after her grandmother died.[1] Travelling to Europe alone was out of the question, but now her aunt was free to accompany her. Catherine would let Adams Street while she was abroad, and aunt and niece were to depart early in February 1909.

Plans were well-advanced before Pattie learned of them, humiliatingly from one of Stella's school friends who, of course, thought Pattie knew. Here was another instance of Catherine usurping her as the

mother. Pattie believed, too, that Catherine had persuaded Stella to the
idea of going abroad, but it is more likely that Stella persuaded her aunt
to accompany her.[2] It may in fact have been Stella who kept it from
Pattie until it was too late, in case she prevented her going. Deakin's
usual prayer of thanksgiving at the end of the year included one dark
note: 'the coming loss of Stella throws its shadow on our future. She
must have her life.'[3]

When Catherine and Stella arrived at Ballara to join the family
for Christmas, there was a terrible scene. Deakin's diary for the next
few days shows him trying to maintain his seaside routine: reading,
gardening, writing letters, having guests for lunch. Catherine's is fuller.
After a 'wretched, painful Christmas Day of silence and sorrow', on
Boxing Day she tried to talk with Pattie and was met with hostility and
bitter accusations about relations with her nieces. 'She never realised
we were hard at work all the time they were with me. She seemed
to think they waited on me and were prejudiced by me against her.'
All her years of devotion serving her dear brother by stimulating the
girls in their work, and saving him expense, all her love and absolute
devotion, seemed 'nullified and in vain'.[4]

Next day, after Alfred 'appealed to P', Stella and Catherine returned
to Melbourne, leaving Deakin and Pattie to a 'night of collapse' and
broken sleep during which Deakin, thinking back to his wedding
night, wrote a small verse, the closest he ever came on paper to criticising
Pattie.

> Sprinkled with blood and wet with tears,
> Timid and tender, since love sears,
> How infantile my bride appears.[5]

For her birthday on New Year's Day, though, he wrote reassuringly
of the joys of sex.

> O call of the Wattle bird! Wooing the morn
> Jet swift, pure, appealing with throb and shy trill—
> We woo a magic more passionate still,

Dividing the dark and all veils that are drawn
Between selves—till we float in freedom up borne
Half-closed lids, witching eyes—a drift and a dream.[6]

Catherine was shocked and bewildered by Pattie's bitterness and anger, naively asking herself how there could be so little trust between two women united by love to the one man. Perhaps she had unwittingly given small causes of offence, she thought, but she also felt that she had given up a great deal for her nieces during 'years of anxious worry and overwork on their behalf' and had forgone her own opportunities for study and a wider circle of friends. This small spurt of self-assertion soon faded. Catherine did not have the emotional strength to defend herself against Pattie. Stella's plans depended on her aunt's co-operation, but they also depended on her father, who was financing the venture and it was no doubt easier for Pattie to vent her anger about Stella's independence to Catherine than to Alfred.

But Pattie's accusations went far beyond this and tore any semblance of civility from their relationship, which never recovered. In 1921, after the man they both loved had died, Pattie wrote a long statement to explain that the breach with Catherine came after 'years of long endurance, suffering and deep humiliations added to heart stabs when children were almost divided from PD'. When Pattie had gone to see Marshall-Hall about Ivy's music lessons, she remembered that he had said, 'Your sister-in-law has forestalled you. Extraordinary person she is. She acts as if she owns the family.'[7]

Deakin was badly shaken by the conflict. When Joseph Cook and his family visited Ballara on 21 January, he was still so 'greatly preoccupied with family affairs' that he was unable to give their discussions about a possible alliance his undivided attention.[8] This is an unusual admission for Deakin, who was adept at remaining detached from the conflicts and negative emotions swirling around him. Pattie would not be mollified. As Stella's embarkation approached, she became 'overwrought' and, instead of joining the rest of the family in Port Melbourne for the farewell rituals on the boat, she visited her close friend Frances Derham.[9]

Deakin brought with him to the ship a heartfelt letter of farewell to his 'Ever dearest sister':

> Where ties of blood & inheritance & sympathy have been tested for fifty years by all kinds of trials there is little that can be said… Despite the differences of sex and the great differences in experience & vocation which this implies our separate spheres have always remained intermingled. We are whatever we are largely owing to each other. My own memories of you go back to the cradle and forward to the grave, tenderness, gratitude and affection being here interwoven with our home our first school and all our period of growth.[10]

Back at Llanarth he watched the boat steaming down Port Phillip Bay from the verandah and a few evenings later on a tram in Bourke Street he thought he saw his sister 'going home to Adams Street…my heart & breath stopped, fluttering still, as I went to my seat remembering that the real you was probably rounding the Leeuwin at the time.'

The renting of Adams Street ruptured Deakin's psychological geography. Catherine's loving gaze had been there all his life. He was her first pupil, and when he was sent away to school at four she was there, her presence in his childhood more continuous than that of their parents. She watched his first performances, listened admiringly to his early literary efforts and shared his intellectual enthusiasms. Later, she witnessed his parliamentary milestones from the gallery, and he would discuss his public life with her. In 1899 he had written to her that 'the least incapacity to see you at will awakens a sense of what I have missed. To have you always at my elbow—at all events within call—has been so lifelong an experience.'[11] Now she was gone: 'Adams Street has ceased to exist for me and there is such a narrowing of my life & feeling that I am not able to realise myself or close the break your going has made.'[12] Catherine's presence had helped him steady his sense of who he was as he confronted the succeeding crises of his political life. He was now facing another, and with a secret fear he shared with no one except his wife.

Deakin and Pattie's marriage had entered a new phase as she became active in public life. Compared with the 1890s, when 'P' barely appears except for notes about her poor health and the very occasional stroll, since their return from London she had become a frequent presence in his daily diaries: her meetings, their social engagements, their activities at Ballara, how well she slept. And his poems to 'the girl with soft brown hair and large brown eyes' he had wedded over half a lifetime ago had become more ecstatic. Their marriage was more companionable than it had ever been, and for his fifty-fourth birthday she wrote a poem for him.[13]

Deakin's final diary entry for 1908 noted his 'failing memory and first sense of age'. Deakin had been farewelling the energies of youth since his thirties, but now, at the age of fifty-three, this was more serious. Loss of memory was arriving insidiously, threatening his capacity to read.

> I find myself unable to synthesize, summarise or even criticise serious books just read—a deadly blow had been dealt at my first and last love—stimulating, elevating, informatory books...to cease to live intellectually as I have lived ever since boyhood—this is an end indeed—much more than a milestone—it is a notice to quit. Unless my memory recovers half my pleasures will have disappeared. But even so that decree must be accepted.

He was forgetting books he had just read, but also the books he had read while his mind was 'keen and retentive—all is obscured—I am down to the dead level of the mass—perhaps below it'.[14] It is hard to judge just how severe Deakin's memory loss was when he wrote this in January 1909. His memory in his prime had been extraordinarily retentive, perhaps photographic, and its falling away at first may simply have brought him closer to more usual experience. But this was the beginning of a terrible decline.

At Ballara over the weekend of 6 and 7 February 1909, Deakin once again thought through his political options, rambling over his familiar territory of the transience and uncertainty of political achievement, whether any particular man is essential to the course of historical events,

before coming to 'the facts of my own case'. He knew he had the opportunity to become prime minister for a third time with a strong party
and the likelihood of doing a great deal of permanently good work for
the country. He expected to win the next election, in 1910, and looked
forward to completing his political tasks. Commonwealth–state financial
arrangements could be put on a new footing; his defence plans could
be bedded down; and he would attend the 1911 Imperial Conference.
Personally he would infinitely prefer not to take office and instead to
advise from the backbench, without the strain on his health and with
more time for domestic life, reading and literary work. In a final note,
he added that none of the crises of the past three and a half years had
unsettled 'the serenity at the core of my heart…fostered by my reading
of the world's scriptures and mystics [this] has now become the kernel
of my inner life—I am in truth at the present moment while most
deeply concerned with and concentrated upon my policy and party
really indifferent to what happens to myself.'[15]

On 12 February 1909 Deakin wrote to Cook that, as the majority
of Liberal Protectionist parliamentarians supported a coalition with
the Anti-Socialist Party, he would now consult his party's supporters
outside parliament.[16] He was warming to Cook, telling Bavin that 'he
is not as black as he has been painted', but he did have 'a real horror of
some of those behind him'. Labor as an ally was hopeless, but

> I am keeping the road open as long as I can…Talking to Cook is
> the only way to prove to them that they have to make their choice…
> My duty to the party is to preserve it alive and if that can only be
> done by a coalition with JC that must follow—but not until the
> other alternatives have been exhausted.[17]

As two opposing parties were rapidly shaping up around him, Deakin
was still standing staunchly in the centre. On speaking tours in Tasmania
and New South Wales, he identified his party's policy achievements as
the 'organic Australian policy': the hundred acts passed since federation,
he said, did not belong to any one party because since 1901 none had a
majority. Passing them always required the co-operation of two.[18]

Once Deakin became persuaded that a fusion of his Liberal Protectionists, Forrest's Anti-Socialist Protectionists and Reid's Anti-Socialist Free Traders was inevitable, he needed a reason to move against Labor. The dreadnought scare, which hit in late March 1909, gave it to him. HMS *Dreadnought*, first launched by the Royal Navy in 1906, was a faster, larger battleship that created a naval arms race between Britain and Germany. The British Admiralty, fearing that Germany was threatening Britain's naval supremacy, had asked parliament to fund up to eight of these expensive monsters of the high seas. Although Britain made no request of its dominions, New Zealand immediately offered to pay for one, and a public campaign sprang up in Australia to follow suit. Andrew Fisher refused to join the panic. In a major speech in Gympie on the last day of March he outlined an ambitious programme for Australia's naval and military defence which built on Deakin's proposals, but went further and faster. He would not, however, commit the government to a dreadnought. After the speech, Deakin cryptically noted, 'Situation more complex than ever.'[19]

As prime minister, Fisher was putting into effect Deakin's dream of an Australian navy, and should have been able to rely on his support. Yet a furious campaign of imperial loyalty was underway. The press, non-Labor politicians and huge public meetings were demanding that Australia offer the Royal Navy a dreadnought. Subscription lists were opened and both the New South Wales and Victorian governments declared that, if the Commonwealth government would not provide Britain with a dreadnought, they would.[20]

Deakin was slow to join the call, but after Fisher's Gympie speech he came out in favour. In a confused and unconvincing speech in Sydney on 7 April, he endorsed Fisher's defence plans; he could scarcely do otherwise, as they were mostly his. But he also argued for a dreadnought: 'The Commonwealth must do its share to prove the unity of Empire.' He asked how Fisher planned to pay for his new Australian navy, and then dismissed the same question for the dreadnought: 'The foreign occupation of Australia…would cost more money than the dreadnought, after we had lost our territory.'[21] The same could be said for the harbour and coastal defences Deakin had proposed and Fisher was committing to.

Deakin's support for the dreadnought was hasty and opportunistic. The British government had not asked for it, and there was no
imminent threat, but it gave Deakin a point of difference from Fisher
with which he felt comfortable. He later wrote to the British journalist
Leo Amery that Fisher's refusal to offer a dreadnought had sealed his
government's doom.[22]

Deakin believed that Fisher was playing for time and intended to
ask for a dissolution of parliament in order to go to the country 'with
the prestige of office'. He also knew that, whenever the election came,
Labor would 'assail all my supporters'.[23] Electoral realities were making
Fusion inevitable, but he needed indignation as well as political logic
to overcome his aversion to joining the conservative obstructionists.
Further complicating his calculations was the antipathy of the *Age* to
any protectionist alliance with the free-trade enemy. David Syme's
fourth son, Geoffrey, was now the proprietor. Deakin found him
ignorant and inexperienced, but he also knew that the *Age* could
shipwreck the coalition venture and set his little party and its sympa-
thisers adrift.

It is not entirely clear when exactly Deakin realised that a permanent
alliance of the non-labour parties was unavoidable; probably sometime
during April 1909, though it was a reluctant recognition and he did not
want to lead the new party. Labor's refusal of electoral immunity to the
good-as-Labor men made it impossible for Deakin's own little band of
Liberals to survive as a separate party.

Deakin decided, he wrote to Catherine, to try the 1904 experiment of
making a coalition from the outside, and then retiring to the backbench
while someone else led. But the experiment failed, as none of Lyne,
Cook or Forrest would countenance serving under either of the others,
so again there was really no one else. The other two non-labour parties
were in straits almost as severe as his own. 'Weak as I was I could have
wrecked both the others easily and on this Labor was relying.' So,
while seeking to withdraw, 'I have become more than ever the pivot of
the whole political situation, the prize fought for and now the unques-
tioned leader of friends and foe.'[24]

Deakin hung on to belief in his agency, even as it was being crushed by the pincer of class politics, telling the readers of the *Morning Post*:

> For reasons known only to himself, which are a *perpetual subject of controversy* in our Press, Mr Deakin pursues his *enigmatic methods* of action...It has become known here that [his friends and supporters] are anxiously pressing him to come to terms with Mr Joseph Cook...To this prompt settlement, *on grounds which can only be guessed* even by his intimates, he remains determinedly opposed...But in spite of Mr Deakin's *persistent elusiveness* the pressure brought to bear upon him...appears so strong that some *unexpected development* must be near at hand.[25]

The italics here are mine, to highlight the way Deakin makes his own mysterious actions and intentions the centre of the story. He would lead, but only if all his policies were accepted. As he had told his English readers in December, 'his first stipulation was that the "national policy" with which he was always identified should be adopted by the new party'.[26]

On 18 May 1909 Deakin wrote to Cook through an intermediary to set out his terms: anomalies in the Tariff Act dealt with in a protectionist manner; workers to get their share of the benefits of protection, and an amendment of the constitution to allow federal regulation of wages; his acceptance of proposals of universal military training and naval coastal defence; priority to be given to the needs of the Commonwealth in the distribution of Commonwealth revenue; and the Commonwealth to take over state debts.[27] It was only eight days till parliament met. Did Deakin expect his ultimatum to be accepted? He told Bavin that it was his personal hope that Cook would refuse and leave him free of the intolerable burden of carrying him and his followers. But then, he later wrote to Amery, 'the apparently impossible happened—Never was a man more taken by surprise than I was—But as my original terms were then accepted, there was no more to be said.' He'd been cornered. With their goal of a united anti-socialist party so close, Reid and Cook were not going to quibble about the details.[28]

In the few days before parliament was to open on the afternoon of Wednesday, 26 May events moved very fast indeed. On Monday, Deakin met with Cook and Forrest and made good progress; on Tuesday, the three met again in the morning and agreed on policies to take to their party rooms later in the day for endorsement. When the Liberals met at 3.30, Deakin tried to defuse the tension with a quip, but William Lyne's anger was soon booming down the corridors. He had fought hard for protection in the hostile political environment of New South Wales and was being asked to embrace the political enemies of a lifetime. The Labor caucus also met on Tuesday afternoon, in gloomy expectation of the end of its second period of government.[29]

That night at a packed Melbourne Town Hall, Deakin launched the Commonwealth Liberal Party, which was designed to give Deakin's Liberals their own organisational base. Standing in front of a map of Australia, he asked his fellow citizens to imagine 'the vastness of the 3,000,000 square miles of territory which is your possession—and for whose present and future you and you alone are responsible'. They must overcome the remnants of old state jealousies and sectional antagonisms, he told them, and think and vote only as citizens of Australia. There was nothing new in this appeal, nor in the broad 'national programme of practical legislation' he outlined. What was new was Deakin's assault on Labor's organisation.

Since his speech at Ballarat in August 1904, Deakin had not attacked his ally's machine. But Labor was no longer his ally and he needed a clear differentiation from Labor's very similar policies, as well as justification for the step he was about to take. The Labor Party, he said, 'has political methods which carry obligations and restrictions to extremes'; small committees make binding decisions 'outside the light of day'; freedom of speech is suppressed more severely than in Turkey or Russia; caucus members 'are compelled to vote against their judgement and consciences'; and from their 'misguided sense of loyalty tens of thousands of voters put themselves in the clutches of a machine'. Let Labor 'never subject either a voter or his representative to the indignity of putting aside the only thing which makes him a man—his judgement and his conscience'. The Commonwealth Liberal Party, by contrast, was not a party of 'mere duplicates', but 'a free union of free members'.[30]

When Deakin's Liberal Protectionists met again the next morning, Lyne continued his dramatic denunciations: 'The Party is being thrown into a boiling cauldron. We are being asked to join men who will hoodwink us in the carrying out of our programme. If the Party does this contemplated thing we will go down, down, down as conservatives.' Shouting, 'It is impossible for me to be friends with "the Chief" any longer for I cannot shake hands with a traitor,' he stormed out.

The dominant mood in the party room, though, was not anger but sadness and resignation. Concluding the meeting, Deakin said he was recommending the union of parties 'only as a last resort...I may be wrong but I can see no other alternative!...If you think as I do that there is no other way, please indicate your position by holding up your right hands.'[31] The result, eleven to three, marked the end of the Liberal Protectionists as a separate parliamentary party. Of the three who failed to raise their hands, only one, John Chanter, joined the Labor Party. Billy Trenwith, the only trade unionist in Deakin's little band, accepted the majority decision and lost his seat to Labor at the next election. The third, George Wise, who held the rural seat of Gippsland, was not threatened by Labor and so had the luxury of maintaining his opposition to the conservatives as an independent liberal.[32]

Later on Wednesday, when the three uniting parties met—Deakin's Liberals, Forrest's Anti-Socialist Protectionists and Reid's Anti-Socialist Free Traders—it was Reid who moved the motion to formalise their union. 'Nothing in my political career has given me greater pleasure,' he said. 'There are now but two parties in the Commonwealth: the Labour Party, or more correctly speaking the Socialistic Caucus Party, and the Party who are opposed to the improper interference with personal liberty and freedom of conscience.'[33] This was Australia's new political landscape: not progressive liberal and obstructionist conservative, but Labor and anti-Labor. Deakin was determined to continue to pursue progressive politics inside the new configuration, but it would be harder than ever to discern the progress of the Ideal in his political work.

•

Deakin was elected leader of the Fusion party, as the new parliamentary grouping called itself. He then advised Fisher of the Liberals' decision to withdraw their support from his ministry, in wording identical to Fisher's to him the previous November, ending with, 'May I add for its members, and especially for myself, that our relations with the Ministry have always been of the most friendly character.'[34]

The next two days in parliament were pandemonium. The galleries were packed when a relaxed Deakin strolled into the chamber and to the Opposition benches, all eyes upon him. The newly united Opposition applauded as he rose to address the House, but he got no further than 'Mr Speaker' before Lyne roared 'Judas!' As the Speaker tried to maintain order amid the hissing and cheering and Lyne's repeated interjections, Deakin argued that the governor-general's speech had been more of an electoral address than a practical outline of the business of the session, but he sat down without moving a motion.[35]

Fisher was angry and wanted to know the charges against his government that warranted it being put out. Deakin responded that he was only repeating what had been done to him last November. It was an acrimonious exchange and the debate continued in that vein for some time, until halted by the Member for Wentworth, Willie Kelly, who moved an adjournment, which Fisher took as a no-confidence motion and duly lost.

Kelly may have been acting on his own initiative, as by convention a no-confidence motion is moved by the leader of the Opposition. When Fisher asked Deakin directly at the end of the night's debate if Mr Kelly had acted with his knowledge, he answered 'Certainly', but if so it was an uncharacteristically provocative move. Willie Kelly was a fashionable young man who oozed class privilege and spoke with an Eton drawl. To allow such a man to dismiss the dignified, work-hardened Labor prime minister would have been a calculated and humiliating class insult, which was not Deakin's style. But, whatever Deakin's knowledge, Labor members took it as an insult and it fuelled their anger at his actions.[36]

The most telling blows were landed by Labor's attorney-general, Billy Hughes. All Deakin's achievements had depended on the support

of Labor, he said, yet he now sat with men whom he had unsparingly
denounced.

> There is not a vested interest in this country now that does not
> acclaim him as their champion. He stands to-day under the banner
> of the Employers' Federation, under the banner of every vested
> interest, of every powerful monopoly. What a career his has been!
> In his hands, at various times, have rested the banners of every
> party in this country. He has proclaimed them all, he has held
> them all, he has betrayed them all.[37]

On Friday, 29 May the attacks on Deakin continued. Again when
he rose to speak Lyne shouted 'Judas!' and Hughes took up the theme
of Christ's betrayer:

> It was then that I heard from this side of the House some mention
> of Judas. I do not agree with that; it is not fair—to Judas, for
> whom there is this to be said, that he did not gag the man whom
> he betrayed, nor did he fail to hang himself afterwards.[38]

As he denounced Deakin, Hughes engaged in extravagant theatrics,
'cupping his hands to his ears and listening in anxious expectancy to
a far off sound..."I am waiting to hear the cock crow," he said.' The
incident was omitted from Hansard.[39]

Hughes's main line of attack on Deakin was for an inconstancy
which he never admitted to, as he 'has an excuse and an explanation
for everything':

> For his is a programme that changes to fit the bewildering circum-
> stances of political warfare. It is the programme of those who from
> time to time are whirled in violent gyration around the honourable
> member. He still remains the same. Parties change. Circumstances
> change. He alone remains constant and unshaken. But yesterday
> he was here. To-day he is there. But the day before he offered to
> stand equal in all things with us...

There is surely some moral obliquity about a nature such as his. No act that he commits, no party that he betrays, no cause that he abandons, affects him at all. He regards himself as the selected and favoured agent of Providence. Everything that he does he does for the very best. He does it because there is nothing else that can be done to conserve the welfare of the people and the interests of the nation. To realize this noble ideal he has assassinated Governments, abandoned friends to the wolves, deserted principles, and deceived the people.[40]

Hughes claimed that this 'political mercenary of Australia' had been prepared to serve in a Labor coalition, turning Deakin's enigmatic passivity into the cunning, self-justifying steering by the chances for power that would mark his own future political career.

33

PRIME MINISTER III

OVER THE WEEKEND Billy Hughes prepared a long case for a dissolution of the parliament for Fisher to present to the governor-general, Lord Dudley; but, as Deakin could assure him that he had the confidence of the House, Dudley decided to let the session run its course till the election due in early 1910. On 1 June 1909 Deakin was sworn in as prime minister for the third and last time, and the next day he finalised his cabinet. It was a complex business to balance the three groupings' strengths and take account of personal antipathies as well as fitness for task, and there were many disappointed men.[1] From Barton's cabinet of kings only Forrest and Deakin were left, and five of the ten were new to the ministry.[2] This was the seventh federal ministry in eight years.

His private secretary, Malcolm Shepherd, watched as Deakin changed from the genial man he was out of office to one who kept all at arms-length.[3] When parliament reconvened, Fisher moved a no-confidence motion. He was angry, driven by a sullen wrath at what he saw as Deakin's betrayal, and determined to defend his government's record. For the next three weeks debate on the motion prevented any progress on the new government's legislation. One Labor windbag spoke for ten hours and the attacks on Deakin were personal. Hughes even raised the spectre of his 'ancient séances',[4] and Lyne continued to make bitter, irrational accusations.

Those who think there has been a deplorable deterioration of parliamentary behaviour since some more courteous past should read the record of the debate in the early hours of Friday, 23 July 1909, the climax of weeks of disgraceful disorder and unrestrained invective. Weary members had been sitting since 3.00 p.m. Thursday. The ostensible object of debate, the Old Age Pension Bill, which in fact Labor supported, had disappeared from view. Instead, members argued about whether a sacred line had been crossed when Lyne refused to withdraw his comment that the ex-convict father of a Queensland Liberal, Littleton Groom, would be turning in his grave to find his son sitting with the conservatives. The pointless rancour finally halted when the Speaker, Frederick Holder, collapsed on the floor of the House crying, 'Dreadful! Dreadful!' Deakin told chastened members that his condition was grave, and he died some hours later.[5]

In the Labor press Deakin was the arch-villain of Fusion, a snob, a toff, a Tory in disguise, whose professed independence and Liberal principles were now exposed as sham by his alliance with all the enemies of the working man who peopled Labor's populist imagination: land sharks, sweaters, monopolists, coal barons, sugar kings, greedy middlemen, the idle rich, the squatters, the money lords, the Associated Banks, the Federation of Employers and so on. These were now the potbellied friends of top-hatted Deakin in Labor cartoons.

Monster rallies were held to denounce the Fusion government, and fifty thousand copies of Hughes's Judas speech were distributed. Led by the rising Labor star Frank Anstey, the vitriol flowed most freely in Victoria, where Fusion finally broke the alliance between the Liberal Protectionists and working men that went back decades, to Graham Berry and beyond. Though its refusal of electoral immunity made Fusion all but inevitable, Labor turned on Deakin with elemental rage, as if he had breached a natural order.[6]

In parliament Deakin calmly batted away the insults and the accusations. He had, he said, played all his political cards on the public table and been constant in his policy commitments. 'In a whirling, changing world, honourable members will find me the one stable, consistent person, with a steady view of my own policy, and a frank criticism of theirs.'[7] But little else was stable. He had the numbers but nothing more: 'no unity, no warmth, no faith and little good will'. Some on his own side openly enjoyed Labor's attacks on him.

The one string to his bow was that cabinet gave him control of the tactics in the House. He requested all ministers without exception to submit their answers to questions to him for approval and that they be constant in their attendance at parliament. Thus he prevented his ministers responding to Labor in kind, as 'Cook and Forrest were all for aggressive and violent measures…to silence the Opposition and crush them by our majority'. Instead, Deakin adopted what he described as 'Fabian tactics', after the Roman Commander Fabius Maximus, who avoided pitch battles against the invading armies of Hannibal in favour of a war of attrition. 'By studied moderation of tone, refusal to resent insult and by the strict suppression of my own speech and that of my friends so far as I could influence them,' he let the storm beat upon them 'until it died of inanition while we meekly and patiently waited until their wrath melted away'. He also used the delay to get his disparate team in hand and to build policy consensus.[8] 'Labor's blundering tactics,' he told Catherine, 'are in fact helping the new party hold together.'[9]

The strain took its toll on his body. He was nervy and restless, with bouts of upset stomach and insomnia, and he lost weight. 'No one,' he told Bavin, 'knows what it cost me to take the course I believed to be right…The wrench was a most trying situation on the nerves as well as the conscience.' In July 1909 he had one of his 'occasional internal collapses'.[10] Whenever possible he escaped to Ballara for the weekend to recuperate with physical exercise, sea bathing and sleep; and sometimes Dr Crivelli brought doses of nerve tonic into the office. By October, though, he could report to Catherine that his weight had recovered.[11]

During August he was preoccupied with negotiating a new financial agreement with the states. The 'Braddon clause', which obliged the Commonwealth to return three-quarters of its customs revenue to the states, was due to expire the following year. Described by Deakin as 'the leg rope on the Commonwealth Constitution', it severely limited the money available to the Commonwealth for its own responsibilities. Two were now pressing: defence and old-age pensions. But the states needed money too, for development and for education, and their expenditure was far greater than the Commonwealth's. Deakin, Cook and Forrest as treasurer met with the premiers for a week of closed discussions in which they argued about the amount to be set in a new system of per capita annual payments. They eventually settled on twenty-five shillings per person, with a special additional payment to Western Australia and a proposal for the Commonwealth to take over the states' debts.[12]

The week of the premiers' conference, he told Catherine, was one of the most important and arduous of his political life, but he was content with the outcome. He would need his steel armour, though, when he ventured into the House.[13] Labor supported the per-capita payment, but the premiers wanted the amount to be fixed in an amendment to the constitution. Even though inflation was low, this seems an extraordinary idea, but Deakin himself had argued for something similar at the Federation Convention in Sydney and he supported the premiers' demand. Without the constitutional guarantee, he told the parliament, the federal parliament could revoke or alter the agreement at any time.[14]

In 1902, anonymously in the *Morning Post*, Deakin had criticised the silence of the constitution on financial relations, which had left the states 'legally free, but financially bound to the chariot wheels of the central government'.[15] Now he hoped that the omission could be rectified, the autonomy of the states protected and the federation saved from unseemly periodic wrangling.

Labor supported a system of per-capita payments, but was completely opposed to the amount being set in the concrete of the constitution, as were many Fusion members. The *Age* was outraged. It had given Fusion only lukewarm support; now it declared war on the government. The agreement sacrificed the prestige of the Commonwealth, it argued. Worse, it made the Commonwealth dependent on high

levels of imports for revenue to meet the constitutionally guaranteed
payments, whereas the aim of protection was to build import-replacing
industries. Deakin's breach with the *Age* now seemed irreparable, with
unsettling consequences for the upcoming election. Deakin barely got
the bill for the referendum through the House. It would be put to the
electorate at the next election.

By October 1909, parliament had become a little more civil, and the
government started to bowl up the bills. 'The turn of the tide had come,
and we took it at the flood.'[16] The site for the new capital was settled,
after years of political jockeying; a defence act passed which provided for
compulsory military training; an Australian coinage legislated, business
law made more uniform and a high commissioner to London finally
appointed. Pressure was on Deakin to accept the appointment; the
governor-general, Lord Dudley, was furious when he refused, and
lectured Pattie in an extraordinary manner. But it went to George Reid,
who skipped off to London to enjoy the rewards of his self-sacrifice.

There were two important items of unfinished business. The first
was a bill for the Commonwealth to take over the Northern Territory
from South Australia, which had been agreed to in 1907. Deakin urged
members to lay aside their state spectacles and focus on the national
issues at stake. The Territory needed to be developed and settled by
the white race, 'otherwise other countries will take it.'[17] If Australia
was a nation for a continent, then the nation had to inhabit the whole
continent, not just the coastal fringe. He made no mention at all of
the indigenous people already living there. The bill was passed the
following year by the Fisher government.[18]

The second piece of unfinished business was to give legislative
form to the New Protection. The High Court had ruled against the
Commonwealth using its power over excise to regulate industrial
conditions. Deakin proposed instead an Interstate Commission to
oversee national wages and conditions and make adjustments if a
state's 'unfair' conditions were giving its producers an advantage in
the national market. It was a clumsy mechanism, and probably not
workable, but it was never to see the light of day.

Deakin invited the premiers to pass parallel legislation to establish their own wages boards, which was an easier option than a referendum, but he got no agreement. Both Labor and the conservative members of Fusion were stubbornly opposed. A referendum remained the Fusion government's policy, but it no longer spoke of a living wage, and Labor plausibly claimed that Deakin's commitment to the working man had been weakened by his new bedfellows.[19]

At the end of the session Deakin wrote to Catherine, who was shivering in Berlin with Stella, that he looked back 'with philosophic content...on the rounding off of my federal service by the achievements of this year. There is a rough completeness about it which is as much as we can hope for in practical life.'[20] It was, he said, 'the finest harvest of any session' yet. 'But the tactics were mine own from first to last. The financial agreement was mine. The Northern Territory mine, the Defence was made a success by my amendment in the office draft.'[21] The note was 'too egotistical' he thought. Perhaps it was, but he had always believed he was central to events in his political life. By the end of 1909 his sense of indispensable agency had become a lonely burden.

The election was to be held on 13 April 1910, and Deakin fully expected 'a sweeping victory'. He would continue as prime minister, tick off the remaining items on his legislative agenda, attend the Imperial Confer- ence in 1911 and then retire to give a new chief time to settle in before the next election, in 1913.[22] It would be the first election in which voters had a choice of only two parties and whichever won would form the government. No longer would ministries be put together by the leader from loose coalitions and independents. Party had won. Two referendum questions would also be voted on: one on the Commonwealth's per-capita payments to the states, and the other authorising the Commonwealth to take over the states' debts.

On 7 February eight thousand people heard the prime minister's policy speech at Ballarat's new Coliseum Picture Palace. The organising narrative was the accomplishments since federation, the growth of national feeling, the legislative achievements and the work still to be done. He attacked Labor for its 'narrow, mechanical uniformity enforced by the constant knee drill in caucus', in contrast to the Liberals' union of free men. In his concluding plea for national unity he revealed his idealised and fanciful notion of the federation as a harmonious and co-operative dovetailing of duties. 'Why should there be animosity between yourself when doing your State business, and you yourself when doing Commonwealth business? The same citizenship underlies both…the same blood runs in the veins of both.'[23]

Ivy came with him to Ballarat and stayed on for a week to canvass. She and Herbert worked hard during the campaign. Herbert was Deakin's right-hand man in the Commonwealth Liberal Party, raising money and making platform speeches. Ivy organised a women's section to counterbalance the more conservative Australian Women's National League. 'Ivy is now a political woman,' he wrote to Catherine, 'engaged almost every day at the CLP office.' With her new confidence in public duties, Pattie too was electioneering. 'You would hardly believe the change in her habits and interests.'[24] Having his family active with him in his public life was a new experience for Deakin: 'I have always been a lonely politician and man working with those whom Fate gave me… never before have I had my own kin by my side in public affairs.'[25]

For the next two months Deakin campaigned hard in Victoria, New South Wales and Queensland. Most meetings he found enthusiastic, though the cheers were fewer, and in Gympie, Fisher's home town, the hall was only half full. The routine, though, was as arduous as ever: speeches and meetings in every town, every day scores of hands to shake, every night a different bed and fitful sleep. He received two serious health warnings in February, and had gastric upsets for much of the campaign, but he pushed through to give his all to his last election campaign.[26]

Deakin was standing on his record, presenting a smooth continuity of practice and principle between his various administrations. Labor attacked his inconstancy, and the betrayal of Fusion, which aligned him with men whose policies he had previously scorned. Labor also attacked the referendum proposal to enshrine the financial agreement with the premiers in the constitution, though it supported the agreement itself. At meetings to support Liberal candidates in Melbourne's working-class suburbs of Richmond, Collingwood and Brunswick,

Deakin was faced with such a hubbub of catcalling and interjections that he could not get a hearing.[27]

The referendum proposal was widely opposed, draining support from the government advocating it. The *Age* campaigned against the government, as Deakin had expected it would. Younger members of the ANA denounced the proposal, arguing it swung the constitution the ANA had fought for too far towards states' rights. This was an ominous sign. The young politically engaged men who had once seen him as their hero were deserting him.[28]

Deakin closed his campaign on election eve where it had begun, in Ballarat at the Coliseum, and spent election day, Wednesday, 13 April, going round the booths. That night he was inside the Ballarat Post Office as the telegraph brought the bad news. The government was routed, with defeats all over Victoria, and he could hear the crowd outside cheering for the *Age*, the Labor Party and the anti-fusionists. He almost lost his own seat, to a relatively unknown miner. The referendum proposal on the financial agreement was lost, but the second, that the Commonwealth take over the states' debts, was accepted. Labor had won a smashing victory, a majority in its own right of forty-two out of seventy-five seats and a clean sweep in the Senate. Most of Deakin's Liberal Protectionists who had followed him into the Commonwealth Liberal Party had lost their seats.[29]

'So the Waterloo of the Liberal Party has come,' he wrote to Catherine, and it 'was wholly unexpected'. For tactical reasons he had always spoken of the possibility of Labor success, but he had in fact expected to achieve a working majority and certainly not this 'absolute transformation'.[30] In the aftermath, he pondered the reasons. The main one, as he saw it, was Labor's superior organisation. The leagues' 'great army of unpaid zealots' had been steadily recruiting for the past three years and on the day were able to get more of their supporters to the polling booths, a crucial advantage in the days before compulsory voting, which did not become law in federal elections until 1924.

The Liberals' greatest loss, Deakin thought, was that Labor had captured the whole of the generation with an interest in politics that came to adulthood in the past three years. If Labor had gained their adherence on its merits, this would indeed be 'a deadly augury for the opponents of the Caucus everywhere'. It would mean that the progressive spirit of young Australia had deserted the Liberal Party and it had become the party of reaction.

This was an unsettling conclusion for Deakin as he tried to discern the deep currents at play in Labor's historic victory, which tolled 'the knell of the existing system'. The universal franchise Liberals had fought for had now, with Labor's organisation, liberated the material concerns of the masses: 'Promises of tangible, visible things, better wages, shorter hours, cheaper living, steady employment and the like' were 'just and right', as the inequities of society were 'glaring, universal, scandalous', but only 'if they are associated with and subordinate to moral and spiritual considerations'. He was well aware that there were material interests on his side of politics too, but he clung to the belief that there were also 'wise, just-tempered, capable and charitable people', well informed on social and political matters, who would resist aggression and self-interest for the national interest.

With Carlyle whispering in his ear, Deakin was still a nineteenth-century idealist who wanted to believe that politics was driven by spirit and ideals, not just by material interests, and that history was moving providentially towards the harmonious transcendence of differences; but he was not optimistic. 'Never before had "class consciousness" been so manifest in the Commonwealth,' he reflected, fuelled by a coalminers' strike in Newcastle and the arrest of its leader, Peter Bowling. Carlyle too can be heard in Deakin's repeated imagery of Labor's mechanical men in a fallen world devoid of the life-giving spirit. Sectarianism also contributed to the Liberals' defeat, with the Orange Lodges driving the Catholic vote into the arms of Labor and dealing another blow to Deakin's dream of a united Commonwealth.[31]

In all Deakin's voluminous reflections on the election defeat, there is no hint of financial anxiety. Ivy was married to a wealthy man, and Stella was soon to be married to David Rivett, who was returning from abroad to a lectureship at the university. He would have his member's allowance, now six hundred pounds per annum, and the fees from three directorships begun in the 1890s: the London Guarantee and Accident Company, the AMP Society and the Union Trustee Company. And he was still writing for the *Morning Post*, though sharing the task with Tom Bavin, who wrote on state matters. This would have brought his annual income to over a thousand pounds a year. There was no thought of resuming legal practice, so we can assume that his investments had prospered sufficiently for him to be able to make provision for his retirement and security for Pattie and Vera in the event of his death. Fisher later offered him an allowance as leader of the Opposition which, characteristically, he declined, though he did gratefully accept the services of a secretary to assist with routine correspondence.[32]

We don't truly know what power means to someone until they lose it. To Deakin by 1910 it meant a burdensome responsibility which was robbing him 'of the peace without which there is neither wisdom nor happiness', he wrote to Catherine.

> A continent was strapped to my shoulders…I had come to a dreadful state of mind ever vibrating in different keys, always planning always apprehensive and always being switched on and off suddenly to a variety of calls that robbed me at last of everything that makes the inner life steadfast and enduring.[33]

Referring to Bunyan's *Pilgrim's Progress*, he wrote in his notebook that 'When Christian's pack fell from his back he did not go on his way more lightly or more rejoicing than I am doing.'[34] After the defeat, he and Pattie retreated to Ballara, where a mellow autumn lasted deep into May. For ten years they had been coming to Point Lonsdale, but his brooding over national problems and party politics had always drawn a veil over nature. Now, bathing in the sea every evening, 'half by sunlight and half by moonlight', he gradually returned to himself.[35]

> Oh birdsong—can it be
> That I at last am free
> This mellow autumn morning time to muse and list to thee

Returning to my own
My self, my life, alone
To privacy, to liberty, fresh seed to be sown.[36]

The world appeared as if new.

> A new Melbourne surrounds me…buildings, shops and other improvements having been so long regarded with unseeing eyes that now they strike me as if fresh creations…Every tram ride, every walk up and down Bourke Street to the House shows me my fellow citizens as freshly as if I were in Italy or France—they could not be more foreign to me than after my long period of indiscriminate obliviousness.

Absorption in politics 'had diverted his mind…from the living world of facts and individuals around me so that I might have been a dweller for that period upon another plane'. Taking refuge when he could in his books had only

> deepened the gulf separating me from actual persons and things…I feel as I pass along the streets like a man who has been blind and recently operated on so that my vision of place and things is becoming restored to me. The nightmare (or daymare) of responsibility is drifting back into the landscape…I return to normal existence.[37]

34

LEADER OF THE OPPOSITION

AS LEADER OF the Opposition, Deakin's political duties were light. With no chance of defeating legislation and so no need for his skills in parliamentary tactics and personal persuasion, he could only criticise, and try to keep up the spirits of his side. Although he would rather have retired, and characteristically offered to resign, there was no one to take over as leader and he would not leave the party in the lurch.[1] He was still by far the Opposition's most effective debater, whose speeches would be reported in detail in the press and so keep the Opposition relevant in the eyes of the public.[2]

A government with a disciplined majority in both houses was a novel situation, and Labor was impatient to exploit its power with a rush of legislation. It completed much of the legislation already in train before the election, albeit with some minor differences. The Commonwealth takeover of the Northern Territory had become bogged down in a dispute over the route of the railway link with Darwin and lapsed when the Fusion government lost office. Labor revived it, and Deakin supported it warmly in his second-reading speech. Labor's Naval Defence Act was also based on the proposals of the Fusion ministry, though where Deakin had intended to raise a loan to finance it Labor would pay for it with a land tax.[3]

As well as completing Deakin's programme, Labor had its own more radical and socialist aims. Many Opposition members opposed Labor for essentially class-based, material reasons, but this was difficult for Deakin, who still identified as progressive. He needed other grounds, and found them in the damage some of Labor's proposals would do to the delicate federal balance of power, tilting it too far towards the Commonwealth. So he argued against Labor's proposal to impose a land tax, both to raise revenue and to break up large landholdings, on the grounds that the constitution retained all the powers over land for the states. This conveniently landed him in the same position as the majority of his party, who vehemently opposed a land tax for class reasons, while maintaining his progressive self-image.[4]

Labor was planning a referendum to expand the Commonwealth's powers. The High Court's rejection of the Excise Tariff Act, which was to give effect to the New Protection, had brought home to Labor the constitutional constraints on the federal government's capacity to improve wages and working conditions. Deakin was still proposing to achieve New Protection through his cumbersome Interstate Commission, but Labor preferred a more direct route, proposing to give to the Commonwealth powers over trade and commerce, wages, conditions and industrial disputes, and corporations and monopolies. It could thus bypass the conservative state upper houses, which regularly frustrated progressive legislation.

Deakin led the opposition to the Constitution Alteration Bill with a major second-reading speech in mid-October 1910. Pattie, Catherine, Stella and Vera were all there to hear him, and he judged it a 'Success'. In the past, Deakin had sometimes used notes when making official speeches to stop himself straying off course or disclosing too much when in office. Now he was relying on notes for names and facts and figures, and to prevent his speeches collapsing into garrulous rambling.[5] The speech was cogent, he was on top of the detail and the relevant history, and he dealt as deftly as ever with queries and interjections. Deakin had been thinking about the constitution since the convention of 1891, and he appealed to this, as well as to the vote of the Australian people at the referenda, to argue against proposals which would recklessly alter the federal balance and leave little for the state governments to do. Deakin was not opposed to the constitution being altered; it had to grow and adapt, and he agreed with some of Labor's intent; but Hughes as attorney-general had handcuffed four of the five proposals together, and was forcing an all-or-nothing choice on voters.[6]

Deakin's political year ended with the publication on 8 December 1910 of an Open Letter to the 'Women and Men of Australia', urging them to reject the proposals.[7] The previous summer at Ballara he had been preparing for the election; this summer it was the referendum, which would be his last campaign. 'Nearing the end—a critical year public and private—perhaps the critical year for my future short or long.'[8]

Deakin spent most of March and April 1911 campaigning in all states except Western Australia. The referendum was held on 26 April and the outcome was a triumph for the Opposition, with every state but Western Australia rejecting the proposals. Fisher, on his way to London for the coronation of George V and the Imperial Conference, had left the leadership of the campaign to Hughes, who had clearly overreached himself, revealing the authoritarian tendencies which were to wreak havoc on the nation a few years later, during the war. The proposed constitutional changes went beyond what had been agreed to by the Labor Federal Conference, and they trod heavily on the toes of state Labor leaders ambitious for their own reforms.

This was the first referendum campaign centred on the distribution of powers in Australia's federation. Convinced that, whatever its legal artificialities, federalism was the only form of government fitted to Australian circumstances, Deakin focussed on the impracticality in a continent the size of Australia of centralising power in a distant capital, remote from the day-to-day lives of Australians and without the capacity to deliver services efficiently, concerns which still hold today.[9] The result was an enormous relief to Deakin. 'We are saved from the precipice over which we could have gone had the majorities been against us, smashing our federal constitution to pieces. To have had to remain in politics a helpless witness of this catastrophe...would have been a dismal prospect.'[10]

In the year since he had lost government in April 1910, with time to write and reflect, Deakin's loss of memory became a major preoccupation. In June 1910 he began writing a memoir of 'the books that filled a sensitive and solitary boyhood', and it cost him 'a terrible effort', as 'what seemed a mountain chain of memories stretching along and beyond my horizon...resolved itself into a series of inconspicuous islets, small, separate, and irregularly scattered, the barren remains of a submerged Atlantis from which to cull a few wave-worn relics of the wonders of my childhood.'[11]

His papers hold many typewritten and hand-corrected drafts, as he tried out different metaphors for the loss of vivid access to his childhood. When he wrote *The Crisis of Victorian Politics* in 1899, twenty years after the events, he was right back in his younger self, seeing the scenes, hearing the conversations and feeling again the exhilaration of his whirl into politics. Now he could not repeat the feat, though in fact he did remember a good deal about the books and authors he had read.

The failure was not just of memory, but also of literary ambition. He had hoped to follow the muse of childhood, Wordsworth, with the boy shaped by books rather than nature. His conclusion—'I am not fit to write'—is histrionic, but it does reveal his knowledge that his once great gifts were falling away, and perhaps too a little vanity.

The memoir was written to be read to a meeting of the Brown Society, a private club started by Ivy and Herbert that met monthly at Winwick to discuss the poems of T. E. Brown, a late-Victorian poet and theologian, to listen to music and to read their essays on literary subjects to each other. Younger men like Ernest Scott and Walter Murdoch, a literary journalist and academic, read papers, and no doubt Deakin wanted to impress them with a well-crafted literary essay.[12]

Even had Deakin's memory been in better shape, he was expecting too much of himself. He had never mastered the literary essay or longer literary forms. His temperament was that of 'the improvisatore...

spontaneous, irregular, rapid'—at its best in sketches and verses and on his feet, the skills of the journalist and speechmaker. The two book-length manuscripts he left, 'The Crisis in Victorian Politics' and 'The Federation Story', are collections of sketches rather than sustained historical narratives.

Deakin had always written in his journals and notebooks when he had the leisure, recording thoughts on his reading, metaphysical speculations, and his shifting moods and psychic energies. From the middle of 1910 he had more leisure than he had had since his youth, but his subject matter was narrowing to his self and his mind's disappearing capacities. He sorted through his old manuscripts, destroying many, précising some, and writing reminiscences of his childhood, parents, schooling and youth. He now wrote not so much to explore the world as to hang on to it and, as his short-term memory faltered, to maintain his grip on his sense of a continuous self.

Over the coming years, until he could write no more, Deakin recorded the decline of his memory; and, while the bitterness of comparison could still be sharply felt, he gave an account of what he had once been.

> Whereas before I moved within a circuit of general conscious-
> ness with a large supply of recognitions around me in addition
> to the full flow of memories more or less individualised that
> always accompanied my consciousness of whatever work was in
> hand...I now move as if on a narrow line, darkness around me,
> with difficulty keeping to that line, the supplementary flashes
> that visit me irregularly coming out of the vague surrounds with
> hardly an indication of their origins or relationships...In anything
> demanding particulars—formerly most came unsought—and
> not in disorder—the subconscious self busily employed supplied
> my consciousness with what it needed...Now I see neither ahead
> nor behind me except for a very little way—I move on a line...
> proceeding blindly.

His judgement, he thought, was not affected. He still held to the same conclusions, but he had lost his control of the arguments and

details they were based on.[13] The once densely woven web of his mind
was losing its connections and his self was slipping away: 'it is plain
that A.D. no longer lives as he was—Another A.D. sits among ruins
picking his way carefully across the debris to the haven of complete
forgetfulness that awaits me.'[14]

As the urgency of his political commitments faded, he became
more aloof. Deakin had often sought strategies of detachment from the
urgency of politics, but just as often he had believed himself to be its
dramatic centre. Previously his sense of disconnection was transitory.
'Now the experience has come to stay.'

> At the House and even in debate there is a strange sense of remote-
> ness and I watch events as if they were part of a play in which my
> part was filled by an amateur acting with real actors...This gives
> me a queer angle of vision since I feel already like a man dead and
> translated, talking to the living, enjoying their society, basking in
> the sunshine, musing pleasantly and completing my little errands
> quietly or sitting at home in myself patiently and cheerfully saying
> 'Knock if you like or if you prefer enter without knocking.'[15]

Sometimes he elaborated his aloofness into the experience of two
selves, an inner and an outer, with the inner shaped by his lifelong love
of reading and recorded in the manuscripts piled in his drawers under
lock and key. 'Living at the heart of things, a most untiring agent in
the executive and legislative life of politics, with pulses oftener at fever
heat than those of the confirmed gambler or speculator, I feel and have
always felt aloof in the sense described.' 'Aloofness', he wrote, 'means
living in one self.'[16] Deakin had learned to live in his self when a boy
and, though it began as a place of fantasy and escape from loneliness,
as his reading matured it became a well-furnished room secluded from
the vexations of political life, a place of deep enjoyment and spiritual
refreshment where he could recuperate his energies.

Deakin's religious life was lived here. He had early rejected an
external God empirically knowable through sensation for an imminent,
in-dwelling God knowable through prayer and intuition, believing

that 'The Kingdom of Heaven is within.' Secular thinkers now need to work hard to grasp the theological dimensions of this and to see how his belief grounded the vicissitudes of his political life in what for him were enduring truths.

He believed that his resilience in public life arose from his reliance on 'the unseen in a spirit of faith at times indistinguishable from fatalism... that whatever happens is the best under the circumstances'. Without some such belief, 'my worrying, anxious temper, always fretting lest I should fall short...or miss the one right moment to act or speak... would have made me incapable of doing even the little I have been able to accomplish.'[17] Deakin's patience and elusiveness as he kept his options open till divine providence showed its hand were grounded in his non-doctrinal religious faith. This is what gave him the fortitude for political life.

He was not, however, without moments of doubt: 'I once thought our Federation a distinct illustration of a real and great victory won against hopeless conditions—Now I am not so sure.' He wondered sometimes at the venality of the masses, and he felt despondent as he watched Labor undertaking tasks that were once his, disheartened 'that it matters so little what one does' and how very slow the 'ascent on the high road'. But mostly, in keeping with his mixture of faith and fatalism, he believed his had been a most fortunate life and he was grateful. So far as he could judge from his observation of his fellows, he had been 'an exceptionally happy man, not envious...Chiefly because I would not at any price change my parents, sister, wife and children.'[18]

Comforting Catherine in May 1909 when she was in Berlin with Stella and very lonely, he had written, 'My sympathy is real...In public affairs with all my good friends and allies I am utterly alone among them all. But belief in unconscious communication with the living loved ones and perhaps with those who have passed on really sustains us.'[19] We should not be distracted by the reference to communication beyond the grave to miss the revelation Deakin makes here about the non-religious sources of his psychological strength. All his life he had been cherished: by his mother, father and sister; his wife and daughters; beyond the family in his early adulthood by Terry, Syme and Pearson.

In politics, older men like Berry and Service were always keen to help him. This love and support had built up a store of deep identifications on which he could draw; a psychoanalyst would call them good objects.

Occasionally he described himself putting on his armour—but the metaphor is misleading.[20] Armour is defensive and the man it protects may not be strong. But Deakin was strong, with an extraordinary capacity to endure political setbacks and physical travail. His strength did not come from battle-hardened defences, but from the core of his self. When he needed to he could retreat into that self and be alone, happy and independent.

The resilience and richness of Deakin's inner world help us to understand a major blind spot in his dealings with Labor. He was genuinely sympathetic to the hardships endured by working-class people and committed to greater social justice, but it was the humanitarian sympathy of an outsider without shared experience. From the security of his cherished and comfortable childhood and the easy successes of his youth, Deakin never understood the grievance and injuries of working-class life, its humiliations and narcissistic wounds. The bitterness and pride which drove men like Billy Hughes or Andrew Fisher or Frank Anstey were a mystery to him, as was their fierce determination that others would have the opportunities denied to them, and their hunger for recognition. Nor did he understand the bonds of solidarity forged by shared deprivation which underlay Labor's commitment to collective political action.

Waking at Ballara on Saturday, 12 November 1910 after a strained and busy week in town, Deakin heard a light-hearted and affectionate voice whispering to him from his 'subconscious self': 'Finish your job and turn in.' Deakin was well read in the emerging field of psychology, much of which overlapped with psychical literature in its theories about human consciousness. Freud had not yet been translated into English, but Deakin was familiar with Frederic Myers, who coined the terms 'subliminal self' and 'stream of consciousness' and argued that the waking, conscious self represents but a small part of the individual. He had too read the writings of William James on the subliminal self and religious experience.

So when he heard the homely, slangy phrase, though it was one he would never use himself, he was sure it was 'the ripe result of my own unconscious meditation'. Still, so closely did the voice express his conscious wishes that he felt obliged to suspect it to make sure it was a message from his best, his 'most receptive and reflective and mature self', and not just a wish. Finally, he had received permission to retire, but the voice had not told him exactly when his job would be finished. This he still needed to determine. 'Will it finish with the Referendum? I hope so—'[21]

The referendum was defeated. Surely his job was now finished and he could 'turn in', but despite his anxious listening, the voice did not come again.[22] So his public life stretched on, at least until the end of 1911. There was still no alternative leader. With another federal election due in 1913, when Hughes was vowing to put the referendum proposals again, he stayed on. Outside the parliament the Liberals were still 'an improvised organisation against the marvellous discipline and efficiency of the caucus and its leagues'.[23] The Commonwealth Liberal Party had not spread beyond Victoria, in fact scarcely beyond Deakin and his family, who provided most of its office bearers: he was president, Herbert Brookes treasurer and chief moneyman, and Ivy the secretary of the women's section.

Victoria had two other non-labour electoral organisations, both avowedly anti-socialist: the People's Party, which had evolved from the Kyabram Movement and was backed by the Victorian Employers' Federation; and the Australian Women's National League, which championed the home as a bastion of freedom and independence against Labor's socialist ambitions. The Commonwealth Liberal Party and the People's Party tried to negotiate a merger during 1911, which failed at the last moment, after the Commonwealth Liberal Party had already dissolved itself in anticipation and renamed itself the People's Liberal Party.

The AWNL was determined to retain its independence as a separate organisation and was furious with the Commonwealth Liberal Party for initiating a women's branch. The Deakinite Liberals were far too close to Labor for the conservative women who ran the AWNL; the Ballarat branch even tried to organise against Deakin in his own electorate. How little did they realise, reflected Deakin, that they might have been the authors of his liberation. Instead, he dealt with their petty intrigues as if all his interests lay in retaining his post.[24]

Herbert, the loyal acolyte, and Ivy, the dutiful daughter, worked tirelessly for the Commonwealth Liberal Party 'personified in Grandpa', as Herbert described it in a letter to Ivy.[25] In July 1911 the party launched a monthly journal, the *Liberal*, which was edited and largely financed by Herbert.[26] Deakin wrote unsigned material for it over the next couple of years, and was likely the author of an article, 'What have the Liberals done?', which appeared in the first issue and rehearsed the progressive achievements of Victorian liberalism: the secret ballot, payment of MPs, extension of the franchise, free education, factory acts and wages boards, and the role of protection in advancing the industrial classes.[27]

With no fresh policies to offer, the *Liberal* fell back on attacking Labor's organisational discipline, with cartoons and articles elaborating the imagery of Labor parliamentarians as cogs and wheels in a machine driven by faceless union bosses. Deakin did not write all the articles but his metaphoric imagination produced these staples of the Liberals' anti-Labor rhetoric, which can still be faintly heard today.

Deakin soldiered on through the rest of 1911 and into 1912, his struggles with his memory recorded in his private writings but still masked in parliament by careful preparation. In August a new editorial team at the *Morning Post* decided that a letter from Australia every three weeks would suffice, so he wound up his partnership with Bavin, and henceforth wrote them all himself. He did consider ceasing altogether, but still valued having a direct voice in London.[28]

Catherine and Stella had returned to Melbourne from abroad early in the year, and he had resumed his regular visits to Adams Street. David Rivett had also returned and was staying at Adams Street until he and Stella were married in November by Charles Strong. They rented a flat nearby in Airlie Street, South Yarra, and later built on a block in Walsh Street that Deakin helped them to buy, repeating William's generosity to his son at the start of his own married life.[29]

Since their return from London, Pattie's community engagement had flourished. This was a source of satisfaction and new friendships, but also of stress and anxiety as she became embroiled in various organisational conflicts. In 1912 she was invited to be the inaugural president of the new Lyceum Club for women university graduates and other women who had distinguished achievements in their own right. Vera reported that when he heard of the invitation, Deakin, 'who had a habit of making light of any serious matter brought forward…by any of his women folk…quipped, "Well, Pattie dear, I evidently had failed to observe that your stockings had recently acquired a faint tinge of blue, but you know how unobservant I am about women's clothes."'[30]

During 1912 Deakin's health worsened. He had lost all zest for public life and was trudging on until he could retire. In April he went to Mildura, the first visit since his failure twenty years earlier to bring peace to the feuding settlers. Now in its semi-jubilee year, the settlement was prospering and Deakin was presented with an address welcoming him as the founder of Victoria's irrigation policy.[31] It must have been a gratifying moment to see his youthful enthusiasm bearing fruit, but the main purpose of his visit was to rally support for the Liberal Party for the coming election and the repeated referendum.

In September he resigned as president of the People's Liberal Party, though he took on one last fight on behalf of his old protectionist colleagues, securing a spot on the party's Senate ticket for Samuel Mauger, a progressive Liberal who had lost his seat to Labor in 1910. It was a furious fight, won despite fierce opposition from the AWNL, which regarded the champion of the anti-sweating league as a dangerous radical.[32]

Parliament resumed in June 1912 and Labor worked it hard. Deakin's speech on Labor's bill for a maternity allowance shows him losing his connection with the progressive direction of Australian politics, as he was pulled to the right by his conservative colleagues and the limits of his own class experience. Labor proposed paying five pounds to all women who gave birth, regardless of marital status and regardless of means. Deakin did not repeat the outrage at the government's condoning of illegitimacy which was animating the conservative press, but he did query the lack of means testing in what Labor intended as a universal benefit free of any hint of charity. Influenced by Pattie's activities, he was wary of the government's capacities to administer the benefit, arguing that it should draw on the experience of the many charitable organisations already in the field.[33]

Deakin still had moments when he thought that perhaps it was his duty to stay on, worried that his strong personal desire for release might be clouding his judgement.[34] But, after another severe bout of illness in September 1912, the decision seemed inevitable and he told Pattie his intentions.[35] She too was having a difficult year. Her mother had endured a lingering death earlier in the year and Pattie had spent many days at her bedside.[36] In October she grew cold in his arms as they lay in bed, almost dying from a bad heart attack. It seemed a 'sign that our exodus from public life is appointed as I felt it must be and have come to long for'.[37]

Deakin's last address to the parliament was late on the evening of Wednesday, 18 December on the mundane issue of the administration of the Postmaster-General's Department.[38] Parliament would not meet again until after the election, to be held in May the following year, but as no one knew Deakin's plans his last address went unremarked. He received no formal farewell from the chamber where he had spent so much of his working life, leaving at midnight to go home to an empty house, the family being already at Ballara for the summer.

When he told Herbert and Ivy of his decision, they were 'absolutely adverse', and he found Herbert's reproaches 'deeply and almost fiercely antagonistic and despairing', leaving him 'more solitary than I have ever been'.[39] He had intended that the public announcement of his resignation would be to his constituents in Ballarat, but when a rumour started to circulate early in the new year he brought the announcement forward, telling a surprised Joseph Cook on 7 January 1913.

The press were informed the following day in a brief announcement in which he cited medical advice, and he sent telegrams to all the Liberal members. Later that day he took the train to Queenscliff with Herbert, who was depressed and silent. Herbert and Ivy were pouring energy, money and time into the Liberal Party, partly from political conviction but mostly because of their devotion to Deakin, and now he was deserting them.

Public assessments of Deakin's contribution were equivocal. Sympathy was expressed for his poor health, admiration for his great gifts and his devotion to duty, and hope that he might return to public life when his health had recovered, perhaps as a senator. At fifty-six, he was still a relatively young man. But the general verdict was that as a leader he had failed.

This was to be expected from the *Argus*, which judged him unable to rise to the responsibilities of office. But the *Age* too claimed that 'leadership was not his forte.' Granting that without his skills in compromise the federal conventions on the constitution might have foundered on party strife, the *Age* nevertheless continued to see Fusion as a huge mistake, and to believe, quixotically, that a strong Liberal Protectionist leader could have prevented it. Sydney's *Catholic Press* and Melbourne's *Advocate* both judged him a public failure, though a most attractive one; and the *Sydney Morning Herald* praised him only for his contribution to irrigation and imperial affairs.

As the two-party system settled into shape, the skills of compromise and negotiation that leaders had needed to build coalitions in the fluid colonial parliaments were being replaced by the fighting skills of the political warrior. Deakin was criticised for elusiveness, hesitancy and prevarication, for weakness of will, and for not being a 'good hater'.[40] The harshest judgements came from the pen of the Labor member for Bourke in the inner northern suburbs of Melbourne, Frank Anstey, who wrote a fourteen-page pamphlet on Deakin's thirty-year career of compromise and betrayal.

Anstey elaborated Billy Hughes's earlier indictment of Deakin for unprincipled inconstancy, as he retold the history of his coalition with the 'Tories' Service and Gillies, the failure of Victoria's Factory Acts, his calling out the troops during the maritime strike, the betrayal of Watson and then of Reid, and so on.[41] As is generally the case in the denunciation of villains, Anstey markedly overestimated Deakin's power and his 'diabolical cunning', but like those more sympathetic to Deakin he was fitting his own explanation into the space Deakin always left open for the guidance of providence.

As the newspapers damned him with faint praise, Deakin woke at Ballara on 9 January 1913 'very weary but a free man…on the knees of his soul thanking God for this very great…and unmerited mercy of release'.[42] Since losing the election, Deakin had written few discrete prayers. Instead, in another notebook, he had recorded reflections which included much more residue of daily practical life. When his memory was at its peak he had no need of these records, but now they helped him keep track of events and his responses. A storm of messages—letters, telegrams and telephone calls—descended on him from friends and supporters, a month later letters arrived from English public men, and he was kept busy replying to them all.

The family marked the end of his parliamentary life by commissioning a portrait from Arthur Woodward, a family friend who taught painting at Bendigo. Sitting on the verandah at Ballara with the Queenscliff headland in the background and book in hand, he is more relaxed than in the rather stiff full-length official portrait Frederick McCubbin painted of him later that year, which hangs in Parliament House in Canberra. Disappointingly, Woodward was not confident he could paint Deakin's mesmeric eyes, so shaded them with his hand.[43]

On Monday, 22 January, Deakin was back in Melbourne to chair his last meeting as party leader. The main item of business was who would replace him. In a tense duel between Cook and Forrest, Cook won by a vote. Forrest was very upset at losing the chance to finally wear the crown and angry with Deakin, whose vote he had expected. But Deakin had been impressed with Cook's diligence as deputy leader and his capable handling of parliament, whereas Forrest was already sixty-five and in poor health. After the vote Deakin handed the chair to Cook. He had felt 'cool, clear and rapid' while conducting the ballot, but he was now overcome with dizziness as the blood rushed to his head. Sitting at the back of the room he saw the meeting 'as if far away and myself an invisible onlooker…My political life is over.'[44]

·

So he said, but he could not let go completely. The next election would be held on 31 May, when Hughes would again try to amend the constitution, and Deakin was soon out campaigning against 'these six drastic and destructive and unreasonable proposals' and urging electors to protect the principles of the constitution for the generations to come.[45] In early April he travelled with Ivy to Tasmania for ten days of campaigning, but it was too much for him and once back he collapsed again in exhaustion. Herbert was insisting he campaign in New South Wales and Queensland, but he refused.[46] He did make a few more campaign speeches, including for Hugh McKay of Sunshine Harvesters, who was the new Liberal candidate for Ballarat, but two weeks before election day he announced that his doctor had forbidden any further public engagements during the campaign, and retired to Ballara.[47]

Vera had decided to follow Stella's footsteps and travel overseas with Auntie Katie as chaperone—in her case, to study music. She had announced her plan to her rather surprised father in March, and early in May she and Catherine sailed for Europe, accompanied by Ida Woodward, Arthur Woodward's daughter, who planned to study art.[48] Seeing them off on the boat, Catherine thought he looked 'very sad and ill' as he told her the doctor's instructions—no more public meetings.[49] She sailed with a heavy heart.

Finally, it was his body rather than the whisperings of his subconscious that forced him from the field. Retrospective diagnosis is difficult, but Deakin's constant monitoring of his health has left a record of symptoms which suggest that he suffered from chronic hypertension over a long period: the likely transient ischaemic attack, or mini-stroke, in 1902, when he thought he had died; his recourse to electromagnetic stimulation; his collapses after the manic activity in London in 1907, and after other periods of intense strain; his episodes of dizziness; his chronic insomnia; his nosebleeds; and finally his deteriorating memory and cognitive capacities. On New Year's Day, 1912, he described another near-death experience in a poem, 'The Crisis':

The life-line through my feeble fingers ran—
My heart beats wavered, weak and very slow—

My gusty breathing, wavering to and fro
Now almost ceased, and then again began.[50]

Given his fitness and his abstemious diet, there was likely a genetic
component in Deakin's condition and, indeed, his two grandmothers
both died of heart disease.[51] In January 1913 he had recorded a blood-
pressure reading in his diary for the first and only time: 164, with the
note that it should be 130, which he achieved a few weeks later. Medical
science was just beginning to understand the long-term effects of high
blood pressure. In May he consulted another doctor, who diagnosed him
as suffering from 'hyperneurasthenia', suggesting that his nerves, not
his heart, were the problem; but even had the diagnosis been correct,
there was little that could have been done, as the drugs then prescribed
to lower blood pressure were of little use.[52] Still, the focus on his nerves
gave Deakin the hope that with sufficient rest his mind would recover
at least some of its former powers.

The absence of an accurate diagnosis of Deakin's condition added
to his personal pain and sense of isolation as, behind his characteristically cheerful demeanour, he fought his disappearing memory and
devised strategies to disguise its extent. It kept hope alive when there
was none, and it encouraged his family and colleagues to believe him
more capable than he was, and so to pressure him to do more than
he could. Having taken on a task, Deakin pushed himself hard to
recapture some of his old efficiencies, only to be confronted again and
again with his incapacity: 'True I have no choice—I cannot be other
than I am—So small, so superficial, so shadowy, so little even reflected
of the man I once was.'[53]

35

'THE WORLD FORGETTING,
BY THE WORLD FORGOT'[1]

NEVER HAD HIS days been 'so barren of events…[they] melted into
each other until it became an effort to remember the day of the week',
Deakin wrote to Catherine on 20 May 1913.[2] It was as if his public life
'never had been and never could have been'.[3] There is a slight morbid
exaggeration here, as he was still engaging in some political activities.
The Liberals had won the election by a single seat and Joseph Cook was
now prime minister. Deakin wrote to each of the defeated candidates,
including to Hugh McKay, who lost the seat of Ballarat to the Labor
candidate by less than four hundred votes.[4] He was still writing for the
Morning Post and would do so for another year yet. Up in town the habits
and sociability of a lifetime carried him along, as he met friends and old
colleagues, and chaired meetings of the AMP Society and the London
Guarantee and Accident Company. He renewed his involvement with
the Society for the Prevention of Cruelty to Animals, enjoyed visiting
exhibitions of new art with Pattie and sat for McCubbin.

But back at Ballara he was isolated and his public life fell away. It was here that he did most of his writing, including further reminiscences of his childhood and youth. Memory is always an unreliable narrator, and one suspects that in his reclusive life by the sea he exaggerated the solitariness of his childhood and the attractions of the literary life to his restless, energetic younger self. By September 1913, after more than three months of quiet, physical exertion and good meals, he was more muscular than he had been for twenty years. His memory at times revived a little, but it was capricious and didn't last.[5] He had expected that, free from the strains of office, his memory would recover completely, but the opposite happened: 'When I stepped out of Parliament in some mysterious fashion all my memories commenced to die or disappear.'[6]

Cook clearly saw a man still competent to undertake public duties and urged him to accept the chairmanship of the Interstate Commission. Deakin was reluctant. Needing to return books to the parliamentary library on 29 July, he went to great lengths to avoid meeting Cook and giving him the chance to press the matter, 'approaching strategically and cautiously from the rear of the House' and using a little-known stairway.

> Arrived at the first floor, felt perfectly safe and at once stepped to the Library door only to meet...face to face with Cook...At once and without hesitation he very gravely appealed to me not to be led by fears of health but to take the Chairmanship of the Interstate Committee. We walked to his office, he strongly urging on my acceptance and I as constantly stating my present inability.

After a night's reflection Deakin wrote to decline the post.[7]

Early in 1914 Cook made him another offer, the presidency of the Australian Commission for the Panama–Pacific International Exposition in San Francisco, to be held the following year to celebrate the opening of the Panama Canal and to display the city's remarkable recovery since the 1906 earthquake. The duties were comparatively light, and it would give him the chance to visit California again. Vera could come, and he thought Catherine too might like to accompany them to see the new world.[8] Cook and Brookes both urged him to accept, believing he would benefit from the stimulation. Physically, he was feeling stronger—so, still hoping for his memory's revival, he accepted.

On 4 June the new governor-general, Munro Ferguson, granted Cook a double dissolution, with an election to be held on 5 September. Labor controlled the Senate and had twice rejected a bill which prohibited preference in public employment for unionists. It was only a little more than a year since the last election, but Cook was frustrated with his one-seat majority and Labor's continual blocking of his measures in the Senate. This was Australia's first double-dissolution election.

As the campaign got underway, Europe was preparing for war after the assassination of Archduke Ferdinand. Britain declared war on Germany on 4 August 1914. Deakin declined to speak at a rally at the Melbourne Town Hall, but he did reluctantly accept Cook's invitation to chair a royal commission to inquire into the supply of foodstuffs during the war, which recommended that foodstuffs were only to be exported within the empire except with the permission of the government.[9] 'That settles poor me,' he wrote, and he struggled with the task.[10]

> At last I have realised what it is to be stripped to the bone; to have no continuity of memory or argument, to live upon impressions that fade or are forgotten in a few minutes and often in a few seconds…My experiences in the Food Supply Commission are absolutely damning and only by the inexhaustible kindness of my good friends there am I able to stagger 'under way'.[11]

Just days after Deakin had accepted the job, Cook lost the election and Fisher returned as prime minister. Labor wound up the commission in November, but Andrew Fisher confirmed plans for Deakin to visit the International Exposition in San Francisco, and offered him a thousand pounds for expenses, insisting that Pattie accompany him.[12] Deakin was surprised. He had thought that with the country at war the visit was likely to be cancelled. Fisher too was unaware of the extent of Deakin's decline, and hoped that Deakin's standing and diplomatic skills would strengthen Australia's relationship with the United States.[13]

In September 1914 Deakin spoke to the seventy former students of Melbourne Grammar who had already volunteered, young men facing danger to protect our freedoms.[14] The world crisis he had long imagined had arrived. His reflective writings from this time, however, have nothing at all on the war, and are preoccupied with his struggles with his memory. Vera and Catherine were in Europe and he urged them to come home by the Cape route as soon as they could get a berth.

Early in 1915 Deakin sailed for California with Pattie and Vera, but only after an unseemly public brawl with Hugh Mahon, Labor's minister for external affairs. An Australian official already in San Francisco had recommended that with the outbreak of war Australia's participation in the exposition should be abandoned and Mahon accused Deakin of covering up the advice, which Deakin denied. Their 'epistolary duel' was carried out in the press, and the *Age* concluded that Mahon was trying to force Deakin's resignation.[15] Even as Mahon continued to attack him, Hughes, who was acting prime minister, rang to confirm his appointment and Fisher's offer of a thousand pounds.[16]

So he and Pattie repeated the journey across the Pacific they had taken in 1885 with the infant Ivy. His greatest relief on boarding the ship, he told Catherine, was 'the absence of all news about the War', which was a great drain on a nervous person such as himself.[17] Later, he wrote to her, 'Of the war I say nothing. When we are successful I will rejoice in a very minor key—there are dead on both sides—there is the dragged out grief and anxiety—there is the endless train of consequences.'[18] He made no mention of Gallipoli and seems to have been oblivious to the excitement back home of a nation eager to prove itself in battle and blood sacrifice.

His duties in San Francisco were mainly ceremonial, and to get what publicity he could for the Australian pavilion. As the United States was keeping out of the war in Europe, Deakin's weak martial spirit helped him avoid the diplomatic blunders of a more belligerent temperament. Opening the Australian exhibition, he read a message from King George V as well as one from Fisher dedicating Australia's contribution 'to the promotion of the arts of peace and abiding friendship with the United

States', and referred to the war only obliquely in his profound sorrow at the untold sacrifices and the disunity among civilised men.[19]

Pattie eased him through the demanding social schedule and smoothed the vexations of his unreliable short-term memory. They enjoyed some touring, travelling down to the Mexican border and visiting Yosemite, and they spent time with George Chaffey, who was developing new irrigation colonies near Los Angeles.

Meanwhile, Mahon, still smarting from being overruled, continued to be unhappy about the venture. Early in May 1915, without consulting Deakin or the other commissioners, he recalled the public servant managing the pavilion. Deakin resigned. In the circumstances of the Gallipoli campaign, this was a small matter, and Fisher accepted his resignation.[20] By early July the Deakins were back in Australia, a month earlier than planned but relieved to be home.

Mahon's persecution of Deakin didn't stop, however. David McGrath, who had won Deakin's old seat of Ballarat for Labor, asked Mahon questions in parliament which implied that Deakin had been double-dipping in availing himself of government allowances. When Deakin handed his report to Fisher, and returned more than six hundred pounds of his thousand-pound allowance, Mahon insisted that the report should have been submitted to him as the responsible minister.[21] It was unbelievably petty. Cook was furious and urged retaliation, but Deakin declined.[22]

To hostile Labor eyes Deakin was still powerful and fair game, and even close friends saw him as more capable than he was. Herbert, who was in the thick of patriotic war work, was vexed at his keeping aloof from public affairs. 'He does not understand my wrecked memory,' Deakin noted resignedly, and has 'exaggerated expectations of my recovery'.[23] He continued to refuse most invitations to speak, and struggled to get his accounts in order to pay the new federal income tax Labor had imposed to help pay for the war.

For much of the year Ivy was ill with a difficult pregnancy, which ended in a stillbirth, and Deakin would sit by her bed for hours and read to her. Many days, his restless nature took him out and about, into town

on various errands, often to Adams Street to chat with Catherine and
to the Base Hospital in St Kilda Road, where Pattie had become the
organiser of the Anzac Buffet, which provided refreshments to soldiers
waiting for embarkation or to be seen at the hospital. Here he would talk
with wounded soldiers and help with various tasks, buttering bread or
sweeping the floor, and he would gallantly escort her home at the end
of the day. Pattie had thrown herself into war work, out of duty but
also as a distraction from the grief of watching her beloved husband's
inexorable decline. Many years later she said that the work 'had come
at a time of deep bereavement and loss', and helped 'to fill the blank'.[24]

From modest beginnings in August 1915, with a few women volunteers, by the end of the war the Anzac Buffet was serving a thousand
soldiers a day. It soon expanded its services beyond tea and sandwiches
to become a place where a soldier could find a sympathetic listener, and
sometimes an advocate. This was Pattie's forte. Charming, but with a
no-nonsense approach to authority, she became 'Intercessor-in-Chief',
ignoring protocol to call on the military brass hats to find out information for a soldier's family or straighten out a muddled pay account.[25]

She was so busy that they now went to Ballara rarely, and then only
for a long weekend. They had changed places, Deakin wrote: 'She is
triumphing. I am withering and indeed withered. Yet I am more than
ever her lover and server. She is my advisor and now my leader in very
many ways.' Meekly accepting his growing dependence on her, he
submitted gratefully to her loving care.[26]

Vera was no longer at home. As soon as she had returned to
Melbourne from the United States she had done a first-aid course and
then gone to Cairo and later London to work with the Red Cross. Her
father was very hurt and did not want her to go. He was partly worried
about the impact on his hard-earned finances, which had to last him
and Pattie for the rest of their lives. But she was determined and he
did not stand in her way.[27]

He was still writing in his notebooks, recording and re-recording
his fragmented, unreliable memory and trying to solve the riddle of
himself. Pen in hand he could steady himself and keep to his train of
thought far better than when he was talking. The literary arts had not

entirely deserted him. They could still be heard in his vivid descriptions
of his inner world and the cadences of his prose.

> Today my books are strangers to me, nothing more than relics
> which I can revise and retain but a few hours at best and usually
> without any return. To live among the scores of books one has
> forgotten, after a public career that now remains wrapped in
> clouds…No banishment was ever more complete—No collapse
> could be ghastlier—In the very midst of my quiet retirement I
> find myself absolutely cut off from my past life, my once clear
> memories, my hopes and aims of simple service—A stranded
> mariner, in a deep sense a solitary, without a memory or the flow
> of speech that once ran always free and sometimes shot higher
> than I can now realise—Kindness and consideration surround
> me, but I have lost even my tongue and fail with my pen to sketch
> with rough outline what I desire to convey…I do not spit these
> censures at my poor over-shadowed brain but having a clearer
> interval than is usual I am trying to set down at least some partial
> aspects of my present exile from public life, from books, from aims
> at usefulness, from old friendships.[28]

He wrote this on 6 November 1915. On 30 December he wrote, 'Not
only has my memory foundered as a whole, but I have now become a
mere juggler with myself—misleading and misconstruing myself…
my helpless attempts to read the riddle of my mind and thought must
be frankly abandoned.'[29]

The diary for 1916 is the last in which Deakin kept a record of his
daily life. Dr Crivelli was still assuring him he could restore his health,
and prescribed two new medicines, to be taken two days apart: Kola
Astier, or caffeine; and Neurosine, which was a cocktail of powerful
drugs used to relieve nervous tension. The American Medical Association regarded it as 'a shotgun nostrum'.[30] He was also having regular
massages.

Nothing seemed to help and Pattie even had to remind him of
their wedding anniversary. In desperation, she decided to consult

specialists in England and America, and they left in late September 1916. John Forrest was on board as far as Perth, and Deakin enjoyed long and friendly talks with him, dismissing their tensions over the leadership when Deakin cast his vote for Cook as caused by 'unintentional passing over'.

Deakin also spent the voyage reading and rereading the bible of the Christian Scientists, Mary Baker Eddy's *Science and Health*, with its assertion of the primacy of our spiritual being and its central message that sickness is a belief rather than a property of matter. The daily diary peters out in October, when they are still on the ship, with displays of the paranoid tendencies that so often accompany dementia. Deakin suspected that the captain was plotting maliciously against them.[31]

In London they were reunited with Vera and the three of them spent Christmas 1916 helping out at the Brighton Red Cross dinner for wounded soldiers, Pattie carving and Deakin waiting on tables. Pattie was very protective and Deakin saw few of his former friends and associates.[32] One who did see them was Colonel Unsworth, who had accompanied the Salvation Army's General Booth to breakfast at Llanarth in 1905: 'He was so different. Sometimes in talk there were flashes of the old Deakin, but, alas! The golden bowl was almost broken, only the kind heart remained.'[33] Neither the British nor American specialists could do anything for him, and early in 1917 Pattie brought him home. 'Life has ended—in truth in fact and in judgement…My memory is but a little fiction, a chance return of the pitiful and withering memorial of AD…Such is my miserable end!'[34]

Deakin's last public utterance was on 19 December 1917, supporting a Yes vote in the second referendum on conscription to be held the following day. Publishing his appeal, the *Argus* editorialised that the Yes case would have greatly benefited from Deakin's public advocacy. There is a copy in his handwriting in his papers, but it is unlikely he composed it. It read in part:

> Fellow Countrymen—I have lived and worked to help you keep Australia white and free…God in his wisdom has decreed that at this great crisis in our history my tongue must be silent owing

to my failing powers. He alone knows how I yearn, my fellow Australians, to help you to say that magic word which shall aid our gallant soldiers and save our civilisation.[35]

'White and free' is not a phrase Deakin ever used, and the self-pitying tone in 'I have lived and worked' is not his. The ghostwriter was probably Herbert Brookes, who was on the executive of almost every major war organisation in Melbourne, a fierce advocate of conscription and now on friendly terms with Billy Hughes.[36]

As Deakin drifted deeper into himself, the harmonious Australia he had once hoped for had become bitterly divided. Andrew Fisher had resigned as Labor's prime minister at the end of 1915 and Hughes had been unanimously elected in his stead. Hughes wanted to introduce conscription to boost flagging recruitment, but many in Labor opposed it, so in 1916 he had appealed over the heads of his party to the people. The referendum was lost, and the Labor Party split. In a manoeuvre just as devious as any he had accused Deakin of, Hughes led twenty-three loyalist Labor parliamentarians into a merger with the Opposition Liberals and became prime minister of the newly named Nationalist government. Deakin's Liberal Party was no longer.

In December 1917 Hughes was trying again with a second referendum, but the campaign was even more divisive than the first, especially in Melbourne, where the Catholic Archbishop, Daniel Mannix, was recommending Catholics to vote No. With Ireland bleeding after the uprising of Easter 1916 and Britain's brutal reprisals, many heeded his voice. Brookes, whose mother was an Ulster Protestant, had a virulent sectarian streak, and was incensed by Mannix's intervention. Likely Brookes offered Hughes Deakin's assistance, and Deakin, barely aware of the tumult outside, obliged.

The rift between Pattie and Catherine continued, with Pattie controlling Catherine's access to her brother. From the beginning of 1917 he seems to have been confined to Llanarth, where Pattie cared for him. Whereas before he could visit Catherine at will, he was now brought to Adams Street every Wednesday in 1917 for lunch and in 1918 in the afternoon. It was heartbreaking for Catherine to watch him grow less and less interested as she tried to make him recall old times. Sometimes she would play the piano for him, and sometimes Stella would be there with her little boy, Rohan, who was born at the beginning of 1917. Deakin had always enjoyed the company of children and he still did. In May 1919 Catherine came home to find him inside the house, looking at books with Rohan.

In London, Vera had become engaged to an Australian soldier and ex-prisoner of the Turks, Tom White. Early in 1919 Ivy cabled her to come home. Alfred was going down fast. On one visit to Adams Street he repeated his father's dying words, 'It will not be long now,' and Catherine thought he knew her. He was brought to see her for her birthday in July, when she turned sixty-nine, but had no realisation of the day. Shortly after his sixty-third birthday, in August, Vera brought him to Adams Street for almost his last visit to the home of his boyhood and youth. He was sad and gentle, and the music made him weep. In mid-September he lapsed into his final illness. Catherine visited him in the breakfast room at Llanarth: 'the darling talked all the time,' his voice strong as if he were orating. 'It was terrible to see.'

On Sunday, 5 October 1919 the family gathered at Llanarth. He whispered farewell and kissed them each in turn, and on Tuesday morning he died. Announcing his death to the House of Representatives that afternoon with the profoundest grief, Hughes said: 'he dies now in the service of his country no less truly than if he had been stricken in the field of battle. His health...broken by the great strain of public duty...He has done great things for Australia and he has died in her service.' The House adjourned for the rest of the day.[37]

In death, the state claimed him. Two days later his body lay in Queen's Hall in the building he had entered forty years before with his resignation speech in his pocket and where he had achieved some of his greatest triumphs. Archdeacon Hindley of Melbourne's Anglican diocese officiated at the state funeral, the leading Liberal William Watt delivered the oration, and the pallbearers were all public men, including Billy Hughes and Joseph Cook but not either of his sons-in-law. Pattie and Ivy seem not to have attended, while Catherine, Vera and Stella watched from the gallery and could not hear the service.

It was, Catherine said, just as we wanted it, 'stately and plain and rich', though perhaps more conventionally religious than Deakin would have chosen. No doubt Charles Strong was not considered suitable to conduct a state funeral. Watt noted that, though he might have had many honours, 'he had died plain Alfred Deakin.'

Crowds watched as the cortege, led by a band playing the 'Dead March' from Handel's oratorio *Saul*, went down Spring, into Collins, then onto Swanston Street and across the Princes Bridge to St Kilda Road, where returned men and nurses watched it pass from outside the Base Hospital. Boys were lined up outside Melbourne and All Saints Grammar schools, and in a gesture of sectarian peace a row of girls stood outside St Mary's Roman Catholic School in Dandenong Road as the motorcade approached the St Kilda Cemetery. He was buried in the non-denominational section in a grave next to William and Sarah.[38] The family chose an open book for his simple headstone, engraved only with his name and the dates of his birth and death.

Pattie mourned him in private:

We lived as lovers from 1881 to 1919, when he left me broken and bruised, a poor frayed end still his and he still mine. Beyond the mist the dawn shall come again: in that day when there is no setting of the sun, we two will march side by side in that Beyond, God's Heaven, there to abide...[39]

36

AFTERLIFE

DEAKIN DIED IN a society traumatised by events in which he had played no part: sixty thousand Australians killed in the war, many more maimed or sent mad, families and communities shrouded in grief, and sectarianism at fever pitch. Herbert Brookes, who had entered the war a Liberal, was now a raging Protestant loyalist, in the thick of the campaign against the disloyal Fenianism of Daniel Mannix and his cowardly Catholic flock.[1] It would have broken Deakin's heart.

The nation-building moment of federation, which was Deakin's triumphant achievement, had been pushed from popular memory by Australia's second birth on the Gallipoli Peninsula and the Western Front. Australians now had other heroes—John Monash, Pompey Elliott, William Birdwood, Harry Chauvel, Simpson and his donkey, sixty-four winners of the Victoria Cross. Before their courage and glorious achievements, winning a referendum or outwitting Joseph Chamberlain over appeals to the Privy Council were nothing.

His family and close friends wanted to commemorate their beloved

Alfred, to recapture the vivid man he was at his height and to honour the sacrifice of his health they believed he had made in the service of the nation. Herbert had already begun working on his papers. On his and Ivy's advice, Pattie commissioned Walter Murdoch to write a biography. Murdoch had been a young journalist, teacher and aspiring man of letters when he and Deakin became friends in 1905, largely on the basis of their shared literary interests. Deakin had written to Murdoch in appreciation of a piece he had written, 'for he was ever the helper and encourager of young men, and especially of young men—being mindful of his own early aspirations—who were learning to write'.[2]

After Murdoch moved to Perth in 1913 to take up the chair of English at the University of Western Australia, they had corresponded. Murdoch was a foundation member of the Brown Society in 1906, and when in Melbourne part of the Winwick circle of artists, musicians, academics and men of affairs which Ivy and Herbert gathered around themselves. He knew and loved Deakin, and he had the literary skills to write a compelling book.

The family made Deakin's private notebooks, with their often anguished self-abnegation, available to him, as well as his unpublished manuscripts. And they shared their memories. Pattie, Catherine and Herbert each read the draft. Catherine, who began the reminiscences she wrote for Murdoch with 'I worshipped the baby as I have the man during all our lives,' requested he soften even the mildest criticism; and Murdoch's scant treatment of Deakin's spiritualism was no doubt encouraged by Herbert, who regarded it as embarrassing nonsense.[3]

Alfred Deakin: A Sketch, published in 1923, is an affectionate, lively book which emphasises Deakin's literary interests and ambitions and suggests that a quiet literary life might have suited him better than politics. But we must judge a man's life not just by what he says but what he does. Murdoch's is the judgement of a man who had himself lived the life of the word, and he did not grasp the compulsion and the pleasure in Deakin's pursuit of politics. He included generous extracts from his writing, letters and speeches, including from the notebooks, which revealed Deakin's long struggle against his failing memory. These, wrote Ernest Scott, were so 'intensely painful, the reader finds that he cannot miss a word of it, and every word stabs him'.[4] Also publicly revealed for the first time was Deakin's anonymous writing for the *Morning Post*. Herbert and Murdoch hoped to follow the *Sketch* with a more comprehensive biography, but its sales were disappointing and the time did not seem ripe. A decade later a cheaper edition sold better.[5]

Pattie was fifty-six when she was widowed and wore mostly black or grey for the rest of her life. For a few years she continued to live at Llanarth and for a time all three daughters lived close by in Walsh Street. The cockatoo which her brothers had given her when she was a small child was still alive. When it heard the front door opening it would call, with Alfred's intonation, 'Is that you, Pattie dear?'[6] After she moved from Llanarth into an apartment, also in Walsh Street, Ivy and Herbert incorporated Llanarth into Winwick and she bought a weekend cottage at Montrose, in the foothills of the Dandenongs, where she could garden and entertain her grandchildren. She continued her public work for women and children to the end, as well as her interest in the welfare of returned soldiers. Pattie died at Ballara in late December 1934, two days before her seventy-first birthday. By then she was living with Vera, Tom and their four daughters. Catherine, still living at The Elms in Adams Street, died three years later.

Ivy, Stella and Vera each fulfilled the wishes of their father that his daughters lead unselfish, family-centred lives, though they were more publicly engaged than he had envisaged when he wrote his strange Testament. Pattie had shown the way, and they followed: confident, energetic, educated women engaged in high-minded good works and bringing up their children to be contributors.

Ivy and Herbert did not abandon their ambition for a more comprehensive biography. Herbert was Deakin's literary executor, and after Pattie's death he became the holder of his papers. In 1944 he edited and published Deakin's *Federal Story*, to limited interest, and in 1948 transferred Deakin's papers to the University of Melbourne, hoping to persuade the professor of history, Max Crawford, to write a new biography.

Winwick was still a magnet for Melbourne's more sedate movers and shakers. Around 1950 John La Nauze, the new professor of economic history at the University of Melbourne, started attending its weekend tennis games. La Nauze was a West Australian and an undergraduate student of Murdoch, with whom he had kept in touch as he pursued his academic career, to Oxford on a Rhodes Scholarship and to university posts in Adelaide, Sydney and Melbourne. In 1956 La Nauze committed to writing the Deakin biography. Amid his other duties, it took him the best part of ten years. Herbert was by then nudging ninety, and assisting La Nauze with his memories brought purpose to his last years. La Nauze recalled that 'these talks became one of his few holds on his past life...and I came to know more about the years from 1900 on to AD's retirement in 1913 than anyone else he could talk to.'[7]

La Nauze's main interest was in Deakin as a nation-builder. His two-volume biography is weighted to the years Herbert knew him. Deakin's childhood, youth and colonial political career are dealt with briskly. Herbert's influence can be felt too in the cursory treatment of Deakin's unconventional spiritual life and his lifelong quest for divine reassurance. Of his marriage he says little more than that he and Pattie 'lived happily ever after'.[8] As was the case for Murdoch and most of Melbourne's middle class, the financial disasters of the early 1890s were best forgotten. These omissions aside, La Nauze's achievement is immense, a meticulously researched and sympathetic biography of the public man which is also a detailed history of the Commonwealth's first decade. I have relied on it heavily.

Since the 1930s the National Library had been coveting Deakin's papers. Once La Nauze had finished with them, the family passed them over. Other papers followed: from the Brookes family; from Catherine, whose papers had ended up with Stella; and from Stella. Catherine saved everything associated with her adored brother, and her diary provides intimate views of family relations. The well-organised files of John La Nauze are now also in the National Library.[9] Pattie's papers are still with Vera's descendants.

Accepting Deakin's papers on behalf of the nation on 3 December 1965 the prime minister, Robert Menzies, said that he regarded Deakin as

Australia's greatest prime minister: 'All the foundational policies, not only in the fiscal field, in the defence field, in the industrial field, the pattern of national policy which we have come to accept so much in Australia was laid down by this remarkable man.'[10] When Menzies was reforming non-Labor politics in 1944, after the wartime collapse of the United Australia Party, it was to Deakin's Liberal Party he turned for a name, 'because we were determined to be a progressive party, willing to make experiments, in no sense reactionary'.[11]

It was almost thirty years since the demise of the first Liberal Party in 1917. Menzies knew that, in the face of Labor's popular and effective wartime government, non-Labor had to shake off its reputation for conservative obstructionism if it were to regain its hold on the future. It had to move back to the centre. 'Liberalism,' he said at the new party's launch in August 1945, 'proposes to march down the middle of the road'.[12] The new party could not be seen just as the defender of the material interests of property and business. The homes of the middle class, which he praised in his speech to the 'Forgotten People', were material, but they were also homes spiritual, and he praised the contribution of the middle class to intellectual and artistic life.

In repeating Deakin's Carlylean emphasis on things of the spirit, Menzies was revealing his political formation in Victoria's high-minded colonial liberalism. By mid-century 'things of the spirit' covered the non-material aspects of life, with few religious connotations, as when Victoria's new Liberal premier, Rupert Hamer, asked in his first budget speech, 'What is the profit…in steadily expanding and improving man's supply of material things, if the things of the spirit are dimmed.'[13] Hamer said this in August 1972, just before Gough Whitlam swept to power, claiming culture, the arts and nature for Labor. Before this transformation of Labor into a hybrid social-democratic and trade-union based party, culture mostly belonged to the Liberals, who viewed Labor as the party of philistine materialism.

By 2001, when the centenary of federation was celebrated, Deakin had faded to a face on an information board, one of the bearded worthies who had made the constitution and after whom things are named: a suburb, an electorate, a university, a lecture series. He no longer lived in the contemporary national imagination. Among the political cognoscenti too he had become more of a cypher than a man, as both parties turned away from the protective policies of the early twentieth century towards racially non-discriminatory immigration and neo-liberalism's faith in open markets. He came to represent the now discarded policies of tariff protection, state paternalism, centralised arbitration, imperial nationalism and the racism of White Australia, policies which were shaped in the early decades of the twentieth century and all but gone by its closing.

The turn against Deakin was most evident in the Liberal Party which, under John Howard, remade itself as the joint bearer of the liberal and conservative traditions in Australian politics, reclaiming the free-trade heritage of George Reid and adopting a reactive social conservatism. With material economic issues now dominating the political agenda, Deakin, Reid and Higgins became counters in ideological arguments which had little to do with the historical context of their actions and decisions.[14]

Yes, Deakin did support protection, White Australia, an active state, centralised industrial relations and imperial nationalism; so, to varying degrees, did most of his fellow Australians. And if they were not whole-hearted supporters of all these policies, they were prepared to live with them. That is why they became Australia's shared policy assumptions for three-quarters of a century. Successful politicians in liberal democracies are not original thinkers: their coin is the currency of the age and society in which they compete for support. So it was with Deakin. It is not to the policies he supported that we should look for his achievements, but to his statecraft and the urgent energy he brought to his political work.

Deakin's greatest legislative achievements came about when he led minority governments, taking support from wherever he could get it and compromising to achieve outcomes he believed were in the long-term national interest. With almost unfailing civility and determined optimism, Deakin turned what others might have regarded as a handicap into an opportunity, arguing that his dependence on Labor to pass legislation, and sometimes on members of the Opposition or on independents, had strengthened rather than weakened his achievements, for it made his government's legislation not just the achievement of one party, but 'organic Australian policy', the fruit of wide Australian experience.

Deakin assumed the existence of a consensual centre, which it was the job of politicians to realise in institutions and legislation. This was the place where politics connected with Australian experience and with the nation's practical needs—for defence, for development, for population, for workable institutions of governance, for civilised wages and working conditions. It was more like the nation's beating heart than an ideological position, and the Liberal Party was for him only ever a means to express it. 'We have consistently put our policy in first place,' he said. 'It is for that policy we have politically lived': 'The policy has made us and not we the policy.'

The political world he entered in 1879 was small and intense, animated by passionate commitments and animosities, as Graham Berry fought the conservative Legislative Council in the name of democracy and the people, imbuing this local colonial struggle with world-historical significance. Whirled into politics by chance, the ardent young Deakin felt himself to be a player in world history, an agent of progressive reform engaged in life-or-death struggles with the obstructionists for the colony's future, never wondering why the fathers of English liberalism took an interest in his progress. Had Victorian politics in the early 1880s been calm and procedural, it is unlikely it would have held him.

When the progressive spirit seemed to have deserted the colony in the early 1890s, and the pressing task was financial repair, his interest flagged until he was drawn into the great national cause of federation, where his oratory lifted it from the haggling over border duties to a test of men's souls. Deakin's speech in Bendigo to the ANA in March 1898 was a turning point in the campaign, but it was not his only contribution. As important was that he was prepared to compromise, because he knew that the moment could pass and history move on; as it has done for Australians who want the nation to become a republic. Always aware of how ephemeral were the moments of political opportunity,

Deakin brought a sense of drama to his political work which at times seemed melodramatic but which focussed the minds of the political class—and his own—on what was at stake if courage failed, and made him ready to compromise.

During the federation campaign Deakin always argued for the broad national view against the parochial and sectional. When the constitution was finally law and the Commonwealth inaugurated, he saw it as the duty of those who had argued for federation to make it work. The constitution provided a framework for the government of the new nation—but it was only a framework. Federal institutions had to be built and federal laws passed for areas of federal responsibility. Support for the federal union slumped in the early years, once voters confronted the expense and the states realised how much they had given up. Trials of strength with the states, as well as the parsimonious, had to be won, as in Deakin's battle to establish the High Court.

There was a real danger that if these early Commonwealth governments failed the new federation itself would fail, foundering on partisan differences, parochial jealousies and personal animosities. Western Australia, after all, was only just in, and thirty years later it would try to secede; and North Queenslanders had not entirely given up their desire for a separate state above the 22nd parallel. Federal sentiment and a wide federal perspective had to be nurtured. Again and again in his speeches after federation, Deakin conjured up the map of Australia, reminding his audience that they were no longer just Victorians or South Australians or Tasmanians; they were now also Australians. This was Deakin's great mission in the federal parliament—to make real the promise of a nation carried in the constitution—and he brought all his gifts, his courtesy and his capacity for unstinting work to the task.

Underpinning all this was his religious sensibility. All his actions were done under the eyes of his loving God. This God could be let down and disappointed, but he was not a wrathful God and in his presence Deakin felt no fear. In his occasional low moments Deakin would reflect that, without the belief in a divine purpose for the universe and without faith in the soul's immortality, it would be easy to live selfishly and in the moment. Deakin did not presume to know what the divine purpose was, only to believe that it existed. It gave him a still point from which to view the small struggles and personal vanities of the political world, and the detachment to contemplate the long view of Australia's historic opportunities and strategic challenges. And it gave him the will to persist.

NOTES

The source of the epigraph is Notes for lecture on Real and Ideal, 18 November 1877, National Library of Australia (NLA) MS 1540/3/156.

INTRODUCTION

1   A. G. L. Shaw, 'Foundation and Early History' in Brown-May and Swan (eds), *The Encyclopedia of Melbourne*, 287.
2   Richard Broome, *The Victorians: Arriving*, 27–34.
3   Geoffrey Serle, *The Golden Age*, 369–81.
4   Medley Notebook, Diary Notes for 1880, 330.
5   Hobart *Mercury*, 26 February 1909; see also speech at Murwillumbah, *Sydney Morning Herald*, 22 March 1909.
6   Paul Kelly, *The End of Certainty*.
7   10 May 1909, *Federated Australia*, 256.
8   Autobiographical Notes, Typescript 3/300, 30 December 1915.
9   *Crisis in Victorian Politics*, 1.
10 Gabay, *Messages from Beyond*, 75.

CHAPTER ONE: IMMIGRANTS' CHILD

1   Red Spine Notebook, 4–6 November 1910, 75–76.
2   Alfred Deakin (AD) wrote two portraits of his parents: on 3 June 1908, the day his mother died, Medley Notebook, 32–35; and on 12 November 1913, Counsel Fees Notebook, 232–34. Catherine's portrait, 'The Parents of AD', is at NLA MS 1540/17/369.
3   Rickard, *Family Romance*, 4–5; Eric Richards, *Britannia's Children*, 149–52; James Hammerton, *Emigrant Gentlewomen*, 31.
4   *New Monthly Magazine*, 1 August 1815, 82. His name is spelt Bills.
5   The parish records for St Teilo's, Llanarth are in the Gwent County Records office. William Bill was overseer in 1817–18 and 1828–29, and deputy overseer in 1824–25. He is last mentioned in the parish accounts in 1833, presumably around the time the family moved to Great Campston near Grosmont.
6   They were buried as out-of-county strays from the parish of Kendle Church across the border in Herefordshire. Burials 443 and 455, parish register, St Teilo's, Llanarth, Gwent County Records Office.
7   William Deakin to Sarah Bill, 15 August 1849, Abergavenny, NLA MS 4913, folder 13.
8   Parish register for St Nicholas, Grosmont, Monmouthshire, Marriages 1837–1900. Copy held at parish and supplied by Vicar Jean Prosser, 23 June 2010; Register of Deaths in the District of South Yarra, 21 December 1892, no. 2466.
9   William Deakin, Voyage Diary, typescript, NLA MS 1540/19/367–94.
10 The two books of poems are in Catherine Deakin's papers, NLA MS 4913, folders 9 and 10; William's poem, folder 2. The poems are discussed more fully in Judith Brett, 'Alfred Deakin's Childhood'.
11 Autobiographical Notes, 1; Advertisement, *Argus*, 26 November 1858.
12 Sands and McDougall Melbourne Directories, 1856–60.
13 Headstone, churchyard, St Teilo's, Llanarth.

14 Clue XV, 4 November 1910; Clue XXXIV, 14 February 1913. The poem was published in 1849 and was Queen Victoria's favourite, giving her solace after the death of Prince Albert.
15 Catherine Deakin (CD), 'My first recollections of my only brother', NLA MS 4913, folder 1.
16 Advertisements, *Bendigo Advertiser*, 14 November 1857; 28 June 1858; *Kyneton Observer*, 11 August 1857.
17 CD, 'My first recollections of my only brother', NLA MS 4913, folder 1.
18 Serle, *The Rush to be Rich*, 91.
19 Autobiographical Notes, 3.
20 Michael Cannon, *Melbourne After the Gold Rush*, 402–08; Bessy Bevan Death Certificate, 27 November 1857, Deaths in the District of Melbourne, 1858, registration no. 480; David Lewis Bill Death Certificate, Deaths of the District of Collingwood, 1859, registration no. 183.
21 Autobiographical Notes, 4.
22 'Books and a Boy', NLA MS 1540/4/112.

CHAPTER TWO: MELBOURNE GRAMMAR

1   Advertisement, *Argus*, 20 June 1863.
2   Autobiographical Notes, 7–8.
3   Title 140–187 was transferred to William Deakin on 31 August 1865. Colony of Victoria, Memorandum of Transfer, 4,993.
4   Leather-bound notebook of William Deakin, 14 October 1884, NLA MS 4913, folder 10.
5   La Nauze, *Alfred Deakin*, 8.
6   CD, Diary, 24 April 1868, 16 May 1869, NLA MS 4913.
7   *Argus*, 2 March 1858.
8   Weston Bate and Helen Penrose, *Challenging Traditions*.
9   'Books and a Boy', NLA MS 1540/4/112.
10 Autobiographical Notes, 12–13.
11 CD, Diary, November 1867, NLA MS 4913; Autobiographical Notes, 4.
12 M. Theobold, *Knowing Women*, 32; Bate and Penrose, *Challenging Traditions*, 16 and 46.
13 Autobiographical Notes, 15.
14 John Thompson, cited by Walter Murdoch, *Alfred Deakin*, 13, note 1.
15 La Nauze, *Alfred Deakin*, 20.
16 Counsel Fees Notebook, 147–49; Manning Clark, 'Bromby, John Edward (1809–1889)', *Australian Dictionary of Biography* (ADB).
17 Testimonial from J. E. Bromby, 9 February 1874, cited in La Nauze, *Alfred Deakin*, 23.
18 Counsel Fees Notebook, 149–50.
19 AD to CD, 31 May 1871, NLA MS 4913, folder 13.
20 Counsel Fees Notebook, 154–57.
21 Counsel Fees Notebook, 151; La Nauze, *Alfred Deakin*, 19.
22 Anon., 'On Boys', *Colonial Monthly*, December 1868, cited in Simon Sleight, *Young People and the Shaping of Public Space*, 41.
23 Serle, *Rush to be Rich*, 382; Australian Bureau of Statistics cat. No. 3105.0.65.001, *Australian Historical Population Statistics*, Table 23. Population, age and sex. Vic., 1861–1891.
24 CD, 'Parents of AD', NLA MS 1540/19/370.
25 The November Matriculation Examinations, *Argus*, 18 December 1871.
26 See Richard Twopeny's bemoaning of the child-centredness of colonial family life in *Town Life in Australia*, 1883, 82–83.
27 CD, 'Parents of AD', NLA MS 1540/19/367.
28 Counsel Fees Notebook, 140–42.

CHAPTER THREE: AFTER SCHOOL

1   Counsel Fees Notebook, 163–64.
2   Counsel Fees Notebook, 157–58; interview, *Punch*, 1 October 1903, 406.

3 Carlyle, *Sartor Resartus*, World Classics Series, 148–49.
4 Stewart, 'Britain's Australia', 17.
5 *Emerson's Nature*, 5.
6 Autobiographical Notes, Typescript, NLA MS 1540/3/300.
7 CD, Diary for 1870, NLA MS 4913.
8 His granddaughter, Judith Harley, told me he suffered from what is now called Irritable Bowel Syndrome, as did her mother, Vera.
9 Counsel Fees Notebook, 160.
10 Waugh, *First Principles*, 20–23.
11 Counsel Fees, 157.
12 Reference from Caroline Anderson, Fairlie House, 5 September 1876, NLA MS 1540/20/165.
13 Two mortgages were raised on Adams Street in August 1874. Certificate of title, Colony of Victoria, Vol. 140, Fol. 27887.
14 CD, Diary, August 1874, NLA MS 4913.
15 Counsel Fees Notebook, 167–70.
16 Old exercise book, NLA MS 1540/3/294, 1–14.
17 Autobiographical Notes, 16.
18 Counsel Fees Notebook, 140-2; H. L. Burney to AD, 27 November 1875, NLA MS 1540/4/110; *Quentin Massy*, NLA MS 1540/4/109.
19 Tregenza, *Professor of Democracy*.
20 Tregenza, *Professor of Democracy*, 68–73.
21 Counsel Fees Notebook, 193.
22 Counsel Fees Notebook, 185.
23 H. B. Higgins, Draft Autobiography, NLA MS 1057/3, 63–64.
24 Counsel Fees Notebook, 165.
25 Smith, 'Religion and Free Thought in Melbourne, 1870–1890', 160–68.
26 Counsel Fees Notebook, 171.
27 H. B. Higgins, Draft Autobiography, NLA MS 1057/3, 59–60.

CHAPTER FOUR: THE PLUNGE INTO SPIRITUALISM

1 Personal Experiences of Spiritism, 1202; Counsel Fees Notebook, 155–56.
2 Personal Experiences of Spiritism, 1394.
3 Personal Experiences of Spiritism, 1208.
4 Editorial, *Harbinger of Light*, May 1875, 814.
5 Advertisements in *Harbinger of Light*, 1879.
6 A Spiritual Diary, Preliminary Record, note 1.
7 CD Diary, 13 May to 29 July 1875.
8 Gabay, *Messages from Beyond*, 34–37.
9 Personal Experiences of Spiritism, 1264–1271; Counsel Fees Notebook, 177–79; CD, 'My first recollections of my only brother', NLA MS 4913, folder 1.
10 Terry (ed.), *Spirit Teachings*, 15–16.
11 Personal Experiences of Spiritism, 1425–26.
12 Personal Experiences of Spiritism, 1424.
13 Personal Experiences of Spiritism, 1415–16.
14 Old exercise book, NLA MS 1540/3/294, 49.
15 Gabay, *The Mystic Life of Alfred Deakin*, 107.
16 Pattie Deakin (PD), 'AD. Reminiscences', NLA MS 1540/19/275.
17 Browne, *The Grand Reality*, 506–07.
18 Browne, *Reasons for the Hope that Is in Me*, 3–20; PD, letter to her grandmother in England, 8 July 1879, NLA MS 4913/2/12.
19 AD to PD, 28 December 1880, letter in family's possession.
20 Counsel Fees Notebook, 230–31.
21 AD to PD, 15 July 1881, letter in family's possession.
22 *Harbinger of Light*, December 1876, 1124.

23 AD, Preface, 9 September 1877, *The Lyceum Leader*.
24 AD, 'The Lyceum', *Harbinger of Light*, July 1878, 1427.
25 *Harbinger of Light*, March 1876, 985; April 1876, 999; also Gabay, *Messages from Beyond*, 191–92.
26 Preface to *New Pilgrim's Progress*.
27 *Harbinger of Light*, February 1878, 1348.
28 Personal Experiences of Spiritism, 1423–34.
29 *New Pilgrim's Progress*, 74.
30 *New Pilgrim's Progress*, 134.
31 A. F. Davies, *Skills, Outlooks and Passions*, 31–32.
32 Rickard, *Family Romance*, 42–43.
33 *New Pilgrim's Progress*, 253.

CHAPTER FIVE: LIBERALS, CONSERVATIVES AND DAVID SYME

1   Wright, *A People's Counsel*, 16–18.
2   Serle, *Rush to be Rich*, 22–24.
3   This much-quoted dismissal of the prerogatives of the colony's wealthiest citizens was made in a speech to his Brighton electorate. *Age*, 24 October 1864.
4   Cited in Gwynneth Dow, 'Higinbotham, George (1826–1892)', ADB. See also, Stuart Macintyre, *A Colonial Liberalism*, 17–65.
5   *Federal Story*, 9.
6   Geoffrey Bartlett, 'Berry, Sir Graham (1822–1904)', ADB; Paul Strangio, 'Broken Heads and Flaming Horses: Graham Berry, The Wild Colonial' in Paul Strangio and Brian Costar (eds), *The Victorian Premiers*, 51–73; Raymond Wright, *A People's Counsel*, 84–90.
7   William Stebb (ed.), *Charles Henry Pearson*, 219.
8   *Fortnightly Review*, cited in Murdoch, *Alfred Deakin*, 53.
9   AD to Charles Pearson, 8 June 1878, NLA MS 2503.
10 *Crisis in Victorian Politics*, 3.
11 *Harbinger of Light*, December 1878; March, July, October 1879.
12 La Nauze, *Alfred Deakin*, 70–71.
13 *Crisis in Victorian Politics*, 5.
14 Deakin's account of his relationship with Syme comes mainly from the autobiographical notes he wrote in 1910, which were based on notes made in 1881 when the two men were close. These are in the Counsel Fees Notebook, 194–210. He used these for the brief description of Syme and the *Age* in *Crisis in Victorian Politics*, but not for the rather woolly introduction he wrote for Ambrose Pratt's 1908 biography, *David Syme: Father of Protection in Australia*. Busy as prime minister, he did not then have time to consult his earlier notes and it has none of their vivid detail.
15 Stuart Macintyre, *A Colonial Liberalism*, ch. 3; Stuart Sayers, 'Syme, David (1827–1908)', ADB; L. F. Whitfield, 'The *Age* and Public Affairs'; Serle, *Rush to be Rich*, 26–31.
16 Counsel Fees Notebook, 194–98.
17 Counsel Fees Notebook, 199–200.
18 *Crisis in Victorian Politics*, 3.
19 *Crisis in Victorian Politics*, 5–6.
20 Counsel Fees Notebook, 204–05.
21 This account of Syme's writings on political economy is based on J. A. La Nauze's essay on Syme in *Political Economy in Australia*. The description of his thinking as tending towards state socialism is on 127. See also Stuart Macintyre, 'David Syme and the Pursuit of Progress' in *A Colonial Liberalism*, 87–114.
22 Counsel Fees Notebook, 200–02.
23 Alfred Deakin, Introduction to Ambrose Pratt, *David Syme*, xi.
24 Denovan, *The Evidence of Spiritualism*, 117.
25 PD, 'AD Reminiscences', NLA MS 1540/19/275.
26 Rodney Cherry to AD, 29 April 1906, NLA MS 1540/1/1396.

CHAPTER SIX: WEST BOURKE

1   *Argus*, 10 February 1879.
2   *Crisis in Victorian Politics*, 10.
3   *Crisis in Victorian Politics*, 26.
4   AD to Christopher Crisp, 23 August 1880, NLA MS 743/269.
5   *Crisis in Victorian Politics*, 27–30.
6   Cited in Pratt, *David Syme*, 270.
7   *Age*, 10 February 1879.
8   *Crisis in Victorian Politics*, 32.
9   *Crisis in Victorian Politics*, 32.
10 Notes from 1879, Counsel Fees Notebook, 216
11 *Argus*, 19 February 1879; *Age*, 19 February 1879.
12 *Age*, 3 March 1879.
13 La Nauze, *Alfred Deakin*, 43.
14 Serle gives an unskilled labourer's annual income as ninety to one hundred and twenty pounds a year. *Rush to be Rich*, 91.
15 *Crisis in Victorian Politics*, 37–39; *Harbinger of Light*, April 1879.
16 Wright, *A People's Counsel*, 84–91.
17 *Crisis in Victorian Politics*, 21–22.
18 *Argus*, 9 July 1879.
19 PD, 'AD Reminiscences', NLA MS 1540/19/275.
20 *Crisis in Victorian Politics*, 41–42.
21 Victorian Parliamentary Debates (VPD), 8 July 1879, 29; 30.
22 *Crisis in Victorian Politics*, 42.
23 *Crisis in Victorian Politics*, 42.
24 *Crisis in Victorian Politics*, 24–26; 45–46.
25 *Crisis in Victorian Politics*, 46–48.
26 *Crisis in Victorian Politics*, 50–51.
27 George Watson, *The English Ideology*, ch. 7.
28 *New Pilgrim's Progress*, 253.
29 15 March 1914, typescript from notebook in family's possession; NLA MS 1540/3/303.
30 Interview with Vera White, 25 December 1981.

CHAPTER SEVEN: 'I AM THE BOY'

1   *Crisis in Victorian Politics*, 51.
2   Personal Experiences of Spiritism, 1301–20; quotes at 1301, 1303, 1320.
3   Personal Experiences of Spiritism, 1311–20.
4   Jennifer M. T. Carter, *Eyes to the Future*, 58–59; Pattie Deakin, 'AD Reminiscences', NLA MS 1540/19/275; Hugh Junor Browne, *Astronomy and its Bearing on the Popular* is dedicated to My Friend Sydney G. Watson Esq., 'A Veteran in the Cause of Truth'.
5   Gabay names Mrs Armstrong as the source of the travel prophecy, *Mystic Life*, 17.
6   Jennifer M. T. Carter, *Painting the Islands Vermilion*.
7   Rickard, *Family Romance*, 69.
8   The account of Deakin's experience is based on four letters to Catherine. AD to CD 30 October and 1, 7 and 10 November 1879, NLA MS 4913/2/13b, and on the entry First Voyage, Trip to Fiji, in Medley Notebook, 332–39.
9   Jennifer M. T. Carter, *Painting the Islands Vermilion*.
10 AD to CD, 7 November 1879, NLA MS 4913, folder 13b.
11 Cited in Stuart Banner, *Possessing the Pacific*, 169–170.
12 *Bacchus Marsh Express*, 24 December 1879.
13 *Bacchus Marsh Express*, 3 January 1880.
14 *Crisis in Victorian Politics*, 53.
15 Professor Hamilton, Full Study of Character of Alfred Deakin, 9 January 1880, NLA MS 1540/5/39-42; Poets and Poetry, NLA MS 1540/4/862.

16 Dean Wilson, 'Explaining the Criminal: Ned Kelly's Death Mask', 55–56.
17 *Bacchus Marsh Express*, 14 February 1880.
18 Personal Experiences of Spiritism, 1315; also Diary Notes for 1880, Medley Notebook, 330.
19 *Argus*, 29 May 1880.
20 *Crisis in Victorian Politics*, 54–55.
21 *Age*, 25 June 1880.
22 *Daily Telegraph*, 14 July 1880.
23 *Crisis in Victorian Politics*, 63–67.
24 James David Barber, *The Presidential Character*, 10.
25 Prophecy noted in Diary, 15 August, 1880, Medley Notebook, 330.
26 A Spiritual Diary Personal and Mundane, 6 August 1880.
27 Letter to editor, *Argus*, 7 December 1881.
28 A Spiritual Diary Personal and Mundane, 10 April 1881.
29 Cards in family's possession.
30 Visit to Madame Siecle, 19 January 1881, NLA MS 1540/5/44.
31 *Crisis in Victorian Politics*, 58–61.

CHAPTER EIGHT: MP AND LOVER

1   VPD, 14 September 1880, 216.
2   Patrick Malone to AD, 29 March 1881; NLA MS 1540/8/47.
3   *Crisis in Victorian Politics*, 74–78.
4   Wright, *A People's Counsel*, 90.
5   *Crisis in Victorian Politics*, 78.
6   Weston Bate, 'Bent, Sir Thomas (1838–1909)', ADB.
7   VPD, 17 May 1882, 351.
8   VPD, 17 August 1882, 1459.
9   *Argus*, 26 January 1881.
10 VPD, 5 October 1881, 242.
11 Medley Notebook, 331.
12 Pattie Deakin, Memoirs, held by the family. Cited in Diane Langmore, *Prime Ministers' Wives*, 5–6.
13 AD to PD, 13 July 1881. Letter in possession of the family.
14 AD to PD, 13, 15 and 18 July 1881. Letters in possession of the family.
15 Rickard, *Family Romance*, 70–72.
16 Interview, Vera Deakin.
17 Pattie Deakin, 'AD Reminiscences', NLA MS 1540/19/275; Langmore, *Prime Ministers' Wives*, 6–10; interview, Vera White.
18 AD to PD, 12 January 1882, 28 September 1881. Letters in possession of family.
19 A Spiritual Diary Personal and Mundane, 14 January 1882. The new beginning is at 68. Deakin only numbered the pages of this notebook until 67.
20 'Carlyle's Reminiscences', A Spiritual Diary Personal and Mundane, 20 January 1882.
21 A Spiritual Diary Personal and Mundane, 22 January 1882.
22 AD to PD, 16 February 1882. Letter in possession of family.
23 Diary, 14 February 1882; Counsel Fees Notebook, 339.
24 Counsel Fees Notebook, 12 November 1913, 231.
25 'Memories', December 1889, Medley Notebook, 1540/3/296, 80.
26 Pattie Deakin, 'AD Reminiscences', NLA MS 1540/19/275; AD to CD, 6 April 1882, 18 April 1882, NLA MS 4913, folder 13a.
27 AD to PD, 15 February 1883. Letter in family possession.
28 Diary, 11 January 1882; Counsel Fees Notebook, 339.
29 Certificate of title, Colony of Victoria, Vol. 1339, Fol. 267621.
30 Small leather pocketbook, NLA MS 4913, folder 10; mortgages and transfers on Adams Street, Certificate of title, Colony of Victoria, Vol. 140, Fol. 27887.
31 'A Complaint', 21 January 1883, Literary Memoranda, NLA MS 1540/3/302.

CHAPTER NINE: JAMES SERVICE, ANNEXATION AND FEDERATION

1   Serle, 'Service, James (1823–1899)', ADB.
2   Charles Pearson to Edith Pearson, 11 March 1883, in William Strutt (ed.), *Charles Henry Pearson*.
3   Serle, *Rush to be Rich*, 91.
4   'Two Paths', 4 March 1883, Literary Memoranda, NLA MS 1540/3/302.
5   Serle, *Rush to be Rich*, 72–73.
6   Register of Deputations, VPRS 986, units 4 and 5, Victorian Public Records Office.
7   VPD, 28 August 1883, 836.
8   Statement by PD mainly on her relationship with CD, 1921. In family's possession.
9   Medley Notebook, 94.
10 Diary for 1883; Medley Notebook, 340–41.
11 Red Spine Notebook, 5 November 1910, 72.
12 Red Spine Notebook from back, 6 May 1911, 17.
13 *Argus*, 15 June 1883.
14 *Argus*, 10 October 1877, cited in Thompson, *Australian Imperialism*, 34.
15 'The Makers of the Colonies: The Hon James Service', *Australasian Review of Reviews*, 1892, 126. This was published anonymously; however, Deakin's diary for 1892 records his writing of it. The only copy of this issue I could locate is held by the Veech Library at the Catholic Institute of Sydney.
16 *Age*, 21 April 1883.
17 Serle, *Rush to be Rich*, 183.
18 *Argus*, 4 July 1883.
19 Thompson, *Australian Imperialism*, ch. 5; Serle, *Rush to be Rich*, ch. 6.
20 *Bendigo Advertiser*, 1 October 1883.
21 AD Speech in reply to governor's speech, VPD, 12 June 1884, 85–86.
22 Thompson, *Australian Imperialism*, ch. 4.
23 J. F. Menadue, *A Centenary History of the Australian Natives Association*, 26; Marian Aveling, 'A History of the Australian Natives Association'.
24 Serle, *Rush to be Rich*, 20–21.
25 Clue 260, 15 July 1888.
26 Clue 3, January 1884.
27 AD to PD, 29 January 1884, 5 February 1984. Letters in possession of the family.
28 In 1887 Browne presented a bound collection of his pamphlets to the Victorian Public Library, now the State Library of Victoria: *Astronomy and its Bearing on the Popular Faith: Or, What Is Truth?*
29 PD Memoirs, cited in Rickard, *Family Romance*, 95.
30 I have used the typescript of this diary at NLA MS 1540/5/815-1054, identifying prayers by date and number.
31 Rodney Cherry to AD, 29 April 1906, NLA MS 1540/1/1396. Cherry was a friend of AD's before he entered parliament.
32 David Derham, 'Derham, Frederick Thomas (1844–1922)', ADB.
33 The Vagabond, 'The Sugar Industry', *Argus*, 8 March 1884.
34 AD to Fred Derham, 30 May 1884 and 1 June 1884, Swallow & Ariell Correspondence.
35 Serle, *Rush to be Rich*, 50
36 'Some northern sugar plantations', *Queenslander*, 10 December 1887; 'The Cairns Sugar Lands', *Brisbane Courier*, 14 November 1892.
37 VPD, June 12 1884, 93, 140.

CHAPTER TEN: IRRIGATION AND THE FACTORY ACTS

1   VPD, 10 October 1883, 1386–92.
2   Valerie Yule, 'McColl, Hugh (1819–1885)', ADB.
3   J. A. Alexander, *The Life of George Chaffey*, 79–81.
4   Summary of 1884 diary, Medley, 341.

5   Hugh Junor Browne, *Reasons for the Hope that Is in Me*, 22–24.
6   PD, 'AD Reminiscences', NLA MS 1540/19/275.
7   AD to Fred Derham, 1 January 1885, Swallow & Ariell Correspondence.
8   Jeffrey Richards, '"Passing the Love of Women": Manly Love in Victorian Society'.
9   PD, 'AD Reminiscences', NLA MS 1540/19/275.
10 PD to CD, 5 January 1885, NLA MS 1540/19/19.
11 US Travel Diary, 29 January 1885; AD to Fred Derham, 10 February 1885, Swallow &
    Ariell Correspondence.
12 US Travel Diary, 11 February 1885, 20–21.
13 J. L. Dow, 'America and Big Things,' *Age*, 20 December 1919, NLA MS 1540/10/106.
14 US Travel Diary, Mexico, 19–24 February, 35–77.
15 US Travel Diary, 161–66.
16 Note, 21 March 1885, NLA MS 1540/10/107.
17 PD to CD, 2 and 14 February 1885, NLA MS 1540/19/13-15 and 20-30.
18 Medley Notebook, 109.
19 AD to Graham Berry, 9 February 1885, copy in La Nauze, NLA MS 5248, folder 61; AD
    to F. T. Derham, 10 Feb 1885, Swallow & Ariell Correspondence.
20 Royal Commission on Water Supply. First Progress Report: Irrigation in Western America,
    1885.
21 [AD], 'The Makers of the Colonies: The Hon. James Service', *Review of Reviews*, 1892,
    106–07.
22 Royal Commission on Water Supply, 11.
23 Royal Commission on Water Supply, 109.
24 Prayer XXI, 23 August 1885; Diary, 3 August 1885.
25 Prayer XXVII, 11 October 1885.
26 VPD, 10 November 1885, 1758.
27 Serle, *Rush to be Rich*, 100–06; T. G. Parsons, 'Alfred Deakin and the Victorian Factory
    Act of 1885'.
28 VPD, 30 June 1896, 94 ff.
29 Diary, 7 March 1884.
30 Serle, *Rush to be Rich*, 98.
31 Clue 75, 18 October 1885.
32 AD to CD, 15 April 1873, NLA MS 4913/2/13a.
33 Lovell's Library, Vol. 9, No. 494. Lovell published cheap editions of British books for the
    American market. The Links notebook has notes to *Past and Present* made on 17 October
    1885, NLA MS 1540/3/5. The underlining in the Lovell copy is at 196, 189, 229.
34 Clue 92, 15 November 1885.
35 Diary, 22 October, 15 and 18 December 1885.
36 Diary, 31 December 1885.
37 AD to Christopher Crisp, 5 January 1886, NLA MS 743/281-3.
38 Raymond Wright, *A People's Counsel*, 90.
39 Diary, 27 January 1886.
40 Diary, 5 March 1886.
41 Serle, *Rush to be Rich*, 40–42.
42 VPD, 22 June 1886, 851.
43 Serle, *Rush to be Rich*, 106; *Argus*, 6 April 1866.
44 VPD, 24 June, 415–47; AD, 'Irrigation in Australia', NLA MS 1540/10/30; Benjamin Rankin,
    'Alfred Deakin and water resources policy in Australia', 124–25.
45 Diary, 5 October 1885; 15 February 1886.
46 VPD, 25 August, 1221; Margaret Glass, *Tommy Bent*.
47 Diary, 14 December 1885.
48 VPD, 15 December 1886, 2912.
49 Diane Barwick, *Rebellion at Coranderrk*, 298–99.

50   G. Nanni and A. James, *Coranderrk: We will Show the Country*, 27; VPD, 16 May 1882, 278; 18 May 1882, 360–61.
51   VPD, 23 September 1890, 1713; Jan Critchett, *Untold Stories*, 98–100.
52   VPD, 7 October 1886, 1810.
53   Patrick Wolfe, *Traces of History,* 47–53.
54   Medley Notebook, 107.
55   Diary, 31 December 1886.

CHAPTER ELEVEN: TRIUMPH IN LONDON

1   Lists at front of 1887 Diary, NLA MS 1540/2/6.
2   Counsel Fees Notebook, 212, written 12 November 1913.
3   La Nauze, 89.
4   AD to CD, 2 February 1887, NLA MS 4913, folder 13c.
5   AD to Fred Derham, 29 January 1887, Swallow & Ariell Correspondence.
6   AD to Fred Derham, 1 February 1887.
7   AD to Fred Derham, 26 February 1887.
8   UK Travel Diary, 207.
9   'Anglo-Colonial Notes', *Otago Daily Times*, 25 May 1887.
10   UK Travel Diary, 24 March 1887, 236.
11   UK Travel Diary, 31 March 1887, 245–49.
12   AD to CD, 7 April 1887, NLA MS 1540/19/43.
13   M. Theresa Earle to AD, 30 May 1887, NLA MS 1540/19/376-9.
14   John Edward Kendle, *The Colonial and Imperial Conferences 1887–1911*, 5–7.
15   Circular of Dispatch from Secretary of State to the Colonies to Sir H. B. Loch, 25 November 1886, NLA MS 1540/9/339.
16   Froude, *Oceana, or, England and Her Colonies*, 15.
17   John Seeley, *The Expansion of England*, 1883, cited in Robert Young, *The Idea of English Ethnicity*, 211.
18   R. G. Menzies, 'Not to Yield', Menzies papers, NLA MS 4936/10, ch. IV.
19   Young, *The Idea of English Ethnicity*, 43 ff.
20   Speech reported in *Argus*, 14 May 1887 and 'Our London Letter, 8 April', *Otago Daily Times*, 25 May 1887.
21   UK Travel Diary, 262–64; Edward A. Arnold to AD, 4 April 1887, NLA MS 1540/9/354.
22   Cited in Roberts, *Salisbury*, 18.
23   Holland to Salisbury, 10 March 1887, cited in La Nauze, 92.
24   Proceedings of the Colonial Conference, 1887, vol. 1, 7.
25   Proceedings of the Colonial Conference, 1887, vol. 1, 24–25.
26   AD to Fred Derham, 6 April 1887.
27   Diary 4, 5 April, 1887; AD to PD, 5 April 1887, cited in Murdoch, 103.
28   AD to Charles Pearson, 15 May 1887, NLA MS 2503.
29   AD to Fred Derham, 6 April 1887; Geoffrey Serle, 'Service, James (1823–1899)', ADB.
30   Address from Horsham ANA, *Argus*, 18 June 1887.
31   'The Imperial Conference', *Otago Daily Times*, 20 April 1887.
32   '1887—A Retrospect', *Australian Insurance and Banking Record*, January 1888, 1–3.
33   'Banquet to the Colonial Delegates', *The Times*, London, 21 April 1887.
34   UK Travel Diary, 337.
35   Diary, 26 April 1887.
36   Cited in Roberts, *Salisbury*, 464.
37   *Federal Story*, 22–23.
38   AD to Fred Derham, 27 April 1887.
39   Salisbury to Holland, 27 April 1887, cited in Andrew Roberts, *Salisbury*, 464.
40   John Edward Kendle, *The Colonial and Imperial Conferences*, 12–16.
41   AD, *Federal Story*, 23.
42   UK Travel Diary, 267, 272, 317–19.

NOTES TO PAGES 138 TO 151

AD to Fred Derham, 15 April 1887.
UK Travel Diary, 322.
'Our London Letter', 18 May, *Otago Daily Times*, 6 July 1887.
AD to Fred Derham, 22 April 1887.
UK Travel Diary, 354.
Report from London, 6 May, *Age*, 11 June 1887.
AD to CD, 7 and 30 April 1887, NLA MS 1540/19/43 and 54.
AD to CD, 30 April 1887, NLA MS 1540/19/57.
UK Travel Diary, 312.
Notes at back of trip diary dated 24 May 1887 on page for 6 July, NLA MS 1540/2/6/111.
AD to PD, 1 May 1887. Letter in family possession.

CHAPTER TWELVE: NATIVE SON

Diary 16, 17 June 1887; 'The Return of Mr Deakin', *Argus*, 18 June 1887.
Age, 17 June 1887.
Interview, Vera White.
AD to Graham Berry, 28 July 1887, La Nauze Papers, NLA MS 5248, folder 61.
Argus, 22 June 1887.
Alexander Sutherland, *Victoria and its Metropolis*, 490.
VPD, 5 July 1887, 247–51.
Argus, 12 July 1887.
Notes at back of 1887 diary on page dated 12 July, NLA MS 1540/2/6.
Gabay, *Mystic Life*, 59–62.
Diary, 13 July 1887.
VPD, 5 October 1887, 1498–99.
Royal Commission on Water Supply, Fourth Progress Report. Irrigation in Egypt and Italy, 18 November 1887.
Royal Commission on Water Supply, Fourth Progress Report, 6.
Robert Putnam, *Bowling Alone*.
Royal Commission on Water Supply, Fourth Progress Report, 23.
Speech at Newmarket, *Argus*, 22 December 1887; Clue 163, 28 December 1887.
Pearson, *National Life and Character*, 84.
Stefan Collini, *Public Moralists*.
National Life and Character, 25–26; 180–81; 227; 259.

CHAPTER THIRTEEN: HIGH BOOM

Prayer XLIV, 22 January 1888.
Diary, 12 April 1888.
Clue 240, 24 May 1888.
Diary, 1 May 1888.
Literary Memoranda, 5 May 1888, NLA MS1540/3/202.
The Chief Secretary at Newmarket, *Argus*, 22 December 1887.
AD to Josiah Royce, 30 June 1888, NLA MS 1540/1/50 (copy); Royce, 'Impressions of Australia', *Scribner's Magazine*, 9, 1891, 79.
Royce, 'Impressions of Australia', 76.
Royce, 'Impressions of Australia', 85.
John Fitzgerald, *Big White Lie*.
Argus, 6 October 1887; 27 October 1887.
Serle, *Rush to be Rich*, 295–96; VPD, 8 December 1887, 2562–64; 2573; 18 December 1887, 2641.
Myra Willard, *History of the White Australia Policy*, 84–88; Serle, *Rush to be Rich*, 298–302.
Knutsford to AD, 24 April 1888, NLA MS 1540/9/57.
Diary, 13 June 1888.
Willard, *History of the White Australia Policy*, 90.

17 Pearson, *National Life and Character*, 16.
18 AD to Josiah Royce, 30 June 1888, NLA MS 1540/1/50 (copy); 'Autumn Has Come', 17 June 1888, NLA MS 1540/3/30-82.
19 Benedict Anderson, *Imagined Communities*.
20 Clue 260, 15 July 1888.
21 Prayer XLV, 15 July 1888.
22 La Nauze, *Alfred Deakin*, 77–79; Rickard, *Family Romance*, 20–22; Langmore, *Prime Ministers' Wives*, 17–19.
23 AD to Charles Dilke, 9 January 1888, British Library, Additional MS 43877, 79–80.
24 Graeme Davison, 'Festivals of Nationhood'; Robert Wilson, *Great Exhibitions: World Fairs, 1851–1937*; CD's diary for 1880, NLA MS 4913.
25 Official Record of the Centennial International Exhibition, 1888–1889, Preface.
26 Graeme Davison, 'Centennial Celebrations' in Graeme Davison et al (eds), *Australians 1888*, ch. 1; Official Record of the Centennial International Exhibition, 176–79.
27 Wray Vamplew (ed.), *Australian Historical Statistics*, 41.
28 Serle, *Rush to be Rich*, 252.
29 Cannon, *The Land Boomers*, 56; *Table Talk*, 9 July 1886.
30 *Banking and Insurance Record*, 1888, 1–5, 582–83, 814–15; Serle, *Rush to be Rich*, 247–48; Ville and Withers, *Cambridge Economic History*, ch. 10.
31 S. M. Inghams, 'Mirams, James (1839–1916)', ADB.
32 AD to Berry, 9 April 1889, La Nauze Papers, NLA MS 5248, folder 61.
33 Diary 28 June, 2 July 1889; Don Garden, *Theodore Fink*, 53–54.
34 Prayers XLVI, XLVII, XLVIII, 5, 12, 19 August 1888. These are all Sundays.
35 VPD, 15 August 1888, 666–67.
36 AD to Dilke, 23 August 1888, British Library, Additional MS 43877, 79-80; Serle, *Rush to be Rich*, 322.
37 AD to Berry, 9 April 1889, La Nauze Papers, NLA MS 5248, folder 61.
38 Diary, 9–15 June 1889.
39 J. A. Alexander, *The Life of George Chaffey*, 174, 161.
40 Gabay, *Mystic Life*, 111.
41 Prayer LXII, 6 July 1889.
42 Erland J. Brock, *Swedenborg and his Influence*. This includes an essay by Al Gabay on Swedenborg's influence on Deakin.
43 'Testament for His Daughters'.
44 This section relies on the detailed reading of Deakin's Gospel according to Swedenborg in Al Gabay, *Mystic Life*, 109–17.

CHAPTER FOURTEEN: 1890—FEDERATION AND THE MARITIME STRIKE

1 *Federal Story*, 17.
2 A. W. Martin, 'Parkes, Sir Henry (1815–1896)', ADB.
3 *Federal Story*, 26–28.
4 John Hirst, *Sentimental Nation*, 93.
5 6 February 1890, Sally Warhaft (ed.), *Well May We Say*, 6.
6 John Lack, 'Service and Gillies' in P. Strangio and B. Costar (eds), *The Victorian Premiers*, 88–89.
7 AD to Charles Dilke, 5 September 1889, British Library, Additional MS 43877/91-4.
8 Stuart Svensen, *The Sinews of War*.
9 Prayer LXXVII, 30 August 1890.
10 Memo on swearing in of special constables, 29 August 1889; Memo from Melbourne Superintendent of Police, 25 August 1890. PROV VPRS 937/P0000/513, The Maritime Strike.
11 *Argus*, 30 August 1890.
12 John V. Barry, 'Price, John Giles (1808–1857)', ADB.
13 Chris Clark, 'Price, Thomas Caradoc (1842–1911)', ADB.

14 VPD, 2 September 1890, 1353.
15 PROV VPRS 937/P0000/513, The Maritime Strike.
16 VPD, 2 September 1890, 1356–59.
17 VPD, 10 September 1890, 1536.
18 Official Record of Centennial International Exhibition, 272.
19 Lack, 'Service and Gillies' in Strangio and Costar (eds), *The Victorian Premiers*, 88–89.
20 VPD, 21 August, 1209.
21 VPD, 21 August 1890, 1218–19.
22 'Optimism', 13 July 1889, Literary Memoranda, NLA MS 1540/3/202.
23 'Above the Speaker', *Argus*, 30 August 1890.

CHAPTER FIFTEEN: ALFRED, PATTIE AND CATHERINE

1 Interview, Vera White.
2 AD to Berry, 9 April 1889; Rickard, *Family Romance*, 80; PD statement on her relationship with CD, 1921.
3 Diary, 28 May 1888, 1 October 1889.
4 Langmore, *Prime Ministers' Wives*, 21; Rickard, *Family Romance*, 80; PD statement on her relationship with CD, 1921.
5 PD, 'AD Reminiscences', NLA MS 1540/19/275.
6 Cited in Rickard, *Family Romance*, 16.
7 Diary, 3 August 1890; Prayer LXXVII, August 1890.
8 Clues, 432, 3 August 1890.
9 Diary, 15 July 1890; Prayer, 20 July 1890.
10 Deana Heath, *Purifying Empire*, 101–06.
11 'Testament for his daughters'.
12 Diary, 15, 18 October 1890.
13 Statement by PD on her relationship with CD, 1921; CD Diary, 10 January to Easter 1891, NLA MS 4913.

CHAPTER SIXTEEN: TANGLED TIMES

1 VPD, 30 October 1890, 2252; 2289–90.
2 Syme to AD, 31 October 1890.
3 Diary, 4 November 1890; 24 November 1890.
4 *Temple and Tomb*, 6.
5 David Walker, *Anxious Nation*, 20–23.
6 *Irrigated India*, 209; Interview with Mr Deakin, Adelaide *Advertiser*, 17 February 1891.
7 *Temple and Tomb*, 148–49.
8 *Irrigated India*, 230–32.
9 Murdoch, *Alfred Deakin*, 169.
10 Lord Cross to AD, 2 April 1891, NLA MS 1540/10/38.
11 Telegram, Philip Mennell to AD, 24 August 1892, NLA MS 1540/10/48.
12 Preface, *Temple and Tomb*.
13 *Irrigated India*, 10.
14 *Temple and Tomb*, 131.
15 *Irrigated India*, 43–47.
16 *Federal Story*, 33.
17 Federation Convention Debates Sydney, 5 March 1891, 86.
18 John Playford, 'Kingston, Charles Cameron (1850–1908)', ADB.
19 VPD, 21 July 1891, 495–96; La Nauze, 'The Name of the Commonwealth of Australia', in Helen Irving and Stuart Macintyre (eds), *No Ordinary Act*.
20 Marilyn Lake, 'Oh to be in Boston Now that Federation's Here'.
21 AD to CD, 1 January 1891, NLA MS 4913, folder 13c.
22 Clue 445, n.d.—late 1890 to mid-1891, NLA MS 1540/3/282-288.
23 *Argus*, 12 June 1891; Diary, 11 June 1891.

24 Prayers, 9 August 1891, 14 August 1891, 4 November 1891, 20 September 1891, 2 November 1891.
25 Notes on Séances, inserted in Diary 1891, NLA MS 1540/2/12/89 and 99. The sittings were on 9 August and 6 September, both Sundays.
26 'Town Talk', 26 November 1891, cutting in NLA MS 4913, folder 2.
27 AD to CD, 11 January 1892, NLA MS 4913, folder 13c.
28 Blainey, *From Gold to Paper*, 86; Banking Record, 1892, 866–67; George Meudell, *Pleasant Career*, 17–18, 280.
29 Red Spine Notebook, 4–11 May 1911, 22 from back.
30 Serle, *Rush to be Rich*, 266–67.
31 *Argus*, 11 August 1893.
32 Diary 24, 25 June, 16, 26 July 1888.
33 *Australasian*, 28 February 1891.
34 *Table Talk*, 13 May 1892, 4 November 1892; *Argus*, 13 April 1893.
35 *Banking Record*, October 1888, 673.
36 *Table Talk*, 4, 11 December 1891; *Argus*, 1 December 1891.
37 Diary, 28 November 1891; Prayer CXX, 28 November 1891.
38 *Bohemia*, 3 December 1891.
39 Prayer CXXI, 2 December 1891.
40 William Bayles to AD, 7 December 1891, NLA MS 1540/20/3.
41 Diary, 3 January 1892.
42 Diary, 18 February 1892.
43 *Federal Story*, 33.
44 VPD, 3 December 1891, 2857–58; J. Waugh, 'The Centenary of the Victorian Voluntary Liquidation Act 1891'.
45 Cannon, *Land Boomers*, 117–25; Ann Mitchell, 'Munro, James (1832–1908)', ADB.
46 Canon, *Land Boomers*, 204–05, 211–12; 152.
47 Garden, *Theodore Fink*, 75–77.
48 Diary, 30 March 1891.
49 AD to Dilke, 11 December 1891, British Library, Additional MS 43877/110.
50 AD to Pearson, 14 December 1892, NLA MS 2503.
51 Invitation, from Progressive Political League, 23 July 1891, NLA MS 1540/8/6; AD's reply, 28 July 1891, NLA MS 1540/8/11; Strangio, *Neither Power nor Glory*, 20–21; *Argus, Age*, 13 April 1892.
52 AD to Dilke, 14 March 1892, British Library, Additional MS 43877/110.
53 Lack, 'David Syme and the Three Stooges' in Strangio and Costar (eds), *Victorian Premiers*, 100–04.
54 J. A. Alexander, *The Life of George Chaffey*, 190–209; *Mildura Cultivator*, 2 July 1892.

CHAPTER SEVENTEEN: THE DEATH OF WILLIAM AND RETURN TO THE LAW

1   Memorandum, 31 October 1892, NLA MS 1540/19/471.
2   PD statement on her relationship with CD, 1921, in family's possession.
3   CD Diary, September 1892 to January 1893, NLA MS 4913.
4   Diary, 2 January 1893.
5   AD to Royce, 3 April 1893, NLA MS 1540/1/203b-c.
6   CD's diary for 1893. The séance was held on 16 April. NLA MS 4913.
7   Clue 529, 28 May 1892, conceived February 1891.
8   AD to Charles Pearson, 14 December 1892, NLA MS 2503; Diary, 1892, pages at beginning.
9   Income-tax assessment notice for year ending 31 December 1894, NLA MS 1540/20/99.
10 prov.vic.gov.au/online-exhibitions/deeming, accessed 22 February 2015.
11 Cannon, *Land Boomers*, 96–100; *Argus*, 4 March 1893.
12 AD to Charles Pearson, 18 March 1893, NLA MS 2503.
13 *Sydney Mail*, 18 March 1893.
14 *Argus*, 2 May 1893.

15 Asa Briggs, 'Melbourne' in *Victorian Cities*.
16 AD speech at dinner, *Age*, 9 December 1895. Deakin repeats this interpretation in his introduction to Ambrose Pratt's 1908 authorised biography of Syme.
17 AD to Charles Pearson, 13 June 1893, NLA MS 2503.
18 Trevor Sykes, *Two Centuries of Panic*, ch. 14; Geoffrey Blainey, *Gold and Paper*, ch. 10, quote 162–63.
19 Charles Pearson, 'The Political Situation in Victoria', *Speaker*, 26 March 1892.
20 Prayer CLXXIX, 11 December 1892.
21 Clues 635, 15 July 1894 (an old note).
22 Clues 622, 22 February 1894.

CHAPTER EIGHTEEN: MIDLIFE

1   *Federal Story*, 53.
2   *Age*, 8 February 1893; *Prahran and St Kilda Chronicle*, 18 February 1893.
3   *Argus*, 15 March 1893.
4   Irving, 'When Quick Met Garran: The Corowa Plan'; Hirst, *Sentimental Nation*, chs 6 and 7.
5   Quartly, 'Victoria' in Irving (ed.), *Centenary Companion to Australian Federation*, 243.
6   AD to Charles Pearson, 18 March 1893, NLA MS 2503.
7   *Argus*, 14 December 1893.
8   Diary, 4 June 1894; *Argus*, 5 June 1894; Quartly, 'Victoria' in Irving (ed.), *Centenary Companion to Australian Federation*, 247–49.
9   John M. Tregenza, 'Pearson, Charles Henry (1830–1894)', ADB; Edith Pearson to AD, 7 June 1894, 29 September 1894, NLA MS 1540/1/154, 272.
10 Cited in Rickard, 'The Quiet Little Man in a Brown Suit' in Strangio and Costar, *The Victorian Premiers*, 110.
11 *Bendigo Independent*, 11 September 1894; *Australasian*, 15 September 1894.
12 *Geelong Advertiser*, 20 September 1894.
13 *Free Lance*, 23 April 1896.
14 *Bendigo Advertiser*, 26 September 1894; *Argus*, 25 September 1894; *Table Talk*, 22 September 1894.
15 W. G. McMinn, 'Reid, Sir George Houston (1845–1918)', ADB.
16 Diary, 25 January 1895 – 5 February 1895.
17 Geoffrey Serle, 'Turner, Sir George (1851–1916),' ADB.
18 *Federal Story*, 68–67.
19 John Lack, 'David Syme and the three stooges', in Strangio and Costar (eds), *Victorian Premiers*, 95–96.
20 'Personal Experiences of Spiritism', 1425.
21 Diary, 5, 6 December 1898.
22 'Personal Experiences of Spiritism', 1451.
23 La Nauze, *Alfred Deakin*, 39.
24 He gave a lecture on Hinduism to the Australian Church, 7 June 1895.
25 Diary, 19 May 1891.
26 Jill Roe, *Beyond Belief*, 69, 91–92, 119; Diary, 24 May 1896.
27 C. R. Badger, *Charles Strong and the Australian Church*; Malcolm Wood, *Presbyterianism in Colonial Victoria*, 339.
28 Jill Roe, *Beyond Belief*, 34–38.
29 Badger, *Charles Strong and the Australian Church*, 226–31.
30 *North Melbourne Courier*, 22 September 1893; Colin Holden and Richard Trembath, *Divine Discontent*, 15.
31 *Prahran Chronicle*, 16 June 1894; Melbourne *Punch*, 14 June 1894, 376.
32 Marian Sawer, *The Ethical State*, 36–38.
33 *Age*, 19 March 1895.

34 John Rickard, *Class and Politics*, 88 passim; John Lack, 'Mauger, Samuel (1857–1936)', ADB; *Argus*, 13 August, 1895.
35 VPD, 12 November 1895, 3149.
36 *Age*, 14 April 1896; *Free Lance*, 23 April 1896.
37 Cited in Murdoch, *Alfred Deakin*, 190.
38 *Colac Herald*, 28 April 1896.
39 Sargood's letter, *Argus*, 23 April 1896; Deakin's response, VPD, 30 June 1896, 94–110.
40 Macintyre, *Winners and Losers*, 48–49; Serle, 'The Victorian Legislative Council 1856–1950'.
41 Diary, June 1896.
42 *Argus*, 4–7 May 1896.
43 Report of the Mildura Royal Commission, Victoria, 1896. Deakin's evidence, 221–35.
44 W. K. Hancock, *Australia*, 71.
45 *Argus*, 17 July 1896.
46 Very frequent diary entries on cycling, 21 August 1895 passim.
47 Clues 624 and 625, 21 May 1894.
48 Advertisement, *North Melbourne Gazette*, 31 July 1896, 3; Diary, June and July 1896; Prayer CCXX, 1 August 1896.
49 Diary, 15 August 1896.
50 AD to CD, 20 December 1898, NLA MS 4953, folder 13c.

CHAPTER NINETEEN: 'THE TIMES THAT TRY MEN'S SOULS'
1   Convention Debates, Adelaide, 30 March 1897, 295, 302.
2   Prayer CCXXIV, 4 April 1897.
3   AD, *Federal Story*, 83–84; Hirst, *Sentimental Nation*, 171–72.
4   Convention Debates, Adelaide, 30 March 1897, 293–98.
5   Convention Debates, Sydney, 20 September 1897, 818.
6   *Argus*, 2 October 1897; 15 October 1897.
7   *Federal Story*, 173.
8   *Federal Story*, 62–64.
9   *Federal Story*, 83.
10 Hirst, *Sentimental Nation*, 176.
11 Hirst, *Sentimental Nation*, 249.
12 *Federal Story*, 86, 88.
13 *Federal Story*, 34–35.
14 Barton to AD, 24 July 1894, NLA MS 1540/11/15.
15 *Age*, 22 August 1899.
16 Sydney Convention Debates, 6 September 1897, 49.
17 Hirst, *Sentimental Nation*, 178–79.
18 *Federal Story*, 92–96; Diary, 14, 15 March 1898.
19 Appendix, *Federal Story*, 175–78. 'The warm life blood of federation' does not appear in the later printed text of the speech, but is quoted in the brief report in the ANA's journal, *Advance Australia*, April 1898.
20 *Argus*, 17 March 1898; Joseph Jones, 'Gay, William (1865–1897)', ADB.
21 *Advance Australia*, April 1898.
22 Federal Story, ch. 14; La Nauze, *Alfred Deakin*, 175–77.
23 Barton to AD, 15 June 1898, NLA MS 1540/11/80-1.
24 Hirst, *Sentimental Nation*, 191–99.
25 Hirst, *Sentimental Nation*, ch. 10; *Federal Story*, ch. 15.
26 *Argus*, *Age*, 27 July 1899.
27 Prayer CCXXVII, 19 June 1897.
28 Prayer CCXXXVII, 3 December 1900.
29 'The Federal Faith', *Prahran Telegraph*, 8 April 1898.
30 Prayer CCXXXIII, 4 June 1898.

CHAPTER TWENTY: LONDON, 1900

1   Herbert Brookes to his angel lover, 11 May 1899, Brookes papers, NLA MS 1924/1/232.
2   Interview, Vera Deakin.
3   AD to Herbert Brookes, 30 August 1899, 3 July 1899, NLA MS 1540/19/65/68.
4   Herbert Brookes to AD, 29 August 1899, NLA MS 1540/19/65.
5   Alison Patrick, 'Brookes, Herbert Robinson (1867–1963)', ADB; Peter Cochrane, 'How Are the Egyptians Behaving?'
6   AD to Herbert Brookes, 15 September 1899, NLA MS 1540/19/70.
7   AD to Herbert Brookes, 1 October 1899, NLA MS 1540/19/75.
8   AD to Herbert Brookes, 27 October 1899 and 23 November 1899, NLA MS 1540/19/78 and 82.
9   Interview, Vera Deakin; AD to Herbert Brookes, 17 September 1899, NLA MS 1540/19/73.
10 Rickard, *Family Romance*, 100.
11 Diaries, 1895–97 passim.
12 AD to Herbert Brookes, 17 September 1899, NLA MS 1540/19/73.
13 AD to CD, 11 March 1891, NLA MS 4913, folder 13c.
14 Rickard, *Family Romance*, 126.
15 Communication from Judith Harley.
16 Diary, January to June 1890; Interview, Vera Deakin; Diane Langmore, *Prime Ministers' Wives*, 21.
17 *Federal Story*, 144.
18 *Federal Story*, 154.
19 *Federal Story*, 162.
20 *Federal Story*, 171.
21 *Argus*, 19 July 1900.
22 VPD, 14 August 1900, 803; *Australasian*, 18 August 1900.
23 Bernhard Wise to AD, 28 July 1899; NLA MS 1540/11/109.
24 *Argus*, *Age*, 17 August 1900.
25 Vice Chancellor of Oxford Sir Thomas Fowler to AD, 17 May 1900, NLA MS 1540/11/482; Diary, 1 December 1900.
26 Diary, 28 March 1900; *Age*, 24 September 1900.
27 La Nauze, Introduction, *Federated Australia*, i, ix.
28 Mennell to AD, 28, 29 November, 5 December 1900, NLA MS 1540/7/8-10; Diary, 28, 29, 30 November 1900. Judith Harley, *My Grandfather's Legacy*.
29 Nicol Dunne to AD, citing Deakin's words, January 1901, NLA MS 1540/12-13.
30 Cited in La Nauze, Introduction, *Federated Australia*, x.
31 *Age*, 30 November 1900; Prayer CCXXXVI, 29 November 1900.

CHAPTER TWENTY-ONE: THE HOPETOUN BLUNDER

1   Until 1977 the name of the electorate was spelt Ballaarat, which was the spelling often also used for the town. However, the modern spelling has been used throughout.
2   Diary, 22 September 1900.
3   Weston Bate, *Lucky City*, 265–66.
4   *Age*, *Argus*, 2 November 1900.
5   Diary, 26 September 1900.
6   La Nauze, *Alfred Deakin*, 261–62.
7   La Nauze, *Alfred Deakin*, 206–07.
8   Barton to AD, 16 November 1900, NLA MS 1540/14/9; AD to Barton, 7 November 1900, NLA MS 51/1/723.
9   AD to Barton, 14 and 19 November 1900, NLA MS 51/1/725 and 727.
10 Barton to AD, 20 and 5 November 1900, NLA MS 1540/14/10 and 6.
11 AD, 'The Approaching Inauguration', 29 November 1900, in *Federated Australia*, 3–6.
12 The following account of the appointment of the first prime minister is based on La Nauze's very detailed 1957 essay *The Hopetoun Blunder*, which includes Deakin's three

crucial letters to Barton in full. These can also be found in the correspondence files for 1900 in Barton's papers at the NLA.

13 Chris Cuneen, 'Lyne, Sir William John (1844–1913)', ADB.
14 *Federal Story*, 105.
15 Hirst, *Sentimental Nation*, 279–88.
16 *Argus*, 21 December 1900.
17 *Argus*, 26 December 1900.
18 'The First Ministry', 31 December 1900, *Federated Australia*, 13–15.
19 *Argus*, 27 December 1900.
20 Counsel Fees Notebook, 13 February 1909, MS 1540/3/290 NLA, 49.
21 Philip Mennell to AD, 10 and 26 May 1901, NLA MS 1540/1/613-6.

CHAPTER TWENTY-TWO: CELEBRATIONS AND BEGINNINGS

1   Diary, 1 January 1900; J. J. Keenan, *The Inaugural Celebrations of the Commonwealth of Australia*.
2   'About People', *Age*, 2 January 1901.
3   salvationarmy.org.au/en/Who-We-Are/History-and-heritage/Australias-first-film-studio, accessed 22 September 2015; Inauguration of the Commonwealth of Australia (1901), clip, aso.gov.au/titles/tv/mister-prime-minister-deakin/clip1/?nojs, accessed 22 September 2015.
4   Henry Gyles Turner, *The First Decade of the Australian Commonwealth*, 16.
5   'Deakin', *United Australia*, 20 August 1901.
6   *Age*, 6 February 1901.
7   Gerald E. Caiden, *Career Service*, 56.
8   *Age*, *Argus*, 7 March 1901.
9   'The Liberal Outlook', *United Australia*, 1 January 1900, 12.
10 Federation Debates, Sydney, 335; Federation Debates, Adelaide, 297–98.
11 'The Liberal Outlook', *United Australia*, 1 January 1900, 11–12; McMillan's Reply, 1 July 1900, 4–5.
12 *Federated Australia*, 26 February 1901, 41–42.
13 For a detailed discussion of the results, see Geoffrey Sawer, *Australian Federal Politics and Law*, 17–18.
14 *Age*, *Bendigo Independent*, 30 March 1900.
15 *Federated Australia*, 2 April 1901, 49–50.
16 Bolton, *Edmund Barton*, 289–91.
17 F. K. Crowley, 'Forrest, Sir John (1847–1918)', ADB.
18 Diary, 6–9 May 1901.
19 *Age*, 10 May 1901.
20 Invitation to Mrs W. Deakin to the Opening Ceremony of the Commonwealth Parliament, NLA MS 4913, folder 3.
21 *Catholic Press*, 9 November 1901.
22 La Nauze, *Alfred Deakin*, 242–43.
23 *Federated Australia*, 4 December 1900, 8.
24 VPD, 14 September 1880, 216.
25 R. D. Garran, *Prosper the Commonwealth*, 155.
26 Diary, 12 July 1901, *Age*, 15 July 1901.
27 Medley, Clue 779, 13–24 June 1901.
28 Prayer CCXXXVII, 4 August 1901.
29 Prayer CCXL, 11 August 1901, 5 a.m.
30 Prayer XLI, 12 August 1901, 4 a.m.
31 Prayer XLI, 12 August 1901, 4 a.m.

CHAPTER TWENTY-THREE: ATTORNEY-GENERAL AND ACTING PRIME MINISTER

1   Commonwealth Parliamentary Debates (CPD), 7 August 1901, 3503.
2   CPD, 12 September 1901, 404–07.

3 See Gwenda Tavan, *The Long, Slow Death of White Australia*, 11–22.
4 J. S. Mill, 'Representative Government' in *Three Essays*, 380.
5 CPD, 12 September 1901, 4805.
6 *Federated Australia*, 8 October 1901, 80.
7 Myra Willard, *History of the White Australia Policy*, 122.
8 CPD, 8 July 1901, 4636.
9 *Federated Australia*, 1 October 1901, 78.
10 CPD, 12 September 1901, 4812.
11 Atlee Hunt Diary, 13 January 1904, NLA MS 1100.
12 *Commonwealth Franchise Act (1902)*.
13 Jennifer Norberry, 'Voters and the Franchise: The Federal Story', Australian Parliamentary Library, Research Paper 17, 2001–02.
14 H. L. Nielsen, *The Voice of the People*; Rickard, *Class and Politics*, 177–79.
15 CPD, 18 March 1902, 10962–87.
16 Diary, 19 December 1901.
17 Prayer LIV, 23 March 1902.
18 AD to Barton, 24 April 1902, NLA MS 1540/14/118.
19 AD to Brookes, 21 April 1902, NLA MS 1540/19/136.
20 Macintyre, *Oxford History*, 46.
21 Bolton, *Edmund Barton*, 238–39.
22 AD to Barton, 24 April 1902, NLA MS 1540/14/118 and 119.
23 Barton to AD, 24 April 1902, NLA MS 1540/14/121.
24 13 February 1909, Counsel Fees Notebook, 49.
25 Atlee Hunt Diary, 1902, 1904, NLA MS 1100.
26 *Argus*, 2 May 1902; Barton to AD, 1 May 1902, NLA MS 1540/14/122; Diary, 1 May 1902.
27 *Age*, 29 May 1902; Diary, 14, 15, 16, 21, 23 May 1902 for meetings with Hopetoun.
28 John Linlithgow (Hopetoun) to AD, 11 June 1902, NLA MS 1540/14/143; La Nauze, 302–03.
29 Diary, 11 July 1902.
30 AD to Herbert Brookes, 17 July 1902, NLA MS 1540/19/142.
31 La Nauze, *Alfred Deakin*, 273.
32 La Nauze, *Alfred Deakin*, 266–70.
33 *Federated Australia*, 1 April 1902, 96–97.
34 Convention Debates, Adelaide, 13 April 1897, 500.
35 *Bendigo Advertiser*, 4 August 1902.
36 Souter, *Acts of Parliament*, 71.
37 Diary, 3 September 1902; CPD, 3 September 1902, 15677 ff.
38 *Federated Australia*, 16 September 1902, 104.
39 CPD, 3 September 1902, 15679.
40 Prayer LVI, 24 August 1902.
41 Adelaide *Advertiser*, 23 September 1904.

CHAPTER TWENTY-FOUR: 1903

1 Medley Notebook, 161–63.
2 Barton to AD, 19 October 1902, NLA MS 1540/14/235.
3 The incident is described in detail in La Nauze, *Alfred Deakin*, 255–57.
4 R. M. Crawford, 'Tom Roberts and Alfred Deakin'.
5 Frederick W. H. Myers, *Human Personality*, 482–85.
6 Hugh Browne, *The Grand Reality*, 506.
7 Zorah Cross, 'Pattie Deakin', Hobart *Mercury*, 11 December 1935; Frank Bongiorno, 'In this world and the next', 189.
8 'Twenty-one years', Medley Notebook, 5 from back.
9 Diary, 3 April 1903; Rickard, *Family Romance*, 105–06.
10 CPD, 9 June 1903, 588.

11 CPD, 9 June 1903, 616.
12 Diary, 9 June, 25 July and 30 July 1903.
13 PD on her relations with CD, 1921. In family's possession.
14 Diary, 23–31 July 1903; *Family Romance*, 106.
15 Prayer LXVIII, 2 August 1903.
16 CPD, 24 July 1903, 2614.
17 CPD, 30 July 1903, 2863–64; 2882–83.
18 CPD, 9 September 1903, 4842, 4850–51.
19 Rickard, *Class and Politics*, 192–94.
20 *Federal Story*, 49–50.
21 Diary, 28 July 1903.
22 Prayer LXXII, 30 August 1903.
23 Diary, 7 September 1903.
24 *Federal Story*, 34.
25 AD to Barton, 17 September 1903, NLA MS 51/1/1258a; Counsel Fees Notebook, 13 February 1909, 49.
26 Prayer LXXIV, 20 September 1903; LXXV, 24 September 1903; Diary, 21–30 September 1903.
27 Newton Wanliss to AD, 30 September 1903, NLA MS 1540/13/13.
28 Melbourne *Punch*, 1 October 1903, 460. The interviews, by 'Lauderdale', were collected into a book in 1904 and republished in a facsimile edition edited by Michael Cannon in 1977. Deakin's home looks modest compared with the mansions of many other of Victoria's representative men.

CHAPTER TWENTY-FIVE: PRIME MINISTER I

1   Hughes and Graham, *Handbook of Australian Government and Politics, 1890–1964*, 467.
2   Cited in Childe, *How Labour Governs*, 18.
3   Judith Brett, *Australian Liberals*, 16–18.
4   *Argus*, 30 October 1903; electionspeeches.moadoph.gov.au/speeches/1903-alfred-deakin, accessed 4 January 2016.
5   *Federated Australia*, 2 and 10 November 1903, 124–27; *Argus*, 30 October 1903.
6   Chamberlain to Mennell, 22 September 1903, NLA MS 1540/1/926.
7   Volume of press clippings, *Morning Post*, 26 September 1903, NLA MS 1540/7374, no. 137.
8   Hammond Hall to AD, 2 November 1903, NLA MS 1540/1/931.
9   McMinn, *George Reid*, 201–02.
10 Sawer, *Australian Federal Law*, 35–36.
11 *Federated Australia*, 9 February 1902, 133–35; *Age*, 2 February 1904.
12 Loveday, P. et al (eds), *The Emergence of the Australian Party System*, ch. 8.
13 Bede Nairn, 'Watson, John Christian (Chris) (1867–1941)', ADB.
14 CPD, 22 March 1904, 779–90.
15 PD to Herbert Brookes, 6 April 1904, NLA MS 1924/1/1237.
16 Hunt Diary, 15 April 1904, 18 April 1904, NLA MS 1100.
17 AD to Bavin, 15 April 1904, NLA MS 560/2/2.
18 CPD, 19 April 1904, 1048.
19 CPD, 21 April 1904, 1244.
20 Prayer XVI, 24 April 1904.
21 AD to Bavin, 27 April 1904, NLA MS 560/2/3.
22 See Hughes, CPD, 20 May 1904, 1381.
23 Prayer XII, 21 February 1904, NLA MS 1540/5/993; Prayer XXVII, 25 February 1904, which has the note: see XII, 21 February, NLA MS 1540/5/1014. As these prayers are out of order in the typescript, I have given the page numbers.

CHAPTER TWENTY-SIX: LABOR IN, LABOR OUT

1 CPD, 27 April 1905, 1247–50.
2 McMinn, *George Reid*, 203.
3 CPD, 19 May 1904, 1335.
4 Forrest to AD, 21 and 25 April 1904, NLA MS 1540/15/346 and 365.
5 Wise to AD, 12 and 20 May 1904, NLA MS 1540/16/35-6 and 48.
6 Wise to AD, n.d. (August 1904?), NLA MS 1540/16/135.
7 Ross McMullin, 'Leading the World' in Faulkner and Macintyre (eds), *True Believers*, 33.
8 Typescript of undated memorandum of understanding, NLA MS 1540/16/877-8.
9 Forrest to AD, 18 May 1904, NLA MS 1540/16/44.
10 CPD, 19 May 1904, 1338–40.
11 Counsel Fees Notebook, 13 February 1909, 49.
12 George Reid, *My Reminiscences*, 233.
13 Prayer XXI, 29 May 1904.
14 AD to Watson, 30 May 1904, NLA MS 1540/16/70.
15 *Argus*, 28 June 1904.
16 *Age*, 2 August 1904.
17 *Age*, 3 August 1904.
18 AD to Syme, 3, 4, 5 and 9 August 1904, NLA MS 1540/16/107, 109-11, 112, 113; Syme to AD, 9 August 1904, NLA MS 1540/16/114.
19 Prayer XXX, 3 August 1904.
20 Prayer XXXII, 11 August 1904.
21 McMinn, *George Reid*, 209.
22 Reid, *My Reminiscences*, 234.
23 Sawer, *Australian Federal Politics and Law*, 38–39.
24 Cited in Palmer, *Henry Bournes Higgins*, 177.
25 Hughes, CPD, 12 August 1904, 4218.
26 Hunt Diary, 12 August 1904, NLA MS 1100.
27 Melbourne *Punch*, 18 August 1904.
28 CPD, 12 August 1904, 4232.
29 Fitzhardinge, *That Fiery Particle*, 154, 168; Fitzhardinge, 'Hughes, William Morris (1862–1952)', ADB.
30 *Age*, 16 August 1904.
31 *Age*, 23 August 1904.
32 CPD, 12 October 1904, 5494.
33 Samuel Mauger to AD, 23 August 1904, NLA MS 1540/16/628.
34 Watson, *Caledonia Australis*.
35 Rickard, 'McLean, Allan (1840–1911)', ADB.
36 CPD, 12 October 1904, 5472–515.
37 Prayer XXVII, 14 July 1904.
38 Therese Radic, 'George Marshall-Hall (1862–1915)', ADB.
39 Prayer XXXV, 23 October 1904.
40 Jessie Strong to Herbert Brookes, 27 February 1901, NLA MS 1924/1/461.
41 Ivy Deakin to Herbert Brookes, 20 January 1903, NLA MS 1924/1/1157.
42 'Confession of My Ideal', March 1904, NLA MS 1240/1/1224.
43 Cited in Rickard, *Family Romance*, 111.
44 Diary, 20 December 1904; Jessie Strong to Herbert Brookes, 25 February 1905, NLA MS 1240/1/1273.
45 PD to Herbert Brookes, 19 December 1905, NLA MS 1240/1/1296; Vera Deakin to Brookes, n.d., NLA MS 1240/1/1299.
46 Pat Jalland, *Australian Ways of Death*, 170–71.
47 La Nauze, 201–02; morningtoncemetery.com/Denominations/Historic-C-of-E/Strachan-Kate, accessed 26 October 2016.

CHAPTER TWENTY-SEVEN: ANOTHER PATH?

1   'M.S.' Written 10–13 April and 12 June 1904, Clue 818, Medley Notebook, 194–98. Gabay discusses the religious meanings of this narrative in *Mystic Life*, 130–32.
2   Gabay, *Mystic Life*, 152. These include an untitled manuscript notebook, MS 1540/5/1506 NLA, begun on 5 April 1905. There is a typescript of this at NLA MS 1540/5/1459-99 which omits some pages. Citations are from both.
3   Untitled manuscript, Typescript, NLA MS 1540/5/1484.
4   Prayer XXV, 16 June 1904; Prayer XXXVII, 29 January 1905.
5   Brookes to AD, 15 February 1905, NLA MS 1924/1/1273.
6   Andrew Thompson, *Imperial Britain*, 67.
7   AD to Leo Maxse, 25 April 1904, NLA MS 1540/7/19.
8   Deakin's further correspondence with Maxse, NLA MS 1540/7/20–38.
9   AD to Forrest, 5 April 1905, cited in La Nauze, *Alfred Deakin*, 381.
10 Untitled manuscript, original, NLA MS 1540/5/1506, 13, 15.
11 Untitled manuscript, typescript, NLA MS 1540/5/1463-4.
12 Untitled manuscript, typescript, 12 April 1905, NLA MS 1540/5/1485.
13 Untitled manuscript, typescript, note added after interview with Booth, NLA MS 1540/5/1462.
14 Colonel Unsworth, 'The Hon. Alfred Deakin', Obituary, NLA MS 1540/23/278.
15 Untitled manuscript, typescript, NLA MS 1540/5/1484.
16 Untitled manuscript, typescript, NLA MS 1540/5/1471.
17 Zachary Gorman, 'Debating a Tiger Cub: The Anti-Socialist Campaign'.
18 Reid to AD, 18 March 1905, NLA MS 1540/16/277.
19 L. F. Crisp, *Australian Federal Labour Party*, 270–73.
20 Syme to AD, 6 April 1905, NLA MS 1540/16/291.
21 Dame Elizabeth Couchman, 'History of AWNL, 1904–45', MS 8713, box 23/6 (a) SLV.
22 Pratt, *David Syme*, 231–32.
23 Lyall Hunt, 'Hackett, Sir John Winthrop (1848–1916)', ADB; Merab Harris Tauman, 'O'Connor, Charles Yelverton (1843–1902)', ADB.
24 *Morning Post*, London, 20 March 1903, Press clippings, NLA MS 1540/7/374, no. 113.
25 *Daily News*, Perth, 15 May 1905.
26 Untitled manuscript, typescript, May 1905, NLA MS 1540/5/1488.
27 Medley Notebook, 29 May 1905, 281.
28 Diary, 31 May 1905.
29 Chapman to AD, 9 and 16 June 1905, NLA MS 1540/16/274 and 371.
30 Beale to AD, 4 June 1905, NLA MS 1540/1/1165.
31 Carruthers to AD, 7 June 1905, NLA MS 1540/16/323.
32 Beale to AD, 11 and 16 June 1905, NLA MS 1540/1/1167 and 1170.
33 Watson to AD, 22 June 1905, NLA MS 1540/16/392.
34 *Age*, 26 June 1905.
35 Reid, CPD, 29 June 1905, 41, 54.
36 AD to Watson, 28 June 1905, NLA MS 1540/16/41.
37 Diary, 28 June 1905.
38 CPD, 29 June 1905, 41–57.
39 CPD, 29 June 1905, 73.
40 CPD, 29 June 1905, 60.
41 CPD, 29 June 1905, 79.
42 AD to Turner, 1 July 1905, NLA MS 1540/16/435 (draft).
43 CPD, 1 August 1905, 412; Diary 28 June 1905.
44 AD to Bavin, 8 July 1905, NLA MS 560/2/13; *Morning Post*, London, 11 August 1905 (written 3 July 1905), NLA MS 1540/7/374, no. 233.
45 Reid, *My Reminiscences*, 242.
46 Counsel Fees Notebook, 48.
47 Reid to AD, 1 January 1905, NLA MS 1540/16/199.

48 McMinn, *George Reid*, 216; Reid's speech at Hawthorn, *Argus*, 23 May 1905.
49 AD to Northcote, 4 July 1905, NLA MS 1540/16/437, copy.
50 *Leader*, 15 July 1905; *Bendigo Advertiser*, 12 July 1905.
51 *Federated Australia*, 3 July 1905, 152.
52 *My Reminiscences*, 249.
53 He did write to Richard Hodgson at the American Society for Psychical Research to request some assistance, but as we only have Hodgson's reply we can only speculate as to what he asked. Diary, 7 September 1904; Richard Hodgson to AD, 18 October 1904, NLA MS 1054/1/1052-3.

CHAPTER TWENTY-EIGHT: PRIME MINISTER II

1   16 October 1904, Medley Notebook, 13–15 from back.
2   Richard Gillespie, 'Dr Thomas George Beckett (1859–1937)', collections.museumvictoria.com.au/articles/2970, accessed 6 June 2016; *Argus,* 6 July 1906.
3   Untitled manuscript, typescript, 10 September 1905 and 22 October 1905, NLA MS 1540/5/1024 and 1489.
4   Diary, 28 July 1905.
5   CPD, 1 August 1905, 414, 417.
6   'The PM's refutation of the Labour Party's Charges' from our Australian Correspondent, NLA MS 1540/15/429.
7   Counsel Fees Notebook, 8 February 1909, 48.
8   CPD, 26 July 1905, 185–86.
9   Melbourne *Herald*, 12 June 1905. The interview was tabled in the Senate on 31 August 1905, Papers Presented to Parliament (Commonwealth), 1905, vol. II, 315–17; Meaney, *Search for Security*, 126.
10 Diary, 2 August 1905; Leo Maxse to AD, 27 September 1905, refers to AD's letter of resignation, 15 August 1905, NLA MS 1540/1/1185.
11 CPD, 26 September 1906, 2457-73; La Nauze, 430–31.
12 AD to CD, 20 May 1915, MS 4913 NLA, folder 13c.
13 Medley Notebook, 1 January 1906, 10 from back.
14 PD to Ivy and Herbert Brookes, 9 January 1906, NLA MS 1924/1/1303.
15 Diary, 2 September 1905.
16 *Ballarat Star*, 19 January 1906, 6; *Barrier Miner* (Broken Hill), 26 January 1906.
17 Melbourne *Punch*, 8 February 1906.
18 *Express and Telegraph* (Adelaide), 26 June 1906.
19 La Nauze, *Alfred Deakin*, 312–13.
20 Malcolm Shepherd, 'Memoirs', NAA A1632, 28.
21 Vida Goldstein to AD, 22 October 1906, NLA MS 1540/15/618.
22 *Argus*, 4 and 5 July 1906.
23 Forrest, Isaacs, Lyne, Chapman, Playford, Groom, Ewing and Keating to AD, 23 August 1906, NLA MS 1540/1/1540a.
24 Bernhard Wise to AD, 14 August 1906; Walter James to AD, 17 August 1906, NLA MS 1540/1/1494 and 1501.
25 AD to Samuel Mauger, 10 September 1912, cited in La Nauze, *Alfred Deakin*, 415–16.
26 Prayers XXVI, 5 August 1906; XXVIII, 1 October 1906; see also XXX, 25 November 1906.
27 The following discussion relies on La Nauze's detailed discussion of policy towards the New Hebrides and British New Guinea in *Alfred Deakin*, chapters 19 and 20, and on Roger Thompson, *Australian Imperialism in the Pacific*.
28 *Federated Australia*, 12 February 1901, 37–38; 11 March 1902, 91–92.
29 La Nauze, *Alfred Deakin*, 444–47.
30 La Nauze, *Alfred Deakin*, 448–49.
31 Lord Elgin to Northcote, 9 March 1906, *New Hebrides Correspondence*, 14.
32 AD to Northcote, 13 June 1906, *New Hebrides Correspondence*, 37–44.
33 Thompson, *Australian Imperialism*, 184–86; La Nauze, *Alfred Deakin*, 451; *New Hebrides Correspondence*, 52.

34 La Nauze, *Alfred Deakin*, ch. 20, has a very detailed discussion of Deakin's dealings with the issue of New Guinea. My much briefer discussion draws on this.
35 Peter Maiden, *Missionaries, Cannibals and Colonial Officers*.
36 CPD, 23 August 1906, 337, 3340, 3345.
37 See letter from H. Eitaki, Consul for Japan, to Barton, 3 May 1901, reprinted in Meaney, *Australia and the World*, 121–22.
38 Meaney, *Search for Security*, 129–33.

CHAPTER TWENTY-NINE: IMPERIALIST

1   *Argus*, 26 March 1906.
2   Speech at Ballarat, 'Protection and Practical Legislation or Anti-Socialism', 24 March 1906.
3   Winthrop Hackett to AD, 2 and 24 April 1906, NLA MS 1540/15/519 and 525.
4   David Syme to AD, 14 and 27 March 1906, NLA MS 1540/15/505 and 513.
5   Winthrop Hackett to AD, 24 April 1906, NLA MS 1540/15/525.
6   Gorman, 'Debating a Tiger Cub', 39–48.
7   F. K. Crowley, 'Cook, Sir Joseph (1860–1947)', ADB; McMinn, *George Reid*, 93.
8   For example, 'The Liberal Party and its Liberal Programme', 29 March 1906, NLA MS 1540/15/1807.
9   Election policy speech, Ballarat, 17 October 1906, electionspeeches.moadoph.gov.au/speeches/1906-alfred-deakin, accessed 12 May 2016.
10 Crisp, *Australian Federal Labour Party*, 159–162.
11 Protection and Practical Legislation, 24 March 1906, 28.
12 Forrest to AD, 10 July 1906, NLA MS 1540/15/559.
13 Watson to AD, 30 May 1906, NLA MS 1540/15/536.
14 Frank Fox, *Bulletin* cutting, 10 May 1906, NLA MS 1540/1/1414.
15 'Election Policy Speech, Ballarat', Melbourne *Herald*, 18 October 1906. Scott is identified as the author in his letter to AD, 20 October 1906, NLA MS 1540/15/614.
16 Watson to AD, 17 December 1906, NLA MS 1540/15/656; McMullin, *Light on the Hill*, 60.
17 AD to Tom Bavin, 27 February 1907, NLA MS 1540/1/38.
18 *Age*, 13 December 1906.
19 Australian Politics and Elections Data base, University of Western Australia, elections.uwa.edu.au/listelections.lasso, accessed 12 May 2016; Sawer, *Australian Federal Politics and Law*, 62–63; Turner, *First Decade*, 132–33.
20 Watson to AD, 17 and 27 December 1906, NLA MS 1540/15/ 656 and 671.
21 AD to Watson, draft, 3 January 1907, NLA MS 1540/1/682.
22 Prayer XXXI, Xmas Day, 1906.
23 Turner, *First Decade*, 133–34; Hunt, 'Federal Memories: 1907 London', NLA MS 1100, folder 17.
24 Diary, 23–24 February 1907; AD to Bavin, 25 February and 1, 6 and 10 March 1907, NLA MS 560/37, 39–41.
25 Prayers XXXIV and XXXV, 1 and 2 February 1907.
26 CD Diary, 5 March 1907, NLA MS 4913.
27 Hunt, 'Federal Memories: 1907 London', NLA MS 1100, folder 17; PD to Ivy and Herbert Brookes, 27 March 1907, NLA MS 924/1/1367.
28 PD to family, cited in Diane Langmore, 26.
29 Chamberlain to AD, 26 April 1906, NLA MS 1540/1/1390.
30 AD to Campbell-Bannerman, 13 April 1907, NLA MS 1540/15/1406-7.
31 La Nauze, *Alfred Deakin*, 500–02; Turner, *First Decade*, 137–38.
32 Morley to Minto (Vice-Roy of India), 2 May 1907, cited in La Nauze, *Alfred Deakin*, 480–81.
33 Speech at 1900 Club, Report, *Argus*, 20 April 1907; Diary, 19, 24 April 1907; Hunt, 'Federal Memories: London 1907', NLA MS 1100, folder 17.
34 Tennyson to AD, n.d. [after April 19] 1907, NLA MS 1540/15/1475.

35 Turner, *First Decade*, 145–46.
36 Richard Jebb, *Studies in Colonial Nationalism*.
37 Diary, April and May 1907; La Nauze, *Alfred Deakin*, 512–13.
38 Counsel Fees Notebook, 13 February 1909.
39 AD to Amery (draft), 26 May 1907, cited in La Nauze, *Alfred Deakin*, 513. I have been unable to locate the original in Deakin's papers.
40 Memorandum of Interview between Mr Deakin and Representatives of the Admiralty, 24 April 1907, NLA MS 1540/15/1606.
41 La Nauze, *Alfred Deakin*, 524–26; Turner, *First Decade*, 139–40; Meaney, *Search for Security*, 141–50.
42 AD to Jebb, 23 July 1906, NLA MS 339/1/4a-b.
43 *Argus*, 17 and 20 May 1907; Turner, *First Decade*, 154.
44 Frank Harris to AD, 19 April 1907, NLA MS 1540/12/1429.
45 Hunt, 'Federal Memories: London 1907', NLA MS 1100 folder 17.
46 PD to Ivy Brookes, 19 April 1907, 3 and 8 May 1907, NLA MS 1924/1/1371, 1372, 1379-82; PD, 'AD Reminiscences', NLA MS 1540/19/275.
47 PD to Ivy, 3 May 1907, NLA MS 1924/1/372.
48 *Argus*, 24 April 1907.
49 Deakin records many of Pattie's meetings in his diary; Diane Langmore, 'Pattie Deakin', in *Prime Ministers' Wives*.
50 La Nauze, *Alfred Deakin*, 148–50.
51 PD, 'AD Reminiscences', NLA MS 1540/19/275.
52 *The Times*, 20 June 1907.
53 Prayer XXXVII, 21 July 1907.

CHAPTER THIRTY: DEFENCE AND THE NEW PROTECTION

1 Forrest to AD, 25, 28 and 30 July 1907, NLA MS 1540/15/727, 731 and 734.
2 Diary, July and August; note 3–4 August 1907, at back.
3 Diary, 9 August 1907.
4 Turner, *First Decade*, 107.
5 Hughes to Jebb, 23 September 1907, cited in La Nauze, *Alfred Deakin*, 424.
6 See Prayers, XXXVII, 25 July 1907; XI, 7 July 1907; XLI, 13 October 1907.
7 Turner, *First Decade*, 176–77.
8 Syme to AD, 8 and 9 October 1907, MS 1540/15/747 and 749.
9 McMullin, *Light on the Hill*, 62.
10 *Federated Australia*, 21 October 1907, 213–14.
11 Murphy, D. J., 'Fisher, Andrew (1862–1928)', ADB; Clem Lloyd, 'Andrew Fisher' in Michelle Grattan (ed.), *Australian Prime Ministers*.
12 CPD, 13 December 1907, 7509–36.
13 Counsel Fees Notebook, 154.
14 Diary, 27 November 1907; CPD, 13 December 1907, 7509–36.
15 'New Protection: Explanatory Memorandum', Papers presented to Parliament, no. 147, 1907–08, vol. 2, 1887–89.
16 These two paragraphs on the New Protection draw on La Nauze, *Alfred Deakin*, 413–14; Macintyre, *Winners and Losers*, 54–56; Isaacs and Macintyre (eds), *The New Protection*, ch. 2; Rickard, *H. B. Higgins*, 171–74; Sawer, *Australian Federal Politics and Law*, 83.
17 La Nauze, *Alfred Deakin*, 432–33.
18 Prayers XLV–XLIX, 25 December 1907 – 12 January 1908.
19 Elizabeth Morrison, *David Syme*, 379–85; Tribute, *Age*, 17 February 1908; Introduction, Ambrose Pratt, *David Syme*.
20 Turner, *First Decade*, 182–83.
21 Prayer LII, 22 March 1908.
22 Diary, 9 April 1907; Counsel Fees Notebook, 13 February 1909, 49; *Argus*, 11 April 1908.
23 La Nauze, *Alfred Deakin*, 433–34; *Age*, 14 April 1908.

24   Diary, 30 April 1908.
25   *Federated Australia*, 20 April 1908, 232–33.
26   CD Diary, June 1908, NLA MS 4913; Prayer LVL, 3 June 1908.

CHAPTER THIRTY-ONE: THE GREAT WHITE FLEET

1   Lake and Reynolds, *Drawing the Global Colour Line*, 196–97. Whitehall edited Deakin's
     letter of invitation before sending it on. Deakin's letter to Reid in the US National Archives
     is cited in Reynolds and Lake, 197.
2   Lake and Reynolds, *Drawing the Global Colour Line*, ch. 7.
3   *Age*, 24 February 1908; Meaney, *Search for Security*, 164–65.
4   Grey to Elgin, 22 February 1908, cited in Meaney, *Search for Security*, 165.
5   Cited in Lake and Reynolds, *Drawing the Global Colour Line*, 200.
6   *Argus*, 16 March 1908.
7   Meaney, *Search for Security*, 166.
8   'The Commonwealth Crisis' was serialised in the *Lone Hand* from October 1908 to August
     1909. In 1909 it was published in book form as *The Australian Crisis*. Meaney, *Search for
     Security*, 159.
9   Meaney, *Search for Security*, 159–62; David Walker discusses Australian invasion narratives
     in *Anxious Nation*, ch. 8.
10   Frank Fox to AD, n.d. 1907, probably December, NLA MS 1540/1/1840; AD's reply to
     Fox is cited in Meaney, *Search for Security*, 160, note 4. I have been unable to locate the
     original, as the NLA references he used do not coincide with the current system.
11   Rodney G. Boland, 'Bedford, George Randolph (1868–1941)', ADB; Correspondence from
     Bedford about Deakin's investment in the Seymour and Leichhardt syndicates, and in a
     pastoral property, NLA MS 1540/20/26, 28, 31.
12   AD to Richard Jebb, NLA MS 339/1/19-20.
13   Meaney, *Search for Security*, Churchill's views cited 164 and 155.
14   *Argus*, 20 August 1908.
15   'The American Fleet', 25 August 1908, *Federated Australia*, 240–41.
16   CD Diary, 29 and 31 August, NLA MS 49113.
17   'The American Fleet', 2 March 1908, *Federated Australia*, 228–30.
18   Meaney, *Search for Security*, 172.
19   Sam Furphy, 'Aboriginal House Names and Settler Australian Identity', 59.
20   Prayer LVIII, 16 August 1908; Prayer LIX, 13 September 1908.
21   McMullin, *Light on the Hill*, 66; Strangio, 'Fusion in Victoria' in Strangio and Dyrenfurth
     (eds), *Confusion*, 150–51.
22   CPD, 6 November 1908, 2136–67.
23   Diary, 31 October – 7 November 1908.
24   CPD, 10 November 1908, 2139–40; Diary, 11 November 1908.
25   'Deakin Falls Again', 16 November 1908, *Federated Australia*, 245.
26   McMinn, *George Reid*, 246–47.
27   *Federated Australia*, 14 December 1909, 248.

CHAPTER THIRTY-TWO: FUSION

1   Diary, 11 June 1908.
2   Statement by PD on her relations with CD, 1921. In family possession.
3   Diary, 15 August 1908; Prayer LX, 12 December 1908.
4   CD, Diary, 1909–10, NLA MS 4913.
5   Diary, 28 December 1908; Clue 92, 28 December 1908, NLA MS 1540/3/282.
6   Medley Notebook, 1 January 1909, 36.
7   Statement by PD on her relationship with CD, 1921. In family's possession.
8   AD to Joseph Cook, 12 February 1909, NLA MS 1540/16/490.
9   Diary, 1, 4 February 1908.
10   AD to CD, 4 February 1909. NLA MS 4913, folder 13.

11 AD to CD, 20 July 1899, NLA MS 4913, folder 13c.
12 AD to CD, 9 February 1909, NLA MS 4913, Folder 13.
13 Medley Notebook, 1 August 1908, 30. This has copies of many of the anniversary poems. 'P. Lovely poem', Diary, 3 August 1910.
14 Clue 17, 17 January 1909, NLA MS 1540/3/282.
15 Counsel Fees Notebook, 6, 7 and 8 February 1908, 37–48.
16 AD to Joseph Cook, 12 February 1909, NLA MS 1540/16/490.
17 AD to Bavin, 18 February 1905, NLA MS 560/2/80.
18 Hobart *Mercury*, 26 February 1909; see also speech at Murwillumbah, *Sydney Morning Herald*, 22 March 1909.
19 Diary, 31 March 1909.
20 Meaney, *Search for Security*, 177–80; La Nauze, *Alfred Deakin*, 553–57.
21 Deakin's speech to the inaugural meeting of the Commonwealth Liberal and Progressive League, *Sydney Morning Herald*, 7 April 1909.
22 La Nauze, *Alfred Deakin*, 555–56, which includes citation of AD to Amery, 12 April 1909.
23 Counsel Fees Notebook, 25 July 1909, 57.
24 AD to CD, 31 May 1909, NLA MS 4913, folder 13b; La Nauze, *Alfred Deakin*, 542–45.
25 *Federated Australia*, 10 May 1909, 256.
26 *Federated Australia*, 21 December 1908, 249.
27 AD to J. D. Farleigh, 18 May 1909, NLA MS 1540/16/576.
28 AD to Bavin, 21 May 1909, NLA MS 560/2/89; AD to Amery, 30/7/1909, cited in La Nauze, *Alfred Deakin*, 545. This argument draws on Sean Scalmer's persuasive account of the free-traders' commitment to fusion in 'Free Traders and the Puzzle of Fusion', in Strangio and Dyrenfurth (eds), *Confusion*.
29 *Argus*, 26 May 1909.
30 'The Liberal Party', pamphlet, NLA MS 1924/18/51.
31 J. Hume Cook, Report of the meeting of the Liberal Protectionist Party, 25 May 1909, The History of the Movement, NLA MS 601/3/63, 1–19.
32 Judith Brett, 'Deakin and the Liberal Protectionists' in Strangio and Dyrenfurth (eds), *Confusion*; Ian Hancock, 'Wise, George Henry (1853–1950)', ADB.
33 Quoted in Hume Cook, The History of the Movement, NLA MS 601/3/63, 29.
34 *Age*, 27 May 1909, printed Deakin's letter to Fisher. His papers have a very heavily scored draft, NLA MS 1540/16/595, which includes the page numbers in Hansard of Fisher's statement in November 1908.
35 *Age*, 28 May 1909.
36 Martha Rutledge, 'Kelly, William Henry (1877–1960)', ADB; CPD, 27 May 1909, 169; La Nauze, *Alfred Deakin*, 567.
37 CPD, 27 May 1909, 132–33.
38 CPD, 28 May 1909, 175.
39 Malcolm Shepherd, 'Memoirs', CRS A1632, NAA, 129.
40 CPD, 29 May 1909, 176–77.

CHAPTER THIRTY-THREE: PRIME MINISTER III

1 Counsel Fees Notebook, 63–64; Diary, 2 June 1909.
2 Turner, *First Decade*, 222–23.
3 Shepherd, 'Memoirs', NAA CRS A1632, 71.
4 CPD, 24 June 1909, 392.
5 CPD, 22 July 1909, 1605–09; Turner, *First Decade*, 230–31.
6 Dyrenfurth, 'Labor's View of Fusion', and Strangio, 'Fusion in Victoria' in Strangio and Dyrenfurth (eds) *Confusion*, 90–99 and 151–53.
7 CPD, 24 June 1909, 380.
8 Counsel Fees Notebook, 14 January 1910, 89–91; comment about ministerial approval, Shepherd, 'Memoirs', NAA CRS A1632, 72–73.
9 AD to CD, 4 August 1909, NLA MS 4913, folder 13.

10 AD to Bavin, 28 June and 18 July 1909, NLA MS 560/2/94 and 97.
11 Diary, July–December 1909; AD to CD, 6 October 1909, NLA MS 4913, folder 13.
12 CPD, 8 August 1909, 3154–63; *Federated Australia*, 23 August 1909, 265–67; La Nauze, *Alfred Deakin,* 587–92.
13 AD to CD, 24 August 1909, NLA MS 4913, folder 13.
14 CPD, 8 August 1909, 3154–61.
15 *Federated Australia*, 1 April 1902, 97.
16 Counsel Fees Notebook, 14 January 1910, 91–92.
17 CPD, 15 October 1909, 4627–29.
18 La Nauze, *Alfred Deakin*, 592–93.
19 La Nauze, *Alfred Deakin*, 579–80.
20 AD to CD, 20 December 1909, NLA MS 4913, folder 13b.
21 Counsel Fees Notebook, 14 January 1910, 92.
22 Counsel Fees Notebook, 6 May 1910, 95–96.
23 'Prime Minister at Ballarat', Commonwealth Liberal Party, Melbourne, 1910, pamphlet, NLA, 22.
24 AD to CD, 12 January 1910, 21 September 1909, NLA MS 4913, folder 13.
25 AD to Ivy and Herbert Brookes, 28 April 1911, after the 1911 referendum. Cited in La Nauze, 610.
26 Diary, January–April 1910.
27 Diary, 2, 4, 6 April.
28 *Age*, 17 March 1910; Letter to the editor, *Argus*, 19 March 1910; Counsel Fees Notebook, 99.
29 La Nauze, *Alfred Deakin*, 600–01; *Age*, 14, 15 April 1910.
30 AD to CD, 19 April 1910, NLA MS 4913, folder 13b.
31 Counsel Fees Notebook, 6 May 1910, 99–107.
32 Diary, 31 August 1910; La Nauze, *Alfred Deakin*, 610.
33 AD to CD, 2 June 1910, NLA MS 4913 NLA, folder 13b.
34 Red Spine Notebook, 28 May 1910, NLA MS 1540/3/28, 16.
35 AD to CD, 21 June 1910, NLA MS 4913h, folder 13c.
36 Medley Notebook, morning, 14 May 1910, 62.
37 Counsel Fees Notebook, n.d. mid-1910 and 2 October 1910, 110 and 115.

CHAPTER THIRTY-FOUR: LEADER OF THE OPPOSITION

1 Diary, 30 June 1910; Red Spine Notebook, 3 September 1910, 40–41.
2 Red Spine Notebook, 27 November 1910, 94–96.
3 CPD, 12 August 1910, 4423 ff; Turner, *First Decade*, 294–95.
4 CPD, 30 August 1910, 2198 ff.
5 Red Spine Notebook, 29 May 1910, 21–24.
6 Diary, 19 October 1910; CPD, 19 October 1910, 4801–28.
7 *Age*, 8 December 1910.
8 Diary, 1 January 1911.
9 Red Spine Notebook, 7 December 1910, 104.
10 Red Spine Notebook, 28 April 1911, 14 from back.
11 'Books and a Boy', NLA MS 1540/4/112-149. He discusses his disappointment with his efforts, 3 September 1910, under the heading 'My Mental Failure', Red Spine Notebook, 41.
12 Rivett, *Australian Citizen*, 51–52.
13 Red Spine Notebook, 24 September 1910, 47–49.
14 Counsel Fees Book, 2 October, 1911, 131.
15 Red Spine Notebook, 24 September 1910, 50.
16 Red Spine Notebook, 6 November 1910, 76–78.
17 Red Spine Notebook, 4 November 1910, 56–58.
18 Red Spine Notebook, 4 November, 27 May and 11 September 1910, 58, 45, and 15.

19 AD to CD, 31 May 1909, NLA MS 4913, folder 13b.
20 For example, AD to CD, 4 August 1909, NLA MS 4913, folder 13.
21 Gabay, *Mystical Life*, 182–84; Red Spine Notebook, 12 and 13 November 1910, 83–92.
22 Red Spine Notebook, 2 June 1911, 37 from back.
23 *Age*, 2 May 1911.
24 *Liberal*, 1:3, September 1911, 61–63; Quartly, 'Political Housekeeping and Fusion' in Strangio and Dyrenfurth (eds), *Confusion*, 180–82; Red Spine Notebook, 10 December 1911, 44–45 from back.
25 Herbert Brookes to Ivy Brookes, 22 December 1910, NLA MS 1924/1/1758.
26 Rivett, *Australian Citizen*, 44, 205.
27 *Liberal*, 1:1, July 1911, 5–6 and 11.
28 AD to Bavin, 9 August 1911, NLA MS 560/2/158.
29 Rivett, *David Rivett*, 52–54.
30 Cited in Diane Langmore, *Prime Ministers' Wives*, 30.
31 *Age*, 26 April 1912.
32 *Age*, 10 September 1912; Quartly, 'Political Housekeeping and Fusion' in Strangio and Dyrenfurth (eds), *Confusion*, 180.
33 CPD, 24 September 1912, 3325–33; Grimshaw et al, *Creating a Nation*, 206–07.
34 See Prayer LXXII, 21 November 1911; Red Spine Notebook, 14 May 1912, 53 from back.
35 Diary, 27 September 1912.
36 Diary, April, May.
37 Red Spine Notebook, 16 October 1912, 58 from back.
38 CPD, 1 December 1912, 7406–08.
39 Diary, 30 December 1912; Red Spine Notebook, 9 January 1913, 63.
40 *Argus*, *Age*, *Sydney Morning Herald*, 9 January 1913; *Catholic Press*, 16 January 1913.
41 Frank Anstey, 'Thirty Years of Deakin', Labor Call, Melbourne, 1913 (pamphlet in NLA).
42 Red Spine Notebook, 9 January 1913, 62–63.
43 Personal Communication, Judith Harley.
44 Diary, 20 January 1913; Red Spine Notebook, 22 and 24 January 1913, 69–70 from back.
45 Speech at Ballarat, *Ballarat Star*, 12 March 1913.
46 Diary, March, April 1913.
47 Diary, 22 April 1913; *Age*, 14 April 1913.
48 Diary, 5 March 1913, 7–8 May 1913; *Bendigo Advertiser*, 7 May 1913.
49 CD Diary, 8 May 1913, NLA MS 4913.
50 Medley Notebook, 76.
51 Sarah Bill died on 25 April 1855, of apoplexy. Death certificate No. 168, Counties of Hereford and Monmouthshire. Catherine Deakin died on 27 August 1854 of valvular disease of the heart. Death certificate No. 426, County Oxford. General Register Office, England. I have not been able to locate his grandfathers' death certificates.
52 Theodore A. Kotchen, 'Historical Trends and Milestones in Hypertension Research', *Hypertension*, 58:4, October 2011; Diary, 8 May 1913; see also conversation between La Nauze and Professor Pansy Wright, professor of physiology at the University of Melbourne, cited in Gabay, *Mystic Life*, 192, n. 13.
53 Autobiographical Notes, Typescript, XVI, 2 October 1914, NLA MS 1540/3/300.

CHAPTER THIRTY-FIVE: 'THE WORLD FORGETTING, BY THE WORLD FORGOT'

1 Poem, 1 January 1914, Medley, 115.
2 AD to CD, 20 May 1913, NLA MS 4913, folder 14.
3 AD to Bavin, 17 September 1913, NLA MS 560/2/173.
4 Diary, 6 June 1913; *Age*, 23 June 1913.
5 AD to Bavin, 17 September 1913, NLA MS 560/2/173; Red Spine Notebook, 4 September 1913, 94 from back.
6 Autobiographical Notes, Typescript, 5 December 1915, Fragments, 58.
7 Diary, 29 July 1913; Red Spine Notebook, 2 August 1913, 89.

8   AD to CD, 9 March 1914, NLA MS 4913, folder 14.
9   *Age*, 1, 8 September 1914.
10   Autobiographical Notes, Typescript, XIV, 30 August 1914.
11   Autobiographical Notes, Typescript, Typed Notes (42), XVI, 2 October 1914.
12   Note at end of 1914 Diary.
13   Day, *Andrew Fisher*, 111–12.
14   *Argus*, 10 September 1914.
15   *Age*, 14, 15 January 1915.
16   Diary, 11–14 January 1915; La Nauze, *Alfred Deakin*, 632–33.
17   AD to CD, 24 January 1915, NLA MS 4913, folder 14.
18   AD to CD, 11 May 1915, NLA MS 4913, folder 14.
19   *Daily Standard* (Brisbane), 12 March 1915.
20   Diary, March–May 1915; *Argus*, 12 May 1915.
21   *Worker* (Brisbane), 1 July 1915; *Australasian*, 28 August 1915.
22   Diary, 19–20 July 1915.
23   Diary, 4 November 1915; 28 October 1915.
24   Diary, July to December 1915; Diane Langmore, *Prime Ministers' Wives*, 38–39.
25   Kristen Thornton, 'Pattie Deakin, Intercessor-in-Chief: A Case Study of Charity during the Great War', unpublished paper.
26   Autobiographical Notes, Typescript, 20 December 1915.
27   Interview, Vera White.
28   Autobiographical Notes, Typescript, 6 November 1915.
29   Autobiographical Notes, Typescript, 30 December 1915.
30   Eric W. Boyle, *Quack Medicine*, 55.
31   Diary, September and October 1916.
32   Interview, Vera White.
33   Colonel Unsworth, 'The Hon. Alfred Deakin', cutting, NLA MS 1540/23/278.
34   19 January 1917, cited in La Nauze, *Alfred Deakin*, 636.
35   *Argus*, 19 December 1917.
36   Rivett, *Australian Citizen*, 56.
37   CD Diary for 1917–19, NLA MS 4913; Interview, Vera White; CPD, 7 October 1919, 1048–49.
38   CD Diary, 9 October 1919, NLA MS 4913; *Argus*, 9 October 1919.
39   Memoir by PD still with family, cited in Rickard, *Family Romance*, 160.

CHAPTER THIRTY-SIX: AFTERLIFE

1   Rivett, *Australian Citizen*, 58–77.
2   Murdoch, *Alfred Deakin*, 307.
3   Rickard, *Family Romance*, 164–65.
4   Review in *Argus*, 28 August 1923.
5   Rivett, *Australian Citizen*, 83–84.
6   Reminiscence, Lilian Deakin Bennett (nee White), November 1972, Queenscliffe Historical Society.
7   Irving and Macintyre (eds), *J. A. La Nauze: No Ordinary Act*, 4–7; La Nauze cited in Rivett, *Australian Citizen*, 202; La Nauze, *Walter Murdoch*, Preface.
8   La Nauze, *Alfred Deakin*, vii, 52.
9   G. T. Powell, 'Modes of Acquisition'.
10   Handing over of the papers of Alfred Deakin to the National Library, 3 December 1965. pmtranscripts.pmc.gov.au/release/transcript-1207, accessed 7 March 2017.
11   Robert Menzies, *Afternoon Light*, 286.
12   Cited in Hancock, *National and Permanent*, 61.
13   VPD, 12 September 1972, 174.
14   Stuart Macintyre, 'Whatever Happened to Deakinite Liberalism?' in Strangio and Dyrenfurth (eds), *Confusion*, 227–48.

SOURCES AND BIBLIOGRAPHY

Alfred Deakin's Papers, NLA MS 1540
Deakin's papers in the National Library of Australia were my major source as I tried to discern the patterns of connection between Deakin's inner world and his life as a public man. Deakin's inner world is well documented in the many private notebooks he kept during his life. These include a prayer diary, 'The Boke of Praer and Praes', begun in 1894 and running to 1913, and a series called Clues, a miscellaneous collection of numbered epigrams, notes on his reading, and reflections on life and the nature of the universe. As these are both dated, they can be easily matched to events.

Deakin wrote one major autobiographical piece, *The Crisis in Victorian Politics*, on his unexpected discovery of politics as his vocation, and had intended when he had the time to continue the story. After he lost the 1910 election he did have more time, but he no longer had the capacity for major literary work. On the basis of notes and diaries, which he then destroyed, he wrote about his early life, and this autobiographical writing is the major source for his childhood and youth, together with some writing by his sister, Catherine, and a few surviving letters. His diary records for 1876 and 1878 to 1883 are digests of the originals compiled long after the events they record, with no indication of what was edited out. His papers also contain a great deal of religious writing, including on his experiences with spiritualism.

All this writing, in multiple notebooks, is difficult to navigate. After his death, Vera White and Herbert and Ivy Brookes made typed copies of the writing of most biographical interest. Much of this is easy to locate in the original, but not all, and some is from notebooks that are still with the family. Where I have been able to locate the original source, I have given it; otherwise I have referred to the typescript, which for the most part is unpaginated. Typed copies were also made of the Clues and the prayer diary. When citing individual Clues and Prayers I have given the number and date, so they can be located in either the manuscript or the typescript.

The most straightforward source is the series of annual diaries he kept from 1884 till 1916, a week to an opening, in which he recorded daily events: appointments, meetings, travel arrangements, where and with whom he ate lunch and dinner, the weather, his state of health and the quality of his sleep. Entries are often cryptic, but they provided me with a reliable spine for the research. In 1887 he had two diaries, one covering his time abroad, and another when he was back home, the first few weeks of January and from mid-June. His papers also include travel diaries of his 1885 trip to the United States to investigate irrigation and his 1887 trip to the Colonial Conference in London. These were transcribed by Catherine from his long letters home.

For the major sources listed here I have given only the name in the endnotes. Less frequently used items and correspondence have full citations.

Autobiographical Notes, NLA MS 1540/3/293.
Autobiographical Notes, Typescript, Extracts by Herbert and Ivy Brookes, NLA
   MS 1540/3/300.
Clues Notebooks, 1884–1909, NLA MS 1540/3/282-288. Typescript extracts transcribed
   by Herbert and Ivy Brookes, NLA MS 1540/3/301.
Counsel Fees Notebook, NLA MS 1540/3/290.
Diaries, 1884–1916, NLA MS 1540/2/1-36.
Medley Notebook, NLA MS 1540/3/296.
Personal Experiences of Spiritism, about 1895, NLA MS 1540/5/1175-1452.
Prayer Diary, 'The Boke of Praer and Praes', NLA MS 1540/5/1457. Typescript at
   NLA MS 1540/5/818. In the endnotes prayers are identified by number and date.
Red Spine Notebook, NLA MS 1540/3/281.
Testament prepared by Alfred Deakin in 1890 for the guidance of his daughters,
   NLA MS 1540/19/356. Referred to in endnotes as 'Testament for his daughters'.
Travel Diary from America, 1885, NLA MS 1540/2/38.
Travel Diary from England and Europe, 1887, NLA MS 1540/2/39.
Spiritual Diary Personal and Mundane, 1880–82, NLA MS 1540/5/1453. This contains
   his séance journal from 1 August 1880 to 1 September 1881. In January 1882 he
   makes a new beginning under the heading 'Memoranda—1882'.

Published Works by Alfred Deakin
In chronological order. Works not published in his lifetime are listed at time of writing.
Quentin Massys: A Drama in Five Acts. J. P. Donaldson, Melbourne, 1875.
*A New Pilgrim's Progress, Purporting to be Given by John Bunyan Through an Impressional
   Writing Medium.* W. H. Terry, Melbourne, 1877.
Preface, 9 September 1877. *The Lyceum Leader: Compiled from the Lyceum Guide
   for the Melbourne Progressive Lyceum by the Conductor.* E. Purton & Co., Steam
   Printers, Melbourne, 1877.
Royal Commission on Water Supply, *First Progress Report: Irrigation in Western
   America.* Victorian Government Printer, 1885.
Royal Commission on Water Supply, *Fourth Progress Report: Irrigation in Egypt and
   Italy.* Victorian Government Printer, 1887.
'The Makers of the Colonies: The Hon. James Service'. *Australasian Review of Reviews*,
   1892, 126.
'Irrigation in Australia'. *The Yearbook of Australia for 1892.* Petherick and Co., London,
   1893, 81–96. Copy at NLA MS 1540/10/30.
Irrigated India: An Australian View of India and Ceylon: Their Irrigation and Agriculture.
   W. Thacker and Co., London, 1893.
Temple and Tomb in India. Melville, Mullen and Slade, Melbourne, 1893.
'The Federal Council of Australasia'. *Review of Reviews*, 1895, 154.
The Federal Story: The Inner History of the Federal Cause. (Written 1900.) Edited by
   Herbert Brookes, Robertson and Mullens, Melbourne, 1944. A new edition, edited
   by John La Nauze, was published by Melbourne University Press in 1963, and a
   further one, edited by Stuart Macintyre, in 1995 under the title *And Be One People:
   Alfred Deakin's Federal Story.* All page references are to this last edition, which was
   also published by Melbourne University Press.
The Crisis in Victorian Politics, 1879–1881. (Written 1900.) J. A. La Nauze and R. M.
   Crawford (eds), Melbourne University Press, Carlton, 1957.
Federated Australia: Selections from the Letters to the Morning Post, 1900–1910. J. A. La

Nauze (ed.), Melbourne University Press, Carlton, 1968. Dates in the endnotes are
for time of writing, not of publication in London six weeks or so later.
'The Liberal Outlook'. *United Australia*, 1:1, January 1900.
'Imperial Federation'. An Address Delivered by the Hon. Alfred Deakin, M.P. at the
Annual Meeting of the Imperial Federation League of Victoria. Echo Publishing,
Melbourne, 1905.
'Protection and Practical Legislation or Anti-Socialism'. Berry, Anderson & Co.,
Ballarat, 1906. NLA.
Introduction. Ambrose Pratt, *David Syme: Father of Protection in Australia*. Ward
Lock & Co., Melbourne, 1908.
'Prime Minister at Ballarat'. Commonwealth Liberal Party, Melbourne, 1910. NLA.

Other Manuscript Sources
Barton, Edmund. NLA MS 51.
Bavin, Thomas. NLA MS 560.
Brookes, Herbert and Ivy. NLA MS 1924.
Cook, J. Hume. NLA MS 601.
Couchman, Dame Elizabeth. State Library of Victoria, MS 8713.
Crisp, Christopher. NLA MS 743.
Deakin, Catherine. Papers. NLA MS 4913.
Deakin Collection, Queenscliffe Historical Museum.
Dilke, Charles. British Library, Additional MS 43877.
Higgins, Henry Bournes. NLA MS 1057.
Hunt, Atlee. NLA MS 1100.
La Nauze, John. NLA MS 5248.
Menzies, Robert Gordon. NLA MS 4936.
Pearson, Charles Henry. Copies of letters to Pearson from Deakin. NLA MS 2503.
Originals in State Library of Victoria.
Shepherd, Malcolm. Memoirs. National Archives of Australia, A1632.
Swallow & Ariell Correspondence. University of Melbourne Archives, 1/6/2. This
contains Deakin's letters to Fred Derham.

Interview
Vera Deakin White. Conducted by Judith and Tom Harley. NLA TRC 4802, Oral
History Collection.

Newspapers, Periodicals and Government Sources
The main newspapers consulted were the *Age* and the *Argus*; however, as Trove now
provides easy access to non-metropolitan and local newspapers and to many weeklies,
others were also consulted, as indicated in the endnotes.
Australian Insurance and Banking Record, 1888–94.
Commonwealth Parliamentary Debates, House of Representatives, 1901–13.
Harbinger of Light, 1876–80. Edited by W. H. Terry. Journal of the Victorian Associa-
tion of Progressive Spiritualists. State Library of Victoria.
Liberal, 1911–14. Edited by Herbert Brookes. Journal of the Commonwealth Liberal
Party. State Library of Victoria.
New Hebrides: Correspondence relating to the Convention with France. House of
Commons, London, 1907.

Official Record of the Centennial International Exhibition, 1888–89. Sands & McDougall, Melbourne, 1890.

Official Record of the Proceedings and Debates of the Australasian Federation Conference, 1890. Government Printer, Melbourne, 1890.

Official Report of the National Australasian Convention Debates, Adelaide, 22 March to 5 May 1897, Government Printer, Adelaide, 1897.

Official Record of the Debates of the Australasian Federal Convention, Second Session, Sydney, 2 to 24 September 1897. Government Printer, Sydney, 1897.

Official Record of the Debates of the Australasian Federal Convention, Third Session, Melbourne, 20 January to 17 March 1898, two vols. Government Printer, Melbourne, 1898.

Parish Records for St Teilo, Llanarth. Gwent County Records Office.

Proceedings of the Colonial Conference, 1887. Colonial Office, London, 1887.

Public Records Office of Victoria. Chief Secretary, Record of Deputations. VPRS 986.

Public Records Office of Victoria. Maritime Strike. VPRS 937 P0000/513.

Sands & McDougall Melbourne Directories, 1856–60.

Victoria, Mildura Royal Commission. Mildura Settlement. Report of the Mildura Royal Commission. Government Printer, Melbourne, 1896.

Victorian Parliamentary Debates, Legislative Assembly, 1879–1900.

Books and Articles Primarily about Deakin

Anstey, Frank. *Thirty Years of Deakin*. Labor Call, Melbourne, 1913. (Pamphlet, NLA.)

Brett, Judith. 'Alfred Deakin's Childhood: Books, a Boy and His Mother'. *Australian Historical Studies*, 1:43, 2012, 61–77.

Crawford, R. M. 'Tom Roberts and Alfred Deakin' in Franz Phillip and June Stewart (eds), *In Honour of Daryl Lindsay: Essays and Studies*. Oxford University Press, Melbourne, 1964.

Harley, Judith. 'My Grandfather's Legacy' in *Alfred Deakin Lectures: Ideas for the Future of a Civil Society*. ABC Books, Sydney, 2001.

Gabay, Al. *The Mystic Life of Alfred Deakin*. Cambridge University Press, Cambridge, 1992.

Lake, Marilyn. 'Looking to American Manhood: The Correspondence of Alfred Deakin and Josiah Royce' in Robert Dixon and Nicholas Birns (eds), *Reading across the Pacific: Australia–United States Intellectual Histories*. Sydney University Press, Sydney, 2010.

La Nauze, J. A. *Alfred Deakin: A Biography*. Melbourne University Press, Carlton, 1965.

Langmore, Diane. 'Pattie Deakin' in *Prime Ministers' Wives: The Public and Private Lives of Ten Australian Women*. McPhee Gribble, Ringwood, Victoria, 1992.

Murdoch, Walter. *Alfred Deakin: A Sketch*. Constable & Co., Sydney, 1923.

Parsons, T. G. 'Alfred Deakin and the Victorian Factory Act of 1885: A Note'. *Journal of Industrial Relations*, June 1973, 206–08.

Rankin, Benjamin. 'Alfred Deakin and Water Resources Policy in Australia'. *History Australia*, 10:2, 2012, 114–35.

Rickard, John. *A Family Romance: The Deakins at Home*. Melbourne University Press, Carlton, 1996.

Woods, Carole. '"My Native Place": Alfred Deakin in Fitzroy'. *Victorian Historical Journal*, 82:2, 2011, 158–74.

Other Books, Articles and Theses

Alexander, J. A. *The Life of George Chaffey: A Story of Irrigation Beginnings in California and Australia*. Macmillan, Melbourne, 1928.

Anderson, Benedict. *Imagined Communities: Reflections on the Origins and Spread of Nationalism*, rev. edn. Verso, London, 1991.

Aveling, Marian (Quartly). 'A History of the Australian Natives Association, 1871–1900'. PhD thesis, Monash University, 1970.

Badger, C. R. *Charles Strong and the Australian Church*. Abacada Press, Melbourne, 1971.

Banner, Stuart. *Possessing the Pacific: Land Settlers and Indigenous People from Australia to Alaska*. Harvard University Press, Harvard, 2007.

Barber, James. *The Presidential Character: Predicting Performance in the White House*. Prentice Hall, New Jersey, 1977.

Barwick, Diane. *Rebellion at Coranderrk*. Aboriginal History Inc., Canberra, 1998.

Bate, Weston. *Lucky City: The First Generation at Ballarat, 1851–1901*. Melbourne University Press, Carlton, 1971.

Bate, Weston and Helen Penrose. *Challenging Tradition: A History of Melbourne Grammar*. Australian Scholarly Publishing, Melbourne, 2002.

Beevers, D. G. 'Sir William Ossler and the Nature of Essential Hypertension'. *Journal of Human Hypertension*, 28, 2014, 15–17.

Bessant, B. *Schooling in the Colony and State of Victoria*. Monograph no. 1, Centre for Comparative and International Studies in Education, La Trobe University, Victoria, 1983.

Blainey, Geoffrey. *Gold and Paper: A History of the National Bank of Australia*. Georgian House, Melbourne, 1958.

Bolton, Geoffrey. *Edmund Barton*. Allen & Unwin, Sydney, 2000.

Bongiorno, Frank. 'In this World and the Next: Political Modernity and Unorthodox Religion in Australia, 1880–1930'. *Australian Cultural History*, 25, 2006, 179–207.

Boyle, Eric W. *Quack Medicine: A History of Combating Health Fraud in Twentieth-Century America*. Praeger, Santa Barbara, California, 2013.

Brett, Judith. *Australian Liberals and the Moral Middle Class: From Alfred Deakin to John Howard*. Cambridge University Press, Cambridge, 2003.

Briggs, Asa. *Victorian Cities*. Odhams Books, London, 1963.

Brock, J. Edward. *Swedenborg and His Influence*. Academy of the New Church, Bryn Athyn, Pennsylvania, 1988.

Broome, Richard. *The Victorians: Arriving*. Fairfax, Syme & Weldon Associates, Sydney, 1984.

Browne, Hugh Junor. *The Holy Truth; Or, The Coming Reformation*. Arthur Hall & Co., London, 1876.

Browne, Hugh Junor (ed.). *The Grand Reality: Being Experiences in Spirit Life of a Celebrated Medium Received Through a Trance Medium*. George Robertson, Melbourne, 1888.

Browne, Hugh Junor. *Reasons for the Hope that Is in Me; Or, Wonderful and Irrefutable Evidence of a Future Life*. W. H. Britten, Manchester, 1891.

Browne, Hugh Junor. *Astronomy and its Bearing on the Popular Faith; Or, What Is Truth?* H. J. Browne, Melbourne, 1887.

Browne, Hugh Junor. *Religion in the Light of Truth and Reason*. H. J. Browne, Melbourne, 1900.

Brown-May, Andrew and Shurlee Swan (eds). *The Encyclopaedia of Melbourne*. Cambridge University Press, Melbourne, 2005.

Caiden, Gerard. *Career Service: An Introduction to the History of Personnel Administration in the Commonwealth Public Service of Australia, 1901–1961.* Melbourne University Press, Carlton, 1965.

Cannon, Michael. *The Land Boomers.* Melbourne University Press, Carlton, 1966.

Cannon, Michael. *Victoria's Representative Men at Home: Punch's Illustrated Interviews by 'Lauderdale'.* Facsimile edition, Today's Heritage, Melbourne, 1977.

Cannon, Michael. *Melbourne after the Gold Rush.* Loch Haven Books, Main Ridge, 1993.

Carlyle, Thomas. *Past and Present.* Lovell's Library edition, 1885 [1843]. In family's possession.

Carlyle, Thomas. *Sartor Resartus.* Oxford University Press, World's Classics series, 1987 [1836].

Carter, Jennifer. *Painting the Islands Vermilion: Archibald Watson and the Brig Carl.* Melbourne University Press, Carlton, 1999.

Carter, Jennifer. *Eyes to the Future: Australia and Her Neighbours in the 1870s.* National Library of Australia, Canberra, 2000.

Childe, Vere Gordon. *How Labor Governs: A Study of Workers' Representation in Australia*, 2nd edn. Melbourne University Press, Carlton, 1964.

Cochrane, Peter. '"How are the Egyptians Behaving?" Herbert Brookes, British Australian'. *Australian Historical Studies*, 30:113, 1999, 303–18.

Collini, Stefan. *Public Moralists, Political Thought and Intellectual Life in Britain, 1850–1930.* Clarendon Press, Oxford, 1991.

Crisp, L. F. *The Australian Federal Labour Party, 1901–1951.* Longmans, Green & Co., London, 1955.

Critchett, Jan. *Untold Stories: Memories and Lives of Victorian Kooris.* Melbourne University Press, Carlton, 1998.

Davies, A. F. *Skills, Outlooks and Passions: A Psychoanalytic Contribution to the Study of Politics.* Cambridge University Press, Cambridge, 1980.

Davison, Graeme. *The Rise and Fall of Marvellous Melbourne.* Melbourne University Press, Carlton, 1978.

Davison, Graeme, J. W. McCarty and Ailsa McLeary (eds). *Australians 1888.* Fairfax, Syme & Weldon Associates, Sydney, 1987.

Day, David. *Andrew Fisher: Prime Minister of Australia.* Fourth Estate, Pymble, New South Wales, 2008.

Denovan, W. D. C. *The Evidence of Spiritualism.* W. H. Terry, Melbourne, 1882.

Faulkner, John and Stuart Macintyre (eds). *True Believers: The Story of the Federal Parliamentary Labor Party.* Allen & Unwin, Sydney, 2001.

Fitzgerald, John. *Big White Lie: Chinese Australians in White Australia.* University of New South Wales Press, Sydney, 2007.

Fitzhardinge, L. F. *That Fiery Particle, 1862–1914: A Political Biography, William Morris Hughes*, vol. 1. Angus & Robertson, Sydney, 1978.

Froude, James Anthony. *Oceana, or, England and Her Colonies.* Longmans, Green & Co., London, 1886.

Furphy, Sam. 'Aboriginal House Names and Settler Australian Identity'. *Journal of Australian Studies*, 26:72, 2000, 59–68.

Gabay, Alfred J. *Messages from Beyond: Spiritualism and Spiritualists in Melbourne's Golden Age, 1870–1890.* Melbourne University Press, Carlton, 2001.

Garden, Don. *Theodore Fink: A Talent for Ubiquity.* Melbourne University Press, Carlton, 1998.

Garran, Robert. *Prosper the Commonwealth.* Angus & Robertson, Sydney, 1958.

Glass, Margaret. *Tommy Bent: 'Bent by Name, Bent by Nature'*. Melbourne University Press, Carlton, 1993.

Goldberg, S. L., and F. B. Smith (eds), *Australian Cultural History*, Cambridge University Press in association with the Australian Academy of the Humanities, Melbourne, 1988.

Gorman, Zachary. 'Debating a Tiger Cub: The Anti-Socialist Campaign'. BA Hons thesis, History, University of Sydney, 2012.

Grattan, Michelle (ed.). *Australian Prime Ministers*. New Holland, Sydney, 2000.

Grimshaw, Patricia, Marilyn Lake, Ann McGrath and Marian Quartly. *Creating a Nation*. McPhee Gribble, Melbourne, 1994.

Hammerton, James. *Emigrant Gentlewomen: Genteel Poverty and Female Emigration, 1830–1914*. Croom Helm, London, 1979.

Hancock, Ian. *National and Permanent? The Federal Organisation of the Liberal Party of Australia, 1944–1965*. Melbourne University Press, Carlton, 2000.

Hancock, W. K. *Australia*. E. Benn, London, 1930.

Heath, Deana. *Pacifying Empire: Obscenity and Moral Regulation in Britain, India and Australia*. Cambridge University Press, Cambridge, 2010.

Hirst, John. *The Sentimental Nation: The Making of the Australian Commonwealth*. Oxford University Press, Melbourne, 2000.

Holden, Colin and Richard Trembath. *Divine Discontent: The Brotherhood of St Laurence, A History*. Australian Scholarly Publishing, Melbourne, 2008.

Hughes, Colin and B. D. Graham. *A Handbook of Australian Government and Politics, 1890–1964*. Australian National University Press, Canberra, 1968.

Irving, Helen. 'When Quick Met Garran: The Corowa Plan'. *Papers on Parliament* no. 32, December 1998.

Irving, Helen (ed.). *The Centenary Companion to Federation*. Cambridge University Press, Melbourne, 1999.

Irving, Helen and Stuart Macintyre (eds). *No Ordinary Act: Essays on Federation and the Constitution by J. A. La Nauze*. Melbourne University Press, Carlton, 2001.

Jalland, Pat. *Australian Ways of Death: A Social and Cultural History, 1840–1918*. Oxford University Press, Melbourne, 2002.

James, Louis. *The Victorian Novel*. Blackwell, Oxford, 2006.

Jebb, Richard. *Studies in Colonial Nationalism*. Edward Arnold, London, 1905.

Keenan, J. J. *The Inaugural Celebrations of the Commonwealth of Australia*. Government Printer, Sydney, 1904.

Kelly, Paul. *The End of Certainty: Power, Business and Politics in Australia*. Allen & Unwin, Sydney, 1992.

Kendle, John Edward. *The Colonial and Imperial Conferences, 1887–1911: A Study in Imperial Organization*. Royal Commonwealth Society, Longmans, London, 1967.

Knaplund, Paul. 'Sir Arthur Gordon on the New Guinea Question, 1883'. *Historical Studies*, 7, 1956, 328–33.

Kotchen, Theodore A. 'Historical Trends and Milestones in Hypertension Research'. *Hypertension*, 58:4, 2011, 522–38.

Lake, Marilyn and Henry Reynolds. *Drawing the Global Colour Line: White Men's Countries and the Question of Racial Equality*. Melbourne University Press, Carlton, 2008.

Lake, Marilyn. 'Oh to be in Boston Now that Federation's Here'. *Papers on Parliament* no. 61, May 2014.

La Nauze, John. *Political Economy in Australia: Historical Studies*. Melbourne University Press, Carlton, 1949.

La Nauze, John. *The Hopetoun Blunder: The Appointment of the First Prime Minister of the Commonwealth of Australia, December 1900*. Melbourne University Press, Carlton, 1957.

La Nauze, John, *Walter Murdoch: A Biographical Memoir*. Melbourne University Press, Carlton, 1977.

Loveday, P., A. W. Martin and R. S. Parker. *The Emergence of the Australian Party System*. Hale & Iremonger, Sydney, 1977.

Macintyre, Stuart. *Winners and Losers: The Pursuit of Social Justice in Australia*. Allen & Unwin, Sydney, 1986.

Macintyre, Stuart. *The Succeeding Age, 1901–1942: Oxford History of Australia*, vol. 4. Oxford University Press, Melbourne, 1986.

Macintyre, Stuart. *A Colonial Liberalism: The Lost World of Three Victorian Visionaries*. Oxford University Press, Melbourne, 1991.

Macintyre, Stuart. *History for a Nation: Ernest Scott and the Making of Australian History*. Melbourne University Press, Carlton, 1994.

McMinn, W. G. *George Reid*. Melbourne University Press, Carlton, 1989.

McMullin, Ross. *The Light on the Hill: The Australian Labor Party, 1891–1991*. Oxford University Press, Melbourne, 1991.

Maiden, Peter. *Missionaries, Cannibals and Colonial Officers: British New Guinea and the Goaribari Affair*. Central Queensland University Press, Rockhampton, 2003.

Martin, Allan. *Robert Menzies: A Life*. Melbourne University Press, Carlton, 1993.

Meaney, Neville. *The Search for Security in the Pacific, 1901–1914*. Sydney University Press, Sydney, 1976.

Meaney, Neville. *Australia and the World: A Documentary History from the 1870s to the 1970s*. Longman Cheshire, Melbourne, 1985.

Menadue, J. E. *A Centenary History of the Australian Natives Association, 1871–1971*. Horticultural Press, Melbourne, 1971.

Meudell, George. *The Pleasant Career of a Spendthrift*. Routledge, London, 1929.

Mill, J. S. 'Representative Government' in *Three Essays*, Oxford University Press, Oxford, 1975 [1861].

Morrison, Elizabeth. *David Syme: Man of the Age*. Monash University Publishing, Clayton, Victoria, 2014.

Myers, Frederick W. H. *Human Personality and its Survival of Bodily Death*. Longman, Green & Co., London, 1903.

Nanni, G. and A. James. *Coranderrk: We Will Show the Country*. Aboriginal Studies Press, Canberra, 2013.

Nielsen, H. L. *The Voice of the People, or, The History of the Kyabram Reform Movement*. Arbuckle, Waddell and Fawkner, Melbourne, 1902.

Norberry, Jennifer. 'Voters and the Franchise: The Federal Story'. Australian Parliamentary Library, Research Paper no. 17, 2001–02.

Palmer, Nettie. *Henry Bournes Higgins: A Memoir*. Harrap, London, 1931.

Pearson, Charles Henry. 'The Political Situation in Victoria'. *Speaker*, 26 March 1892.

Pearson, Charles Henry. *National Life and Character: A Forecast*. Macmillan, London, 1893.

Pierce, Peter (ed.). *The Cambridge History of Australian Literature*. Cambridge University Press, Cambridge, 2009.

Powell, Graeme. 'Modes of Acquisition: The Growth of the Manuscript Collection of the National Library of Australia'. *Australian Academic and Research Libraries*, 22:4, 1991, 74–80.

Pratt, Ambrose. *David Syme: Father of Protection in Australia*. Ward, Lock & Co., Melbourne, 1908.

Putnam, Robert. *Bowling Alone: The Collapse and Revival of American Community*. Simon & Schuster, New York, 2000.

Radic, Therese and Suzanne Robinson (eds). *Marshall-Hall's Melbourne: Music, Art and Controversy, 1891–1915*. Australian Scholarly Publishing, Melbourne, 2012.

Reid, George Houston. *My Reminiscences*. Cassell, London, 1917.

Richards, Eric. *Britannia's Children: Emigration from England, Scotland, Wales and Ireland Since 1600*. Hambledon and London, London, 2004.

Richards, Jeffrey. '"Passing the Love of Women": Manly Love in Victorian Society' in J. A. Mangin and James Walvin (eds), *Manliness and Morality: Middle Class Masculinity in Britain and America, 1840–1940*. Manchester University Press, Manchester, 1987.

Rickard, John. *Class and Politics: New South Wales, Victoria and the Early Commonwealth, 1890–1910*. Australian National University Press, Canberra, 1976.

Rickard, John. *H. B. Higgins: The Rebel as Judge*. Allen & Unwin, Sydney, 1984.

Rivett, Rohan. *Australian Citizen: Herbert Brookes, 1867–1963*. Melbourne University Press, Carlton, 1963.

Rivett, Rohan. *David Rivett: Fighter for Australian Science*. Rivett, Melbourne, 1972.

Roberts, Andrew. *Salisbury: Victorian Titan*. Weidenfeld & Nicholson, London, 1999.

Roe, Jill. *Beyond Belief: Theosophy in Australia 1879–1939*. University of New South Wales Press, Sydney, 1986.

Royce, Josiah. 'Impressions of Australia'. *Scribner's Magazine*, 9, 1891, 76–87.

Sawer, Geoffrey. *Australian Federal Politics and Law, 1901–1929*. Melbourne University Press, Carlton, 1956.

Sawer, Marian. *The Ethical State? Social Liberalism in Australia*. Melbourne University Press, Carlton, 2003.

Serle, Geoffrey. 'The Victorian Legislative Council 1856–1950'. *Historical Studies*, 6:22, 1954, 186–203.

Serle, Geoffrey. *The Golden Age: A History of the Colony of Victoria, 1851–1861*. Melbourne University Press, Carlton, 1963.

Serle, Geoffrey. *The Rush to be Rich: A History of the Colony of Victoria, 1883–1889*. Melbourne University Press, Carlton, 1971.

Sleight, Simon. *Young People and the Shaping of Public Space in Melbourne, 1870–1914*. Ashgate, London, 2013.

Smith, F. B. 'Religion and Free Thought in Melbourne, 1870–1890'. MA thesis, University of Melbourne, 1960.

Souter, Gavin. *Acts of Parliament: A Narrative History of the Senate and House of Representatives Commonwealth of Australia*. Melbourne University Press, Carlton, 1988.

Stebb, William (ed.). *Charles Henry Pearson: Fellow of Oriel and Education Minister of Victoria*. Longman, Green & Co., London, 1900.

Strangio, Paul and Brian Costar (eds). *The Victorian Premiers, 1856–2006*. Federation Press, Sydney, 2006.

Strangio, Paul. *Neither Power nor Glory: 100 Years of Political Labour in Victoria*. Melbourne University Press, Carlton, 2012.

Strangio, Paul and Nick Dyrenfurth (eds). *Confusion: The Making of the Australian Two-Party System*. Melbourne University Press, Carlton, 2009.

Sutherland, Alexander. *Victoria and its Metropolis: Past and Present*. McCarron, Bird, Melbourne, 1888.

Svensen, Stuart. *The Sinews of War: Hard Cash and the 1890 Maritime Strike*. University of New South Wales Press, Sydney, 1995.

Sykes, Trevor. *Two Centuries of Panic: A History of Corporate Collapses in Australia*. Allen & Unwin, Sydney, 1998.

Tavan, Gwenda. *The Long, Slow Death of White Australia*. Scribe, Melbourne, 2005.

Terry, W. H. (ed.). *Spirit Teachings: Oral, Impressional and Automatic. Received at Dr J. B. Motherwell's Circle*. W. H. Terry, Melbourne, 1908.

Theobald, Marjorie. *Knowing Women: Origins of Women's Education in Nineteenth Century Australia*. Cambridge University Press, Cambridge, 1996.

Thompson, Andrew. *Imperial Britain: The Empire in British Politics, c. 1880–1932*. Longman, Harlow, 2000.

Thompson, Roger. *Australian Imperialism in the Pacific: The Expansionist Era, 1820–1920*. Melbourne University Press, Carlton, 1980.

Thornton, Kristen. 'Pattie Deakin, Intercessor-in-Chief: A Case Study of Charity during the Great War'. Unpublished paper.

Tregenza, John. *Professor of Democracy: Life and Work of Charles Henry Pearson*. Melbourne University Press, Carlton, 1968.

Turner, Henry Gyles. *The First Decade of the Australian Commonwealth*. Mason, Firth & McCutcheon, Melbourne, 1911.

Twopeny, Richard. *Town Life in Australia*. Elliot Stock, London, 1883; Penguin Facsimile Edition, 1973.

Vamplew, Wray (ed.). *Australian Historical Statistics*. Fairfax, Syme & Weldon Associates, Sydney, 1987.

Ville, Simon, and Glenn Withers, *Cambridge Economic History*. Cambridge University Press, Cambridge, 2015, ch. 10.

Walker, David. *Anxious Nation: Australia and the Rise of Asia, 1850–1939*. University of Queensland Press, Brisbane, 1999.

Warhaft, Sally (ed.). *Well May We Say…: The Speeches that Made Australia*. Black Inc., Melbourne, 2004.

Watson, Don. *Caledonia Australis: Scottish Highlanders on the Frontier of Australia*. Collins, Sydney, 1984.

Watson, George. *The English Ideology: Studies in the Language of Victorian Politics*. Allen Lane, London, 1973.

Waugh, John. *First Principles: The Melbourne Law School, 1857–2007*. Miegunyah Press, Carlton, 2007.

Waugh, John. 'The Centenary of the Victorian Voluntary Liquidation Act'. *Melbourne University Law Review*, 18, 1991, 170–74.

Whitfield, L. F. '*The Age* and Public Affairs, 1861–1881'. MA thesis, University of Melbourne, 1950.

Willard, Myra. *History of the White Australia Policy to 1920*. Melbourne University Press, Carlton, 1978.

Wilson, Dean. 'Explaining the Criminal: Ned Kelly's Death Mask'. *La Trobe Journal*, 69, 2002, 51–58.

Wilson, Robert. *Great Exhibitions: World Fairs, 1851–1937*. National Gallery of Victoria, Melbourne, 2007.

Wolfe, Patrick. *Traces of History: Elementary Structures of Race*. Verso Press, London, 2016.

Wood, Malcolm. *Presbyterians in Colonial Victoria*. Australian Scholarly Publishing, Melbourne, 2008.

Wright, Raymond. *A People's Counsel: A History of the Parliament of Victoria, 1856–1990*. Oxford University Press, Melbourne, 1992.
Young, Robert. *The Idea of English Ethnicity*. Blackwell, Oxford, 2008.

Websites
Australian Dictionary of Biography. adb.anu.edu.au. In endnotes I have given only the author of the individual article.
Australian Politics and Elections Database, University of Western Australia. elections. uwa.edu.au/listelections.lasso, accessed 12 May 2016.
collections.museumvictoria.com.au/articles/2970, Richard Gillespie, 'Dr Thomas George Beckett (1859–1937)', accessed 6 June 2016; *Argus*, 6 July 1906.
Election Policy Speech, 1903. electionspeeches.moadoph.gov.au/speeches/1903-alfred-deakin, accessed 4 January 2016.
Election Policy Speech, 1906. electionspeeches.moadoph.gov.au/speeches/1906-alfred-deakin, accessed 12 May 2016.
Inauguration of the Commonwealth of Australia (1901, film clip). aso.gov.au/titles/tv/mister-prime-minister-deakin/clip1/?nojs, accessed 22 September 2015.
morningtoncemetery.com/Denominations/Historic-C-of-E/Strachan-Kate, accessed 26 October 2016.
Online exhibition on the Deeming Case. prov.vic.gov.au/online-exhibitions/deeming, accessed 22 February 2015.
pmtranscripts. pmc.gov.au/release/transcript-1207, accessed 7 March 2017.
salvationarmy.org.au/en/Who-We-Are/History-and-heritage/Australias-first-film-studio, accessed 22 September 2015.

LIST OF ILLUSTRATIONS

INDEX